MW01042719

Hand Made, Hand Played

Hand Made, Hand Played
The Art & Craft of Contemporary Guitars

Robert Shaw

 LARK BOOKS

A Division of Sterling Publishing Co., Inc.
New York / London

Editor:
Cassie Moore

Art Director:
Travis Medford

Production Editor:
Linda Kopp

Assistant Editors:
Amanda Carestio
Susan Kieffer

Front cover
Frans Elferink
Moderne, 2006
Photo by Martin Philippo

Spine, title, half title, and page 3
Johann Gustavsson
JG Bluesmaster '59
Custom, 2006
Photo by Matte Henderson

Front flap
Don Morrison, Donmo
Resonator Guitars
Rustbucket Tricone, 2006
Photo by Mark Thomson

Title and half title
Jean Larrivée,
Jean Larrivée Guitars
LV-10 KOA, 2000
*Photo by F. Miyazaki, Blue G
Acoustic Guitars, Tokyo*

Page 2
Otto D'Ambrosio
Prelude #7, 2006
*Photo by David Perluck
Photography*

Page 5
John Greven
OM Custom Sunburst, 2004
*Photo by F. Miyazaki, Blue G
Acoustic Guitars, Tokyo*

Back cover
Dale Unger, American
Archtop Guitars
White Lightning, 2002
Photo by Ray Baldino

Back flap
David Myka
Myka Sungazer, 2005
Photo by Robert Taylor

Library of Congress Cataloging-in-Publication Data

Shaw, Robert, 1951-
  Hand made, hand played : the art & craft of contemporary guitars / Robert
Shaw.
    p. cm.
  Includes bibliographical references and index.
  ISBN 978-1-57990-787-7 (hc-plc with jacket : alk. paper)
  1. Guitar makers. 2. Guitar--Pictorial works. I. Title.
  ML1015.G9S512 2008
  787.87'192--dc22

                                2008007972

10 9 8 7 6 5 4 3 2

Published by Lark Books, A Division of
Sterling Publishing Co., Inc.
387 Park Avenue South, New York, NY 10016

Text © 2008, Robert Shaw
Photography © 2007, Artist/Photographer as specified

Fender®, Stratocaster®, Strat®, Telecaster®, Tele®, Relic®, Precision Bass®, Jazz Bass®, and the
distinctive headstock and body designs of those guitars are trademarks of Fender Musical Instruments Corp.
All rights reserved. Used with permission.

Gretsch®, Falcon ™, and the distinctive headstock and body design of the Billy-Bo Jupiter Thunderbird are
trademarks of Fred W. Gretsch Enterprises, Ltd., and are used herein with express written permission.
All rights reserved.

The Double Neck Harp Guitar design is a trademark of William Eaton. Used with permission.

Distributed in Canada by Sterling Publishing,
c/o Canadian Manda Group, 165 Dufferin Street
Toronto, Ontario, Canada M6K 3H6

Distributed in the United Kingdom by GMC Distribution Services,
Castle Place, 166 High Street, Lewes, East Sussex, England BN7 1XU

Distributed in Australia by Capricorn Link (Australia) Pty Ltd.,
P.O. Box 704, Windsor, NSW 2756 Australia

The written instructions, photographs, designs, patterns, and projects in this volume are intended for the personal
use of the reader and may be reproduced for that purpose only. Any other use, especially commercial use, is
forbidden under law without written permission of the copyright holder.

Every effort has been made to ensure that all the information in this book is accurate. However, due to differing
conditions, tools, and individual skills, the publisher cannot be responsible for any injuries, losses, and other
damages that may result from the use of the information in this book.

If you have questions or comments about this book, please contact:
Lark Books
67 Broadway
Asheville, NC 28801
828-253-0467

Manufactured in China

All rights reserved

ISBN 13: 978-1-57990-787-7

For information about custom editions, special sales, premium and corporate purchases, please contact
Sterling Special Sales Department at 800-805-5489 or specialsales@sterlingpub.com.

For information about desk and examination copies available to college and university professors, requests
must be submitted to academic@larkbooks.com. Our complete policy can be found at www.larkbooks.com.

Contents

This book is dedicated to the memory of my mother, Terry Shaw, who taught me to love music, books, nature, and all things of beauty.

Robert Shaw

The Art and Craft of the Contemporary Guitar

We are living in the greatest age of guitar building in history. A renaissance of guitar making was set off by the sea changes in popular culture and music that took place in the 1960s, when seemingly everyone was inspired to learn to play a guitar or knew someone who did. Thanks to now legendary artists such as Joan Baez, The Beatles, Bob Dylan, the Rolling Stones, and Joni Mitchell and manufacturers such as Fender, Gibson, Gretsch, and Martin, the guitar became the most popular instrument in the world. Inevitably, some of the baby boomers who picked up guitars in the '60s began building their own instruments, and, as musicians grew older and more sophisticated, they sought (and could afford) more and better guitars. This synergy has continued to expand and mature, and today there are more highly skilled luthiers at work, making more outstanding instruments, than ever before.

The rise of the guitar began with the great American folk boom—or as many now call it, "The Great Folk Scare"—of the late 1950s and early 1960s. During this period, traditional, if variously authentic, folk music by guitar-strumming groups such as the Chad Mitchell Trio; The Kingston Trio; The Limeliters; the New Christy Minstrels; and Peter, Paul, and Mary reached the top of the charts. Below the level of mass popularity, roots-oriented and socially conscious artists like Baez, Dylan, Phil Ochs, Odetta, and Pete Seeger intersected with the Civil Rights Movement and other social causes; long lost bluesmen of the 1920s and 1930s—including Sleepy John Estes, Mississippi John Hurt, Skip James, Son House, and Bukka White—were rediscovered and given brief second careers; and country and Bluegrass masters such as Lester Flatt, Don Reno, and Doc Watson flatpicked with blazing speed and precision, all helping to bring the guitar to new prominence.

A somewhat parallel scene took place in Britain, where Lonnie Donegan led a '50s craze for "skiffle," a loose amalgam of American jug band music, gospel, and blues played on cheap guitars accompanied by simple, homemade instruments. His biggest hit, which reached number one in Britain in 1956 and climbed into the top ten in America, was a version of Leadbelly's "Rock Island Line." Donegan, and what he called his "mongrel music," set off a massive increase in guitar sales in Great Britain. Many of the key musicians of the coming "British Invasion," including Mick Jagger, Pete Townshend, Van Morrison, and Ray Davies, got their start playing or listening to skiffle. Also influenced by the craze,

♠ Mississippi John Hurt enjoyed a revival during the early '60s.
Courtesy of the Hulton Archive, Getty Images
Photo by the Frank Driggs Collection

♠ Country legend Doc Watson played his part in the American folk boom.
Courtesy of the Michael Ochs Archives, Getty Images
Photo by Michael Ochs Archives

The Beatles perform on *The Ed Sullivan Show*.
Courtesy of the Hulton Archive, Getty Images
Photo by CBS Photo Archive

" We are living in the greatest age of guitar building in history. "

a Liverpool schoolboy named John Lennon formed a skiffle band called The Quarry Men in 1957, later drafting a couple of other kids named Paul McCartney and George Harrison to join him.

On February 9, 1964, just over two months after John F. Kennedy's assassination, The Beatles played *The Ed Sullivan Show* before 73 million viewers—the largest audience in television history—and tens of thousands of young turks decided on the spot that they had to learn to play guitar (and maybe have hordes of girls scream at them, too). Guitar sales soared to unprecedented levels that year and continued to climb throughout the next decade, bolstering several guitar manufacturers toward new growth. In 1965, for example, C.F. Martin & Co. built a new 64,000 square foot factory, producing more than 10,000 guitars in its first year and more than 20,000 instruments annually by 1971.

Ironically, if not surprisingly, as major manufacturers like Fender, Gibson, and Gretsch ramped up production to meet demand in the 1960s and 1970s, quality went down. Larry Acunto, co-publisher of *20th Century Guitar* magazine, explains: "…the small, often family-owned companies started selling out to the major corporations. In 1965, CBS bought Fender, and Fender went downhill pretty quickly. In 1967, Norlin bought Gibson, and Baldwin bought Gretsch. All of these big companies were going into the guitar business, and they didn't have a clue as to what they were doing. At that point, American guitar manufacturing went right down the tubes."

In the meantime, a new generation of independent hand builders, led by pioneers such as James D'Aquisto, Michael Gurian, Jean Larrivée, Jon Lundberg, and Richard Schneider, was headed in the opposite direction. These artists explored the fine points of guitars made before the corporations stepped in, and designed new instruments that incorporated their discoveries, experiments, and inventions.

As was the case with many of the handcrafts that found new life amidst the counterculture of the '60s and '70s, *lutherie* (the hand building or repair of plucked

Located on North Street in Nazareth, Pennsylvania, the historic Martin Factory served as the company's main guitar-making facility from 1859 to 1964.

● Legendary classical luthier Manuel Velázquez works on a piece in his shop.

8

> **" We were a bunch of eccentric, odd-ball misfits, operating between the cracks. "**

and bowed stringed instruments) was so far below the radar as to be nonexistent. In America, guitars were produced in factories; the only hand builders worthy of apprenticeship made traditional classical guitars, not the acoustic and electric steel-strings popularized by the folk boom and the British Invasion. So many young builders turned first to the Old World traditions.

Irving Sloane's *Classic Guitar Construction*, published in 1964, was for years the only printed resource available to budding builders. Many of those who did not have access to a living craftsman built their first guitars following Sloane's instructions. A lucky few found mentors who could teach them. Pioneering acoustic steel-string guitar builder Michael Gurian, for example, studied with legendary classical luthiers Eugene Clark, David Rubio, and Manuel Velázquez, all of whom were working in New York City in the mid-1960s. He started his career building classical guitars, lutes, and Armenian ouds. In Canada, Jean Larrivée followed a course parallel to that of Gurian; after graduating from playing Duane Eddy riffs to classical guitar at age 20, he studied with classical luthier Edgar Mönch, who was then working in Toronto.

But America is the country where the steel-stringed guitar was born, and, within a few years, cultural and economic forces led most members of the first generation of independent builders to concentrate on steel-stringed instruments. For the most part, they had to make it up as they went along. There was no tradition of steel-string hand building to learn from and no established lutherie profession to join. "We were a bunch of eccentric, odd-

ball misfits, operating between the cracks," says Ervin Somogyi. "It was terra incognito." Nashville guitar guru, dealer, and author George Gruhn adds, "When I first opened my shop in 1970, I used to joke that if I lost a finger on my left hand for each independent luthier producing fine quality handmade guitars, I would still have at least as many usable digits left as Django Reinhardt." (The count would be three; Reinhardt's left hand was badly burned when he was 18, rendering his ring and pinkie fingers unusable for playing.)

The arcane, highly specialized archtop tradition hung on by a thread due to the efforts of James D'Aquisto, who had apprenticed with the great New York-based archtop builder John D'Angelico in the 1950s and early 1960s. D'Aquisto almost single-handedly kept the art of archtop building alive after his master's death in 1964. In 1970, he was by far the most prominent missing digit on George Gruhn's metaphoric hand. Happily, a few

● Archtop builder John D'Angelico poses with musician Johnny Smith and then apprentice Jimmy D'Aquisto.

ambitious young builders like Bob Benedetto, Roger Borys, John Monteleone, and Phil Petillo chose to follow the demanding path of archtop building as the decade wore on, giving D'Aquisto the chance to act as a bridge to the great tradition in which he had apprenticed and worked for so long.

But most of the new hand builders chose to look further into the past for models and found them in guitars made years earlier by Fender, Gibson, Martin, Gretsch, and other manufacturers. Many, like Jon Lundberg and Mario Martello in Berkeley, Božo Podunavac in Chicago, and Matt Umanov in New York, cut their teeth as repairmen and learned lutherie from the inside out by taking old guitars apart and putting them back together, discovering literally what made them tick and what made one instrument sound better than another. Lundberg ran *the* Berkeley guitar shop in the early '60s, which apparently everyone passed through. He built a reputation for retopping old Martin archtops with X-braced flattop soundboards, a trick that Marc Silber brought back to New York in the early 1960s and practiced at his seminal Fretted Instruments shop in Greenwich Village.

Michael Gurian began building steel-strings in the late 1960s and moved to New Hampshire in 1971. There he founded Gurian Guitars, Ltd., building a few thousand instruments before a string of bad luck and a major fire forced him to close shop a decade later. Gurian continues to play a pivotal role in the world of acoustic guitars, supplying custom parts to Martin, Taylor, and other manufacturers around the world. An astonishing number of today's most respected luthiers apprenticed with Gurian, including renowned classical builder Thomas Humphrey, Froggy Bottom Guitars founder Michael Millard, the eclectic and innovative builder Joe Veillette, and William Cumpiano and Jonathan Natelson. Cumpiano and Natelson went on to write *Guitarmaking: Tradition and Technology*, the standard textbook on lutherie since its publication in 1985.

Again paralleling Gurian, Jean Larrivée started his own company in 1971, building distinctive high quality acoustic steel-strings. From 1971 to 1977, Jean Larrivée Guitars grew steadily, moving four times to ever-larger spaces and employing a steady stream of apprentices, most notably Sergei de Jonge, William "Grit" Laskin, and Linda Manzer, all of whom are now part of any short list of the world's premier luthiers. Larrivée's company has continued to grow over the years and is now manufacturing several dozen guitars a day in two factories, one in Vancouver and the other in southern California, where he lives.

Another pioneer of high quality acoustic building was Stuart Mossman, an accomplished flatpicker who began producing dreadnought-shaped instruments in Winfield, Kansas, in 1970. His company's early literature makes his viewpoint clear: "We at Mossman are disgusted with what has happened to the quality of goods produced in this country. Quality has been sacrificed for quantity. Mass production has gotten out of hand. Craft has almost been completely eliminated from our society. This vile abomination (of plywood) is currently being perpetuated on the unsuspecting guitar-playing public on a grand scale. We at Mossman considered plywood briefly one day and unanimously decided that plywood makes the best cement forms available. We do not now nor will we ever stoop to the level of plywood construction, and we apologize for our contemporaries who have lowered the station of our craft by using laminated backs and sides." Mossman's operation grew steadily and was producing 1,000 guitars a year by 1975, when a fire destroyed the company's entire supply of rosewood. The company recovered quickly, but Mossman survived only as a small manufacturer, never regaining the prominence of his early years.

9

♠ Some of the world's premier luthiers got their start under Jean Larrivée, creator of this LV-10 KOA, 2000.
(page 97)

♠ Using only high-end woods, Stuart Mossman was dedicated to the philosophy of quality over quantity.
Golden Era Deluxe #4662, 1977 (page 148)
Stuart Mossman
National Music Museum
The University of South Dakota
Photo by Bill Willroth, Sr.

♠ Jefferson Airplane performs at the Naumberg Bandshell in Central Park, New York City, August 15, 1972.
Courtesy of the Hulton Archive, Getty Images

♠ Alembic Guitars' #1 For Jack Casady, 1972, helped launch a new genre in high-end instrument building.

On the West Coast, a young luthier named Steve Klein began shaking things up in the early 1970s with his radical acoustic guitars. Rather than modeling his work after existing examples, Klein was one of the first builders to rethink the instrument and produce completely original designs. Working from novel bracing concepts developed for the classical guitar by the physical chemist Dr. Michael Kasha, Klein built steel-string guitars that were different both inside and out; his model featured a huge, voluptuous body shaped like an oval sitting atop and intersecting a much larger circle. As would many builders after him, Klein hung around clubs and concert venues, befriending roadies and managers for the chance to show his work to stars like Stephen Stills and Doc Watson, who gave him valuable feedback, and Joni Mitchell, who eventually commissioned her own Klein guitar.

Even more radical than Klein was the avant-garde jazz guitarist Allan Gittler, who in the mid-1970s designed one of only two musical instruments ever to reach the collection of the Museum of Modern Art in New York. Gittler took an extreme, minimalist approach, seeking to remove everything from the guitar that was not essential to its function. Among the parts he deemed nonessential were the body and neck, which ultimately left him with a fishbone-shaped skeleton that still boggles the minds of luthiers and musicians alike. Thirty-five years later, Mike Stevens, who ran Fender's first custom shop, still calls the original Gittler one of his favorite guitar designs of all time.

Also working on the plugged-in side of things were electronics wizard and design engineer Ron Wickersham and his artist wife, Susan. In 1969 in Santa Rosa, California, the pair co-founded a company called Alembic and began customizing guitars and sound systems for the likes of Jefferson Airplane; the Grateful Dead; and Crosby, Stills, and Nash. Designing specialized electronics and pickups for existing instruments ultimately led to designing and building guitars from the ground up. The first Alembic bass, made for Jefferson Airplane bassist Jack Casady, was completed in 1972 and cost more than $4,000, an absolutely staggering price at the time. The following year, the Wickershams negotiated an agreement with a distributor and began manufacturing a standardized high-end instrument. Susan Wickersham recalls, "Many people thought that no one would be interested in an instrument so dedicated to excellence that the price was unheard of for production instruments. I guess they were wrong, weren't they? It was the advent of an entirely new genre in instrument building."

That genre, sometimes called the "boutique guitar," has grown exponentially over the past 30 years. There are now hundreds of independent luthiers and small shops

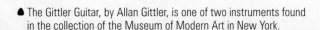

♠ The Gittler Guitar, by Allan Gittler, is one of two instruments found in the collection of the Museum of Modern Art in New York.

all over the United States, Canada, Great Britain, Europe, Japan, and beyond building high quality instruments that sell from a few thousand dollars to prices well into five figures. Some of these men and women—yes, there are female guitar builders, several of whom are among the most respected artisans at work today—have been making guitars for decades, while others have come to the field only in the past eight to 10 years.

The advent of the World Wide Web in the mid-1990s helped fuel the expansion of guitar building. The Internet leveled the playing field for small entrepreneurs by making it far easier for consumers, builders, and retailers to find each other and by helping advance the careers of many luthiers, dealers, and consultants. Players and collectors can now easily visit hundreds of individual luthiers' sites, view and compare detailed photographs of instruments, listen to guitars being played, and even choose customized options like specialty woods, inlay, and electronics. Specialists like Chris Kamen of Classic Guitars International, Cliff Cultreri of Destroy All Guitars, Paul Heumiller of Dream Guitars, and Richard Glick of Fine Guitar Consultants act as middlemen, representing the work of selected independent luthiers while also negotiating sales and commissions for their clients.

Another major effect of the downturn in guitar manufacturing quality was the growth of interest in "vintage" guitars, made before the pioneer manufacturers were either bought out or lowered standards so they could significantly increase production. This trend began in the late '60s and early '70s with players who rediscovered and exploited the capabilities of older instruments like pre-war Martin and Gibson acoustics and discontinued '50s electrics such as the original Gibson Les Paul, the Flying V, and the Gretsch White Falcon. As certain guitars became associated with individual musicians—Albert King and his Flying V, Jimmy Page and his vintage Les Paul, B.B. King and his Gibson ES-335 "Lucille," or Jimi Hendrix and his Fender Stratocasters—the demand for similar instruments grew and prices for rare originals climbed.

By the late 1980s and early 1990s, collectors were paying tens or even hundreds of thousands of dollars for prime examples of vintage guitars. It's estimated that by the mid-90s, there were more than 80 vintage guitar shows held each year in the United States alone, with total annual sales of more than $200 million. Following suit, independent luthiers began to make far less costly (and

11

♠ Jimi Hendrix plays his Fender Stratocaster.
Courtesy of the Michael Ochs Archives, Getty Images
Photo by Joel Axelrad

♠ Albert King performs with his Gibson Flying V.
Courtesy of the Hulton Archive, Getty Images
Photo by the Frank Driggs Collection

often arguably better built) instruments based on hard-to-find classics by Fender, Gibson, Martin, and other companies. The Martin OM–45 was one of the first models to follow this progression; very few were ever made and, after fingerpickers rediscovered the virtues of the model, demand quickly outstripped supply. Fingerstyle pioneer Eric Schoenberg worked with luthier Dana Bourgeois to design a cutaway version of the OM and then teamed with Martin to produce it on a commercial scale. The collaboration marked the start of Martin's reproduction of historic models, a move that was eventually followed by the other big companies.

♠ Made expressly for Schoenberg Guitars by C.F. Martin & Co., the Schoenberg Soloist, 1988, was based on the Martin OM-45 and produced on a commercial scale.
(page 164)

Fender, Gibson, and Martin all also opened custom shops in the late 1980s, allowing them to cater to the desires of well-heeled individual clients and to compete more directly with small specialty builders. By the mid-1990s, they had all followed the independents' lead and were issuing their own reproductions of long discontinued models. Today, this trend has reached extremes and includes, for example, Fender limited editions, guitars that are accurate down to the tooling marks and scuffed surfaces of the originals and retail for $10,000 or more.

The explosion of instrument building in the past 25 years has been led by independent luthiers, many of whom work alone in small, one-man shops. They build their instruments by hand, with an attention to detail that factories cannot afford and with higher quality woods and more technical skill than in any previous era. The versatile English luthier Ralph Bown explains the merits of this time-consuming, labor-intensive approach this way: "I've always felt quite strongly that a guitar is really only 'handmade' if it's made by one pair of hands from start to finish, whatever many respected manufacturers may claim—i.e.,

> *"Factories aim for exact clones, not treating each component on an individual basis."*

one person has an overview of the instrument and brings their judgment and intuition to bear on every aspect of it. I think that's the only way really exceptional guitars will ever get made. If you think about it, that, along with the scope to customize, is the most valuable thing any individual luthier has to offer, so it's worth hanging on to."

"Factories aim for exact clones, not treating each component on an individual basis," adds Canadian luthier Michael Heiden. "Handmade means made by the hands of one craftsman. What is so great is that we all do it a bit differently. Buyers have a

♠ Ralph Bown designs and builds his guitars from start to finish in his studio in York, England.

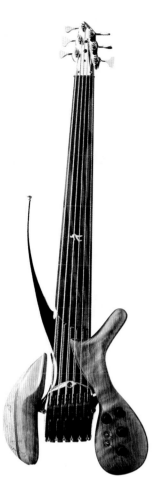

◆ Michael Spalt explores the potential of each piece of wood, as evident in his Spalt Magma 601, 2004. (page 403)

vast array of choices." As Heiden suggests, the art of lutherie is all about differences and the goals and methodologies expressed through the builder's knowledge of and engagement with every detail of the process.

Los Angeles luthier Michael Spalt explains the process this way: "If you look at instruments, no matter how close the tolerances, or how exactly they may look the same, each one will be different—each piece of wood has a different potential and unlocking it is where the true art happens. All traditional high-level crafts are aware of this. Old Japanese carpentry texts deal with the art of finding the right tree, grown in the right spot, harvested the right way, used the right way, etc. It all culminates in a piece of work where respect and understanding for the material and the beauty of its functional interpretation feeds the soul." Guitar builder Scott MacDonald echoes Spalt, saying: "My work is organic. I work with something that was alive, something that grew in the ground and died. I build [with] it, and it's changed from a lifeless substance to one that's alive again. I feel like an alchemist. I'm transforming something back to the living. I'm generating life from something that once lived in a different form."

The enormous expansion of individual craftsmanship and creative energy has been driven and inspired by players, who are willing to pay a premium for the soul nourishment and personal satisfaction that they believe only a custom-built guitar can deliver. They bring their needs and ideas to luthiers and work closely with them through the design and building processes. "Most folks have owned and played at least one instrument, some lots," explains Michael Heiden. "Some don't care what it is; it's just a tool, and they don't get too emotional about it. Others really care and know exactly what it is; they need and adore it like a very special friend. They come to me when they know what it is they want and can't find it in the stores or want something that is a bit different, if not unique. I feel I do my best work when they can tell me in very clear terms what it is they need."

The intimate relationship between luthier and client is the currency of the current revival, the fuel that feeds the twin engines of builder and player. Classical builder Greg Byers says that, aside from two older luthiers who served as mentors, "my biggest influences are the players who have evaluated my guitars. The most important thing an aspiring builder can do is go to the best players he or she can find and listen—truly listen—to how they sound and what they say. Listen critically and listen to criticism!"

◆ Pictured in his shop in Huntington, New York, Scott MacDonald of S.B. MacDonald Custom Instruments likens his building process to alchemy.

Rick Davis, who builds his Running Dog acoustic guitars in a small shop outside his rural Vermont home, is typical of today's custom builders when he outlines his process: "Body style, tonal properties, neck profile, and cosmetic appointments are chosen through consultation. One pair of hands then builds the guitar. Select materials are used throughout. The woods are carefully chosen for a particular instrument, giving consideration to personal preferences for tone and aesthetics. Each soundboard is carefully tap-tuned to give full voice to the instrument. Wooden bindings and wood-and-abalone or gemstone rosettes complement and complete the body, fingerboard, and headstock. Inlays are hand-cut to your specification."

The highly respected electric guitar builder Michael DeTemple is less specific but equally adamant about the importance of creating instruments that are tailor-made for each client. "My goal," he tells potential customers on his website, "is to make a guitar that once in your hands is undeniably an inspiration to your playing. Undeniably *the* best-feeling and best-sounding guitar you've ever held. *The* guitar that draws you to it every time you see it. *The* guitar that you have to pick up because you feel you have no choice. *The* guitar that you will feel is *your* guitar for the rest of your life. *The* guitar that is undeniably yours."

As with any handcraft in our highly competitive technological world, building guitars by hand is not an easy way to make a living. It demands a complex combination of technical and business skills to succeed. Archtop builder Steve Andersen says he never could have imagined the breadth of skills he has had to learn in the course of his 25 years as an independent luthier. "Photography, bookkeeping, tool design and construction, metalworking, advertising, customer relations, computer skills, tonewood harvesting and processing, carbon graphite composites, and electronics are all skills I've acquired over the years. Of course, learning these things has improved my instruments, but if I'd had a clue when I first ventured into guitar making, I might have opted for something a bit 'easier.'"

And for all that, the monetary rewards can also be problematic. A few luthiers, primarily classical and archtop specialists, are in such demand that clients have to wait years to get one of their instruments, but the majority work much closer to the edge. Most high quality hand builders can only produce between 10 and 15 instruments a year, and even though their guitars retail for thousands of dollars each, their profit margins are often fairly slim. David King, who builds 10 to 12 electric bass guitars a year in Portland, Oregon, calculates the financial side of his work this way: "Total time [per instrument]: about 100 hours over three months; cost of wood: $200 to $500; metal and plating: $100; electronics: $300; strings, screws, oil, etc: $25. I figure I can make

▲ Rick Davis consults closely with clients to build guitars like the Cherry Concert Jumbo, 2004.
(page 73)

Rick Davis works in his shop in Richmond, Vermont. ▲

14

● Steve Andersen has been building archtops such as The Gold Standard (2005), here, for 25 years.
(page 191)

But economics is not what drives most hand builders. Innovator Ken Parker, who has seen his share of business ups and downs, says firmly, "Even if I were living in a cardboard box, I'd still be making guitars." Canadian electric bass builder Sheldon Dingwall speaks for most luthiers when he says, "Building instruments to me is the most fascinating and fulfilling experience imaginable. It is the meeting place between the technical world of physics and engineering and the emotional world of soul and passion." Paul Norman, who builds Forbidden Fruit Guitars, adds, "I have been, in order, a finish carpenter, an architect, an actor, a theater technician, a theatrical scene designer, a designer/draftsman, a printed wiring board designer, and a software engineer, the latter for over 20 years. Having proven myself to be only a fair guitar player after years of instruction, I figured I would give guitar construction a shot. Late bloomers rejoice! I have found the synthesis of all my previous experiences."

Unlike many professionals, luthiers are in general not particularly competitive among themselves, and most are happy to share their knowledge and enthusiasm with their peers. Many guitar makers are members of the Guild of American Luthiers (GAL), which was established in 1972 and now has members in over 30 countries around the world, and/or the Association of Stringed Instrument Artisans (ASIA), which was founded in 1988 "to help provide a sense of community and professionalism to the field of stringed instrument making and repair." Each organization shares technical and resource information, publishes an informative magazine, and offers its members a biennial symposium full of workshops, lectures, and other helpful presentations. And retail guitar shows, another development of the '80s and '90s that brings dozens of luthiers together to show their latest creations, are often as much about networking and catching up with old friends as they are about business.

$15 an hour if I don't screw up too much. If I add in wood shopping, travel, time messing with computers, time cleaning the shop and rebuilding machinery, time harassing, threatening, and cajoling suppliers and talking to earnest customers, I can count on $5 an hour." More than a few experienced builders supplement their sales by sharing their expertise with others. Many choose to write how-to books and articles, take in apprentices, consult with novices, or teach courses online, at guitar shows, professional gatherings, or lutherie schools like the Roberto-Venn School of Lutherie in Phoenix, Arizona, and Charles Fox's American School of Lutherie in Portland, Oregon.

Despite their camaraderie and the high level of their current achievements, many luthiers worry about the future of their chosen profession. Technology has brought enormous changes to the business of building guitars in recent years. Builders can now use CAD (Computer-Aided Design) and CAM (Computer-Aided Manufacturing) to plan and execute their work with a precision that is beyond the capabilities of the human hand. Computer Numerically Controlled milling machines (CNCs), which have a margin of error as low as one ten-thousandth of an inch, make it possible to create highly detailed copies of individual parts and models with little or no variation from one to the next.

CNCs are being used by all the major manufacturers and some small builders, while many other builders buy parts from companies that supply precision pre-cut necks, bridges, rosettes, inlay, and other instrument pieces.

Like most technology, CAD and CAM are a mixed blessing. Their precision has made extraordinary things possible—perhaps most notably the astonishing inlay work of the late Larry Sifel and his compatriots at Pearl Works, Inc.—but these programs can also provide a lazy builder with an easy way to cut corners. In the hands of a wizard like Sifel, the new technologies can be used to bring the traditional art of lutherie into the twenty-first century, but the mechanized precision they offer can also lead builders away from engagement with the particularities of their work and materials. In the service of less imaginative or ambitious builders, they could spell disaster for the future of lutherie.

Recalling his early days as a classical builder, Michael Gurian told *American Lutherie* magazine, "Today everyone needs the table saws, the band saws, every kind of power equipment under the sun. But I could go out and be a gypsy, head out with a little valise, and in that valise I would have all the tools and woods necessary for three guitars. A couple of planes, some good chisels, some rope..." "I see a lot of people tooling up and assembling computer-made parts," adds Ervin Somogyi, "but, for me, that's something different from lutherie. I don't see many young people interested in investing the time to really learn how to make a guitar. I hope the guitar will provide a perpetual haven

♠ Luthiers Michihiro Matsuda and Mario Beauregard flank their former teacher and master builder Ervin Somogyi at the Healdsburg Guitar Festival in California.

for the creative misfits, but I'm inclined to think that the classical builders will be the guardians of the analytic mindset a luthier needs."

Others see reason to be optimistic. Jeff Elliott, who has been crafting superb classical, harp, and acoustic guitars for more than 40 years, points out that a big part of the appeal of guitar playing and building is the refuge they can offer from the pervasive world of technology. The Internet can connect us with people, ideas, and products all over the planet, but, like television, it can also distract and disconnect us from our immediate surroundings and the richness of everyday interactions and experiences. The Luddite Kentucky poet Wendell Berry, who deliberately chooses to write only with pen or pencil on paper, has advised budding poets, "Live a three-dimensioned life; stay away from screens." As something that can also be done without computers, the Internet, or even electricity, the building and playing of instruments can humanize us and put us in touch with traditions of self-sufficiency, hand work, and the shared language of music that stretch as far back into human history as we can look. Traditional lutherie is, after all, about the work of the hand and, ultimately, about

◀ The detailed inlay on the OM-Night Dive Limited Edition, 2004, was a collaboration between Pearl Works, Inc., Martin, and William "Grit" Laskin.
(page 118)

touch, the most primal and connecting of human senses. In a letter to his friend Juan Martinez Sirvent, Antonio de Torres, the father of the Spanish classical guitar, explained, "My secret is one you have witnessed many times, and one that I can't leave to posterity, because it must with my body go to the grave, for it consists of the tactile senses in my finger pads, in my thumb and index finger that tell the intelligent builder if the top is or is not well made, and how it should be treated to obtain the best tone from the instrument."

Whatever the future holds, the present is a moment without precedent in the history of the guitar. As Chris Martin IV, CEO of the C.F. Martin & Co., puts it, "There have never been guitars built on Earth as good as the ones being built today." Both the quality of workmanship and materials are at an all-time high as creative luthiers explore the use of every conceivable type of tonewood and go to extraordinary lengths to find rare and exotic timber. Every kind of guitar ever made is being made today, from exacting reproductions of Renaissance and Baroque instruments crafted with period hand tools to electrics built with space-age materials and the latest advances in electronics. The entire history of the guitar is at the disposal of today's builders, and both the guitar's history and future can be told through the amazing instruments they are creating.

" Not bad for a bunch of hippies. "

This book showcases guitars designed and built by a host of the finest artisans of the past 25 years—almost all of whom are still at work today—and the remarkable variety of high quality instruments they are making. The collection is extensive and includes, among others, elegant parlor guitars for quiet living room picking; wildly shaped electric guitars for crashing rock and roll; tenor, baritone, and bass guitars; guitars with seven, eight, 10, 12, or even more strings; guitars with metal bodies and inset resonators; guitars with hand-carved tops, two necks, or multiple or unconventionally shaped sound holes; guitars made specifically for Bluegrass, folk, blues, rock, and jazz musicians; European gypsy guitars, Spanish flamenco and classical guitars; and beyond.

"Not bad for a bunch of hippies," says Ervin Somogyi, surveying the field he has helped to build with a wry smile. "It's a good time to be alive," adds Jeff Elliott.

17

Manuel Velázquez's hands rest on guitar tops. ♠

ACOUSTIC GUITARS

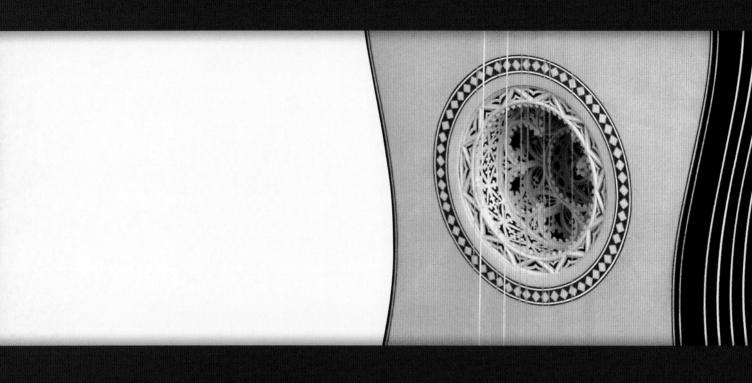

HISTORIC

While the origins of the guitar remain obscure and hotly debated, instruments similar to the modern guitar can be traced to the ancient Near East and probably were introduced to Europe during the Crusades. A variety of plucked stringed instruments, most with bowl-shaped backs like those of the Arabic oud and the later Renaissance lute and Neapolitan mandolin, were popular in Europe during the Middle Ages. Four- and five-stringed fretted instruments evolved in Europe during the fourteenth and fifteenth centuries, and a flat-backed, six-coursed relative of the guitar, the vihuela, appeared in early sixteenth-century Spain. Five-course guitars, strung with pairs of gut strings, were common throughout Europe by the mid-1600s and continued to be made until the late 1700s, when the first guitars with six single strings emerged.

Interest in Renaissance, Baroque, and early Romantic-era music began to grow in the 1960s and eventually made its way from the academy to public awareness. As the popularity of early music has grown, so has the demand from performers for historically correct period instruments, and today, a number of luthiers specialize in building accurate and highly playable versions of early guitars and related instruments.

After Antonio Stradivari, Cremona, Italy, 1680

S tephen Barber and Sandy Harris are lute makers who also build reproductions of early plucked instruments, including Baroque guitars. The pair is among the most experienced builders of early instruments, with a combined experience of more than 50 years and close to 1,000 instruments completed.

Although Antonio Stradivari is best known for his violins and other bowed instruments, he designed and made a variety of instruments, including harps, lutes, mandolins, and guitars. Two Stradivari guitars are known to be in existence; this replica is patterned after a guitar in the collection of the Ashmolean Museum at Oxford University in England.

Like other Baroque-era guitars, the Stradivari has five courses, but differs from most other guitars of the period in its 12-fret neck (two frets longer than usual). The bridge required special attention because, as Barber explains, "It has distinctive triangular cut-outs for the strings instead of drilled holes, allowing some adjustment to the string spacing within each course—and to the string height; this feature also allows the soundboard more flexibility."

The bridge "moustachios" are missing from the original Stradivari. They were reconstructed for the copy from ultraviolet light examinations of the original, and by studying a watercolor of the instrument made in the 1880s.

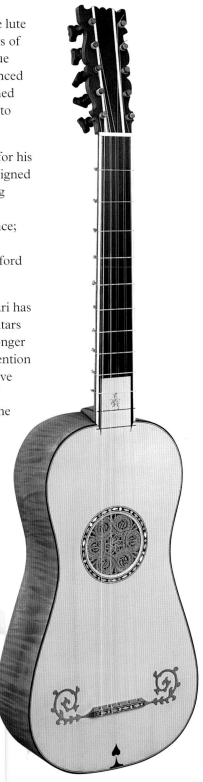

21

SPECIFICATIONS

BODY AND SIDE WOODS: Maple

TOP WOOD: Spruce

NECK WOOD: Maple

FRETBOARD MATERIAL: Ebony

FRETBOARD INLAY: Bone edges

HEADSTOCK DECORATION: Ebony, bone

SOUND HOLE INLAYS: Pearwood, mother-of-pearl

BRIDGE: Pearwood

BINDING: Ebony, boxwood

♠ **After Antonio Stradivari, Cremona, Italy, 1680, 2003**
Stephen Barber and Sandy Harris, Lutemakers
London, England

Richard E. Bruné

Baroque Guitar after Voboam

*R*ichard Bruné began building guitars in 1966. In the late 1960s, he lived in Mexico City, where he studied anthropology and played flamenco guitar professionally in various troupes in Mexico and around the United States. He moved to Chicago in 1972 and says that a year later, "I gave up any pretensions of being a professional guitarist and dedicated myself full time to lutherie."

Bruné has repaired and built copies of many historic instruments over the years; his restorations include instruments by such renowned luthiers as Domingo Esteso, Ignacio Fleta, Santos Hernandez, Hermann Hauser I, Louis Panormo, José Ramirez, Johann Gottfried Scherzer, and Antonio de Torres.

A passionate and opinionated student of guitar history, Bruné was the first elected president of the Guild of American Luthiers.

Baroque-era guitars were smaller and lighter than modern classical instruments, with a shallower body, shorter scale length, and adjustable frets made of tied-on gut. Strings were also gut, which is much quieter than modern synthetics. They were generally more ornately decorated than earlier instruments and were used both to provide accompaniment for singing and as a solo instrument.

They were five-course instruments, tuned as are the top five strings of a modern instrument (A, D, G, b, e,). Although this example carries 10 strings, the first (highest) course was often a single string, and the other four were doubles, with the fourth and fifth courses usually strung in octaves, like a modern 12-string guitar. The second and third courses were strung as unisons, like a mandolin (thus Aa, Dd, GG, bb, e). Some guitarists also strung the fifth course in unison, and tuned the strings up an octave (aa, Dd, GG, bb, e).

Baroque Guitar after Voboam, 1977 ▶
Richard E. Bruné
Evanston, Illinois

SPECIFICATIONS

BODY AND SIDE WOODS: Ebony

TOP WOOD: German spruce

BODY WIDTH, LOWER BOUT: 10¹³⁄₁₆ inches (27.5 cm)

NECK WOOD: Ebony veneered over Spanish cedar

FRETBOARD MATERIAL: Ebony, ivory

FRETBOARD INLAY: Ivory

HEADSTOCK DECORATION: Ebony, ivory

SOUND HOLE INLAYS: Ebony, ivory, parchment (sheepskin)

BRIDGE: Ebony

NUT AND SADDLE: Ivory nut

TUNING MACHINES: Boxwood pegs

BINDING: Ebony, ivory

SCALE LENGTH: 25.4 inches (64.5 cm)

NECK WIDTH AT NUT: 1⅞ inches (4.8 cm)

NUMBER OF FRETS: 16

BRACING: Voboam style

FINISH: Oil finish

BODY DEPTH: 3¾ inches (9.5 cm)

BODY LENGTH: 18⁹⁄₁₆ inches (47.2 cm)

OVERALL LENGTH: 37⁹⁄₁₆ inches (95.4 cm)

U.S. SUGGESTED RETAIL PRICE: $20,000

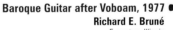

23

HISTORIC

Classical Guitar after Torres F.E. 08

Antonio de Torres (1817–1892) is the most influential Spanish guitar builder of all time. His 155 surviving instruments remain the standard on which the tradition of Spanish luthiery stands. Torres completely redefined the guitar in the mid-nineteenth century, bringing together a variety of construction concepts into a whole so perfectly conceived and balanced that almost every builder since has either copied or built upon his models.

Describing an 1875 Torres she once owned, Beverly Maher of the Guitar Salon said, "It is truly a miracle that such a simply constructed guitar can sound like this. I brought the Torres to Manuel Velàzquez to clean, polish, and secure a couple of cracks. Manuel and his son, Alfredo, and guitarists Virginia Luque, Mike Petrovich, and builder Robert Desmond all gathered to hear the Torres. Virginia played it (still with very old strings), and all of us teared up. Can a guitar of this age have clarity, balance, projection, and brightness? Absolutely! It is a magical instrument."

This guitar is a copy of an instrument that won Torres the bronze prize in an 1858 exhibition in Seville and brought him to prominence. It was the most elaborate of his designs. Brian Cohen's copy contains more than 92 feet (28 m) of handmade double-herringbone purfling, and over 100,000 individual wood inlay blocks set in the complicated geometric pattern on the back, ribs, and top. Cohen works in a very traditional manner and says any nineteenth-century guitar maker stepping into his workshop would instantly recognize the tools, materials, and techniques he employs. He still uses an original nineteenth-century treadle circular saw, a treadle lathe, and countless original fine hand tools. "It is only by working the woods directly by hand in the traditional methods that the authentic and full potential of the wood can be realized," says Cohen.

SPECIFICATIONS

BODY AND SIDE WOODS: Slab-cut figured maple

TOP WOOD: Spruce

BODY WIDTH, LOWER BOUT: 13⅝ inches (34.5 cm)

NECK WOOD: Cedar

FRETBOARD MATERIAL: Ebony

HEADSTOCK DECORATION: Ebony, maple, satinwood, padauk

SOUND HOLE INLAYS: Ebony, maple, rosewood, padauk, mother-of-pearl

BRIDGE: Rosewood, mother-of-pearl

NUT AND SADDLE: Bone

TUNING MACHINES: David Rodgers silver

BINDING: Ebony, holly, maple

SCALE LENGTH: 25.6 inches (65 cm)

NUMBER OF FRETS: 19

BRACING: Torres, 7 fans

FINISH: French polish

BODY DEPTH: 4⁵⁄₁₆ to 4⅜ inches (11 to 11.2 cm)

BODY LENGTH: 18⁵⁄₁₆ inches (46.6 cm)

U.S. SUGGESTED RETAIL PRICE: $18,000

◄ **Classical Guitar after Torres F.E. 08, 1999**
Brian Cohen
Guildford, England

After Johann George Stauffer

ernhard Kresse makes both modern classical guitars and reproductions of early nineteenth-century instruments by Lacôte, Panormo, Ries, and Stauffer. Modern guitars, reproductions, and restored original instruments coming out of his workshop have been widely used for concert performance and recordings by such artists as Duo Arte en Parte, Manuel Barrueco, Duo Ghiribizzo, Marco Schmidt, Raphaella Smits, Pavel Steidl, and Brigitte Zaczek.

Although best known today as C.F. Martin's mentor, the Viennese luthier Johann George Stauffer (1778–1853) was, in his own right, one of the finest and most influential guitar makers of the nineteenth century. His guitars were once played by Franz Schubert as well as by contemporary virtuosi such as Luigi Legnani and Johann Kaspar Mertz.

Around 1815, Legnani worked with Stauffer on a new guitar design, which included such innovations as a sloped back, an adjustable "keyed" neck, and a 22-fret "flying" fingerboard that wasn't attached to the soundboard, but instead extended over it, as on a violin or cello. However, Kresse believes the most important specifications for Stauffer's "Legnani-model" were the stronger body (at the waist) and bowed neck.

◄ **After Johann George Stauffer, 2006**
Bernhard Kresse
Cologne, Germany

25

SPECIFICATIONS

BODY AND SIDE WOODS: Flamed maple

TOP WOOD: Spruce

BODY WIDTH, LOWER BOUT: 11¹³⁄₁₆ inches (30 cm)

NECK WOOD: Maple

FRETBOARD MATERIAL: Ebony

SOUND HOLE INLAYS: Ebony and maple

BRIDGE: Colored pearwood

NUT AND SADDLE: Ebony and metal

TUNING MACHINES: Rodgers

BINDING: Ebony and maple

SCALE LENGTH: 25.25 inches (64.1 cm)

NECK WIDTH AT NUT: 1¹³⁄₁₆ inches (4.7 cm)

NUMBER OF FRETS: 22

BRACING: Transversal bars

FINISH: Shellack

BODY DEPTH: 2⁹⁄₁₆ to 3⅛ inches (6.5 to 8 cm)

BODY LENGTH: 17¾ inches (45 cm)

OVERALL LENGTH: 38³⁄₁₆ inches (97 cm)

U.S. SUGGESTED RETAIL PRICE: $5,800

Dane Hancock

Tárrega Torres FE 17 Reproduction

Among Antonio de Torres's most significant innovations was his bracing pattern, which, along with the slight arch he gave to his tops and backs, allowed him to trim his body woods thinner than anyone had ever done before. Torres's revolutionary design placed horizontal bars above and below the sound hole, with seven short struts arranged across the lower bout like the ribs of a fan above a V-shaped bottom brace. This bracing allowed the extremely thin soundboard to move quite freely.

This superb reproduction by Dane Hancock is a replica of one of Antonio de Torres's most famous instruments. Torres had built the guitar in 1865 for his personal use, but it was later acquired by the great guitarist and composer Francisco Tárrega in 1869.

Tárrega was 17 when his patron purchased the instrument for him, and he played it until the top caved in from constant use 20 years later. Tárrega's protégé and biographer, Emilio Pujol, recalled the instrument this way: "It was made from maple, with

the soundboard in spruce, the neck and the head in cedar, and the fingerboard in ebony. The size was slightly smaller than the usual one. Its sound hole and contours were bordered with the finest of inlays of a pale green shade with double herringbone purfling; on the head, the back, and the ribs was an exquisite rectangular meander inlay. In addition to the spontaneity of the sound, there was its clear, warm timbre as if it were of gold. The balance between bass and treble was proportionally exact in volume and the duration of its vibrations equally generous throughout the fingerboard."

♠ **Tárrega Torres FE 17 Reproduction, 2005**
Dane Hancock, Dane Hancock Master Guitars
Mount Tamborine, Australia

SPECIFICATIONS

BODY AND SIDE WOODS: Master-grade European flamed maple

TOP WOOD: Master-grade quartersawn German spruce

BODY WIDTH, LOWER BOUT: 14⁵⁄₁₆ inches (36.4 cm)

NECK WOOD: Quartersawn Spanish cedar

FRETBOARD MATERIAL: African black ebony

HEADSTOCK DECORATION: Brazilian rosewood veneer with timber Greek key inlays

SOUND HOLE INLAYS: Natural and dyed inlaid timber mosaic

BRIDGE: Brazilian rosewood with mother-of-pearl tie blocks and inlays

NUT AND SADDLE: Select bone

TUNING MACHINES: Reischl machines, silver hand engraved with black mother-of-pearl buttons

BINDING: Brazilian rosewood

SCALE LENGTH: 25.5 inches (64.8 cm)

NECK WIDTH AT NUT: 2 inches (5 cm)

NUMBER OF FRETS: 19

BRACING: Traditional fan

FINISH: French polish

BODY DEPTH: 3¹¹⁄₁₆ inches (9.4 cm)

BODY LENGTH: 19 inches (48.3 cm)

OVERALL LENGTH: 38¹⁵⁄₁₆ inches (98.9 cm)

U.S. SUGGESTED RETAIL PRICE: $9,500

26

Vihuela de Mano

The vihuela was an early Spanish ancestor of the guitar that was very common in the fifteenth and sixteenth centuries but became obsolete after the development of the Baroque guitar. While only a couple of original vihuelas survive, a rich body of music was written for the instrument, and several modern luthiers have created versions of the vihuela for performers of Spanish Renaissance music. The vihuela de mano was a six-course instrument with pairs of strings tuned either G, C, F, a, d, g, or C, F, Bb, a, d, g. It was played with the fingers.

SPECIFICATIONS

BODY AND SIDE WOODS: Pearwood

TOP WOOD: Engelmann spruce

BODY WIDTH, LOWER BOUT: 11¼ inches (28.5 cm)

NECK WOOD: Cherry

FRETBOARD MATERIAL: Ebony

FRETBOARD INLAY: Ivory

HEADSTOCK DECORATION: The core, integral with the wood of the neck, is cherry, veneered front and back with apple wood inlaid with ebony and ivory lines.

SOUND HOLE INLAYS: Rose in sound hole, in gothic style, is built up from two lower layers of cut parchment and an upper layer of carved wood.

BRIDGE: Carved out of apple wood; top surface of ebony with ivory edging

NUT AND SADDLE: Bone nut

TUNING MACHINES: Plum wood tuning pegs

BINDING: Maple, shallowly inlaid into the edge (for protection, around the soundboard only)

SCALE LENGTH: 23 inches (58.5 cm)

NECK WIDTH AT NUT: 2 inches (5 cm)

NUMBER OF FRETS: 10

BRACING: Light lateral bracing of quartered spruce

FINISH: Several thin coats of oil varnish, padded on

BODY DEPTH: 2⅜ to 4¼ inches (6 to 11 cm)

BODY LENGTH: 15½ inches (39.5 cm)

OVERALL LENGTH: 33¾ inches (86 cm)

U.S. SUGGESTED RETAIL PRICE: $6,000

Joel van Lennep describes himself as "a lute builder whose first and foremost love has always been music itself." Van Lennep has been building lutes and vihuelas since 1969. He began his instrument building career with harpsichords and clavichords, but has concentrated solely on lutes and vihuelas since 1975.

This instrument was built by van Lennep for the lutenist and guitarist Hopkinson K. Smith, a world-renowned specialist in solo music for early plucked instruments. "My goal in designing and constructing this instrument," says van Lennep, "was to work within what is known from the scant historical record of iconographic and musically circumstantial evidence on one hand, and the only two surviving historical instruments on the other. Within this framework, I have tried to create the best instrument for sound, playability, and appearance that my taste, materials, knowledge, and abilities allow. All of my designs, as well as the instruments themselves, remain works in progress."

Vihuela de Mano, 2002 ◄
Joel R. van Lennep
Rindge, New Hampshire
Courtesy Hopkinson K. Smith, Basel, Switzerland

27

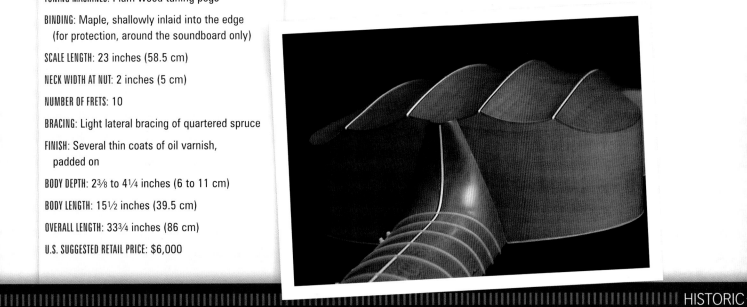

CLASSICAL & FLAMENCO

The classical guitar is an Old World form, developed in the mid-nineteenth century by the Spanish luthier Antonio de Torres, whose friend, the composer Francisco Tárrega, established a repertoire of music written specifically for the instrument. The guitar was brought to worldwide attention by the Spanish virtuoso Andres Segovia in the early twentieth century. Segovia, whose primary instrument was actually built by the German luthier Hermann Hauser I, broadened the instrument's appeal by combining expressive performances of Spanish classical guitar music with early Romantic guitar music by Fernando Sor and Mauro Giuliani and transcriptions of lute music by Bach and other Baroque composers. Musicians such as Julian Bream and John Williams have continued to expand the repertoire of the classical guitar over the

years by commissioning a variety of works from contemporary composers, and luthiers around the world continue to refine and expand the instrument's structure and sonic capabilities.

Flamenco guitars are close relatives of classical instruments, typically built with lighter and less expensive woods and used exclusively for the performance of flamenco, a highly stylized form of folk music and dance developed by Andalusian peasants during the late eighteenth and early nineteenth centuries.

Spruce Top Classical

David Argent's background in tool making and experimental engineering combines with his experience as a guitar player to give him a rare skill set as a luthier. He uses the lattice bracing and arched back approach developed by fellow countryman Greg Smallman. Argent is one of the few builders using Smallman-type lattice bracing whose spruce top guitars are equal or superior to his cedar tops. Although he has only been building for 10 years, his reputation has grown to the point where his name is now mentioned in the same breath as Smallman and Jim Redgate, who have long been considered Australia's preeminent luthiers.

Argent is known for the precision of his handwork. The highly refined parabolic arch of his Brazilian rosewood backs give his guitars a powerful, focused sound that is complemented by the ringing clarity of the spruce soundboards. His colorful new rosette, introduced in 2006, is based on Sturt's desert pea, which is South Australia's floral emblem.

Spruce Top Classical, 2006 ▶
David Argent, David Argent Guitars
Black Forest, South Australia
Courtesy of Chris Kamen,
Classic Guitars International,
Santa Barbara, California

29 ▶

SPECIFICATIONS

BODY AND SIDE WOODS: Brazilian rosewood
  (*Santos Palisander*)

TOP WOOD: Spruce

BODY WIDTH, LOWER BOUT: 14⁹⁄₁₆ inches (37 cm)

NECK WOOD: Brazilian mahogany

FRETBOARD MATERIAL: Indian ebony

HEADSTOCK DECORATION: Brazilian rosewood

BRIDGE: Padauk

NUT AND SADDLE: Bone

TUNING MACHINES: Schaller

BINDING: American walnut

SCALE LENGTH: 25.6 inches (65 cm)

NECK WIDTH AT NUT: (5.2 cm)

NUMBER OF FRETS: 20

BRACING: Lattice braced

FINISH: Acrylic lacquer

BODY DEPTH: 3⁷⁄₈ to 4¼ inches (9.8 to 10.8 cm)

BODY LENGTH: 19⁵⁄₁₆ inches (49 cm)

OVERALL LENGTH: 39¹⁄₁₆ inches (99 cm)

Joaquín Rodrigo Centenary Guitar

Simon Ambridge's guitars are inspired by the instruments of Antonio de Torres, Santos Hernandez, and Hermann Hauser I. "By combining design elements from these great makers with my own ideas," he says, "I produce instruments which are traditional in style, relatively lightly built, and very responsive." As a baby boomer born in 1951, Ambridge's interest in guitars coincided with the explosion of pop music in the 1960s, and the first guitar he made was a solid bodied electric. By the late 1970s, he had built a copy of a Martin 0-45 and (with the help of fellow luthier Kevin Aram) his first Torres-style classical guitar.

Ambridge built this guitar to commemorate the centenary of the birth of the blind Spanish composer Joaquín Rodrigo, who is best known for his concertos for guitar and orchestra. The adagio of Rodrigo's Concierto de Aranjuez, written in 1939, is one of the most familiar pieces of twentieth-century classical music. The haunting melody was adapted by Miles Davis on his album *Sketches of Spain*, and has been used in many movies, television shows, and commercials over the years. In the liner notes to *Sketches of Spain*, Miles Davis expresses the subtle power of Rodrigo's melody: "That melody is so strong that the softer you play it, the stronger it gets, and the stronger you play it, the weaker it gets."

SPECIFICATIONS

BODY AND SIDE WOODS: Brazilian rosewood

TOP WOOD: European spruce

BODY WIDTH, LOWER BOUT: 14½ inches (36.7 cm)

NECK WOOD: Honduran cedar

FRETBOARD MATERIAL: Ebony

HEADSTOCK DECORATION: Carved ebony, snakewood, and engraved sterling silver monogram

SOUND HOLE INLAYS: Natural and dyed veneers and mosaic

BRIDGE: Brazilian rosewood, snakewood inlays, and mosaic

NUT AND SADDLE: Fossil ivory

TUNING MACHINES: David Rodgers sterling silver sideplates and fossil ivory buttons

BINDING: Snakewood

SCALE LENGTH: 25.6 inches (65 cm)

NECK WIDTH AT NUT: 2$\frac{1}{16}$ inches (5.2 cm)

NUMBER OF FRETS: 19

BRACING: Fan strutted

FINISH: French polish

BODY DEPTH: 3⅝ to 3⅞ inches (9.2 to 9.8 cm)

BODY LENGTH: 19⅛ inches (48.5 cm)

OVERALL LENGTH: 38⅞ inches (98.8 cm)

Joaquín Rodrigo Centenary Guitar, 2000 ▶
Simon Ambridge, Ambridge Guitars
Dartington, England

31

Imperial

$\mathcal{P}$aulino Bernabé is one of Spain's preeminent classical builders and, by extension, one of the most highly regarded luthiers in the world. He began building guitars in the Ramirez workshop in 1954, where he stayed for 15 years before leaving because he felt the work was becoming too mechanized. Bernabé wanted to return to building entirely by hand.

Unlike many builders, Bernabé is also an accomplished guitarist himself. He studied for many years with Daniel Fortea, who in turn had studied with the legendary Franciso Tárrega, giving Bernabé a direct line to the heart of the Spanish tradition.

Bernabé says he and his son start with "fantastic wood that's very old. Some of our woods have been aged 100 years. You cannot make a great guitar without great wood; only then can we start to consider the design. My objective is to create guitars with more power and projection, suitable for large concert halls, while still maintaining the other characteristics of a superlative musical instrument—balance, sustain, refinement, and beautiful sound."

The Imperial is the Bernabés' top-of-the-line model and the epitome of the contemporary Spanish guitar.

♠ **Imperial, 2005**
Paulino Bernabé
Madrid, Spain
Courtesy of Chris Kamen, Classic Guitars International, Santa Barbara, California

SPECIFICATIONS

BODY AND SIDE WOODS: Brazilian rosewood

TOP WOOD: Spruce

BODY WIDTH, LOWER BOUT: 14⅝ inches (37.1 cm)

NECK WOOD: Mahogany, cedar

FRETBOARD MATERIAL: Ebony

BRIDGE: Brazilian rosewood

NUT AND SADDLE: Bone

TUNING MACHINES: Fustero

SCALE LENGTH: 25.6 inches (65 cm)

NECK WIDTH AT NUT: 2¹⁄₁₆ inches (5.2 cm)

NUMBER OF FRETS: 19/20

BRACING: Fan

FINISH: French polish

BODY DEPTH: 4⅛ inches (10.5 cm)

BODY LENGTH: 19⁵⁄₁₆ inches (49.1 cm)

OVERALL LENGTH: 39½ inches (100.3 cm)

Edmund Blöchinger

Llobet Model

*T*he master guitarist Pepe Romero, who has worked closely with Edmund Blöchinger for many years, calls him "one of the greatest luthiers in the world today." Both Pepe and his brother Celin often play Blöchinger guitars on stage, and they've joined Blöchinger in a quest to find ways to lower a guitar's action without diminishing the tension at the bridge. Many elements of Blöchinger's guitars, including the shapes of his fingerboards, fretting, and necks, have been designed to achieve this goal.

Blöchinger came to woodworking naturally: his grandfather was a retired forest master who walked with the boy in the spruce forests that surrounded his home and taught him how to judge which trees would yield the best lumber. Blöchinger initially trained and worked as a cabinetmaker but began studying guitar making in the early 1980s. He still selects all the wood for his guitar tops and cuts the trees himself.

◀ **Llobet Model, 2004**
Edmund Blöchinger
Dorfen, Germany
Collection of David Collette, Courtesy of
Guitar Salon International

SPECIFICATIONS

BODY AND SIDE WOODS: Brazilian rosewood

TOP WOOD: European (Alpine) spruce

BODY WIDTH, LOWER BOUT: 1 1/16 inches (35.7 cm)

NECK WOOD: Central American mahogany

FRETBOARD MATERIAL: Ebony

FRETBOARD INLAY: Mother-of-pearl (fret markers on 5, 7, 9) on the side of the fingerboard

HEADSTOCK DECORATION: Brazilian rosewood veneer

SOUND HOLE INLAYS: Ebony, Brazilian rosewood, maple

BRIDGE: Brazilian rosewood

NUT AND SADDLE: Bone

TUNING MACHINES: Reischl "superstar" gold-plated, bone buttons and rollers

BINDING: Maple

SCALE LENGTH: 25.6 inches (65 cm)

NECK WIDTH AT NUT: 2 1/6 inches (5.3 cm)

NUMBER OF FRETS: 19

BRACING: Traditional "Torres" 7-fan

FINISH: French polish, hand-rubbed shellac

BODY DEPTH: 3 3/4 inches (9.5 cm)

BODY LENGTH: 18 3/4 inches (47.6 cm)

OVERALL LENGTH: 38 inches (96.5 cm)

U.S. SUGGESTED RETAIL PRICE: $20,000

Spruce and Maple Classical Guitar

Greg Byers tried a lot of different things as a young man. He started out studying architecture at the University of California at Berkeley, dropped out, worked at a biochemistry lab, joined the Vietnam War resistance movement and narrowly avoided prison on a technicality after refusing induction into the army. He hitchhiked through Europe (but never got to Spain), went to pottery school and spent several years as a stoneware potter, returned to school to study biology, earned a PhD in Ecology and Evolutionary Biology at the University of Arizona, and spent half a year in Puerto Rico working on hummingbird-flower community ecology. It was there that he, a self-described "old steel-string folkie/rocker," fell for the nylon-string guitar.

In 1981, Byers took a course with José Romanillos, whom he says showed him that luthiery is "more than just gluing sticks together. He gave me reason to think my life's work could touch the creative, the spiritual, and the rational in equal measure," says Byers. "This is what I had been looking for."

Byers believes his background in science gives him a somewhat unusual perspective on the making of guitars. "Along with greatly valuing the intuitive approach that most luthiers live by," he says, "I also have the qualifications to bring the scientific method to bear on the art of luthiery. I see the potential for this particularly on the acoustical issues that sometimes seem mysterious and/or insurmountable." Thus far, he has performed intense scientific study of intonation and devised an improved solution to that age-old problem. He is currently seeking funding for a study that would use spectrum analysis of played notes and recordings of resonant frequency series to access the qualities of different soundboard materials and bracing methods.

SPECIFICATIONS

BODY AND SIDE WOODS: European maple

TOP WOOD: European spruce

BODY WIDTH, LOWER BOUT: 14½ inches (36.8 cm)

NECK WOOD: Mahogany

FRETBOARD MATERIAL: Ebony

HEADSTOCK DECORATION: Headstock joined with V-joint, ebony faceplate

SOUND HOLE INLAYS: Maple, pear, cedar, koa, rosewood, and magnolia

BRIDGE: Honduran rosewood

NUT AND SADDLE: Bone

TUNING MACHINES: Sloane

BINDING: Brazilian rosewood

SCALE LENGTH: 25.6 inches (65 cm)

NECK WIDTH AT NUT: 2 1/16 inches (5.3 cm)

NUMBER OF FRETS: 20

BRACING: Modified fan

FINISH: French polish

BODY DEPTH: 3 15/16 inches (10 cm)

BODY LENGTH: 19 5/16 inches (49.1 cm)

OVERALL LENGTH: 38 15/16 inches (99 cm)

U.S. SUGGESTED RETAIL PRICE: $9,500

♠ Spruce and Maple Classical Guitar, 2003
Gregory Byers, Byers Guitars
Willits, California

11-String Terz Guitar

odolfo Cucculelli built furniture with his father before he began crafting guitars in the late 1970s. He builds instruments in many styles following models by José Ramírez, Santos Hernández, Domingo Esteso, and Antonio de Torres, and crafts eight-, 10-, and 11-stringed guitars as well as standard six-stringed classical and flamenco forms.

Eleven-string guitars like this first came to attention through Göran Söllscher's acclaimed performances of the Bach lute suites and English Renaissance lute music on an instrument made by the Swedish luthier George Bolin. Also called Alto Guitars, these are small-bodied instruments tuned a third above normal pitch. The top seven strings are attached to a normal peghead while the four lowest (generally tuned D, C, B, Bb) are attached to a separate, staggered head that allows each string to be a different length. The fingerboard is also staggered, ending well above the sound hole on the lower strings, but extending over it on the highest. The sound hole itself is oval, so all the strings pass over the open sound chamber, just as they would on a standard six-string.

35

◀ **11-String Terz Guitar, 2002**
Rodolfo Cucculelli
Cella Monte, Italy

SPECIFICATIONS

BODY AND SIDE WOODS: East Indian rosewood sides

TOP WOOD: Italian Alpine spruce

BODY WIDTH, LOWER BOUT: 13⅝ inches (34.6 cm)

FRETBOARD MATERIAL: Brazilian rosewood

HEADSTOCK DECORATION: Veneered with ebony

BRIDGE: East Indian rosewood

NUT AND SADDLE: Bone

TUNING MACHINES: Schaller

SCALE LENGTH: 21.8 inches (55.4 cm)

NECK WIDTH AT NUT: 3⅝ inches (9.3 cm)

FINISH: Shellack

BODY DEPTH: 3⅞ to 4⅛ inches (9.8 to 10.5 cm)

BODY LENGTH: 16⅙ inches (40.7 cm)

OVERALL LENGTH: 36⁹⁄₁₆ inches (92.9 cm)

CLASSICAL & FLAMENCO

Custom Concert Classical, Left Handed

*B*ob Desmond is a protégé of Manuel Velázquez, whom he has lived near since the maestro retired to Florida in 1992. Maestro Velázquez has allowed Desmond to visit his workshop frequently and watch him at work, and Desmond says that Velázquez has shown him, through his own instruments, what qualities a great guitar should possess.

Encouragement and support from Velázquez and other luthiers including Robert Ruck and Jeffrey Elliott ultimately led Desmond to devote himself to luthiery full time after a 30-year career as a professional photographer. Desmond continues to take photos, including many wonderful portraits of his friend and mentor, and is also a singer/songwriter and artist. He says he goes about his daily work "with maestro Velázquez's teachings always in mind, attempting to build world-class instruments in the style of Torres, Hauser, and Santos Hernandez. The work that I do is not easy, and that's what I like about it."

Desmond is a perfectionist who produces only six guitars a year. Everything is completely handmade, including his custom parquetry and intricate rosettes. His intention is to make guitars that are very musical and that play easily, with a sound that is clear and sweet, and has a good amount of sustain.

♠ **Custom Concert Classical, Left Handed, 2006**
Robert Boyd Desmond, Desmond Guitars
Orlando, Florida

SPECIFICATIONS

BODY AND SIDE WOODS: Brazilian rosewood

TOP WOOD: German spruce

BODY WIDTH, LOWER BOUT: 14 9/16 inches (37 cm)

NECK WOOD: Mahogany

FRETBOARD MATERIAL: Ebony

HEADSTOCK DECORATION: Brazilian rosewood headstock with mother-of-pearl clover

SOUND HOLE INLAYS: Custom handmade rosette with mother-of-pearl tulips

BRIDGE: Indian rosewood

NUT AND SADDLE: Bone

TUNING MACHINES: David/Robert Rodgers, England

BINDING: Flamed koa with maple and Brazilian rosewood purflings

SCALE LENGTH: 25.6 inches (65 cm)

NECK WIDTH AT NUT: 2 3/32 inches (5.3 cm)

NUMBER OF FRETS: 19

BRACING: Torres fan with open harmonic bar

FINISH: Top is French polished and the rest of guitar oil varnished

BODY DEPTH: 3 7/8 inches (9.8 cm)

BODY LENGTH: 19 3/32 inches (48.5 cm)

Eight-String Classical Guitar with Cutaway

Although six-stringed instruments became the norm in the nineteenth century, guitars with added strings continue to have advocates today. The most common variation is the eight-string, which usually has two added bass strings, tuned to D and A below low E respectively (A, D, E, A, D, g, b, e). The Belgian classical guitarist Raphaella Smits plays an eight-string tuned this way. When asked by *Classical Guitar* magazine why she plays an eight-string, Smits responded, "It is not that I prefer eight to six strings, but that a lot of the music I'm playing benefits from the extra bass strings. The additional seventh and eighth strings give a more full sound. And the seventh string is sometimes very useful for a better, more convenient left-hand fingering."

Jeffrey Elliott is one of America's most highly respected classical guitar makers, with a varied client list that includes Julian Bream, Earl Klugh, Leo Kottke, Burl Ives, and Ralph Towner. Elliott is noted for his rosettes, which he calls "the visual focal point of the guitar, the aesthetic centerpiece, and the maker's signature. I enjoy being creative here," he explains, "integrating the rosette into the instrument's overall aesthetic theme, which is often suggested by the woods themselves." In addition to traditional mosaic designs, he offers rosettes of naturally figured wood and can flank either a traditional mosaic or figured wood with delicate chip carving.

SPECIFICATIONS

BODY AND SIDE WOODS: Brazilian rosewood

TOP WOOD: Western red cedar

BODY WIDTH, LOWER BOUT: 14⅜ inches (36.6 cm)

NECK WOOD: Spanish cedar

FRETBOARD MATERIAL: African ebony

HEADSTOCK DECORATION: Front and back are Brazilian rosewood and maple veneer, with signature head design

SOUND HOLE INLAYS: Mosaic central band, bordered by Brazilian rosewood, satinwood, maple, and holly lines

BRIDGE: Brazilian rosewood with mammoth ivory tieblock inlays

NUT AND SADDLE: Mammoth ivory

TUNING MACHINES: David E. Rodgers (England); scalloped nickel-silver sideplates, engraved; mammoth ivory buttons

BINDING: East Indian rosewood

SCALE LENGTH: 25.8 inches (65.5 cm)

NECK WIDTH AT NUT: 27⅗ inches (70 cm)

NUMBER OF FRETS: 19

BRACING: Traditional Torres/Hauser fan bracing modified for my open-harmonic bar design

FINISH: Traditional French polish (shellac)

BODY DEPTH: 4⅛ inches (10.5 cm) at end

BODY LENGTH: 19 inches (48.2 cm)

OVERALL LENGTH: 40⅜ inches (102.5 cm)

U.S. SUGGESTED RETAIL PRICE: $20,000

37

♠ **Eight-String Classical Guitar with Cutaway, 2000**
Jeffrey R. Elliott, Jeffrey R. Elliott Guitars
Portland, Oregon

Felipe V Flamenco Concert Guitar

*F*elipe and Mariano Conde's family has been building guitars for more than 100 years. The Conde Hermanos (Conde Brothers) were trained by their father and uncle, Mariano and Faustino Conde, who in turn worked together as apprentices under their uncle, Domingo Esteso. Before opening his own shop in 1915, Domingo worked with the legendary Manuel Ramirez, and he was one of the architects of the modern flamenco guitar. Conde guitars have been played by such masters as Vicente Gomez, Paco de Lucia, David Moreno, and Sabicas, as well as by such well-known rock and jazz musicians as David Byrne, Leonard Cohen, Al Di Meola, Bob Dylan, and John McLaughlin.

The Felipe V, named after the street address of their shop in Madrid, is the top of the Conde Brothers' line and one of the finest and most sought after flamenco guitars in the world. Although the Condes also offer this model in Brazilian rosewood, this example features the traditional flamenco combination of a cedar top with Spanish cypress back and sides.

38

SPECIFICATIONS

BODY AND SIDE WOODS: Spanish royal cypress

TOP WOOD: Spruce

BODY WIDTH, LOWER BOUT: 14¾ inches (375 mm)

NECK WOOD: Cedar

FRETBOARD MATERIAL: Ebony

SOUND HOLE INLAYS: Different wood types and colors

BRIDGE: Avalon and mother-of-pearl

NUT AND SADDLE: Bone

TUNING MACHINES: Maximum precision machine head

BINDING: Different wood types and colors

SCALE LENGTH: 25.6 inches (65 cm)

NECK WIDTH AT NUT: 2⅛ inches (5.3 cm)

NUMBER OF FRETS: 19

FINISH: Shellac varnish, fine marquetry details in top, back, sides, and neck

BODY DEPTH: 4⅛ inches (10.5 cm)

BODY LENGTH: 19⅛ inches (48.5 cm)

OVERALL LENGTH: 38½ inches (98 cm)

U.S. SUGGESTED RETAIL PRICE: $20,518

♠ **Felipe V Flamenco Concert Guitar, 2004**
Conde Hermanos
Madrid, Spain

Eight-String Brahms Guitar

This unique guitar was designed by the late David Rubio following concepts of the innovative Scottish virtuoso Paul Galbraith.

The name Brahms Guitar comes from Galbraith's arrangement of the Brahms Variations on an Original Theme, Opus 21A for Piano, which he initially transcribed for six-string guitar. Although he was generally pleased with the arrangement, Galbraith found he still had two significant problems to overcome. "Firstly, I was worried by a certain incompleteness in the bass," he says. "The other problem was that, for much of the piece, my left hand was stretched to its limits."

Galbraith's ultimate solution was to extend the range of the guitar by adding two outer strings, a high string tuned a fourth above the standard high E-string, which would allow him to play more high notes in first position, and an extra bass string tuned a fifth below low E. Galbraith took his ideas to the great English luthier David Rubio, who found a solution in the orpharion, a Renaissance-era member of the cittern family with fanned frets and a slanted bridge and nut that gave it a range of string lengths, longer for the bass notes and shorter for the trebles.

Rubio's design proved an immediate success, and Galbraith has used the instrument ever since in his quest to expand the guitar's capabilities and repertoire. Galbraith supports the Brahms Guitar with a metal end pin, which allows him to hold it upright, like a cello, and mounts the pin in a resonator box that increases the volume and density of the instrument's sound. Since David Rubio's death in 2000, the development of the Brahms Guitar has passed to his former apprentice Martin Woodhouse, who inherited his wood supply and many of his techniques.

SPECIFICATIONS

BODY AND SIDE WOODS: Brazilian rosewood

TOP WOOD: European spruce

BODY WIDTH, LOWER BOUT: 14 11/16 inches (37.3 cm)

ELECTRONICS: Schlemper 40W amp system, with external Sennheiser micro-mic set-up

NECK WOOD: Honduran mahogany

FRETBOARD MATERIAL: Ebony

HEADSTOCK DECORATION: Brazilian rosewood headplate and white and black veneers. (Design is an elongated version of the standard Rubio head design.)

SOUND HOLE INLAYS: Standard Rubio rosette

BRIDGE: Brazilian rosewood, modified classical design

NUT AND SADDLE: Bone

TUNING MACHINES: Custom-made Rodgers eight-string tuners

BINDING: Brazilian rosewood

SCALE LENGTH: 1st string 24.2 inches (61.5 cm); 8th string 25.6 inches (65 cm)

NECK WIDTH AT NUT: 2 7/16 inches (6.3 cm)

NUMBER OF FRETS: 20

BRACING: Soundboard has modified fan bracing with a thin bridge graft following the angle of the bridge. Back uses standard classical three-bar bracing.

FINISH: Oil varnish

BODY DEPTH: 3 3/4 inches (9.6 cm) at the neck end; 3 15/16 inches (10 cm) at the endlock

BODY LENGTH: 19 5/8 inches (49.8 cm)

OVERALL LENGTH: 40 1/8 inches (102 cm)

◆ **Eight-String Brahms Guitar, 1994**
David Rubio
Cambridge, England

39

Model C3 Concert Classical

Michael Greenfield's new double top concert-sized guitar incorporates a number of decidedly nontraditional design elements, including concentric circular acoustic radiators (developed in collaboration with acoustic physicist Dr. Evan B. Davis), a single offset sound hole on the upper bout's treble side, a single secondary side sound port, and a proprietary arrangement of asymmetrical, elongated fan bracing on the soundboard. Greenfield says the result is an instrument with exceptional volume, projection, and clarity. "It's very quick and responsive, with belllike highs, complex partial harmonics, a tight, articulate bass, and a strong, well-defined midrange."

Greenfield's wood of choice for all of his soundboards is now Lutz or Roche spruce (*Picea glauca* + *P. sitchensis* = *P. lutzii*), a naturally occurring hybrid cut from stands on the eastern interior slopes of British Columbia's coastal mountain range, where Sitka and white spruce commonly overlap and interbreed. Hybridization also occasionally takes place between white and Engelmann spruce in this region, meaning three-way crosses are also possible. Whatever its exact genetic makeup, Lutz can be of extraordinary quality, and Greenfield says he doubts he will ever find a finer tonewood.

◀ **Model C3 Concert Classical, 2006**
Michael Greenfield, Greenfield Guitars
Montreal, Quebec, Canada

SPECIFICATIONS

BODY AND SIDE WOODS: Brazilian rosewood

TOP WOOD: Double top, alpine spruce

BODY WIDTH, LOWER BOUT: 14¾ inches (37.5 cm)

NECK WOOD: Spanish cedar

FRETBOARD MATERIAL: Ebony

BRIDGE: Brazilian rosewood

NUT AND SADDLE: Bone

TUNING MACHINES: Sloane

BINDING: Ebony

SCALE LENGTH: 25.75 inches (65.5 cm)

NECK WIDTH AT NUT: 2¹⁄₁₆ inches (5.2 cm)

NUMBER OF FRETS: 21

BRACING: Asymmetrical, elongated fan

FINISH: Lacquer

BODY DEPTH: 4⅛ inches (10.5 cm)

BODY LENGTH: 19⁵⁄₁₆ inches (49 cm)

OVERALL LENGTH: 39⅜ inches (100 cm)

U.S. SUGGESTED RETAIL PRICE: $14,700

Greg Smallman Classical

W hen Greg Smallman started building classical guitars in 1972, Australian instruments and luthiers weren't taken seriously. Realizing that he'd have to offer something extraordinary to receive the international recognition he sought, he went back to first principals. By 1980, he had developed a substantially new approach to classical luthiery.

What he came up with was an elaborate crisscross "lattice" bracing system of short lightweight balsa struts reinforced with carbon fiber and coupled with unbraced sides and a slightly arched back, both made from heavy, laminated rosewood. This combination allowed him to use a much thinner, lighter, and more responsive soundboard than previous builders. These innovations give his guitars a wider frequency response in combination with a less percussive sound, and a significant increase in volume.

The world renowned guitarist and fellow Australian, John Williams, bought one of Smallman's new guitars in 1981 and has championed his work ever since, bringing worldwide attention to his novel instruments.

Smallman continues to experiment with his design. In 1990, he added a truss rod similar to those used in steel-string guitars and more recently has replaced the traditional rosewood bridge with lighter weight padauk. In late 1998, he produced two guitars with no neck heel, and in 2001, he produced an adjustable neck which allows the player to adjust the action without detuning or altering the saddle. Smallman's current guitars include a small armrest on the lower bass side. The armrest makes the guitar more comfortable for the player and, at the same time, prevents his arm from touching and dampening the soundboard.

Smallman's sons Damon and Kym began working alongside their father in 1994, and they produce their own highly regarded instruments as well as assisting with their father's designs.

41

SPECIFICATIONS

BODY AND SIDE WOODS: Brazilian rosewood

TOP WOOD: Cedar

BODY WIDTH, LOWER BOUT: 14⁵/₁₆ inches (36.4 cm)

● **Greg Smallman Classical, 2002**
Smallman & Sons
Melbourne, Australia
Courtesy of Chris Kamen, Classic Guitars International,
Santa Barbara, California

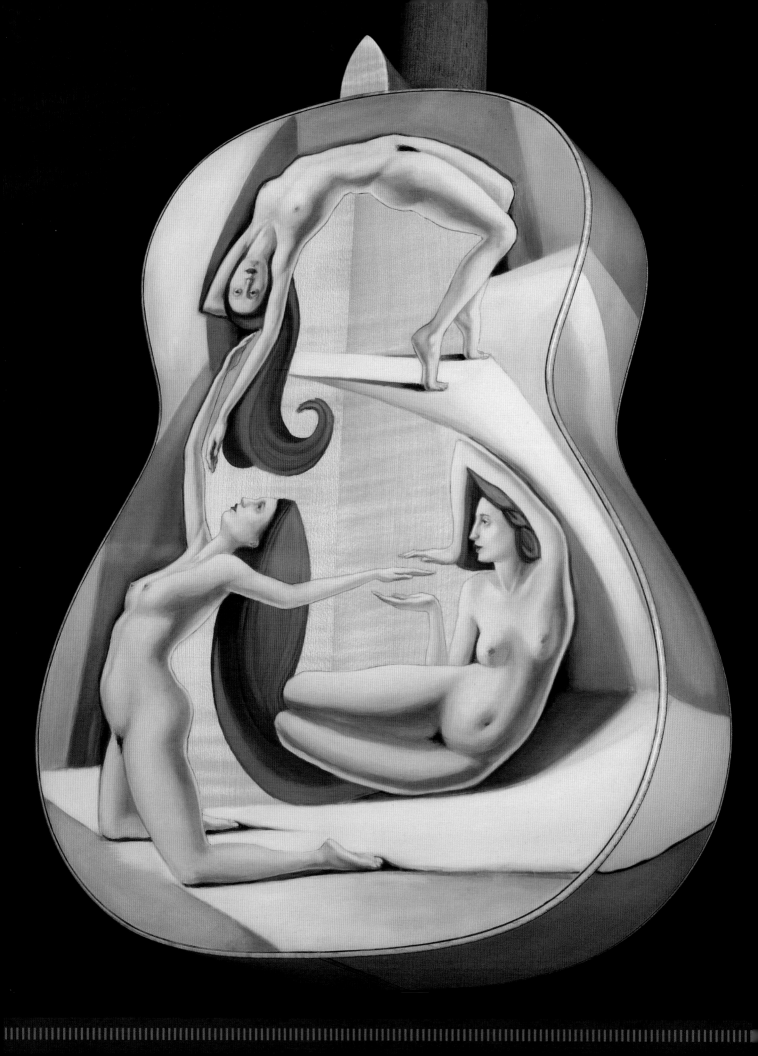

Millennium Hand-Painted Edition #1, "Les Acrobats"

The large open areas of plain wood on many Renaissance and Baroque instruments, including the backs of guitars, violin family instruments, and the protective tops of harpsichords, were often decoratively painted. The renowned classical guitar builder Thomas Humphrey, whose father was a painter and silversmith, has teamed with oil painter and muralist Tamara Codor to revive this tradition. "Tamara has a unique style of combining classical painting with abstract modernism," says Humphrey, "just like my concept for the Millennium guitar." Humphrey's patented Millennium design, introduced in 1985, is distinguished by its sloped face and raised fingerboard.

This guitar, first in a series, features three female acrobats in midflight. Humphrey says the unique construction of this guitar, which differs slightly from his Millennium models in order to accommodate the painting, also resulted in improved sound. "Some really great 'guitar ears' have seen and played this guitar," he says, "and they have told me they think it's the best-sounding ever."

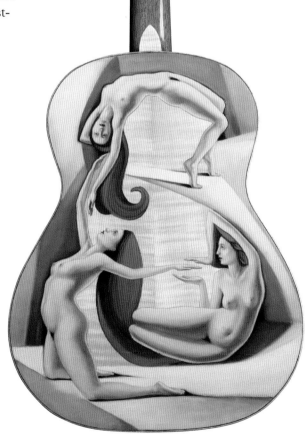

43

SPECIFICATIONS

BODY AND SIDE WOODS: Maple laminated over Brazilian rosewood

TOP WOOD: Cedar

BODY WIDTH, LOWER BOUT: 14¾ inches (37.5 cm)

NECK WOOD: Spanish cedar

FRETBOARD MATERIAL: African ebony

HEADSTOCK DECORATION: Brazil rosewood overlay

SOUND HOLE INLAYS: Wood mosaic

BRIDGE: Brazil rosewood

NUT AND SADDLE: Bone

TUNING MACHINES: Gotoh

BINDING: Maple

SCALE LENGTH: 25.6 inches (65 cm)

NECK WIDTH AT NUT: 2¹⁄₁₆ inches (5.2 cm)

NUMBER OF FRETS: 20

BRACING: Lattice

FINISH: Shellac top and lacquer over oil paint

BODY DEPTH: 4½ inches (11.4 cm)

BODY LENGTH: 19 inches (48.3 cm)

OVERALL LENGTH: 42 inches (106.7 cm)

U.S. SUGGESTED RETAIL PRICE: $42,000

♠ **Millennium Hand-Painted Edition #1, "Les Acrobats," 2006**
Built by Thomas Humphrey
Painted by Tamara Codor
Gardiner, New York

Laurie Williams Classic

*L*aurie Williams builds steel- and nylon-stringed guitars from various types of kauri, a native New Zealand species. The top of this classical guitar is recently cut kauri, which has great resonance, while the back and sides are built from kauri logs that were buried under peat swamps on New Zealand's north island thousands of years ago and remained undisturbed until recent times. Carbon dating suggests these ancient kauri logs are between 30,000 and 45,000 years old.

Whitebait is the name given to describe the bear claw-like lines that occasionally occur in kauri. The outrageously flamed whitebait on this instrument comes from a small ancient kauri log dug up around

1998. Williams describes the timber as "just fantastic to look at, with a chatoyance normally associated with shells like mother-of-pearl. The high flame with intense whitebait concentration, as well as the beautiful dark golden color, is what makes this so exceptional. No one in the industry has seen the likes of it before or since, and it is doubtful whether we shall see it again."

Because his stock of kauri is so limited, Laurie Williams is building just two instruments a year with the wood.

◆ **Laurie Williams Classic, 2005**
Laurie Williams, Laurie Williams Guitars
Mangonui, New Zealand

SPECIFICATIONS

BODY AND SIDE WOODS: New Zealand Williams whitebait ancient kauri

TOP WOOD: New Zealand modern kauri

BODY WIDTH, LOWER BOUT: 14½ inches (36.8 cm)

NECK WOOD: Whitebait ancient kauri

FRETBOARD MATERIAL: Ebony

HEADSTOCK DECORATION: Snakewood

SOUND HOLE INLAYS: Rose

BRIDGE: Snakewood

NUT AND SADDLE: Mammoth ivory

TUNING MACHINES: Gotoh 510

BINDING: Snakewood

SCALE LENGTH: 25.6 inches (65 cm)

NECK WIDTH AT NUT: 2 1/16 inches (5.2 cm)

NUMBER OF FRETS: 20

BRACING: Williams modified fan bracing

FINISH: Lacquer

BODY DEPTH: 3 7/8 inches (9.8 cm)

BODY LENGTH: 18 7/8 inches (48 cm)

OVERALL LENGTH: 38 5/8 inches (98 cm)

U.S. SUGGESTED RETAIL PRICE: $30,000

Cedar Double Top

$\mathcal{M}$atthias Dammann has pioneered the so-called "double top" guitar, which has a soundboard made of a sandwich of extremely thin tonewood "skins" surrounding a core of synthetic aerospace material. The material has a honeycomb structure, and, like the beehives it imitates, is light but deceptively strong. A composite double top is lighter by about 25 percent and stronger than a conventional wooden soundboard. Also, instruments with double tops are louder and more responsive than a normal guitar.

The noted classical guitarist David Russell told *Acoustic Guitar* magazine that his Dammann weighs much less than most other instruments he has used. "It has a very powerful sound which makes it easier to play with an orchestra," continues Russell. "The sound is very flexible. Often cedar top guitars force you into one sound, but this one gives a big fat sound if I want it and a thin, bright, sparkling sound when I want that."

◀ Cedar Double Top, 2006
Matthias Dammann
Passau, Germany
Courtesy Chris Kamen, Classic Guitars International,
Santa Barbara, California

SPECIFICATIONS

BODY AND SIDE WOODS: Brazilian rosewood

TOP WOOD: Cedar double top

BODY WIDTH, LOWER BOUT: 14⅜ inches (36.5 cm)

NECK WOOD: Mahogany, Spanish cedar

FRETBOARD MATERIAL: Ebony/Brazilian rosewood

BRIDGE: Brazilian rosewood

NUT AND SADDLE: Bone

TUNING MACHINES: Sloane/Rodgers

SCALE LENGTH: 25.6 inches (65 cm)

NECK WIDTH AT NUT: 2⅛ inches (5.4 cm)

NUMBER OF FRETS: 10/20

BRACING: Fan inspired under double top

FINISH: French polish

BODY DEPTH: 4¼ inches (10.8 cm)

BODY LENGTH: 19⅜ inches (49.2 cm)

OVERALL LENGTH: 38⅞ inches (98.7 cm)

Concert Classical

Michael Cone built his first classical guitar in 1969 after hearing Julian Bream play an instrument by the French luthier Robert Bouchet (1898–1986). Not long after he began building, he stumbled on an 1803 guitar by the Spanish luthier Juan Pagés at a garage sale in Maine. Pagés (1742–1821) was one of the first builders to experiment with fan bracing, and the guitar gave Cone insight into Pagés five-fan bracing and other eighteenth-century construction techniques.

Another important influence on Cone's developing approach was Marten Cornelissen, a master violin maker. "Cornelissen was able to measure and evaluate Stradivari and Guarnari instruments at the Smithsonian," Cone recalls, "and he was generous and forthcoming with his knowledge. As I applied his experience and method with violins to the classical guitar, a quality of tone emerged that can best be described as singing, rich, warm, clear and brilliant, with excellent projection, separation, and sustain."

Cone's guitars follow Torres's pattern, but he uses both traditional fan bracing and his own "bent fan" bracing, which he developed after studying Dr. Michael Kasha's designs and hearing examples of radial-braced instruments. "I tried bending the braces in the center instead of using separate braces," Cone explains, "and accomplished the sound I was looking for—a traditional guitar sound, only more so." Cone also enhanced the effect of the bracing by carefully varying the thickness of the soundboard as had Stradivari and Guarneri.

Cone suspended guitar production between 1987 and 1998 while he pursued his interest in robotics and computer software. He resumed limited production of classical guitars in 1998, and in 1999, he moved to Maui, where he continues to build "the finest guitars I am capable of."

SPECIFICATIONS

BODY AND SIDE WOODS: Brazilian rosewood

TOP WOOD: European spruce

BODY WIDTH, LOWER BOUT: 14⅝ inches (37.1 cm)

NECK WOOD: Spanish cedar

FRETBOARD MATERIAL: Ebony

FRETBOARD INLAY: Mother-of-pearl

HEADSTOCK DECORATION: Carved ebony

SOUND HOLE INLAYS: Wood mosaic

BRIDGE: Honduran rosewood

NUT AND SADDLE: Pre-ban ivory

TUNING MACHINES: Sloane artist

BINDING: Brazilian rosewood, maple

SCALE LENGTH: 25.6 inches (65 cm)

NECK WIDTH AT NUT: 2¹⁄₁₆ inches (5.3 cm)

NUMBER OF FRETS: 20

BRACING: Soundboard, five fan; back, two V braces

FINISH: Lacquer

BODY DEPTH: 3¹³⁄₁₆ inches (9.7 cm)

BODY LENGTH: 19½ inches (49.5 cm)

OVERALL LENGTH: 39⅞ inches (101.3 cm)

U.S. SUGGESTED RETAIL PRICE: $11,000

♠ **Concert Classical, 2004**
Michael Cone, Michael Cone Classical Guitars
Maui, Hawaii

47

Concert Nylon Crossover Guitar #19

att Mustapick delights in combining exotic woods with striking pattern and/or color including bloodwood, zebrawood, cocobolo, curly koa, sapele, bear claw Sitka spruce, and African mahogany. This nylon string features a redwood top, koa trim, and Malaysian blackwood back and sides. Malaysian blackwood is a nickname for a dense, heavy ebony species (*Diospyros ebonasea*) that some luthiers compare in quality to Brazilian rosewood and African blackwood.

Mustapick's Concert Nylon Crossover is intended to offer the rich warmth of nylon strings, with all the responsiveness, clarity, and projection of a fine classical guitar, combined with the 14-fret geometry and playability that steel-string players are familiar with. The Concert Nylon's soundboard bracing pattern follows the classical tradition, and the waist of the guitar is advanced toward the fingerboard so that more of the lower bout surrounds the bridge.

48

♠ **Concert Nylon Crossover Guitar #19, 2005**
Matthew Mustapick, Mustapick Handmade Guitars
Soquel, California

SPECIFICATIONS

BODY AND SIDE WOODS: Malaysian blackwood

TOP WOOD: Redwood

BODY WIDTH, LOWER BOUT: 14⅜ inches (36.5 cm)

FRETBOARD MATERIAL: Ebony

HEADSTOCK DECORATION: Macassar ebony

BRIDGE: Ebony

NUT AND SADDLE: Bone

TUNING MACHINES: Gotoh deluxe

BINDING: Curly koa

SCALE LENGTH: 25.75 inches (65.4 cm)

NECK WIDTH AT NUT: 1⅞ inches (4.8 cm)

NUMBER OF FRETS: 20

BRACING: Classical strut bracing

FINISH: Nitrocellulose lacquer applied by
  Addam Stark

BODY DEPTH: 4⅛ inches (10.5 cm)

BODY LENGTH: 19⅜ inches (49.2 cm)

OVERALL LENGTH: 40½ inches (102.9 cm)

U.S. SUGGESTED RETAIL PRICE: $4,600

José Oribe

Gran Suprema 664 Concert Model & Gran Suprema Flamenco

José Oribe was a 23-year-old machinist working in the aerospace industry when he first heard a classical guitar. The sound mesmerized him and changed the direction of his life, leading him first to selling classical guitars, and then, in 1962, to begin building them in his garage.

Within a few years of building his first guitar, Oribe was already recognized as among the foremost luthiers in the world. His extensive experience as a factory machinist informed his approach to production, and he maintains a remarkable level of personal oversight building both classical and flamenco guitars.

Oribe still controls every aspect of production; he chooses all the parts for every instrument, matches the woods for color and grain, selects the correct soundboard, and decides which rosette design to use. The guitars are made in batches of anywhere from eight to 17 at a time, and although they take several years to complete, batches are in constant process of assembly, so orders are usually filled quickly. Oribe says he purchased "a lifetime supply of woods" in the 1960s, so components can be made and cured several years in advance. As a result, the long list of celebrated artists who have played Oribe guitars includes Chet Atkins, Earl Klugh, Michael Lorimer, Jiro Matsuda, Frederick Noad, Angel and Pepe Romero, Sabicas, and David Tanenbaum.

◀ **Gran Suprema 664 Concert Model, 2005**
José Oribe, Oribe Guitars
Vista, California

49

Gran Suprema Flamenco, 2005 ▶
José Oribe, Oribe Guitars
Vista, California

SPECIFICATIONS

BODY AND SIDE WOODS: Rarest Brazilian rosewood, birdseye maple, and true Spanish cypress

TOP WOOD: Spruce and cedar

NECK WOOD: Mahogany and Spanish cedar with ebony reinforcements

FINISH: French polish shellac

Jim Redgate
Lattice-Braced Concert Guitar

im Redgate has been building his lattice-braced classical guitars for more than 20 years. Like fellow Australian Greg Smallman, Redgate builds his guitars with an arched braceless back to improve their volume and projection and uses lightweight carbon fiber reinforcements under the soundboard. While not as thin as Smallman's, Redgate's soundboards are much lighter than traditionally braced examples, and his guitars are therefore more responsive, energy efficient, and louder than traditional classical instruments.

Redgate points out that carbon fiber is both lighter and stronger than wood. It allows the soundboard to flex to increase response without danger of giving out like wood braces can, and fiber-reinforced tops are also less likely to be affected by adverse humidity conditions than traditionally braced soundboards.

The Croatian classical virtuoso, Ana Vidovic, is now playing a Redgate exclusively. She says, "When I got it and began to play, I immediately knew that this was the instrument that I want to be playing for a long time. The most amazing thing was that the sound had so much power and beauty, and that it was so easy to play. I felt like I could just make music and not worry about the projection. This guitar has it all."

♠ Lattice-Braced Concert Guitar, 2006
Jim Redgate, Jim Redgate Guitars
Adelaide, Australia
Courtesy of Chris Kamen, Classic Guitars International, Santa Barbara, California

SPECIFICATIONS

BODY AND SIDE WOODS: Brazilian rosewood

TOP WOOD: Spruce

BODY WIDTH, LOWER BOUT: 14¹¹⁄₁₆ inches (37.4 cm)

NECK WOOD: Honduran mahogany

FRETBOARD MATERIAL: Black ebony

SOUND HOLE INLAYS: Rosette handcrafted from 4,000 pieces of Australian wood

BRIDGE: Padauk

TUNING MACHINES: Fustero tuners

BINDING: Australian jarrah

SCALE LENGTH: 25.6 inches (65 cm)

NECK WIDTH AT NUT: 2¹⁄₁₆ inches (5.2 cm)

FINISH: Catalysed nitrocellulose, hand-cut full gloss with satin soundboard

BODY DEPTH: 3⁷⁄₈ to 4¹⁄₈ inches (9.8 to 10.5 cm)

BODY LENGTH: 19⁷⁄₁₆ inches (49.4 cm)

Flamenco Blanca

lamenco guitars are traditionally built with cedar tops and cypress bodies, whereas classical instruments are normally crafted from spruce and rosewood. Cypress is lighter than rosewood and produces a brighter, more aggressive sound. The preference among flamenco players may originally have arisen simply because cypress guitars were cheaper than rosewood ones, but the difference in tonal quality sealed the bargain and has helped define the sound of flamenco. Because flamenco guitarists often use the top of their guitars percussively, traditional flamenco guitars have a plastic or turtle shell plate called *el golpeador* on one or both sides of the sound hole to protect the surface from the sharp blows of the player's hand.

Manuel Reyes Sr., who opened his first shop in 1949, has been one of the world's most admired flamenco builders for decades, and his waiting list now extends beyond 20 years. Reyes was a flamenco guitarist before he began building, and his instruments have always been highly favored by working musicians. This example from the 1980s has traditional friction tuning pegs rather than machine heads.

51

SPECIFICATIONS

BODY AND SIDE WOODS: Spanish cypress

TOP WOOD: Spruce

BODY WIDTH, LOWER BOUT: 14⅝ inches (37.1 cm)

NECK WOOD: Mahogany/cedar

FRETBOARD MATERIAL: Ebony

BRIDGE: Rosewood

NUT AND SADDLE: Bone

TUNING MACHINES: Fustero

SCALE LENGTH: 25.8 inches (65.5 cm)

NECK WIDTH AT NUT: 2¹⁄₁₆ inches (5.3 cm)

NUMBER OF FRETS: 19

BRACING: Fan

FINISH: French polish

BODY DEPTH: 3⅞ inches (9.8 cm)

BODY LENGTH: 19⅛ inches (48.6 cm)

OVERALL LENGTH: 39½ inches (100.3 cm)

♠ **Flamenco Blanca, 1987**
Manuel Reyes Sr.
Córdoba, Spain
Courtesy of Chris Kamen, Classic Guitars International,
Santa Barbara, California

Robert Ruck
Classical Guitar

Robert Ruck, who is entirely self-taught as a luthier, began building full-time when he was 20 and has long been considered one of the greatest classical luthiers in the world. Although he is a prolific builder who averages about 30 guitars a year and has completed more than 900 over the course of his career, he felt compelled to stop taking new orders for good when his waiting list stretched beyond 300 instruments.

Ruck experiments constantly with design elements, and many of his recent instruments feature what he calls "acoustic ports," which are small round auxiliary sound holes, 13/16 inch (2.1 cm) in diameter, cut through the sides of the upper shoulders, one on either side of the heel. The ports are situated 2½ inches (6.4 cm) from the centerline of the heel and centered on each side, and they surround the player with sound.

Kenny Hill, who has been producing a model designed by Ruck for several years, explains the acoustic port concept this way: "The guitar is an air pump. So, thinking about a guitar with just one normal sound hole, and seeing it as a sort of diaphragm, it's clear that there is an 'air flow' bottleneck there at the sound hole, and for that instant while a column of air is moving out, it actually prevents air from moving in, and vice versa. This causes a temporary vacuum or pressure to occur inside the instrument. If you open up a hole somewhere else, you free up the top, just like opening the vent hole on a gas can." Ruck offers the acoustic ports as a free option to his clients, and guitars with ports come with rosewood plugs should the guitarist want to close one or both.

SPECIFICATIONS

BODY AND SIDE WOODS: Indian rosewood

TOP WOOD: Western red cedar

BODY WIDTH, LOWER BOUT: 14½ inches (36.8 cm)

NECK WOOD: Honduran mahogany

FRETBOARD MATERIAL: Ebony

SOUND HOLE INLAYS: Traditional mosaic

BRIDGE: Brazilian rosewood

NUT AND SADDLE: Bone

TUNING MACHINES: Gotoh

BINDING: Rosewood with purflings of maple and rosewood

SCALE LENGTH: 25.6 inches (65 cm)

NECK WIDTH AT NUT: 2⅛ inches (5.4 cm)

NUMBER OF FRETS: 19

BRACING: Nine fan braces symetrically placed

FINISH: Synthetic varnish

BODY DEPTH: 4 inches (10.2 cm)

BODY LENGTH: 19⁵/₁₆ inches (49.1 cm)

U.S. SUGGESTED RETAIL PRICE: $12,500

♠ **Classical Guitar, 2001**
Robert Ruck, Ruck Guitars
Eugene, Oregon

A Series Classical Guitar

*G*ary Southwell is a student of historical guitars who makes dead-on reproductions of nineteenth-century instruments by Lacôte, Panormo, Schertzer, and Stauffer as well as his own highly original designs. Unlike most contemporary guitars, his A Series is based not on Torres and the Spanish tradition, but on the Viennese tradition exemplified by Stauffer and his student Schertzer.

Viennese guitars are known for their bright, responsive sound and technical innovations. The A Series incorporates two of Stauffer's innovations—an adjustable neck (A stands for adjustable), which Southwell has refined so that the player can adjust the string height or action "in seconds if need be," and a raised fingerboard that extends out over the soundboard like a violin rather than being glued to it. The guitar also has a cutaway, an armrest for comfort, and an unusually shaped headstock that echoes the shape of the cutaway, balancing the design in a novel and very distinctive way.

The cutaway was designed at the request of American virtuoso David Starobin, a leading champion of both early nineteenth-century Romantic and contemporary classical guitar who has had about 300 pieces written for him.

53

SPECIFICATIONS

BODY AND SIDE WOODS: Indian rosewood

TOP WOOD: European spruce

BODY WIDTH, LOWER BOUT: 14$^{15}/_{16}$ inches (38 cm)

NECK WOOD: Figured maple

FRETBOARD MATERIAL: Ebony

HEADSTOCK DECORATION: Ebony

SOUND HOLE INLAYS: Ebony/oak/engraved bone

BRIDGE: Indian rosewood

NUT AND SADDLE: Lignum vitae

TUNING MACHINES: Rodgers

BINDING: Ebony

SCALE LENGTH: 25.4 inches (64.6 cm)

NECK WIDTH AT NUT: 2 inches (5 cm)

NUMBER OF FRETS: 20

BRACING: Southwell curved bracing system

FINISH: Oil varnish

BODY DEPTH: 3$^3/_8$ to 4$^5/_{16}$ inches (8.5 to 11 cm)

BODY LENGTH: 18$^1/_8$ inches (46 cm)

OVERALL LENGTH: 37$^{15}/_{16}$ inches (96.3 cm)

U.S. SUGGESTED RETAIL PRICE: $12,000

♠ **A Series Classical Guitar, 2006**
Gary Southwell, Southwell Guitars
Nottingham, England

Classical Concert Guitar

Theo Scharpach, who began building guitars in 1976, says he has never understood why other makers narrow their product line. Following the lead of craftsmen of the eighteenth and nineteenth centuries, whom he believes were much more versatile, Scharpach produces one of the widest ranges of acoustic instruments of any contemporary luthier, including six- and 12-stringed flattops, archtops, Selmer jazz guitars, nylon-stringed jazz and parlor guitars, and octave mandolins. His curiosity has also led him to try his hand at South American guitar relatives like the tiple, requinto, and charango, as well as double necks, long necks, eight-strings, harp guitars, and even a hurdy-gurdy, which took him more than half a year to build over a six year period.

"I am very interested in the history of the guitar," says Scharpach, "simply because that is knowledge we get for free, but we should move further. I appreciate the guitar of Torres, but I would not make a classical concert guitar by copying Torres. I wanted to develop guitars that added something to the history of guitar making." Scharpach's classical model, which took 15 years to develop, incorporates a number of radical concepts intended to improve acoustics, including a double soundtable resonator separated by a bracing system from the back of the guitar, a unique semi-cutaway on the upper treble bout, a raised fingerboard, and an inlaid carbon fiber neck reinforcement. The result of these innovations is a guitar with pronounced sustain, distinct separation of notes within chords, and greatly reduced extraneous string noise.

SPECIFICATIONS

BODY AND SIDE WOODS: Brazilian rosewood

TOP WOOD: German spruce

BODY WIDTH, LOWER BOUT: 14³⁄₁₆ inches (36 cm)

NECK WOOD: *Cedrela odorata*, optional ebony veneered neck

FRETBOARD MATERIAL: Ebony

HEADSTOCK DECORATION: Ebony veneer with maple and ebony layers of veneer

SOUND HOLE INLAYS: Laser cut marquetry of ebony, mahogany, palisander, and maple veneers

BRIDGE: Brazilian rosewood

NUT AND SADDLE: Mammoth ivory

TUNING MACHINES: Custom designed by Rodgers Machines

BINDING: Brazilian rosewood with maple and rosewood purfling

SCALE LENGTH: 25.6 inches (65 cm)

NECK WIDTH AT NUT: 2¹⁄₈ inches (5.3 cm)

NUMBER OF FRETS: 24

BRACING: Non-traditional custom Scharpach design

FINISH: High gloss finish with cellulose, original mixture of different lacquer components with shellac parts

BODY DEPTH: 3³⁄₄ to 4¹⁄₈ inches (9.5 to 10.5 cm)

BODY LENGTH: 19⁷⁄₁₆ inches (49.4 cm)

OVERALL LENGTH: 41⁵⁄₁₆ inches (105 cm)

U.S. SUGGESTED RETAIL PRICE: $12,880

▲ **Classical Concert Guitar, 2005**
Designed by Theo Scharpach
Built by Theo Scharpach and Menno Bos,
Scharpach Guitars
Groessen, The Netherlands

Series II Concert Guitar

Philip Woodfield

*P*hilip Woodfield is both a luthier and an accomplished player who believes it is vital that an instrument "feels right," with a neck shape and action that are comfortable and nonrestrictive. "A guitar must feel satisfying to play," he explains. "It has always been my aim to produce guitars that have clarity, sustain, and good separation of notes. What I love to hear are guitars that sing."

Woodfield says the drive behind his Series II is to produce more volume from a top of traditional thickness. Like his Series I, the Series II is loosely based on traditional designs inspired by Torres and Hauser, but the soundboard of the Series II guitar is braced with carbon fiber-reinforced struts. While most luthiers who incorporate carbon into their bracing couple this approach with an extremely thin, lightweight soundboard, Woodfield chose not to change the top itself. He says the guitars are "very bright in sound and, particularly in the hands of a strong player, they are loud."

Woodfield took the figure on this instrument's unique headstock design from a Roman artifact in the British Museum.

SPECIFICATIONS

BODY AND SIDE WOODS: Brazilian rosewood

TOP WOOD: European spruce

BODY WIDTH, LOWER BOUT: 14½ inches (36.8 cm)

NECK WOOD: Mahogany

FRETBOARD MATERIAL: Ebony

HEADSTOCK DECORATION: Ebony, figured maple, engraved with a figure taken from Roman antiquity

SOUND HOLE INLAYS: Ebony, figured maple

BRIDGE: Brazilian rosewood

NUT AND SADDLE: Bone

TUNING MACHINES: Schaller

BINDING: Brazilian rosewood, boxwood lines

SCALE LENGTH: 25.6 inches (65 cm)

NECK WIDTH AT NUT: 2 1/16 inches (5.3 cm)

NUMBER OF FRETS: 20

BRACING: Lattice model and fan model

FINISH: French polish

BODY DEPTH: 3¾ to 3 15/16 inches (9.5 to 10.1 cm)

BODY LENGTH: 19 1/8 inches (48.6 cm)

OVERALL LENGTH: 39 1/16 inches (99 cm)

55

◆ **Series II Concert Guitar, 2004**
Philip Woodfield
East Sussex, England
Courtesy of Chris Kamen, Classic Guitars
International, Santa Barbara, California

FLATTOP

The first modern acoustic flattop guitars were built by Christian Frederick Martin Sr. in the 1850s, and his innovations were developed and codified by The Martin Guitar Company over the course of the nineteenth and early twentieth centuries. Martin's signal innovation was X bracing, so-called for the spruce braces that cross between the central sound hole and the bridge, thereby providing strong support for the guitar's top at its weakest point and allowing the use of thinner, more responsive wood for the soundboard.

All of Martin's nineteenth-century guitars were relatively small-bodied instruments, built for use with catgut strings. In the 1890s Carl and August Larson created the first X-braced guitars specifically made to handle the added pressure of steel strings. The Larsons' breakthrough was followed by Martin, Gibson, Lyon & Healy, and other American manufacturers in the early decades of the twentieth century, and steel-string flattops became the guitar of choice for a long line of seminal American musicians including Jimmie Rodgers, Robert Johnson, Gene Autry, Hank Williams, Elvis Presley, and Bob Dylan.

The steel-string acoustic flattop remains immensely popular today. Martin and Gibson still produce superb examples of the form, and they have been joined by a host of talented independent luthiers who have analyzed, revived, and improved upon older models and continue to explore and refine the materials and techniques of flattop lutherie.

Green Series
Millennium Oak Special Edition

SPECIFICATIONS

BODY AND SIDE WOODS: Mahogany

TOP WOOD: Alaskan Sitka spruce

BODY WIDTH, LOWER BOUT: 16⅜ inches (416 mm)

NECK WOOD: Mahogany and sycamore

FRETBOARD MATERIAL: Ebony, bound with rosewood and sycamore

HEADSTOCK DECORATION: Oak Leaf inlaid and headstock bound with rosewood and sycamore

SOUND HOLE INLAYS: Hand-inlaid rosewood and sycamore

BRIDGE: Brazilian rosewood

NUT AND SADDLE: Ox bone

TUNING MACHINES: Gotoh SG381

BINDING: Rosewood

SCALE LENGTH: 25.5 inches (64.8 cm)

NECK WIDTH AT NUT: 1¾ inches (4.4 cm)

NUMBER OF FRETS: 20

BRACING: A.X.E. configuration with Alaskan Sitka spruce

FINISH: Satin, nitrocellulose

BODY DEPTH: 4¾ inches (12.2 cm)

BODY LENGTH: 20⅛ inches (51.2 cm)

OVERALL LENGTH: 41¼ inches (104.8 cm)

U.S. SUGGESTED RETAIL PRICE: $4,895

Many parts of the British Isles celebrated the arrival of the Millennium in 2000 by planting oak saplings. Three of these "millennium oaks" were planted in a wildfowl reserve near Avalon Guitars and helped inspire the Avalon "Green" Millennium Oak Special Edition.

The Avalon Millennium Oak Special Edition bears the epithet "Green" because of Avalon Guitars' responsible use of precious tonewoods through minimizing waste. Not only is the guitar inspired by nature, it also represents nature's limited resources. Each guitar has an actual leaf from one of the "millennium oaks" inlaid on the headstock beneath the company's hand-carved myrtlewood logo, and the sound hole and bridge design also draw inspiration from nature's colors and lines.

Avalon Guitars, established in 2000, grew out of the renowned Lowden Guitar operation in Northern Ireland. The company was formed to allow some of Lowden's finest craftsmen to become involved in designing as well as building guitars.

♦ **Green Series Millennium Oak Special Edition, 2004**
Avalon Guitars
Newtownards, Northern Ireland

African Rose Bushongo

The father-son team of Bruce and Matt Petros crafts their limited-edition African Rose guitars from a combination of two rare and beautiful woods, with tops of curly redwood felled in the late-nineteenth century and backs and sides of highly figured bubinga (*Guibourtia tessmannii*), also known as African rosewood.

The redwood comes from logs that sank on their way to a mill at the mouth of the Big River in Mendocino, California, in the mid-1800s and were uncovered more than a hundred years later by bridge builders drilling to sink piling. The bubinga is from a single tree that yielded what the Petroses call "the most striking and elegant figure we have ever seen, [with] a deep, even, and consistent curl."

Bruce Petros has been building acoustic guitars since 1972, and Matthew officially joined the family business in 2000. All of the guitars the two men build feature "pre-stress arched tops," created by gluing on preshaped braces all at once in a vacuum jig to ensure a perfect fit. The Petroses adhere to this time-consuming process because they believe it dramatically increases the strength and stability of the top while enhancing the instrument's tonal response and volume. Another unusual feature of Petros guitars is their handmade tuner buttons, which in the case of the African Rose are carved from Brazilian boxwood.

SPECIFICATIONS

BODY AND SIDE WOODS: Curly African rosewood

TOP WOOD: Century-old curly redwood

BODY WIDTH, LOWER BOUT: 15½ inches (39.4 cm)

NECK WOOD: Mahogany

FRETBOARD MATERIAL: African ebony

HEADSTOCK DECORATION: Petros inlay of mother-of-pearl

SOUND HOLE INLAYS: Bushongo tribal textile design in boxwood

BRIDGE: African ebony

NUT AND SADDLE: Fossilized walrus ivory

TUNING MACHINES: Gotoh 310s with handmade boxwood buttons

BINDING: Boxwood

SCALE LENGTH: 25.5 inches (64.8 cm)

NECK WIDTH AT NUT: 1 13/16 inches (4.6 cm)

NUMBER OF FRETS: 20

BRACING: Petros scalloped symmetrical bracing of Sitka spruce

FINISH: Polyurethane

BODY DEPTH: 4½ inches (11.4 cm)

BODY LENGTH: 19½ inches (49.5 cm)

OVERALL LENGTH: 40½ inches (102.9 cm)

U.S. SUGGESTED RETAIL PRICE: $22,500

♦ African Rose Bushongo, 2006
Bruce and Matt Petros, Petros Guitars
Kaukauna, Wisconsin

59

Jeff Babicz
Signature Series Colossal

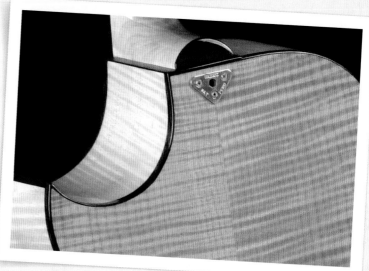

*J*eff Babicz's guitars employ three unique solutions to problems inherent to traditional flattops. Most notably, Babicz's "lateral compression soundboard" anchors the strings directly to the lower part of the soundboard rather than the bridge, thereby spreading string tension across the top of the guitar and reducing the need for interior bracing. Babicz explains, "When you detune a drumhead and tap it, you get very little sound, but when you tune it to pitch and tighten the drum head, volume is released and it becomes alive acoustically. This is exactly what occurs with my new, patent-pending acoustical system. Tonally, there is an extreme balance not only across the strings but also up the neck. Notes ring true past the fifth fret. The classic choked bass notes are freed...once and for all. Another benefit to the design is a much more relaxed string feel to the player especially when bending notes [because] a longer portion of the string is used overall."

Second, instead of being glued down, the "torque-reducing split bridge" is attached to the top with special fasteners that allow it to be easily moved to optimize intonation. Finally, the neck can be adjusted simply by turning a key with an Allen wrench, allowing the player to change the string height and action at will.

◄ **Signature Series Colossal, 2006**
Jeff Babicz, Babicz Guitars
Newburgh, New York

SPECIFICATIONS

BODY AND SIDE WOODS: Master-grade flamed maple

TOP WOOD: Master-grade Adirondack spruce

BODY WIDTH, LOWER BOUT: 17 inches (43.2 cm)

NECK WOOD: Master-grade Honduran mahogany

FRETBOARD MATERIAL: Ebony

FRETBOARD INLAY: Paua abalone

HEADSTOCK DECORATION: Babicz logo in mother-of-pearl with Babicz initial logo in paua abalone over Brazilian rosewood

SOUND HOLE INLAYS: Paua abalone

BRIDGE: Ebony

NUT AND SADDLE: Tusq nut and compensated tusq saddle

TUNING MACHINES: Grover mini gold plated

BINDING: Cocobolo

SCALE LENGTH: 25.5 inches (64.8 cm)

NECK WIDTH AT NUT: 1¾ inches (4.4 cm)

NUMBER OF FRETS: 20

BRACING: Adirondack spruce

FINISH: Nitrocellulose lacquer

BODY DEPTH: 4¾ inches (12.1 cm)

BODY LENGTH: 21⅛ inches (53.7 cm)

OVERALL LENGTH: 42 inches (106.7 cm)

U.S. SUGGESTED RETAIL PRICE: $8,000

"Barbecue Bob"
Stella-Style 12-String

This beautifully crafted guitar was inspired by the smaller type of ladder-braced Stella 12-string played by Robert Hicks, known as "Barbecue Bob," a popular 1920s recording artist who helped define the Atlanta-style of acoustic blues. Hicks was discovered by Columbia Records talent scout Don Hornsby in 1926 while cooking and singing in an upscale barbecue joint outside Atlanta. Hornsby gave Hicks his moniker, had publicity photos taken of him in his white chef's apron, and recorded his first hit 78, "Barbecue Blues," early in 1927. Barbecue Bob went on to record sixty-two sides for Columbia before dying of influenza-related pneumonia in 1931 at age 29. He ranks with Willie McTell, who played a larger bodied 12-string, as the greatest and most influential of early Atlanta bluesmen.

"Barbecue Bob" Stella-Style 12-String, 2002 ►
Ralph S. Bown, Bown Guitars
York, England

SPECIFICATIONS

BODY AND SIDE WOODS: Spanish cypress back and sides, with a light honey sunburst

TOP WOOD: Sitka spruce

BODY WIDTH, LOWER BOUT: 14½ inches (36.8 cm)

SOUND HOLE INLAYS: Tortoise-shell and marquetry trim

BRIDGE: 6-pin

SCALE LENGTH: 26½ inches (67.4 cm), long Stella scale

NECK WIDTH AT NUT: 2 inches (5 cm)

BODY DEPTH: 3½ inches (8.9 cm) tapering to 4 inches (10.8 cm)

Beardsell 2G Slotted Sunburst

As a quick glance at any of his instruments reveals, Allan Beardsell is a maverick with his own ideas about how a guitar should look and sound.

The 2G is the smaller of two acoustic steel-string models that Beardsell makes, and it features his three most prominent design elements: a small, unusually shaped sound hole, a pair of sound side ports he cuts into the bass side of his guitars, and a unique interior structure. Beardsell says the side ports give more bass end to the player, but he feels they don't reduce the guitar's projection because that is the job of the soundboard. "Placement and number of openings is, in my view, irrelevant," he

continues, "except to the comfort of the player. The fact that I didn't omit the front sound hole altogether is because I simply didn't think it would look right!" The sound hole has an odd shape, reminiscent of Mario Maccaferri "Gypsy jazz" guitars, and is set in the active area of the top in the upper bout, where Beardsell feels "the nice trebles exist."

The soundboard is lattice-braced, and the sides are laminated to make them as stiff as a drum rim. Beardsell views the guitar sides as a mounting platform not only for the top but for the back, as well, which he supports with Kasha-style radial braces. The guitar also has a "Laskin" armrest, a beveled cut in the bass side of the lower bout invented by fellow Canadian luthier William "Grit" Laskin. The armrest allows the player to position his picking arm in a more comfortable and ergonomically sensible angle to the strings.

♠ Beardsell 2G Slotted Sunburst, 2006
Allan Beardsell, Beardsell Guitars
Winnipeg, Manitoba, Canada

SPECIFICATIONS

BODY AND SIDE WOODS: Quilted maple

TOP WOOD: Red spruce

BODY WIDTH, LOWER BOUT: 15¼ inches (38.7 cm)

ELECTRONICS: LR Baggs Imix

NECK WOOD: Honduran mahogany

FRETBOARD MATERIAL: Brazilian rosewood

HEADSTOCK DECORATION: Black pearl logo, Brazilian rosewood over/underlay

SOUND HOLE INLAYS: Raised lip (Brazilian rosewood) sideports, blue herringbone top hole

BRIDGE: Brazilian rosewood

NUT AND SADDLE: Bone

TUNING MACHINES: Waverly 3-on-a-plate (engraved) with snakewood buttons

BINDING: Brazilian rosewood

SCALE LENGTH: 24.65 inches (62.6 cm)

NECK WIDTH AT NUT: 1¾ inches (4.4 cm)

NUMBER OF FRETS: 20

BRACING: X on top, radial/transverse on back

FINISH: Nitrocellulose lacquer - Sunburst

BODY DEPTH: 4⅝ inches (11.7 cm)

BODY LENGTH: 18⅞ inches (47.9 cm)

OVERALL LENGTH: 40¼ inches (102.9 cm)

U.S. SUGGESTED RETAIL PRICE: $4,100

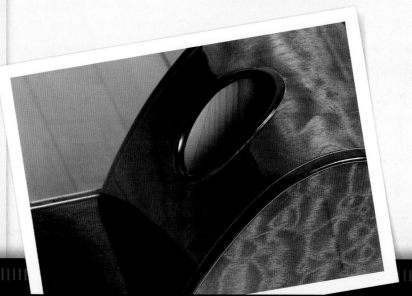

Genesis G2 12-Fret

The Genesis represents Tom Bills's take on the acoustical theories of Dr. Michael Kasha and the Kasha-influenced guitars of Richard Schneider and Boaz Elkayam.

Bills was exhibiting his archtops at a local guitar show when he first encountered Boaz's work. "One guitar caught my eye immediately. I remarked to a friend what an odd-looking thing to not have a hole in the front of the guitar. As I approached it to get a closer look, Boaz picked up the guitar and strummed a first position E chord. That one strum changed my life. I didn't know anything about classics then, but I knew the sound I was looking for when I heard it."

Bills describes what he heard as "a full spectrum sound that leaps from the guitar." "You can't say this guitar is loud so much as you can say it projects," explains Bills, "or say that it vibrates so much as you can say it responds." Putting the sound hole in the center of the top effectively cuts the soundboard in half and requires heavy interior bracing to make up structurally for the giant hole cut in the middle of all the string tension. The heavy bracing keeps the upper bout stiff, so only the area from the sound hole down to the tail of the guitar top is really used for producing sound.

Kasha theorized that moving the sound hole to the bass or treble side of the upper bout would create a greatly enlarged vibrating diaphragm and taking the hole completely off the top would improve things even further.

SPECIFICATIONS

BODY AND SIDE WOODS: Brazilian rosewood

TOP WOOD: Bear claw Sitka spruce

BODY WIDTH, LOWER BOUT: 14½ inches (36.8 cm)

ELECTRONICS: K&K pickup

NECK WOOD: Honduran mahogany

FRETBOARD MATERIAL: Ebony

FRETBOARD INLAY: Ivory falling leaf with paua shell purfling

HEADSTOCK DECORATION: Book-matched Brazilian rosewood with lace wood veneer

SOUND HOLE INLAYS: Ebony and lacewood binding

BRIDGE: Brazilian rosewood

NUT AND SADDLE: Ivory

TUNING MACHINES: Gilbert tuners

BINDING: Macassar ebony with lacewood purfling and paua shell border on top of guitar

SCALE LENGTH: 25.4 inches (64.5 cm)

NECK WIDTH AT NUT: 2 inches (5 cm)

NUMBER OF FRETS: 20

BRACING: Non-traditional

FINISH: Nitrocellulose

BODY DEPTH: 4½ inches (11.4 cm)

BODY LENGTH: 19½ inches (49.5 cm)

OVERALL LENGTH: 40¾ inches (103.5 cm)

U.S. SUGGESTED RETAIL PRICE: $13,000

◀ **Genesis G2 12-Fret, 2005**
Tom Bills, Tom Bills Custom Guitars
St. Louis, Missouri

Nick Lucas Tribute Model

*M*arc Beneteau has been building guitars since 1974, the year he wisely decided he did not want to make his living as a musician and met the seminal Canadian luthier Jean Larrivée. More than 30 years later he says he feels "fortunate indeed" to follow a career that he "would gladly have as a hobby."

Beneteau says his new Nick Lucas Tribute Model is only loosely based on Gibson's famous Nick Lucas acoustic flattop of the 1930s. Though not meant to be a copy of the Gibson, it takes many of its cues from the compact but surprisingly powerful original. "The body shape is the same, as is the sound hole size and location," says Beneteau. "I've also kept the unique '13 frets to the body' design. Otherwise though, it is pure Beneteau in regard to headstock shape, bindings, sound hole inlay, bracing, and so on."

Although he is largely forgotten today, Nick Lucas was a pioneer instrumentalist and singer enormously popular in the 1920s and '30s. Born Dominic Nicholas Anthony Lucanese in Newark, New Jersey, his 1922 recordings of his own *Pickin' The Guitar* and *Teasin' The Frets* were the first commercial jazz guitar records ever, and he went on to record many of the great early songs from Tin Pan Alley. His biggest hit was the original recording of "Tip-Toe Through the Tulips with Me," which sold more than a million copies in 1929. Both the song and Lucas's distinctive falsetto vocal style were greatly admired by the young Herbert Khaury, later to be known as Tiny Tim.

SPECIFICATIONS

BODY AND SIDE WOODS: Brazilian rosewood

TOP WOOD: Adirondack spruce

BODY WIDTH, LOWER BOUT: 14⅞ inches (37.8 cm)

NECK WOOD: Mahogany

FRETBOARD MATERIAL: Brazilian rosewood

FRETBOARD INLAY: Mother-of-pearl Nick Lucas pattern

HEADSTOCK DECORATION: "B" (Beneteau) in mother-of-pearl

SOUND HOLE INLAYS: Brazilian rosewood

BRIDGE: Brazilian rosewood

NUT AND SADDLE: Bone

TUNING MACHINES: Waverly vintage-style tuners

BINDING: Flamed maple

SCALE LENGTH: 25 inches (63.5 cm)

NECK WIDTH AT NUT: 1¾ inches (4.4 cm)

NUMBER OF FRETS: 19

BRACING: Modified X-bracing pattern

FINISH: Lacquer

BODY DEPTH: 4⁵⁄₁₆ inches (11 cm)

BODY LENGTH: 19½ inches (49.5 cm)

OVERALL LENGTH: 39½ inches (100.3 cm)

U.S. SUGGESTED RETAIL PRICE: $7,100

▲ **Nick Lucas Tribute Model, 2004**
Marc Beneteau, Beneteau Guitars
St. Thomas, Ontario, Canada

FLATTOP

CB Super Style 42

Chris Bozung

hris Bozung's CB Guitars are the instruments of choice for more than a few Bluegrass flatpickers, many of whom consider his meticulously crafted guitars the equal of the vintage Martin and Gibson dreadnoughts they are modeled upon.

In addition to a roster of smaller dreadnoughts, Bozung also produces this interpretation of the classic Gibson Super Jumbo of the 1930s. The biggest, most powerful instrument he has ever made, the CB Super has a larger, more rounded top than his dreadnoughts, and features such design touches as a double-bound sound hole, pointed-end fingerboard, and Bozung's own unique take on the Gibson trademarked "Moustache" bridge. Where the original pre-war Super Jumbo guitars featured a 16⅞-inch lower bout, Bozung's version has a slightly smaller X-braced 16½-inch body, which he says helps to focus the tone and eliminate unwanted bass overtones. Bozung scallops his braces, which gives the Super a combination of a vintage Gibson's booming bass and a Martin's clear treble notes.

66

🔺 **CB Super Style 42, 2004**
Chris Bozung, CB Guitars
Fairview, Tennessee

SPECIFICATIONS

BODY AND SIDE WOODS: Cocobolo

TOP WOOD: Engelmann spruce

BODY WIDTH, LOWER BOUT: 16½ inches (41.9 cm)

NECK WOOD: Honduran mahogany

FRETBOARD MATERIAL: Ebony

FRETBOARD INLAY: CB rose vine

HEADSTOCK DECORATION: CB rose bud

SOUND HOLE INLAYS: CB double ring with abalone

BRIDGE: CB moustache bridge, ebony with rose inlays

NUT AND SADDLE: Bone

TUNING MACHINES: Gold-plated Grover vintage-style

BINDING: Grained ivoroid with style 42 abalone purfling

SCALE LENGTH: 25.4 inches (64.5 cm)

NECK WIDTH AT NUT: 1¹¹⁄₁₆ inches (4.3 cm)

NUMBER OF FRETS: 20

BRACING: Forward-shifted scalloped X

FINISH: Hand-stained vintage sunburst

BODY DEPTH: 4⅞ inches (12.4 cm)

BODY LENGTH: 20⅝ inches (52.4 cm)

OVERALL LENGTH: 41¼ inches (104.8 cm)

U.S. SUGGESTED RETAIL PRICE: $4,250

Compass Rose Acoustic Guitar

*A*lthough he has been building guitars for more than forty years, Rick Turner says he didn't want to get into building acoustics until he felt he had enough design elements in place to make something truly unique. "There are plenty of folks making great Martin- and Gibson-inspired guitars," says Turner. "But there are other avenues to explore and other issues to address than creating a brand-new 1930s-sounding guitar."

One of the main avenues Turner explored was the Howe-Orme guitars of the late 1890s, which featured a patented "raised longitudinal belly ridge" and adjustable necks. "I'd seen a Howe-Orme in the earliest days of my lutherie apprenticeship in 1963 in Boston," Turner recalls, "and that guitar showed me that there was no tone to be lost in going away from a traditional dovetailed neck joint, and in fact there might actually be a lot of tone gained by freeing the fingerboard from the top of the instrument. Add to that feature the ability to nearly instantly raise or lower the action, and you've got a great concept."

The only trouble with the Howe-Orme design was that it put too much pressure on the upper bout. Turner wanted to avoid deadening the upper bout with extra bracing or an enlarged headblock, and found the answer to the problem when he visited a medieval Gothic cathedral in France. As he contemplated the flying buttresses that supported the upper walls and made the soaring inner vault possible, he had an epiphany: why not try adding internal flying buttresses to a guitar that would distribute string pressure more evenly?

The buttresses worked very well indeed; this latest incarnation of the concept features four of them, along with a cantilevered fingerboard and "reverse kerfing," which increases stiffness around the rim without adding weight.

◀ **Compass Rose Acoustic Guitar, 2006**
Rick Turner, Turner Renaissance Guitars
Santa Cruz, California

67

SPECIFICATIONS

BODY AND SIDE WOODS: Brazilian rosewood

TOP WOOD: Engelmann spruce

BODY WIDTH, LOWER BOUT: 16¼ inches (41.3 cm)

NECK WOOD: Mahogany laminated

FRETBOARD MATERIAL: Pakka wood

BRIDGE: Rosewood

Carolina Grand Auditorium Baritone

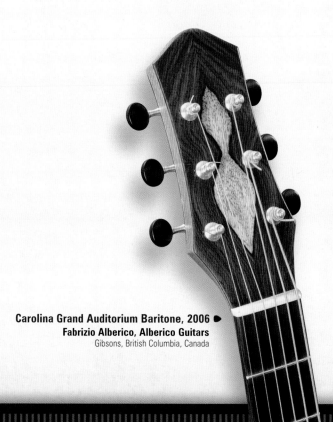

Carolina Grand Auditorium Baritone, 2006 ►
Fabrizio Alberico, Alberico Guitars
Gibsons, British Columbia, Canada

I am not sure my parents knew it," says Fab Alberico, "but as soon as they named me, they created a woodworker. What else could I be, given that *Fabrizio* means 'craftsman' and *Alberico* means 'tree'? And since my grandmother was a D'Addario of the famous string-making family, you could say I was destined to become a luthier."

Alberico became obsessed with fingerstyle guitar while in college, and both his classical and acoustic guitars are aimed squarely at fellow fingerstyle players. He apprenticed with fellow Canadian Sergei de Jonge, a renowned classical builder who has successfully brought many of his ideas on construction and bracing over to the steel-string guitar. Like his mentor, Alberico is a firm believer that less is more and likes to let the lines and woods of his guitars speak for themselves. An adherent and admirer of the Arts and Crafts aesthetic, one of Alberico's guiding mantras is Gustav Stickley's dictum, "There is nothing more highly embellished than a simple thing well done."

This stunning example of Alberico's work is a 28-inch scale-length baritone with back, sides, and head veneer from a set of Nicaraguan cocobolo, "the likes of which I've never seen before," exclaims the builder. Alberico resawed the wood himself from a log he uncovered while visiting an exotic wood supplier several years ago.

SPECIFICATIONS

BODY AND SIDE WOODS: Nicaraguan cocobolo

TOP WOOD: German spruce

BODY WIDTH, LOWER BOUT: 16 inches (40.6 cm)

ELECTRONICS: McIntyre Feather

NECK WOOD: Honduran mahogany

FRETBOARD MATERIAL: Ebony, bound with cocobolo

HEADSTOCK DECORATION: Cocobolo veneers, front and back

SOUND HOLE INLAYS: Cocobolo, paua shell, figured maple

BRIDGE: Ebony

NUT AND SADDLE: Fossilized walrus ivory

TUNING MACHINES: Alessi

BINDING: Cocobolo

SCALE LENGTH: 28 inches (71.1 cm)

NECK WIDTH AT NUT: 1⅞ inches (4.8 cm)

NUMBER OF FRETS: 19

BRACING: Spruce

FINISH: Nitrocellulose lacquer

BODY DEPTH: 4⅝ inches (11.7 cm)

BODY LENGTH: 20 inches (50.8 cm)

OVERALL LENGTH: 42½ inches (108 cm)

U.S. SUGGESTED RETAIL PRICE: $8,300

The Big Bang

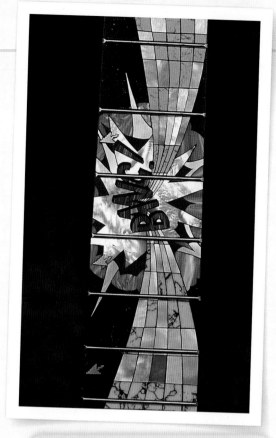

William "Grit" Laskin says the complex inlay on this guitar was the result of a lengthy series of e-mail and phone conversations with a client in France. "The correspondence could fill a novella, or so it seemed," Laskin jokes, "but it was a wonderful discussion of the artists who have meaning for him (principally Magritte and Lichtenstein) as well as his love of mathematics and symbolism in images. There is much that is left to interpretation in this inlay, but one of the more whimsical elements is the fact that the small rectangular shapes emerging from the Big Bang are actually binary code. The darker stone is a '1,' and the shell is a '0.' The code spells out 'stone' and 'shell.' And the position markers are computer cursor arrows, cut from silver."

Although his incomparable inlay work has brought him worldwide recognition, Grit Laskin is first and foremost a superb luthier whose work is admired by such fellow masters as Bob Benedetto, Bill Collings, Roger Sadowsky, and Bob Taylor. He originated the built-in ergonomic armrest and ribrest edge beveling and was the first instrument maker to receive Canada's most prestigious national craft award, the Saidye Bronfman Award for Excellence. Four of his guitars are in the permanent collection of the Canadian Museum of Civilization, Canada's equivalent of the Smithsonian, and he is a founder of the Association of Stringed Instrument Artisans (ASIA) and the author of the first code of ethics for the luthier's trade. Laskin also has recorded four albums of his own music, written a novel, and produced a book about his guitars and inlays titled *A Guitarmaker's Canvas*.

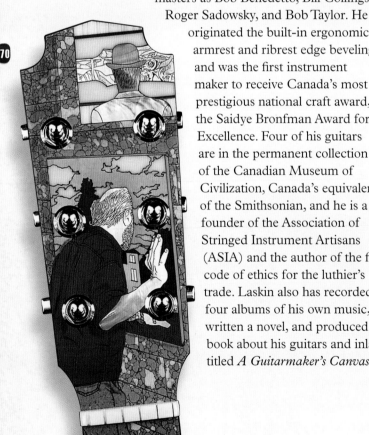

◀ **The Big Bang, 2005**
William "Grit" Laskin
Toronto, Ontario, Canada

SPECIFICATIONS

BODY AND SIDE WOODS: Ziricote

TOP WOOD: Sitka spruce

BODY WIDTH, LOWER BOUT: 15 inches (38 cm)

NECK WOOD: Brazilian rosewood, oil finish

FRETBOARD MATERIAL: Ebony

FRETBOARD INLAY: Various stone, shell, silver, engraved

HEADSTOCK DECORATION: Various stone, shell, silver, engraved

SOUND HOLE INLAYS: Wood and shell

BRIDGE: Ebony

NUT AND SADDLE: Bone

TUNING MACHINES: Schaller

BINDING: Curly maple

SCALE LENGTH: 25 inches (63.5 cm)

NECK WIDTH AT NUT: 1¾ inches (4.4 cm)

NUMBER OF FRETS: 18

BRACING: Spruce

FINISH: Lacquer

BODY DEPTH: 3¾ to 4⅛ inches (9.5 to 10.5 cm)

BODY LENGTH: 19¹¹⁄₁₆ inches (50 cm)

OVERALL LENGTH: 39⅜ inches (100 cm)

U.S. SUGGESTED RETAIL PRICE: $18,000

Bettie on Red

*G*rit Laskin says that the client who commissioned this dramatic guitar is not only a serious collector of "all things Bettie Page," but also has a tattoo of her on his arm. "The inlay was based on the photo that was the model for his tattoo," explains Laskin, "although I had to draw in most of her legs."

Bettie Page, "The Queen of Curves," was one of the most popular and controversial pinup girls of the 1950s. A voluptuous beauty with black bangs and a smile that *Playboy* magazine described as "suggesting forbidden fruit as well as apple pie," Page was named "Miss Pinup Girl of the World" in 1955 and appeared as the centerfold in *Playboy*'s January 1955 issue. Her often provocative cheesecake photographs violated a host of the era's sexual taboos and earned her a reputation as "The Bad Girl Next Door." The photos ultimately led to a U.S. Senate Committee investigation, after which Page quit modeling and disappeared from the public eye. Her whereabouts remained a mystery for more than 40 years, during which

time she grew into a modern popular culture icon, a fact she was oblivious to until the press finally located her in 2000. Today, Page is more popular than she was 50 years ago, in part because of the 2006 film, *The Notorious Bettie Page*, which introduced her legend to audiences born long after her career had ended.

SPECIFICATIONS

BODY AND SIDE WOODS: Brazilian rosewood

TOP WOOD: Sitka spruce

BODY WIDTH, LOWER BOUT: 15 inches (38 cm)

NECK WOOD: Mahogany

FRETBOARD MATERIAL: Ebony

FRETBOARD INLAY: Stone and shell, engraved

SOUND HOLE INLAYS: Wood and shell

BRIDGE: Ebony

NUT AND SADDLE: Bone

TUNING MACHINES: Schaller

BINDING: Ebony

SCALE LENGTH: 25.6 inches (65 cm)

NECK WIDTH AT NUT: 1¾ inches (4.4 cm)

NUMBER OF FRETS: 18

BRACING: Spruce

FINISH: Lacquer

BODY DEPTH: 3¾ to 4⅛ inches (9.5 to 10.5 cm)

BODY LENGTH: 19¹¹⁄₁₆ inches (50 cm)

OVERALL LENGTH: 39⅜ inches (100 cm)

U.S. SUGGESTED RETAIL PRICE: $15,000

♠ Bettie on Red, 2005
William "Grit" Laskin
Toronto, Ontario, Canada

SSS (Standard Steel String) Custom Bubinga

Sergei de Jonge is best known for his outstanding classical guitars, and the graceful lines of his standard steel-string model are influenced by traditional classical design. The front, back, and sides of this unusual custom version are built from bubinga (also known as African rosewood), a beautiful, dense rose-colored Central African hardwood that is strikingly striped with purple. The guitar also features a sound port on the upper left bout, which both increases bass response and projects sound up toward the player.

Like fellow Canadian masters William "Grit" Laskin and Linda Manzer, Sergei de Jonge apprenticed with Jean Larrivée. He now teaches comprehensive four- and five-week courses in classical and acoustic guitar, and most of his six children have learned at his side. His oldest daughter Josia now builds classical guitars full-time and is developing a reputation that rivals her father's. The de Jonge School of Lutherie courses include hands-on, five-days a week instruction in his workshop, as well as the option of staying at the old farm where he lives outside Ottawa, Ontario. He teaches every aspect of the building process from start to finish, and students come home with their own handmade guitar at the end of the course.

SPECIFICATIONS

BODY AND SIDE WOODS: Bubinga

TOP WOOD: Bubinga/spruce sandwich top

BODY WIDTH, LOWER BOUT: 15½ inches (39.4 cm)

NECK WOOD: Bubinga

FRETBOARD MATERIAL: Ebony

HEADSTOCK DECORATION: Ebony headplate

SOUND HOLE INLAYS: Spalted maple and abalone

BRIDGE: Ebony

TUNING MACHINES: Alessi tuners with black pearl buttons

BINDING: Ebony and abalone top purfling

NECK WIDTH AT NUT: 1¾ inches (4.4 cm)

▲ SSS (Standard Steel String) Custom Bubinga, 2006
Sergei de Jonge, de Jonge Guitar Company
Chelsea, Quebec, Canada

Cherry Concert Jumbo

Rick Davis says the challenge of his Concert Jumbo was to make a larger guitar that maintained the melodic quality of a smaller instrument while adding the bass response associated with the Jumbo/Dreadnought class. "Running Dog's Concert Jumbo has the sonority of larger instruments," asserts Davis, "a strong mid-range, and a pure, clear treble. Suited to fingerstyle as well as flatpicking, it is responsive and lively."

Davis is an advocate of building with "alternative" North American woods such as cherry, maple, sycamore, and walnut that allow him to make fine guitars without what he describes as "the destructive baggage of (often) irresponsibly harvested Central American rosewoods and mahoganies." This particular guitar is an example of the direction Davis is heading—trying to focus on the woods rather than on added decoration. "Consider it a Shaker-inspired guitar," he explains, referring to the nineteenth-century American religious sect known for their exquisite, minimalist furniture, baskets, and other utilitarian handcrafts. He adds, "There's more to come in this vein."

Davis named his company after his beloved golden retriever running companions, and each of his instruments features an inlay of his running dog logo on the headstock or as the ninth- or twelfth-fret position marker.

♠ **Cherry Concert Jumbo, 2004**
Rick Davis, Running Dog Guitars
Richmond, Vermont

SPECIFICATIONS

BODY AND SIDE WOODS: American flamed cherry

TOP WOOD: Adirondack red spruce

BODY WIDTH, LOWER BOUT: 15¾ inches (40 cm)

NECK WOOD: Mahogany

FRETBOARD MATERIAL: Ebony

FRETBOARD INLAY: Maple leaves, executed in green abalone

HEADSTOCK DECORATION: Maple leaves, green and red abalone

SOUND HOLE INLAYS: Cherry, wood veneers

BRIDGE: Ebony

NUT AND SADDLE: Bone

TUNING MACHINES: Schaller mini

BINDING: Ebony

SCALE LENGTH: 25.4 inches (64.5 cm)

NECK WIDTH AT NUT: 1¾ inches (4.4 cm)

NUMBER OF FRETS: 21

BRACING: X-braced

FINISH: Lacquer

BODY DEPTH: 4½ inches (11.4 cm)

BODY LENGTH: 20 inches (50.8 cm)

OVERALL LENGTH: 35 inches (88.9 cm)

U.S. SUGGESTED RETAIL PRICE: $3,500

OM-45 Deluxe

Introduced in 1929, the groundbreaking OM (for Orchestra Model) was the first truly modern flattop guitar. Designed specifically to carry steel strings, the new model was the first Martin to offer 14 frets clear of the body and a long 25.4-inch string scale, both of which became industry standards by the mid-1930s. The OM-45 was the highest priced guitar Martin had ever built and few were made; only forty OM-45 standards were produced between 1930 and 1933, when the model was discontinued, and another 14 were made of the much fancier OM-45 Deluxes, all built in 1930.

The combination of a relatively small body and long scale neck made the OM a very lively and responsive instrument, and its wide, thin neck proved ideal for fingerpicking. Fingerstyle players like Eric Schoenberg and Stefan Grossman rediscovered the virtues of the OM in the 1960s and '70s. In part because the remaining originals have become so eagerly sought and expensive— only five of the original fourteen OM-45 Deluxes are accounted for, and their value is now well over $100,000—modern interpretations are now part of the repertory of most of today's master builders. Julius Borges's elegant OMs are widely considered the equal of the rare originals. Although he also makes a more simply decorated 28-style version (as did Martin), his OM-45's exquisite mother-of-pearl trim offers an appropriate visual counterpart to the model's renowned acoustic qualities.

SPECIFICATIONS

BODY AND SIDE WOODS: Brazilian rosewood

TOP WOOD: Adirondack spruce

BODY WIDTH, LOWER BOUT: 15 inches (38.1 cm)

NECK WOOD: Mahogany

FRETBOARD MATERIAL: Ebony

FRETBOARD INLAY: Pale red abalone

HEADSTOCK DECORATION: Abalone

SOUND HOLE INLAYS: Abalone heart

BRIDGE: Ebony

NUT AND SADDLE: Bone

TUNING MACHINES: Gold plated, engraved Waverlys with mother-of-pearl buttons

BINDING: Ivoroid

SCALE LENGTH: 25.4 inches (64.5 cm)

NECK WIDTH AT NUT: 1¾ inches (4.4 cm)

NUMBER OF FRETS: 20

BRACING: Traditional X bracing of Adirondack spruce

FINISH: Nitrocellulose lacquer

BODY DEPTH: 4⅛ inches (10.5 cm)

BODY LENGTH: 19⅜ inches (49.2 cm)

OVERALL LENGTH: 39¾ inches (101 cm)

U.S. SUGGESTED RETAIL PRICE: $24,500

♦ **OM-45 Deluxe, 2004**
Julius Borges, Borges Guitars
Littleton, Massachusetts

FLATTOP

16-Inch Jumbo

$\mathcal{M}$ ike Doolin was a professional musician long before he started building guitars, but maintaining and modifying the electric guitars he played led him into lutherie. As a player, Doolin says he always wanted guitars that gave him full access to all the frets. Since he was dissatisfied with all the instruments he tried, he ultimately designed guitars with extra deep cutaways that worked the way he wanted.

Building a similarly accessible acoustic guitar proved to be a much more difficult proposition. "The shoulders of a non-cutaway guitar form a convex curve," explains Doolin, "which is a very rigid structure, like an eggshell. Adding a cutaway changes this to a concave curve, which is a very flexible structure, like a leaf spring. Since the rigidity of the neck-to-body juncture is a critical factor in guitar tone, directly affecting sustain and midrange response, the challenge in designing a cutaway is to recover the lost rigidity."

Doolin's solution to the acoustic double-cutaway dilemma is a system of internal bracing that he says supports the neck at least as well as the convex shoulders of a non-cutaway. He laminates mahogany and graphite to form rigid flying braces which are let into the headblock and extend to the sides at the waist. This transfers the load of string tension on the neck directly to the convex curves of the lower bout and restores sustain and midrange response so it is equal to or better than a non-cutaway.

Doolin says an extra benefit of his double-cutaway design is the consistency of tone in all registers. "Since all of the frets are on the neck, rather than the highest being over the body," he explains, "the high registers have a ringing, harplike sustain which blends perfectly with the lower range of the instrument."

SPECIFICATIONS

BODY AND SIDE WOODS: Brazilian rosewood

TOP WOOD: Sitka spruce

BODY WIDTH, LOWER BOUT: 16 inches (40.6 cm)

ELECTRONICS: B-band A1

NECK WOOD: Honduran mahogany

FRETBOARD MATERIAL: Ebony

FRETBOARD INLAY: Pearl side dots

HEADSTOCK DECORATION: Pearl logo

SOUND HOLE INLAYS: Spalted beech

BRIDGE: Ebony

NUT AND SADDLE: Bone

TUNING MACHINES: Gotoh 510

BINDING: Curly maple

SCALE LENGTH: 25.5 inches (64.8 cm)

NECK WIDTH AT NUT: 1¹¹⁄₁₆ inches (4.3 cm)

NUMBER OF FRETS: 20

BRACING: Scalloped X

FINISH: Polyester

BODY DEPTH: 4 inches (10.2 cm)

BODY LENGTH: 20 inches (50.8 cm)

OVERALL LENGTH: 40 inches (101.6 cm)

U.S. SUGGESTED RETAIL PRICE: $8,000

◆ **16-Inch Jumbo, 2006**
Michael Doolin, Doolin Guitars
Portland, Oregon

Dovetail Madness

$\mathcal{H}$oward Klepper began fiddling with guitars in 1968 and was part of the remarkable Berkeley scene of the 1970s, which included such prominent luthiers as Larry Jameson, Mario Martello, Steve Klein, Jon Lundberg, Ralph Novak, Marc Silber, Ervin Somogyi, and Michael Stevens. He quit building to pursue an academic career in the late 1970s, but after a nineteen-year hiatus, he shed his academic robes and returned to woodworking, focusing first on turned vessels and then once again on guitars.

The aptly named Dovetail Madness, on which every part of the guitar is built from joined wood of contrasting colors, is a showpiece for Klepper's extraordinary woodworking skills. The guitar also features Klepper's unique bracing system, which employs long, scalloped longitudinal braces and cutout cross braces in the style made famous among classical builders by Bouchet. The cross braces are topped with a carbon fiber/epoxy composite. Klepper likes to use this system on larger guitars and says that in comparison to X-braced instruments, guitars with his system are more balanced toward the midrange. "They are loud and project strongly," he says. "One person described them as sounding as if the sound was originating out in front of the guitar."

77

SPECIFICATIONS

BODY AND SIDE WOODS: Osage orange and East Indian rosewood; inner sides of mahogany; double recurved sides

TOP WOOD: European spruce and western red cedar

BODY WIDTH, LOWER BOUT: 16 inches (40.6 cm)

NECK WOOD: Mahogany, osage orange, and East Indian rosewood

FRETBOARD MATERIAL: Gabon ebony and Brazilian tulipwood

FRETBOARD INLAY: Mother-of-pearl

HEADSTOCK DECORATION: Walnut burl, maple burl, ebony, mother-of-pearl

SOUND HOLE INLAYS: Walnut burl

BRIDGE: Gabon ebony and Brazilian tulipwood

NUT AND SADDLE: Bone

TUNING MACHINES: Sperzel

BINDING: Cocobolo

SCALE LENGTH: 25.4 inches (64.5 cm)

NECK WIDTH AT NUT: 1¾ inches (4.4 cm)

NUMBER OF FRETS: 20

BRACING: Klepper style spruce and carbon fiber composite

FINISH: Nitrocellulose lacquer

BODY DEPTH: 4⁵⁄₁₆ inches (11 cm)

BODY LENGTH: 20¾ inches (52.7 cm)

U.S. SUGGESTED RETAIL PRICE: $12,000

♦ **Dovetail Madness, 2004**
Howard Klepper, Klepper Guitars
Santa Rosa, California

Style-45 Custom Koa Cutaway

$\mathcal{E}$d Foley's acoustic guitars are among the most highly regarded being made for country and Bluegrass pickers today; Bill Monroe owned one, as do Monroe's son and grandson, George Jones, Charlie Daniels, George Strait, and Joe Diffie who ordered two for himself and three for his band after playing a Foley for the first time.

Foley's grandfather, a renowned furniture builder whose work is in the Smithsonian, taught him to love wood as a child, and Foley refinished antique furniture before he began building guitars in 1988. He is known for his meticulous craftsmanship, which often includes elaborate fingerboard, bridge, and pickguard inlay, as well as the inlaid longhorn skull trademark that graces the headstock of each Foley guitar.

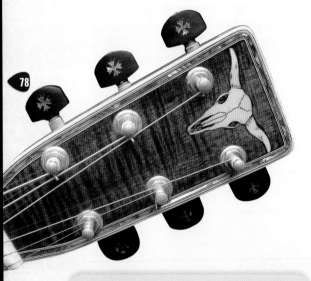

78

◀ **Style-45 Custom Koa Cutaway, 1990**
Ed Foley, Foley Guitars
Andover, New Jersey

SPECIFICATIONS

BODY AND SIDE WOODS: Figured koa

TOP WOOD: Spruce

BODY WIDTH, LOWER BOUT: 14⅞ inches (37.8 cm)

NECK WOOD: Mahogany

FRETBOARD MATERIAL: Ebony

FRETBOARD INLAY: Snowflakes

HEADSTOCK DECORATION: Koa headplate, abalone trim

SOUND HOLE INLAYS: Abalone

BRIDGE: Ebony with abalone snowflakes

TUNING MACHINES: Schaller gold with ebony buttons and abalone inlays

NECK WIDTH AT NUT: 1⅝ inches (4.2 cm)

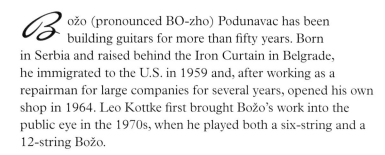

Bell Western Requinto

*B*ožo (pronounced BO-zho) Podunavac has been building guitars for more than fifty years. Born in Serbia and raised behind the Iron Curtain in Belgrade, he immigrated to the U.S. in 1959 and, after working as a repairman for large companies for several years, opened his own shop in 1964. Leo Kottke first brought Božo's work into the public eye in the 1970s, when he played both a six-string and a 12-string Božo.

Bozo apprenticed in the old world tradition of his homeland, and his highly ornate instruments, festooned with abalone and pearl, look like no one else's. He makes six to eight flattops, classical guitars, and archtops each year, all on custom order. His Bell Western designs, which include the ¾-size Requinto, have a fuller than normal lower bout and contoured back that combine to give the body a belllike shape that he says allows for clearer deep tones and shimmering highs with extended harmonics.

◀ **Bell Western Requinto, 1966**
Božo Podunavac, Bozo Guitars
East Englewood, Florida

79

SPECIFICATIONS

BODY AND SIDE WOODS: Rosewood

BODY WIDTH, LOWER BOUT: 13⅝ inches (34.6 cm)

NECK WOOD: Mahogany

FRETBOARD MATERIAL: Ebony

FRETBOARD INLAY: Ebony

HEADSTOCK DECORATION: Abalone

SOUND HOLE INLAYS: Abalone

BRIDGE: Ebony

NUT AND SADDLE: Bone

BINDING: Curly maple, rope and abalone purfling

SCALE LENGTH: 25.4 inches (64.6 cm)

NECK WIDTH AT NUT: 1¾ inches (4.4 cm)

NUMBER OF FRETS: 16 (to body)

BRACING: X bracing

FINISH: Lacquer

BODY DEPTH: 4¼ inches (10.8 cm) (at thickest)

BODY LENGTH: 18 inches (45.7 cm)

OVERALL LENGTH: 41 inches (104.1 cm)

U.S. SUGGESTED RETAIL PRICE: $22,000

Todd Cambio
Fraulini Francesca 12-String

odd Cambio named his business after his great-grandfather, Silvio Fraulini, a skilled stonemason and carpenter from Fiumalbo, Italy, and Cambio's guitars bear the names of Silvio's American-born daughters.

Cambio's Italian heritage is also connected to the guitars he fell in love with and is now trying to emulate: the gutsy, ladder-braced six- and 12-strings made in the 1920s and 1930s in places where there were large pockets of Italian immigrants—"Places like New Jersey (Oscar Schmidt), Chicago (Lyon and Healy, Regal, Tonk Bros.), and New Orleans (Gruenwald)," Cambio explains.

Italian luthiers helped introduce the 12-string guitar to North America. The instrument is in some ways a throwback to the double-coursed guitars of the Renaissance and Baroque eras that went completely out of fashion with the advent of guitars with six single strings around the dawn of the nineteenth century. Ladder-braced twelve-strings created and projected a huge sound, and a number of now legendary blues guitarists, including "Barbecue Bob" Hicks, Lonnie Johnson, Leadbelly, and Blind Willie McTell, took them up for that reason.

The Francesca is an auditorium-sized instrument based on the classic ladder-braced Oscar Schmidt designs of the early twentieth century. Both Leadbelly and Willie McTell used 12-string guitars of this design, and, as their recordings testify, the instrument's combination of body size and ladder-bracing creates what Cambio describes as "a huge, brawny sound that bowls over player and listener alike."

80

SPECIFICATIONS

BODY AND SIDE WOODS: Mahogany

TOP WOOD: German spruce

BODY WIDTH, LOWER BOUT: 16 inches (40.6 cm)

NECK WOOD: Mahogany

FRETBOARD MATERIAL: Ebony

FRETBOARD INLAY: Mother-of-pearl position markers

HEADSTOCK DECORATION: Brazilian rosewood veneer

SOUND HOLE INLAYS: Mosaic purfling

BRIDGE: Ebony pyramid bridge

NUT AND SADDLE: Bone

TUNING MACHINES: Alessi custom-made tuning machines

BINDING: Ivoroid

SCALE LENGTH: 26.5 inches (67.3 cm)

NECK WIDTH AT NUT: 1¹⁵⁄₁₆ inches (4.9 cm)

NUMBER OF FRETS: 12

BRACING: Ladder braced

FINISH: Nitrocellulose lacquer on body, French polish on neck

BODY DEPTH: 4¼ inches (10.8 cm)

BODY LENGTH: 21⅛ inches (53.7 cm)

OVERALL LENGTH: 43⅛ inches (109.5 cm)

U.S. SUGGESTED RETAIL PRICE: $5,000

Fraulini Francesca 12-String, 2006 ▶
Todd Cambio, Fraulini Guitars
Madison, Wisconsin

FLATTOP

Model B 13-Fret

Nigel Forster apprenticed with the highly regarded British luthier Stefan Sobell just after graduating from secondary school in the late 1980s and remained with him except for a two-year hiatus until 2003. He has been building guitars of his own design ever since and describes his Model B as "rather like a long-bodied OM with a clear and powerful, yet sweet voice and a strong, smooth bass."

Forster believes design is the most important factor in the creation of a top-notch instrument, and, in addition to Sobell, most admires the work of classical builders Antonio de Torres and Hermann Hauser I. "The most beautiful instrument I have ever seen is a tired 1930s Hauser in a museum in Rome. So simple and elegant…Design should be discussed far more by players than what rosewood is the best," Forster continues. "Choice of timber will certainly help color the sound, but design is what gives sound its shape and power. Fine instruments come from a combination of thoughtful design, great craftsmanship, and finally, wonderful timber."

The wonderful timber Forster used for this instrument's back and sides is English sycamore. Its warm, light color and dramatic pattern provide a striking complement to the guitar's European spruce top. English sycamore (*Acer Campestre*) is actually a member of the maple family and is not closely related to American sycamore (*Platinus Occidentalis*). The wood is lighter in color than any North American maple, running from lustrous white to pale yellowish white, and can be highly figured. It is often used for violin backs and for early woodwinds such as recorders and shawms.

82

SPECIFICATIONS

BODY AND SIDE WOODS: English sycamore

TOP WOOD: Italian spruce

BODY WIDTH, LOWER BOUT: 15⁵⁄₁₆ inches (39 cm)

ELECTRONICS: Optional

NECK WOOD: 1908 Cuban mahogany

FRETBOARD MATERIAL: Ebony

FRETBOARD INLAY: White pearl

HEADSTOCK DECORATION: Rio veneer

SOUND HOLE INLAYS: Rope trim

BRIDGE: Ebony

NUT AND SADDLE: Bone

TUNING MACHINES: Gotoh

BINDING: Indian rosewood

SCALE LENGTH: 25.4 inches (64.5 cm)

NECK WIDTH AT NUT: 1¾ inches (4.4 cm)

NUMBER OF FRETS: 19, 13 to the body

BRACING: Laminated X brace

FINISH: Malamine

BODY DEPTH: 4⅜ inches (11.2 cm)

BODY LENGTH: 20 inches (51 cm)

OVERALL LENGTH: 40½ inches (103 cm)

U.S. SUGGESTED RETAIL PRICE: $7,000

◄ **Model B 13-Fret, 2004**
Nigel Forster, NK Forster Guitars
Newcastle-upon-Tyne, England

Franklin 12-String

*N*ick Kukich founded Franklin Guitars in 1976 and, after a hiatus in the 1990s, is again making his highly regarded OM and Jumbo model flattops.

Kukich was one of the first luthiers to build guitars based on Martin's Orchestra Model of the late 1920s and early 1930s, which was the company's first guitar with 14 frets clear of the body. His version of the OM was championed by the influential American blues and fingerstyle guitarist Stefan Grossman, and it became John Renbourn's main axe after he and Grossman began playing and recording together in the late 1970s. Renbourn says, "From the point of view of workmanship, Nick's guitars must have something really special—other makers have picked it up, full of the joys of spring, only to lower it slowly down in brooding silence! From my point of view, I love the overall balance."

This extremely rare Franklin 12-string, based on the classic ladder-braced Stella and Regal 12s of the 1920s and 1930s, is a testament to the clean, simple, "less-is-more" power that distinguishes all of Kukich's work.

Franklin 12-String, 1993 ▶
Nick Kukich, Franklin Guitar Company
Rocheport, Missouri

SPECIFICATIONS

BODY AND SIDE WOODS: Mahogany

TOP WOOD: Spruce

BODY WIDTH, LOWER BOUT: 15¼ inches (38.7 cm)

NECK WOOD: Mahogany

FRETBOARD MATERIAL: Ebony

FRETBOARD INLAY: Pearl

HEADSTOCK DECORATION: Pearl "F" logo

SOUND HOLE INLAYS: Wood dyed white and black

BRIDGE: Rosewood dyed black

NUT AND SADDLE: Ivory

TUNING MACHINES: Schaller mini

BINDING: Ivoroid

SCALE LENGTH: 26.5 inches (67.3 cm)

NECK WIDTH AT NUT: 1¹⁵⁄₁₆ inches (4.9 cm)

NUMBER OF FRETS: 19

BRACING: Ladder

FINISH: Nitro lacquer

BODY DEPTH: 4³⁄₃₂ inches (10.4 cm)

BODY LENGTH: 20⅞ inches (53 cm)

OVERALL LENGTH: 42½ inches (108 cm)

SJ-14 Ergo Noir

Charles Fox

Charles Fox has been a leading figure among American luthiers for more than thirty years. In 1973, he founded the School of the Guitar Research & Design Center—the first school for guitar makers in North America—and was later a founder of both the American School of Luthiery and the biennial Healdsburg Guitar Festival, one of the world's leading showcases for acoustic instruments. Through the two schools and many other efforts, Fox has been one of the most influential teachers in the field, and his methods have been studied and adopted by many younger luthiers over the years.

Fox's new Ergo guitar combines a number of recent design trends, including a wedge-shaped body, elevated fingerboard, and doubletop soundboard, to form what he describes as "one emphatic statement of the current state of the art." The Ergo grew out of Fox's interest in applying the new technology of the doubletop, which was developed by classical guitar makers, to the acoustic steel-string. His soon-to-be-patented "ultra low-mass parabolic soundboard," which sandwiches two veneer-like pieces of master-grade tonewood around a 1/16-inch (1.6 mm) core of high-tech honeycomb material, weighs 40 percent less than a normal solid wood soundboard, and yet, despite its weight, is so strong that it does not require the X braces that support most wooden soundboards.

◀ **SJ-14 Ergo Noir, 2005**
Charles Fox, Charles Fox Guitars
Portland, Oregon

SPECIFICATIONS

BODY AND SIDE WOODS: Brazilian rosewood

TOP WOOD: Thin skins of spruce and cedar, sandwiching hollow honeycomb core

BODY WIDTH, LOWER BOUT: 16¼ inches (41.3 cm)

ELECTRONICS: Custom, embedded sensors

NECK WOOD: Honduran mahogany

FRETBOARD MATERIAL: Gaboon ebony, epoxy graphite

HEADSTOCK DECORATION: Brazilian rosewood, book-matched

SOUND HOLE INLAYS: Amboina burl, abalone shell

BRIDGE: Brazilian rosewood

NUT AND SADDLE: Legal ivory

TUNING MACHINES: Gotoh

BINDING: Ebony, maple, fiberboard

SCALE LENGTH: 25.6 inches (65 cm)

NECK WIDTH AT NUT: 1¾ inches (4.4 cm)

NUMBER OF FRETS: 24

BRACING: Top, none; back, radial

FINISH: Waterborne lacquer

BODY DEPTH: 4⁵⁄₁₆ inches (10.9 cm)

BODY LENGTH: 20.6 inches (52.3 cm)

OVERALL LENGTH: 42⅛ inches (106.9 cm)

U.S. SUGGESTED RETAIL PRICE: $23,500

Gibson
SJ-200 Custom Vine

*T*he initials SJ stand for Super Jumbo, the aptly named 16⅞ dreadnought model Gibson set loose upon the world in 1937. Billed as "The King of the Flattops," the SJ-200 has remained in Gibson's line ever since and ranks with Martin's D-28 as the most widely played and imitated acoustic guitar of all time. The first

SJ-200 was built for singing cowboy and movie star Ray Whitley, a peer of the legendary Gene Autry, and featured a torch inlay on its headstock, large blocks of pearl on the fretboard, and a curvaceous moustache-shaped bridge.

The SJ-200's booming rhythm sound, impressive size, and flashy ornamentation made it an ideal stage guitar, and it has been played by a diverse roster of rock, country-and-western, folk, and blues stars over the years, including Roy Rogers, Lefty Frizzell, Elvis Presley, Buddy Holly, Reverend Gary Davis, Dave Van Ronk, Bob Dylan, George Harrison, Keith Richards, Pete Townshend, and Emmylou Harris. With its elaborate fingerboard and pickguard vine inlay, the SJ-200 Vine is the most decorated Super Jumbo ever offered by Gibson.

◄ **SJ-200 Custom Vine, 2000**
Gibson Guitar Corporation Custom Shop
Bozeman, Montana

SPECIFICATIONS

BODY AND SIDE WOODS: Flamed maple

TOP WOOD: Spruce

BODY WIDTH, LOWER BOUT: 16¾ inches (42.5 cm)

NECK WOOD: Maple

FRETBOARD MATERIAL: Ebony

FRETBOARD INLAY: Abalone vine inlay

HEADSTOCK DECORATION: Abalone vine inlay with script Gibson logo

BRIDGE: Ebony mustache bridge

TUNING MACHINES: Waverly gold tuners with engraving

NECK WIDTH AT NUT: 1¾ inches (4.6 cm)

Ebony Parlor Guitar

$\int$ mall-bodied "parlor" guitars were the norm in the nineteenth and early twentieth centuries, when all guitars were strung with gut and plucked with the fingers. Until the mid-1870s, the largest model offered by Martin, the size 0, measured only 13½ inches (34.3 cm) across its lower bout, while the smallest standard model was a mere 11¼ inches (28.6 cm) wide. The 00, introduced in 1874, brought the maximum width up to a whopping (for then) 14⅛ inches (35.9 cm), still pretty small by today's standards.

Parlor guitars went out of favor during the Jazz Age, but have made a comeback in recent years, especially among fingerstyle players.

Rob Girdis's parlor guitars are among the most admired being made today. He says the little instruments consistently draw two comments. "The first one is amazement at how much sound is coming out of such a small guitar. The second is usually it sounds as good as it looks."

Girdis enjoys building parlors because he can use extra-fine materials that aren't large enough for other models and has more leeway to decide where the pattern will work best aesthetically. "And," he adds, "one last reason these are fun to build is that they are just too cute!"

SPECIFICATIONS

BODY AND SIDE WOODS: African ebony

TOP WOOD: Sitka spruce

BODY WIDTH, LOWER BOUT: 12⁹⁄₁₆ inches (31.9 cm)

NECK WOOD: Honduran mahogany

FRETBOARD MATERIAL: Macassar ebony

FRETBOARD INLAY: Boxwood

HEADSTOCK DECORATION: Macassar ebony, black/white fiber, koa

SOUND HOLE INLAYS: Koa, black and white fiber, black and white plastic dots

BRIDGE: Ebony

NUT AND SADDLE: Bone

TUNING MACHINES: Waverly

BINDING: Boxwood, koa, black/white fiber

SCALE LENGTH: 25.2 inches (64 cm)

NECK WIDTH AT NUT: 1¾ inches (4.4 cm)

NUMBER OF FRETS: 18

BRACING: Traditional X bracing on soundboard, Sitka spruce; koa back braces

FINISH: Nitrocellulose lacquer

BODY DEPTH: 3¾ inches (9.5 cm) at tail, 3⅜ inches (8.6 cm) at heel

BODY LENGTH: 18½ inches (47 cm)

OVERALL LENGTH: 37½ inches (95.3 cm)

U.S. SUGGESTED RETAIL PRICE: $7,500

Ebony Parlor Guitar, 2006 ▶
Robert Girdis, Girdis Guitars
Seattle, Washington

87

12-String Guitar

J Thomas Davis began building guitars in a basement workshop while working on a music degree in the mid-1970s. The shop was moved to a storefront in Grandview Heights, Ohio, in 1977 and relocated to its present location in 1993. The shop now employs four people dedicated to restoring and servicing fretted instruments (both electric and acoustic), while Tom spends his time building individual handmade instruments like this 12-string. Davis's varied and distinguished client list includes Pierre Bensusan, Ged Foley of Patrick Street, Arlo Guthrie, James Hetfield of Metallica, Leo Kottke, Manus Lunny, and Amy Ray of Indigo Girls fame.

This instrument's neck, back, and sides are Claro (Spanish for clear or bright) walnut, a wood cut from the stumps of West coast orchard walnut trees, which are created by grafting an English walnut (*Juglans regia*) scion to a rootstock of either black walnut (*Juglans nigra*) or California walnut (*Juglans hindsii*). The wood near the graft tends to be variegated in color, with beautiful dark brown and tan marbled figure. Claro walnut lends itself to work with hand and power tools, has good strength and bending properties, and takes finishes well. It is used mainly for gunstocks and high-quality furniture, but Davis and a few other American luthiers have discovered its virtues as well.

12-String Guitar, 1983 ▶
J. Thomas Davis
Columbus, Ohio

SPECIFICATIONS

BODY AND SIDE WOODS: Sapele

TOP WOOD: Redwood

BODY WIDTH, LOWER BOUT: 16⅝ inches (42.2 cm)

ELECTRONICS: Under saddle pickup

NECK WOOD: Honduran mahogany laminated with maple

FRETBOARD MATERIAL: Indian rosewood

FRETBOARD INLAY: Abalone

HEADSTOCK DECORATION: Abalone

SOUND HOLE INLAYS: Abalone

BRIDGE: Indian rosewood with ebony bridge pins

NUT AND SADDLE: Bone

TUNING MACHINES: Schaller M-6 mini

BINDING: Marquetry purfling and wooden binding

SCALE LENGTH: 25.6 inches (65 cm)

NECK WIDTH AT NUT: 1¹⁵⁄₁₆ inches (4.9 cm)

NUMBER OF FRETS: 20

BRACING: X bracing

FINISH: Lacquer

BODY DEPTH: 4¾ inches (12.1 cm)

BODY LENGTH: 20½ inches (52.1 cm)

OVERALL LENGTH: 42¾ inches (108.6 cm)

U.S. SUGGESTED RETAIL PRICE: $5,850

Carp Guitar

*E*rvin Somogyi built his first guitar in 1971 and, through his highly original work and extensive teachings and writings, has established himself as one of the most admired and influential American luthiers. As he proudly states, "I have taught and influenced many of the younger generation of American luthiers."

Somogyi attributes much of his professional success to the critical thinking skills he learned as a college English major. "I learned to look at something which someone had created and examine it closely, identify which of its elements worked and which ones didn't, to think analytically about the connections of its parts, and to compare it to other work. The skill of being able to analyze serious written work has translated usefully to my being able to understand, and being able to make, better soundboxes."

This modified dreadnought is designed for musicians who sit when they play. It differs from a standard dreadnought in its waist, which is defined, like a that of a classical guitar, and positioned higher up on the instrument, thereby shifting its center of gravity and making it easier to balance in the lap. Somogyi is also a highly skilled and creative woodcarver who makes boxes and decorative carvings, and he often carves elaborate patterns that extend from the sound hole of his guitars to encompass nearly an entire side of the upper bout.

◄ **Carp Guitar, 1998**
Ervin Somogyi
Oakland, California

SPECIFICATIONS

BODY AND SIDE WOODS: Brazilian rosewood

TOP WOOD: Sitka spruce

BODY WIDTH, LOWER BOUT: 15⅜ inches (39.1 cm)

NECK WOOD: Quartersawn Honduran mahogany

FRETBOARD MATERIAL: Macassar ebony, bordered with rosewood binding and maple purfling strips

FRETBOARD INLAY: Abalone shell

HEADSTOCK DECORATION: Brazilian rosewood, ebony and maple veneers; proprietary headstock design

SOUND HOLE INLAYS: Abalone, rosewood, ebony, maple

BRIDGE: Hand-sculpted Brazilian rosewood

NUT AND SADDLE: Bone

TUNING MACHINES: Schaller

BINDING: East Indian rosewood

SCALE LENGTH: 25.25 inches (64.1 cm)

NECK WIDTH AT NUT: 1¾ inches (4.4 cm)

NUMBER OF FRETS: 21

BRACING: Proprietary version of X bracing

FINISH: Nitrocellulose lacquer back, sides, and neck; French polish on face

Nashville Dreadnought

*I*ntroduced in 1931 and officially added to the company's catalog pricelist in 1934, Martin's revolutionary dreadnought model featured a deep, stout body form with a 15⅝-inch lower bout, more than ½ inch (1.3 cm) wider than the OM and 000. The model, named for Britain's massive dreadnought battleships, was indeed a cannon, projecting powerful bass notes and a loud, clear sound that allowed the guitar to hold its own as a rhythm instrument in an ensemble and echo the ringing solo lines of fiddles, mandolins, and banjos.

Nashville Guitar Company founder Marty Lanham became interested in instrument repair in 1964, when he brought a couple of his old Gibsons to a reputable shop in San Francisco. "When I got them back," he recalls, "I could see the guy's handprint in the glue on the back of the mandolin. I knew that I could do better work than that."

When Lanham and his Bluegrass band moved to Nashville in 1972, his day job was in the repair shop at Gruhn Guitars, then as now one of world's leading dealers in high-quality stringed instruments. During his eight years with Gruhn, he worked on what he describes as "a constant parade of the finest instruments in the world," including Hank Williams's Martin D-45, Lester Flatt's D-28, and two of Jimmie Rodgers's guitars. Today, Lanham's own dreadnoughts are compared favorably to pre-World War II Martins, and his client list reads like a who's who of Nashville's best pickers.

SPECIFICATIONS

BODY AND SIDE WOODS: Tasmanian blackwood, rosewood

TOP WOOD: Bearclaw Sitka spruce

BODY WIDTH, LOWER BOUT: 15⅝ inches (39.7 cm)

NECK WOOD: Mahogany

FRETBOARD MATERIAL: Ebony

FRETBOARD INLAY: African snail shell

HEADSTOCK DECORATION: Shell, inlaid NGC logo

SOUND HOLE INLAYS: Abalone

BRIDGE: Ebony

NUT AND SADDLE: Bone

TUNING MACHINES: Waverly

BINDING: Tortoise-shell plastic

SCALE LENGTH: 25.4 inches (64.5 cm)

NECK WIDTH AT NUT: 1¹¹⁄₁₆ inches (4.3 cm)

NUMBER OF FRETS: 21

BRACING: Spruce

FINISH: Nitrocellulose lacquer

BODY DEPTH: 4⅞ inches (12.4 cm)

BODY LENGTH: 20 inches (50.8 cm)

U.S. SUGGESTED RETAIL PRICE: $8,500

Nashville Dreadnought, 1998 ▶
Marty Lanham, Nashville Guitar Company
Nashville, Tennessee

FLATTOP

Henry's Dream Guitar

*M*ichael Keller is an acoustic guitar player who began building guitars in 1975, under the tutelage of renowned classical luthier Jeffrey Elliott. Then living in Portland, Oregon, he also had the opportunity to meet and learn from such other masters as Jimmy D'Aquisto, Michael Gurian, and Robert Lundberg, all of whom passed along their uncompromising, perfectionist standards.

Keller builds a wide range of acoustic flattops, from a massive 18-inch (45.7 cm) jumbo to a half-size, all of which are offered with a host of options for clients to choose from. He has also instituted online documentation of his current work, which allows his customers and any other interested parties to watch new work, as it is created, step-by-step.

This ornately inlaid parlor guitar is a showcase for Keller's decorative skills.

Henry's Dream Guitar, 2004
Michael Keller, Keller Custom Guitars
Rochester, Minnesota

SPECIFICATIONS

BODY AND SIDE WOODS: Brazilian rosewood

TOP WOOD: Adirondack

BODY WIDTH, LOWER BOUT: 14½ inches (36.8 cm)

ELECTRONICS: Baggs dual source

NECK WOOD: Ebony center, maple, and mahogany, 5 piece laminate

FRETBOARD MATERIAL: Ebony

FRETBOARD INLAY: White, gold, and black mother-of-pearl, red abalone, paua abalone

HEADSTOCK DECORATION: White mother-of-pearl and paua abalone

SOUND HOLE INLAYS: Rose pattern marquetry with paua abalone rings

BRIDGE: Ebony

NUT AND SADDLE: Ivory

TUNING MACHINES: Gotoh 510 with pearl knobs

BINDING: Ivoroid

SCALE LENGTH: 24 inches (61 cm)

NECK WIDTH AT NUT: 1¹¹⁄₁₆ inches (4.3 cm)

NUMBER OF FRETS: 19

BRACING: Scalloped adirondack

FINISH: Gloss lacquer

BODY DEPTH: 3⅝ inches (9.2 cm)

BODY LENGTH: 18⅝ inches (47.3 cm)

OVERALL LENGTH: 39¼ inches (99.7 cm)

U.S. SUGGESTED RETAIL PRICE: $25,000

Santa Cruz H-13 Fret Trio

$\int$ anta Cruz founder Richard Hoover began building guitars and carved-top mandolins in 1972, turning his focus to the steel-string acoustic guitars for which his company is known in the mid-1970s. He developed a hands-on "bench style" approach for the company and purposefully limits production to ensure that each guitar receives individualized attention. More than half of the guitars Santa Cruz builds are custom orders, and every guitar top is graduated and tuned by hand to attain maximum resonance and sustain, ensuring a high level of consistency of sound within each standard model line. "By limiting the number of instruments we build," says Hoover, "we can practice a style of lutherie born from a genuine love of the guitar, as opposed to a production line approach that might favor greater numbers at the expense of our attention to detail."

Santa Cruz's new H-13 Fret combines a 12-fret guitar's resonance with a 14-fret's access to create an instrument that is ideally suited to fingerpicking. Despite its small form, the H-13 Fret's body depth approaches that of a much larger dreadnought-sized guitar, producing extra volume and bass support to bolster its rich tone. The H-13 Fret is offered in a wide range of woods, including (L-R): Adirondack spruce top with mahogany sides and back, redwood top with sycamore sides and back, and German spruce with maple sides and back.

93

Santa Cruz H-13 Fret Trio, 2003 ▶
Richard Hoover, Santa Cruz Guitar Company
Santa Cruz, California

SPECIFICATIONS

BODY AND SIDE WOODS: Mahogany

TOP WOOD: Sitka spruce

BODY WIDTH, LOWER BOUT: 14⅝ inches (37.1 cm)

NECK WOOD: Ebony overlay

HEADSTOCK DECORATION: SCGC inlay

SCALE LENGTH: 25.4 inches (64.5 cm)

NECK WIDTH AT NUT: 1¾ inches (4.4 cm)

NUMBER OF FRETS: 13

Eric Bibb's Custom Built Ebony Fylde Guitar

*R*oger Bucknall was nine when he began building guitars in his father's garage. "I made a guitar from plywood and painted it pink," he recalls. "It had flowers on it. Oh dear. After that, I made a canoe (went on holiday in it), a greenhouse (sold it), model planes and boats (crashed and sunk), and set fire to my sister (it was her own fault, and she's better now)."

After earning a degree in mechanical engineering at the University of Nottingham, Bucknall worked for a company that made industrial sound recording devices before setting up his first guitar manufacturing operation on the Fylde (rhymes with wild) coast of Lancashire in 1973. "At this point," says Bucknall, "the only available guitars were American-influenced, but the guitars I was making were very 'English,' suited to the styles of the emerging players in this country." Those players included such legends of the British folk scene as Martin Carthy, Archie Fisher, Gordon Giltrap, Bert Jansch, Nic Jones, Dave Pegg, John Renbourn, and Martin Simpson.

This recent guitar was built for the American blues guitarist Eric Bibb, who has been playing Fylde guitars for several years. "Eric asked me to make him a guitar with a cedar top, and I had just taken delivery of some wonderful Macassar ebony," says Bucknall. "The opportunity of [supporting] the softest of timber soundboards with the hardest body was too good to miss! This radical mixing of timbers doesn't always work, but in this case it's been a success—plenty of power from the heavy back and sides, but warmth and resonance from the cedar top. And it looks fantastic. Eric says it's the best guitar he has ever owned! This sort of commission, with plenty of freedom for me to work, is what keeps me interested and my designs moving forward."

◀ **Eric Bibb's Custom Built Ebony Fylde Guitar, 2006 Roger Bucknall, Fylde Guitars** Penrith, England

SPECIFICATIONS

BODY AND SIDE WOODS: Figured Macassar ebony

TOP WOOD: Western red cedar

BODY WIDTH, LOWER BOUT: 15 9/16 inches (39.5 cm)

NECK WOOD: American cherry and black ebony

FRETBOARD MATERIAL: Ebony

FRETBOARD INLAY: Pearl, diamonds

HEADSTOCK DECORATION: Macassar ebony

SOUND HOLE INLAYS: Colored-wood marquetry

BRIDGE: Ebony

NUT AND SADDLE: Bone

TUNING MACHINES: Gotoh SGL 510 High ratio

BINDING: Siricote

SCALE LENGTH: 25.5 inches (64.8 cm)

NECK WIDTH AT NUT: 1 3/4 inches (4.4 cm)

NUMBER OF FRETS: 20

BRACING: X brace

FINISH: Gloss

BODY DEPTH: 4 1/4 inches (10.8 cm)

BODY LENGTH: 18 5/8 inches (47.3 cm)

OVERALL LENGTH: 39 3/4 inches (101 cm)

U.S. SUGGESTED RETAIL PRICE: $7,500

FLATTOP

The Saddle Pal

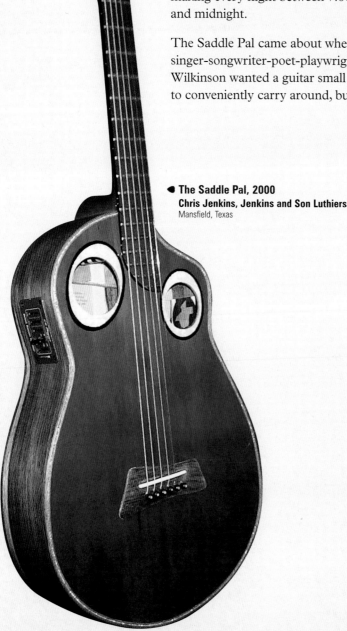

Chris Jenkins is a veterinarian who still practices full time at Creature Comfort Animal Clinic in Arlington, Texas. He is also a skilled luthier whose guitars are being played by many professional musicians, including singer-songwriters Sara Hickman and Christine Lavin. Jenkins takes his second profession of guitar making seriously, focusing his surgical skills on his passion for guitar making every night between 7:00 P.M. and midnight.

The Saddle Pal came about when singer-songwriter-poet-playwright Andy Wilkinson wanted a guitar small enough to conveniently carry around, but with a "sound as big as Texas." Although the guitar is only 13 inches (33 cm) across the lower bout, it has a balanced tone and a huge voice. National Fingerstyle Champion Todd Hallowell says of The Saddle Pal, "It's truly amazing that such a small instrument can have such a huge sound."

Jenkins says that The Saddle Pal lends itself to non-traditional sound hole placements. "Moving the sound hole into the shoulder(s) of the upper bout effectively makes the guitar sound larger than it really is," he explains.

◄ The Saddle Pal, 2000
Chris Jenkins, Jenkins and Son Luthiers
Mansfield, Texas

96

SPECIFICATIONS

BODY AND SIDE WOODS: Southeast Asian rosewood

TOP WOOD: Western red cedar

BODY WIDTH, LOWER BOUT: 13 inches (33 cm)

ELECTRONICS: LR Baggs LB 6

NECK WOOD: Honduran mahogany, hard maple laminate

FRETBOARD MATERIAL: Indian ebony

HEADSTOCK DECORATION: Crushed mother-of-pearl

SOUND HOLE INLAYS: Crushed mother-of-pearl

BRIDGE: Indian rosewood

NUT AND SADDLE: Bone

TUNING MACHINES: Sperzel locking

BINDING: Southeast Asian rosewood with crushed mother-of-pearl purfling

SCALE LENGTH: 25 inches (63.5 cm)

NECK WIDTH AT NUT: 1¾ inches (4.4 cm)

NUMBER OF FRETS: 18

BRACING: Sitka spruce, Jenkins triplex pattern

FINISH: Nitrocellulose lacquer

BODY DEPTH: 3½ inches (8.9 cm) upper bout, 4 inches (10.2 cm) lower bout

BODY LENGTH: 19½ inches (49.5 cm)

OVERALL LENGTH: 37½ inches (95.3 cm)

U.S. SUGGESTED RETAIL PRICE: $5,200

LV-10 KOA

Jean Larrivée began hand building guitars in the 1960s and opened Larrivée Guitars in 1971. Larrivée's company grew steadily from a small shop into Canada's largest and most successful guitar manufacturer and, just days before the September 11 tragedy, opened a United States facility in 2001 to complement its 33,000 square foot operation in Vancouver. Happily, the company weathered the economic downturn brought on by the terrorist attack and is now producing more guitars than ever before. Despite its size, Larrivée is still a family-run business, and his wife and three children are all part of the management team.

The LV-10 is part of Larrivée's top-of-the-line "Rosewood Master Series," although this special custom order example is built entirely of highly figured Hawaiian koa. The elaborate vine fingerboard and bridge inlay are also custom additions to the standard model. Larrivée's 16-inch (40.6 cm) L model is an extremely versatile guitar, which Larrivée says "can handle pretty much everything you throw at it. Even hardcore dreadnought players are sometimes caught off-guard by this body."

LV-10 KOA, 2000 ◗
Jean Larrivée, Jean Larrivée Guitars
Vancouver, Canada

SPECIFICATIONS

BODY AND SIDE WOODS: Koa

TOP WOOD: Koa

BODY WIDTH, LOWER BOUT: 16 inches (40.6 cm)

NECK WOOD: Mahogany

FRETBOARD MATERIAL: Ebony

FRETBOARD INLAY: Tree of life abalone inlay

HEADSTOCK DECORATION: Larrivée logo

SOUND HOLE INLAYS: Abalone

BRIDGE: Ebony with abalone inlay

BINDING: Curly maple binding and abalone top purfling

NECK WIDTH AT NUT: 1¾ inches (4.4 cm)

The Famiglio Project Guitars

*T*his matched pair of guitars, a six-string and a 12-string, was commissioned by George Famiglio of Sarasota, Florida. Richard Glick of Fine Guitar Consultants arranged the commission and was involved in initial discussions between the artist and patron.

Ervin Somogyi recalls, "The image of the court jester came up repeatedly in our discussions, [as did] the image of a turtle emerging from its shell and becoming a rabbit. Clearly, if a creature of swift independence coming out of some kind of protective and hardened but no longer useful shell was to be the main theme, then the jester, the turtle, and the rabbit were to be the main images. Finally, Mr. Famiglio sent me a packet of Xeroxes of images of Picasso's cubist-period work, which he was particularly attracted to. I was to create an allegory of coming-out or metamorphosis, in cubist style, for him."

"I thought that something rendered in cubist style should have depth and texture comparable to that which real cubism can convey," Somogyi continues, "so these images, which are relieved, flat, inlaid, carved, glued, textured, undercut, incised, and recessed, exist on four separate physical levels of their 'canvases,' the upper bouts of the guitars."

Somogyi cut all the relieved wooden elements from the guitar tops, and added inlays of ebony, rosewood, mother-of-pearl, and abalone shell. He did all the cutting, carving, and incising strictly by hand, with surgical scalpels and Japanese carving tools, and cut the mother-of-pearl bubbles with a jeweler's saw. The bubbles were also engraving by hand, and their shaping and polishing was done with hand files and a Dremel Moto-Tool. Somogyi calculates that each of the designs represents combinations of about 160 separate elements, techniques, procedures, and materials, and that each took about 60 hours to execute.

SPECIFICATIONS

BODY AND SIDE WOODS: Brazilian rosewood

TOP WOOD: Sitka spruce

BODY WIDTH, LOWER BOUT: 15 inches (38.1 cm), six-string; 16 inches (40.6 cm), 12-string

ELECTRONICS: B-Brand under saddle pickup

NECK WOOD: Honduran mahogany

FRETBOARD MATERIAL: Macassar ebony

FRETBOARD INLAY: Abalone shell

HEADSTOCK DECORATION: Hand-carved and shaped proprietary design

SOUND HOLE INLAYS: Ebony, spruce, mother-of-pearl, abalone shell

BRIDGE: Brazilian rosewood

NUT AND SADDLE: Ivory, plus fossil ivory bridge pins

TUNING MACHINES: Schaller

BINDING: Rosewood with holly and ebony purflings

SCALE LENGTH: 25.25 inches (64.1 cm)

NECK WIDTH AT NUT: 1¾ inches (4.4 cm), six-string; 2 inches (5 cm), 12-string

NUMBER OF FRETS: 21 on each

BRACING: Maker's variant of X bracing

FINISH: Lacquer on back, sides, and neck; French polish on faces

BODY DEPTH: 5 inches (12.7 cm) at bottom, 4 inches (10.2 cm) at body/neck joint

BODY LENGTH: 22 inches (55.9 cm), six-string; 22½ inches (57.2 cm), 12-string

OVERALL LENGTH: 42 inches (106.7 cm), six-string; 44 inches (111.8 cm), 12-string

♠ **The Famiglio Project Guitars, 2003**
Ervin Somogyi
Oakland, California

Milwaukee Custom 54/45

$\mathcal{R}$udolph Blazer and Wilhelm Henkes have built a reputation as two of Europe's most fastidious traditional craftsmen. They collect classic 1920s and 1930s Martins, Gibsons, Larsons, and Stellas and build reproductions that look—and sound—very close to the originals they revere.

Willi Henkes says, "We are taking care of the old art and old craftsmanship as much as we can. The guitars we are building are made very old-fashioned and traditionally, with techniques and materials that have been used a long time."

The Henkes & Blazer Milwaukee is a jumbo-sized guitar based on the Larson Brothers' Euphonon, made in the 1930s. Although the Larson Brothers are not nearly as well known as Martin or Gibson because they did not market their instruments under their own name,

their prodigious output of guitars, mandolins, and other stringed instruments stands with Martin and Gibson at the pinnacle of American fretted instrument making. The Milwaukee 54/45 is the most decorated of the Henkes & Blazer guitars, showing off their mastery of inlay as well as their precise traditional building skills.

Milwaukee Custom 54/45, 2002 ▶
Rudolph Blazer and Wilhelm Henkes,
Henkes & Blazer Antique Acoustics
Tuebingen, Germany

SPECIFICATIONS

BODY AND SIDE WOODS: Brazilian rosewood

TOP WOOD: Alpine spruce

BODY WIDTH, LOWER BOUT: 16⅝ inches (42.2 cm)

NECK WOOD: American mahogany

FRETBOARD MATERIAL: Madagascar ebony

FRETBOARD INLAY: Abalone, mother-of-pearl, goldfish, Tahiti, snail

HEADSTOCK DECORATION: Abalone, mother-of-pearl

SOUND HOLE INLAYS: Abalone, mother-of-pearl engraved, wood marquetry

BRIDGE: Madagascar ebony, abalone engraved

NUT AND SADDLE: Ivory

TUNING MACHINES: Waverly gold, engraved

BINDING: Ivoroid celluloid, abalone, wood purfling

SCALE LENGTH: 25.3 inches (64.3 cm)

NECK WIDTH AT NUT: 1¾ inches (4.4 cm)

NUMBER OF FRETS: 19

BRACING: X bracing, laminated alpine spruce

FINISH: Nitrocellulose

BODY DEPTH: 4 inches (10.2 cm)

BODY LENGTH: 20⅞ inches (53 cm)

OVERALL LENGTH: 41⁹⁄₁₆ inches (105.6 cm)

U.S. SUGGESTED RETAIL PRICE: $25,230

Tenth Anniversary CM Custom

*I*n honor of the company's tenth anniversary, Huss & Dalton decided to build a limited edition of ten of their CM model guitar, six with Brazilian rosewood backs and sides and koa binding/rosette options, and four with Koa backs and sides and Brazilian rosewood binding/rosette options. This is one of the four koa guitars, which also features Shenandoah vine custom inlay designed by the company's own inlay artist, Brian Dickel.

The CM is a smaller-bodied dreadnought form with deep sides, and it packs a punch not unlike its bigger brothers in the Huss & Dalton line. The CM's elegant design includes a soft bent cutaway, maple bindings, abalone rosette, and an understated 12th-fret scroll fingerboard inlay.

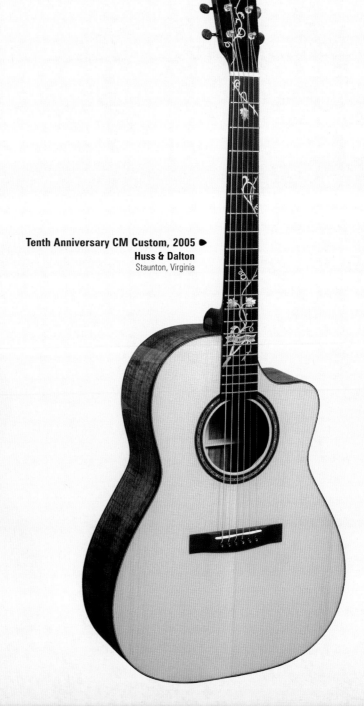

Tenth Anniversary CM Custom, 2005 ▶
Huss & Dalton
Staunton, Virginia

SPECIFICATIONS

BODY AND SIDE WOODS: Highly figured koa

TOP WOOD: Red spruce

BODY WIDTH, LOWER BOUT: 15¼ inches (38.7 cm)

NECK WOOD: Mahogany

FRETBOARD MATERIAL: Ebony

FRETBOARD INLAY: Shenandoah vine with Huss & Dalton 10th Anniversary scroll—abalone and pearl shell, custom designed and drawn by Brian Dickel, cut by Bill Swank

HEADSTOCK DECORATION: Shenandoah vine custom designed and drawn by Brian Dickel and Huss & Dalton logo located at top of headstock—abalone and pearl shell, cut by Bill Swank

SOUND HOLE INLAYS: Custom Brazilian rosewood and abalone rosette

BRIDGE: Ebony

NUT AND SADDLE: Bone

TUNING MACHINES: Gold Waverly machines with snakewood buttons

BINDING: Brazilian rosewood

SCALE LENGTH: 25.4 inches (64.5 cm)

NECK WIDTH AT NUT: 1¾ inches (4.4 cm)

NUMBER OF FRETS: 20

BRACING: Red spruce bracing, forward shifted scalloped X

FINISH: Gloss polyurethane

BODY DEPTH: 4⅝ inches (11.7 cm)

BODY LENGTH: 20 inches (50.8 cm)

OVERALL LENGTH: 40¾ inches (103.5 cm)

U.S. SUGGESTED RETAIL PRICE: $8,500

New Parlor Guitar, Peonies

Steve Kauffman has been a woodworker since he was five and claims he had exhausted all the reading materials on woodworking in the San Francisco library system by the time he was 15. He started playing guitar when he was 11 and began building steel-strings at 20. After building a dozen instruments, Kauffman approached legendary California designer and luthier Steve Klein. Klein told Paul Schmidt, the author of *Art That Sings: The Life and Times of Luthier Steve Klein*, that when they met in 1979, Kauffman was "already a full-blown luthier with chops even better than mine—he's faster and cleaner than I ever was. He wanted to come and apprentice with me, which was sort of difficult to fathom." The two began an ongoing collaboration, with Kauffman eventually taking over much of the building of Klein designs.

Kauffman's New Parlor is one of his own designs, which combines the slim, elegant profile of a nineteenth-century parlor guitar with a lower bout only slightly smaller than a traditional dreadnought "cannon." Like all of Kauffman's work, the guitar features a high-density rosewood neck and a top supported by the Kasha-influenced radial-fan tone bracing system he developed with Steve Klein. Asymmetrical tone braces lie under the bridge, radiating out to drive and control the top over a wide spectrum of frequencies. The area between the bridge and sound hole is supported by a "flying brace" (also pioneered by Steve Klein) which links a small area of the top to the guitar's sides at the waist. Kauffman explains that the flying brace provides the top with firm support where it is most needed while not inhibiting areas needing less structural support.

New Parlor Guitar, Peonies, 2002 ▶
Steven Kauffman, Kauffman Lutherie
Lafayette, California

SPECIFICATIONS

BODY AND SIDE WOODS: Brazilian rosewood

TOP WOOD: Sitka spruce

BODY WIDTH, LOWER BOUT: 14½ inches (36.8 cm)

NECK WOOD: Brazilian rosewood

FRETBOARD MATERIAL: Ebony

FRETBOARD INLAY: Ivory, mother-of-pearl, gold

HEADSTOCK DECORATION: Multiple veneer layers of ebony, rosewood, and holly

SOUND HOLE INLAYS: Rosewood, ebony, mother-of-pearl, abalone, ivory

BRIDGE: Ivory

NUT AND SADDLE: Ivory

TUNING MACHINES: Waverly

BINDING: Holly

SCALE LENGTH: 25.5 inches (64.8 cm)

NECK WIDTH AT NUT: 1¹³⁄₁₆ inches (4.6 cm)

NUMBER OF FRETS: 18

BRACING: Radial fan, in red spruce, carbon fiber

FINISH: Lacquer

BODY DEPTH: 4 inches (10.2 cm)

BODY LENGTH: 20⅝ inches (52.4 cm)

OVERALL LENGTH: 41¼ inches (104.8 cm)

U.S. SUGGESTED RETAIL PRICE: $20,000

The Del Vezeau Model Baritone

*T*his baritone guitar, built for Canadian guitarist and composer Del Vezeau, employs Ralph Novak's patented Fanned-Fret system. By placing the bridge at a steep angle and manipulating the scale length and fret spacing of the bass side of the neck relative to the treble side, the Novak system allows each string to have its own optimal vibrating length instead of the standard compromise of a single length for all. Because fret spacing is wider for the long bass scale and closer for the short treble scale, the Novak Fanned-Fret system is particularly useful in guitars with extended bass ranges like this baritone. The combination of scale lengths creates greater tension on the low strings and correspondingly decreased tension on the high strings for a more even feel across the neck. Dead spots are minimized, allowing each string to speak with its own unique harmonic voice. Perhaps best of all, optimizing scale length and fret spacing for each string also provides superior intonation and clarity.

Like other baritone instruments (and voices), baritone guitars are pitched lower than normal. Baritones can be tuned as low as A, D, G, c, e, a'—five notes below a standard guitar, although many players choose to tune a step higher, B, E, A, d, f#, b'.

The Del Vezeau Model Baritone, 2005 ●
Michael Greenfield, Greenfield Guitars
Montreal, Quebec, Canada

103

SPECIFICATIONS

BODY AND SIDE WOODS: Black acacia

TOP WOOD: Sitka spruce

BODY WIDTH, LOWER BOUT: 17 inches (43.2 cm)

ELECTRONICS: D-tar

NECK WOOD: Mahogany, maple, walnut laminate

FRETBOARD MATERIAL: Ebony

HEADSTOCK DECORATION: Mother-of-pearl "g" logo

SOUND HOLE INLAYS: Spalted maple, paua heart

BRIDGE: Ebony

NUT AND SADDLE: Black tusq

TUNING MACHINES: Waverly

BINDING: Ebony

SCALE LENGTH: 27.5 to 30 inches (69.9 to 76.2 cm)

NECK WIDTH AT NUT: 1 13/16 inches (4.6 cm)

NUMBER OF FRETS: 20

BRACING: Lattice

FINISH: Lacquer

BODY DEPTH: 4 5/8 inches (11.7 cm)

BODY LENGTH: 20 3/4 inches (52.7 cm)

OVERALL LENGTH: 44 inches (111.8 cm)

U.S. SUGGESTED RETAIL PRICE: $16,500

OM Custom Sunburst

*J*ohn Greven has been building guitars for more than 40 years and is widely recognized for his deep knowledge of the classic acoustic guitars of the 1930s. He learned his craft while working for dealer George Gruhn in Nashville in the late 1960s and early 1970s, and says that the sounds of the vintage Martin and Gibson models he encountered there continue to haunt and drive him. "I can still hear that 1939 D-45, that 1935 000-28, and a handful of other extraordinary instruments that are the benchmark of tonal excellence for me," says Greven. "While I have reached this goal only every so often—when each facet of a build worked perfectly and the stars aligned momentarily—tonal ghosts of the great guitars past have emerged from the sound holes of my guitars, lending hope that it just might be possible to achieve true vintage sound with a brand new instrument."

This sunburst OM is a prime example of Greven's ability to channel the guitars of yore, bringing the past into the future. Greven's OM is patterned after the classic Martin Orchestra Model of the early 1930s, and, like that instrument, is ideal for fingerpicking.

OM Custom Sunburst, 2004 ▶
John Greven
Portland, Oregon

SPECIFICATIONS

BODY AND SIDE WOODS: Brazilian rosewood

TOP WOOD: Spruce

BODY WIDTH, LOWER BOUT: 15 inches (38.1 cm)

NECK WOOD: Mahogany

FRETBOARD MATERIAL: Ebony

FRETBOARD INLAY: Abalone slotted diamonds and snowflake

HEADSTOCK DECORATION: Abalone torch inlay

SOUND HOLE INLAYS: Abalone

BRIDGE: Ebony

TUNING MACHINES: Gotoh gold tuners

NECK WIDTH AT NUT: 1¾ inches (4.4 cm)

BRACING: Scallop bracing

FINISH: Sunburst

The Hapa

The Hapa, 2006 ▶
Steve Grimes, Grimes Guitars
Kula, Hawaii

Steve Grimes lives on the island of Maui, home to the 10,000 foot dormant volcano Haleakala and a hotbed of resurgent native culture and music. Grimes built his first double sound hole guitars in collaboration with the Hawaiian slack key master Keola Beamer. Since slack key revolves around alternate tunings with deep lowered (slackened) bass notes, Beamer wanted a guitar that could handle bass sound well. By splitting the normal central sound hole into two smaller holes and moving them to the sides of the fingerboard, they allowed a larger, uninterrupted portion of the soundboard to vibrate and thereby improved the guitar's bass response.

The original Beamer model had two equal-sized sound holes. In the Hapa model, the sound holes are asymmetrical, with the larger of the two on the bass side of the upper bout. Having the bigger hole nearest the player's ear makes the sound of the guitar seem even fuller and louder to the musician than the Beamer. In both models, the combined area of the two sound holes is similar to that of a conventional round hole guitar.

Hapa is Hawaiian pidgin for "half" and is often used in reference to the many islanders who are part white. It's also the name of Maui's most acclaimed musical group, led by New Jersey-born Barry Flanagan and native Hawaiian Nathan Kawai Aweau.

105

SPECIFICATIONS

BODY AND SIDE WOODS: Options: Highly figured Koa, various rosewoods, various maples

TOP WOOD: Options: German, Sitka, Engelmann, Carpathian, and cedar

BODY WIDTH, LOWER BOUT: Options: Classic, OM, and 16 inches (40.6 cm)

TUNING MACHINES: Gotoh 510 Special or Schaller

SCALE LENGTH: 25.5 inches (64.8 cm)

NECK WIDTH AT NUT: 1¹¹⁄₁₆ to 1¾ inches (4.3 to 4.4 cm)

NUMBER OF FRETS: 12-fret model: 20; 14-fret model: 22

BRACING: European or Carpathian spruce

FINISH: Nitrocellulose lacquer

BODY DEPTH: OM: 4⅛ inches (10.5 cm); 16-inch (40.6 cm) model: 4⁵⁄₁₆ inches (11 cm)

BODY LENGTH: OM: 19¾ inches (50.2 cm); 16-inch (40.6 cm) model: 20½ inches (52.1 cm)

OVERALL LENGTH: 41½ inches (105.4 cm)

U.S. SUGGESTED RETAIL PRICE: $6,600

A Man's Journey

This unique guitar's decorated headstock and fretboard were inspired by the colorful narrative inlay work of Canadian master William "Grit" Laskin.

The inlay tells the story of his client's life. Maingard's daughter Lucinda suggested that the images appear on ivory pages falling out of a book of life, and his client commissioned Chinese artist Wang Peng to draw the pictures the inlay is based on.

Maingard explains that his client was a fine guitar player, painter, philosopher, and musician. "The soccer boots recall his youth as a champion junior soccer player," says Maingard. "This image flows into the 'palette of colors' that he used on his last painting—the red dripping from the palette indicates the blood spilt in his journey and, as a healer, a changing adventure day by day. The bird symbolizes the freedom that he feels having achieved and crossed these major thresholds in his life. The infinity sign links the music that he makes, the songs that he sings. The open books circling the sound hole are many lives past and future, spiraling out of the music and his dance of life."

🌢 **A Man's Journey, 2004**
Marc Maingard, Maingard Guitars
Cape Town, South Africa

SPECIFICATIONS

BODY AND SIDE WOODS: Cocobolo

TOP WOOD: Swiss-European spruce

BODY WIDTH, LOWER BOUT: 15 15/16 inches (40.5 cm)

ELECTRONICS: L.R. Baggs

NECK WOOD: Brazilian mahogany

FRETBOARD MATERIAL: Ebony

SOUND HOLE INLAYS: Abalone

BRIDGE: Hand-carved ebony

NUT AND SADDLE: Ivory

TUNING MACHINES: Waverly gold engraved

BINDING: Macassar ebony

SCALE LENGTH: 25.4 inches (64.5 cm)

NECK WIDTH AT NUT: 1 3/4 inches (4.4 cm)

NUMBER OF FRETS: 21

BRACING: X brace with variations

FINISH: Catalyzed finish, German

BODY DEPTH: 3 3/4 to 4 5/8 inches (9.5 to 11.8 cm)

BODY LENGTH: 20 1/8 inches (51 cm)

OVERALL LENGTH: 41 5/8 inches (105.7 cm)

U.S. SUGGESTED RETAIL PRICE: $16,000

Experimental Guitar

Grit Laskin built this experimental guitar after listening to a symphonic performance and observing that the harp, even though a plucked nylon-strung instrument like the guitar, was able to project its sound above the rest of the orchestra. He realized that the key difference between the two instruments was the harp's soundboard, which was tilted at a 35-degree angle rather than the parallel positioning of a conventional guitar. Laskin wondered what would happen if he built a guitar with a 25-degree soundboard tilt, as close to a harp's 35-degree angle as he felt was possible.

This odd-looking and ergonomically challenged instrument was the result. The nylon strings were also attached like a harp's, with the ball ends inserted through the bridge from inside the guitar, by means of a hinged access door in the endblock. Laskin asked a renowned classical player to test the guitar, and he declared the sound "orchestral" but found the body angle very difficult and uncomfortable to deal with. Laskin says he then drew up plans for a second instrument with a reduced 18-degree soundboard angle and a redesigned back shape, but those plans remain on his drawing board.

◀ **Experimental Guitar, 1988**
William "Grit" Laskin
Toronto, Ontario, Canada
Collection of the Canadian Museum of Civilization

SPECIFICATIONS

BODY AND SIDE WOODS: Indian rosewood

TOP WOOD: Sitka spruce

BODY WIDTH, LOWER BOUT: 14 9/16 inches (37 cm)

NECK WOOD: Curly maple

FRETBOARD MATERIAL: Ebony

BRIDGE: Rosewood

NUT AND SADDLE: Bone

TUNING MACHINES: German, handmade

BINDING: Ebony

SCALE LENGTH: 26.4 inches (66 cm)

NECK WIDTH AT NUT: 2 1/16 inches (5.2 cm)

NUMBER OF FRETS: 19

BRACING: Red cedar

FINISH: Lacquer

BODY DEPTH: 7 5/16 inches (18.5 cm) at deepest point

BODY LENGTH: 19 1/2 inches (49.5 cm)

OVERALL LENGTH: 39 3/8 inches (100 cm)

Royal Hawaiian Koa Jumbo Cutaway

*I*n addition to the guitars he is best known for, James Goodall has built (and plays) concert flutes, Baroque oboes, recorders, English horns, dulcimers, hammered dulcimers, and mandolas, as well as other instruments of his own invention. He also painted seascapes before he built his first guitar in 1972, and he traded one of his canvases to buy the wood he needed for the project.

Goodall has lived and worked in Hawaii since 1992, and his business has grown from a one-man shop building 40 instruments a year to an operation with 13 employees that ships 10 instruments a week. His Royal Hawaiian Model is built entirely of koa, a distinctively figured wood unique to the islands. Top quality koa is increasingly expensive and hard to find because of its popularity among luthiers and home decorators, but geography is in Goodall's favor and he makes sure he "gets there" first.

Unlike many builders, Goodall refuses to use any plastics, preferring to bind his instruments solely with strips of wood. For this all-koa guitar, Goodall chose purpleheart (*Peltogyne paniculata*), an exotic tropical wood which, after being cut and exposed to light, turns a rich purple color that is a perfect complement to the warm reddish glow of curly koa.

● **Royal Hawaiian Koa
Jumbo Cutaway, 2004
James Goodall, Goodall Guitars**
Kailua Kona, Hawaii

SPECIFICATIONS

BODY AND SIDE WOODS: Quilted/flamed Hawaiian koa

TOP WOOD: Quilted/flamed Hawaiian koa

BODY WIDTH, LOWER BOUT: 17 inches (43.2 cm)

NECK WOOD: Honduran mahogany

FRETBOARD MATERIAL: Ebony

FRETBOARD INLAY: Island scene

HEADSTOCK DECORATION: Mother-of-pearl peghead border and matching koa

SOUND HOLE INLAYS: Mother-of-pearl

BRIDGE: Ebony

NUT AND SADDLE: Fossilized walrus ivory

TUNING MACHINES: Gold Schallers with ebony buttons

BINDING: Purpleheart

SCALE LENGTH: 25.5 inches (64.8 cm)

NECK WIDTH AT NUT: 1¾ inches (4.4 cm)

NUMBER OF FRETS: 20

BRACING: Modified X pattern

FINISH: Catalyzed urethane

BODY DEPTH: 4⅝ inches (11.7 cm)

BODY LENGTH: 21 inches (53.3 cm)

OVERALL LENGTH: 42 inches (106.7 cm)

U.S. SUGGESTED RETAIL PRICE: $11,994

Michael Heiden

Mark O'Connor Jumbo

Michael Heiden has played fiddle, mandolin, and guitar in numerous folk, Bluegrass, and swing bands over the years and has been repairing and building guitars and mandolins since the early 1970s.

Heiden is particularly known for his player-friendly Jumbos and Dreadnoughts, which are favorites with many Bluegrass guitarists, and for his F-5 style mandolins, which are among the most respected interpretations of Lloyd Loar's classic design available today. This Jumbo was custom made for multi-instrumentalist Mark O'Connor, who, although best known for his astonishing fiddling, is also a wizard on guitar and mandolin. Like Heiden, O'Connor is a genre hopper; he has composed and recorded not only Bluegrass, but also classical and jazz (including two violin concertos), and worked and recorded with such other masters as Béla Fleck, Stéphane Grappelli, Wynton Marsalis, and Tony Rice.

♠ **Mark O'Connor Jumbo, 1991**
Michael Heiden, Heiden Stringed Instruments
Chilliwack, British Columbia, Canada

SPECIFICATIONS

BODY AND SIDE WOODS: Indian rosewood

TOP WOOD: Engelmann spruce

BODY WIDTH, LOWER BOUT: 17 inches (43.2 cm)

ELECTRONICS: LR Baggs

NECK WOOD: Figured Eastern maple

FRETBOARD MATERIAL: Ebony

HEADSTOCK DECORATION: Logo

SOUND HOLE INLAYS: Wood strips

BRIDGE: Ebony

NUT AND SADDLE: Bone and Tusq

TUNING MACHINES: Schaller

BINDING: Ebony on body, ivoroid on neck

SCALE LENGTH: 25.4 inches (64.5 cm)

NECK WIDTH AT NUT: 1 11/16 inches (4.3 cm)

NUMBER OF FRETS: 20

BRACING: Light X brace

FINISH: Nitrocellulose lacquer

BODY DEPTH: 4 inches (10.2 cm)

BODY LENGTH: 21 inches (53.3 cm)

U.S. SUGGESTED RETAIL PRICE: $6,875

L-45.7, Roses

Steve Klein's 45.7 is named for its size. The measurement in centimeters across the lower bout is 45.7 centimeters, just short of 18 inches, which makes this is a very big guitar indeed, 2⅜ inches (6 cm) wider than a Martin dreadnought and more than a full inch (2.5 cm) wider than the so-called "King of Guitars," the Gibson Super Jumbo.

To integrate his design aesthetically, Klein drew the radii of both bout forms from the same compass point and centered a relatively small circular sound hole at the intersection of the two shapes.

The 45.7's bracing is based on the radical concepts developed by Dr. Michael Kasha and classical luthier Richard Schneider, but Klein added his own twists. Long and extremely thin tone bars intersect with the bridge plate, architectural flying braces offer support without touching the top, and the arms of the traditional X brace are removed so that only the front half touches the top. The guitar also has a zero fret, an added fret wire placed about 5 mm from the nut. The nut still controls the spacing of the strings, but the zero fret controls string height, thereby eliminating some intonation problems. Advocates of the zero fret also believe that it helps ensure that open and fretted strings have the same sound.

◄ L-45.7, Roses, 1995
Steve Klein
Vineburg, California
Collection of Jeff Doctorow

SPECIFICATIONS

BODY AND SIDE WOODS: Brazilian rosewood

TOP WOOD: Sitka Spruce

BODY WIDTH, LOWER BOUT: 18 inches (45.7 cm)

NUMBER OF FRETS: 14

The Cherub Guitar

Master luthier Jim Olson, who is himself no slouch at inlay, once said to Harvey Leach, "I don't know why you mess around with simple guitars; there are plenty of us doing that. If I could do inlays like you, that's all I'd do."

Leach, who has done inlay work for C.F. Martin, McCollum, Modulus, PRS, Pensa, and Kevin Ryan as well as his own guitars, has been following Olson's suggestion of late. "A while back I came to a realization," he says, "... as much as I love building simple guitars, what really excites me is inlay work and building from the rarest and most exotic woods available. I hope to push the limits of what can be done with a simple jeweler's saw and some of nature's greatest artwork."

The Cherub Guitar is the most highly decorated Leach guitar thus far and a masterpiece of inlay art, with elaborately detailed inlays made from more than a dozen different types of shell, gemstones, and other materials.

SPECIFICATIONS

BODY AND SIDE WOODS: Brazilian rosewood with sapwood

TOP WOOD: Bearclaw Sitka spruce

BODY WIDTH, LOWER BOUT: 15 inches (38.1 cm)

NECK WOOD: Walnut and maple

FRETBOARD MATERIAL: Ebony

FRETBOARD INLAY: Double intertwined vine with shell and stone

HEADSTOCK DECORATION: Same vine as fretboard, ending with a cherub painting the Leach logo

SOUND HOLE INLAYS: Very fine vine with silver wire, stone, and shell

BRIDGE: Ebony with vine inlay similar to the fretboard

NUT AND SADDLE: Fossilized mammoth ivory

TUNING MACHINES: Grovers

BINDING: Crushed shell

SCALE LENGTH: 25.4 inches (64.5 cm)

NECK WIDTH AT NUT: 1¾ inches (4.4 cm)

NUMBER OF FRETS: 21

BRACING: Modified X bracing

FINISH: High-gloss lacquer

BODY DEPTH: 4½ inches (11.4 cm)

OVERALL LENGTH: 40 inches (101.6 cm)

U.S. SUGGESTED RETAIL PRICE: $28,000

The Cherub Guitar, 2002 ▶
Harvey Leach, H. G. Leach Guitars
Cedar Ridge, California

FLATTOP

The Little Manzer

*T*his diminutive instrument is not a toy but rather a six-string "tenor" or "terz" guitar, pitched a fourth higher than a normal steel-string and tuned A, D, G, C, E, A. The body form is basically the same as a standard Manzer acoustic, and the workmanship and detailing are as exacting as any of Linda Manzer's other work.

Manzer has been building guitars since the 1960s and, like William "Grit" Laskin and several other notable Canadian luthiers, apprenticed with Jean Larrivée in the 1970s. With the help of a part-time assistant, she currently makes 15 to 18 instruments a year and was sufficiently backordered that she stopped taking new orders in 2006 to catch up with the backlog. She says that most people who visit her shop are surprised how "low tech" she is. "I love working by hand and making all the parts," she explains. "I make everything for my guitars here, except the obvious—like machine heads and truss rods, which are made by a machinist friend. [Recently] Pearl Works has cut the intricate Manzer pearl logo, but all other inlay on my guitars, I design and do from 'scratch.' I slot fingerboards one by one, bend all my wood and occasionally I even go to lumber yards to crawl around two-story-high piles of wood, looking for those elusive, fabulous boards of curly maple."

◀ **The Little Manzer**
Linda Manzer, Manzer Guitars
Toronto, Ontario, Canada

Deluxe Model 2000

*B*ernie Lehmann's Model 2000 reflects his experience and interest in Medieval and Renaissance instruments. He trained with master luthier Owen Shaw, who helped establish Boston as a center for early music in the 1970s. While apprenticing with Shaw, Lehmann worked on classical guitars, lutes, vihuelas (a Spanish precursor of the guitar), viols de gambas, and medieval fiddles called rebecs and vielles, which he still makes. He says what he learned from building this wide array of instruments "is how to make strings efficiently drive the enclosed volume of air: Different forms, same rules of tone production."

The body and sides of the Model 2000 are built from ribbed staves instead of two or three large pieces of wood, as were Renaissance lutes, vihuelas, and guitars. The ribbed, vaulted back increases the guitar's volume by focusing the sound towards the sound hole and greatly enhances its projection and carrying power. Lehmann says the highly arched design of the back also makes the guitar very comfortable to hold "because the sides are narrowest at the lower bout— right where the player's arm rests. The guitar feels like a thin body instrument but sacrifices nothing in interior volume. The unique structure of the back provides surprising strength without any bracing being necessary." The guitar also includes a side sound port in the upper bout that sends sound up toward the player. "As far as I can tell," Lehmann posits, a sound port is "as close as we get in this life to something for nothing. It doesn't detract at all from the sound in front, and it just adds to the player's enjoyment."

◀ **Deluxe Model 2000, 2001**
Bernard Lehmann, Lehmann
Stringed Instruments
Rochester, New York

115

SPECIFICATIONS

BODY AND SIDE WOODS: Quilted mahogany

TOP WOOD: Bearclaw Sitka spruce

BODY WIDTH, LOWER BOUT: 15 inches (38.1 cm)

NECK WOOD: Peruvian mahogany

FRETBOARD MATERIAL: Ebony

HEADSTOCK DECORATION: Ivory and carved celtic motif

SOUND HOLE INLAYS: Pierced rosette

BRIDGE: Brazilian rosewood

NUT AND SADDLE: Bone

TUNING MACHINES: Rodgers Lacote style

BINDING: Ivoroid

SCALE LENGTH: 25.6 inches (65 cm)

NECK WIDTH AT NUT: 2 inches (5 cm)

NUMBER OF FRETS: 20

BRACING: Hauser-style fan

FINISH: Lacquer

BODY DEPTH: 4¼ inches (10.8 cm)

BODY LENGTH: 19⅝ inches (49.8 cm)

OVERALL LENGTH: 40¾ inches (103.5 cm)

U.S. SUGGESTED RETAIL PRICE: $12,400

Model 1887 Travel Guitar

Bernie Lehmann says he designed this removable-neck travel guitar for fingerstyle guitarists who are "tired of those wimpy, little puny-sounding guitars that sound like a door harp." Unlike them, the Lehmann Model 1887 Travel Guitar and his new gypsy travel guitar, dubbed "The Gypsy Caravan," are full-sized instruments "that set up in minutes and easily fit in a suitcase or the overhead bin of an airplane. No tools are necessary to take the guitar apart or set it up again; the neck slides off with a pull on the strap pin, and the strings are kept tangle free by a keeper bar that slides into the bridge."

♥ **Model 1887 Travel Guitar, 2004**
Bernard Lehmann, Lehmann
Stringed Instruments
Rochester, New York

The origin of these travel guitars can probably be traced to Lehmann's college study of Experimental Design at Syracuse University, where he says the idea was to create art pieces more than functional musical instruments. "They were half art pieces, half concoctions, but most of them worked. It's important to me to advance the art of luthiery," he continues. "Not by doing copies of what's been done already but by experimentation. I like to make each instrument different. It's an artistic expression for me. Every single instrument I've made has been different in some way. Each instrument is a new challenge. I don't like repetition."

116

SPECIFICATIONS

BODY AND SIDE WOODS: Indian rosewood

TOP WOOD: Adirondack spruce

BODY WIDTH, LOWER BOUT: 15 inches (38.1 cm)

NECK WOOD: Mahogany

FRETBOARD MATERIAL: Ebony

FRETBOARD INLAY: Mother-of-pearl deco design

HEADSTOCK DECORATION: Abalone

SOUND HOLE INLAYS: Abalone and ebony

BRIDGE: Ebony and bone

NUT AND SADDLE: Bone

TUNING MACHINES: Waverly

BINDING: Ivoroid

SCALE LENGTH: 25.5 inches (64.8 cm)

NECK WIDTH AT NUT: 1¾ inches (4.4 cm)

NUMBER OF FRETS: 22

BRACING: Lehmann X

FINISH: Lacquer

BODY DEPTH: 4¼ inches (10.8 cm)

BODY LENGTH: 19⅝ inches (49.8 cm)

OVERALL LENGTH: 40½ inches (102.9 cm)

U.S. SUGGESTED RETAIL PRICE: $4,760

OM-Night Dive Limited Edition

*N*ight Dive was a collaborative effort between Canadian master luthier and inlay artist William "Grit" Laskin, the technical inlay wizards of the late Larry Sifel's Pearl Works, and the craftspeople of C.F. Martin & Co.

Laskin's design for the elaborate pictorial inlay that covers the headstock and fingerboard was painstakingly executed by Pearl Works and then assembled and lacquered by Martin. The inlay, depicting shell divers above and below the water surface, a retrieval boat, a shell cutter, and an observer, forms a visual allegory for the process of harvesting and processing shell into the small slabs that inlayers use. All but the divers are real people involved in the world of shell and inlay: Larry Sifel works at the saw, Chuck Erikson (Sifel's partner, who is known as The Duke of Pearl) retrieves the shell from the divers, and Grit Laskin peers over the edge of the uppermost boat, just an onlooker to the stages of the process that he, as the inlay artist and end user, does not participate in.

Night Dive was made in a combined edition of Dreadnought and OM models, limited to 100 guitars.

● OM-Night Dive Limited Edition, 2004
C.F. Martin & Co.
Nazareth, Pennsylvania

SPECIFICATIONS

BODY AND SIDE WOODS: Brazilian rosewood

TOP WOOD: Bearclaw Sitka spruce

BODY WIDTH, LOWER BOUT: 15 inches (38.1 cm)

NECK WOOD: Genuine mahogany

FRETBOARD MATERIAL: Genuine black ebony

FRETBOARD INLAY: Unique William "Grit" Laskin designed

HEADSTOCK DECORATION: Night dive inlay

SOUND HOLE INLAYS: Style 45 with abalone pearl inlay

BRIDGE: Genuine black ebony

NUT AND SADDLE: Genuine bone

BINDING: Black

SCALE LENGTH: 25.4 inches (64.5 cm)

NECK WIDTH AT NUT: 1¾ inches (4.4 cm)

NUMBER OF FRETS: 20

BRACING: Martin scalloped X bracing

FINISH: Polished gloss nitrocellulose lacquer

BODY DEPTH: 4⅛ inches (10.5 cm)

BODY LENGTH: 19⅜ inches (49.2 cm)

OVERALL LENGTH: 39½ inches (100.3 cm)

U.S. SUGGESTED RETAIL PRICE: $19,999

Custom M1 Cutaway

*I*n addition to doing repair work for Gryphon Stringed Instruments, Michi Matsuda makes 10 to 12 custom guitars a year, and, although he is still taking new orders, his waiting list now stretches to about three years.

Each of Matsuda's guitars is unique, personal, and individual, even if it is one of his basic models. "Although a guitar is designed primarily to be the tool of a performer," he explains, "I am also making visual and auditory art. My custom instruments not only meet the physical and technical needs of the performer, they are also creative, expressive works from my imagination. It is my hope that my artistic expression will inspire guitarists to even greater creative heights."

Matsuda builds two steel-string guitar body designs, the M1, which is a modified OM, and the M2, which is a modified 00. His forms are spare and elegant with just enough ornamentation to pull them back from starkness. His workmanship is as impeccable as his design sense, both of which are much admired by fellow luthiers.

◀ **Custom M1 Cutaway, 2006**
Michihiro Matsuda
Oakland, California

119

SPECIFICATIONS

BODY AND SIDE WOODS: Brazilian rosewood

TOP WOOD: Italian spruce

BODY WIDTH, LOWER BOUT: 15½ inches (39.4 cm)

NECK WOOD: Mahogany

FRETBOARD MATERIAL: Ebony

SOUND HOLE INLAYS: Spalted maple

BRIDGE: Brazilian rose and ebony

NUT AND SADDLE: Bone

TUNING MACHINES: Gotoh 510

BINDING: Rosewood

SCALE LENGTH: 25.25 inches (64.1 cm)

NECK WIDTH AT NUT: 1¾ inches (4.4 cm)

NUMBER OF FRETS: 20

BRACING: Matsuda X bracing

FINISH: Nitrocellulose lacquer

BODY DEPTH: 4⅜ inches (11.1 cm)

BODY LENGTH: 19⅜ inches (49.2 cm)

OVERALL LENGTH: 40½ inches (102.9 cm)

#1,000,000 with Larry Robinson Inlay

*I*t took the family-owned C.F. Martin & Co. 171 years to reach serial number 1,000,000, so not surprisingly the company decided to pull out all the stops on this milestone guitar. No expense was spared, and the resulting museum piece is by far the most elaborate instrument in the company's history and one of the most decorated guitars ever. It is also an anomaly among Martins, which have always prided themselves on their spare elegance. As a 1920s catalog puts it, "Martin designs are notable for rich dignity and neatness. There is only a little ornament, and this is in good taste."

Master inlay artist Larry Robinson designed the intricate inlays of abalone, mother-of-pearl, sea snail, 18-karat gold, white gold, and precious gems (including diamonds, emeralds, rubies, sapphires, and aquamarines) that cover the back, fingerboard, headstock, rosette, pickguard, and inset sound hole rosette of the dreadnought model guitar. Robinson spent nearly two years hand cutting the pieces with a jeweler's saw, fabricating the designs, and gluing them into carefully incised wood, while world-class engraver Dave Guilietti engraved all the gold elements.

The inlaid and engraved pictures that cover the guitar tell the story of the Martin company. On the back, there's a portrait of C.F. Martin, Sr.; above that, angels hold instruments important to Martin's history—a ukulele, a concert guitar, a mandolin, and a dreadnought.

Near the heel of the neck, two cherubim hold a Stauffer guitar from the German shop where C.F. Martin apprenticed when he was 15. On the front, the pickguard is inlaid with the tools of the trade: drawknife, mallet, jeweler's saw, and the inverted top of a Martin guitar showing the X bracing invented by C.F. Martin and credited with revolutionizing acoustic guitars.

"If Martin has a coat of arms," says national sales manager Bruce Mariano, "that's it."

▲ **#1,000,000 with Larry Robinson Inlay, 2004**
C.F. Martin & Co.
Nazareth, Pennsylvania

SPECIFICATIONS

BODY AND SIDE WOODS: Brazilian rosewood

TOP WOOD: Adirondack spruce

BODY WIDTH, LOWER BOUT: 15⅝ inches (39.7 cm)

NECK WOOD: Genuine mahogany

FRETBOARD MATERIAL: Genuine black ebony

FRETBOARD INLAY: Unique Larry Robinson hand-cut inlay

HEADSTOCK DECORATION: Unique Larry Robinson hand-cut inlay

SOUND HOLE INLAYS: Unique Larry Robinson inlay with soundhole rose

BRIDGE: Genuine black ebony with Robinson inlay

NUT AND SADDLE: Fossil ivory

TUNING MACHINES: Gold-engraved Waverly butterbean

BINDING: Grained ivoroid

SCALE LENGTH: 25.4 inches (64.5 cm)

NECK WIDTH AT NUT: 1¾ inches (4.4 cm)

NUMBER OF FRETS: 20

BRACING: Martin scalloped X bracing

FINISH: Polished gloss nitrocellulose lacquer

BODY DEPTH: 4⅞ inches (12.4 cm)

BODY LENGTH: 20 inches (50.8 cm)

OVERALL LENGTH: 40¼ inches (102.2 cm)

U.S. SUGGESTED RETAIL PRICE: Priceless, not for sale

Grand Concert Cutaway "Bevel Edge Model"

$\mathscr{M}$arc Maingard says the beveled edge on the front and back of what is now his favorite guitar model was inspired by William "Grit" Laskin and Kevin Ryan. "When I first saw the bevel edge on Grit Laskin's guitar, I was very inspired to try it for myself. It totally takes out the stress that one experiences on one's forearm in playing guitar."

Because luthiers were few and far between in South Africa, Maingard got started by repairing his own guitar in the early '70s, which led to steady work as a repairman. To further his skills, he apprenticed with an English cabinetmaker and spent a year making violins and cellos before working for the Santa Cruz Guitar Company in the United States for three years. He later studied archtop building with Jimmy D'Aquisto and also spent time with Martin, Gibson, and Ovation. He is now the sole authorized South African repair person for the three companies.

122

Grand Concert Cutaway, ▶
"Bevel Edge Model," 2005
Marc Maingard
Cape Town, South Africa

SPECIFICATIONS

BODY AND SIDE WOODS: Indian rosewood

TOP WOOD: German spruce

BODY WIDTH, LOWER BOUT: 16 1/16 inches (40.8 cm)

NECK WOOD: Honduran mahogany

FRETBOARD MATERIAL: Ebony with African blackwood binding

HEADSTOCK DECORATION: Stalitzin bird of paradise inlay in various stones and "M" pearl logo

SOUND HOLE INLAYS: African tribal art design rosette using triangle maple

BRIDGE: Ebony

TUNING MACHINES: Waverly gold tuners

BINDING: African blackwood binding and curly maple top purfling

NECK WIDTH AT NUT: 1 3/4 inches (4.4 cm)

Malabar 13-Fret

*E*d Claxton got his start as a luthier in the late 1960s when he took a course in North African geography at the University of Texas at Austin. The teacher happened to be the legendary Nubian oud player and ethnomusicologist Hamza El Din, and Claxton soon found himself building one of the ancient lutelike relatives of the guitar for himself.

Claxton built his first guitar in 1971 and landed a job as the guitar tech in one of Austin's most popular guitar shops, which soon led to commissions from the parade of out-of-town musicians who frequented the shop. One of his best known clients was Jimmy Buffett, with whom Claxton also shared a passion for wooden boats. After helping to restore historic barques in Europe and Galveston, Claxton and his wife moved to Maine where he built custom wooden boats and furniture for a dozen years, leaving guitars far behind.

123

♠ **Malabar 13-Fret, 2006**
Ed Claxton
Santa Cruz, California

SPECIFICATIONS

BODY AND SIDE WOODS: Brazilian rosewood

TOP WOOD: German spruce

BODY WIDTH, LOWER BOUT: 14¾ inches (37.5 cm)

NECK WOOD: Mahogany

FRETBOARD MATERIAL: Ebony

FRETBOARD INLAY: 12th fret pearl inlay

SOUND HOLE INLAYS: Wood marquetry

BRIDGE: Ebony

TUNING MACHINES: Alessi tuners with black pearl buttons

NUMBER OF FRETS: 13

Premier Series F-35

After years of running a production-line factory, the renowned Irish luthier George Lowden now works alongside a small team of craftsmen that he trained to create a high standard of quality control and consistency.

Lowden says he designed this comfortable mid-sized guitar around 1982 to provide players with a tighter, more focused sound than his other models. The F-35 was created to respond equally well to a variety of playing styles and has been used by both Alex De Grassi and Richard Thompson.

Lowden has been voicing his guitars with an original strut carving system he calls the "dolphin" profile since the 1970s. Dolphin profile bracing is curved, carefully carved to optimize the soundboard's vibrations without adding extra weight.

◄ **Premier Series F-35, 2006**
George Lowden,
George Lowden Guitars
Downpatrick, Northern Ireland

SPECIFICATIONS

BODY AND SIDE WOODS: Figured claro walnut

TOP WOOD: Western red cedar

BODY WIDTH, LOWER BOUT: 16¹⁵⁄₁₆ inches (430 mm)

NECK WOOD: Mahogany, rosewood, and walnut

FRETBOARD MATERIAL: Ebony

FRETBOARD INLAY: Rosewood and sycamore

HEADSTOCK DECORATION: East Indian rosewood with mother-of-pearl inlay

SOUND HOLE INLAYS: Abalone, rosewood, sycamore, walnut, and mahogany

BRIDGE: Brazilian rosewood

NUT AND SADDLE: Tusq/Bone

TUNING MACHINES: Gotoh 510

BINDING: Figured sycamore with sycamore, rosewood, and mahogany purflings

SCALE LENGTH: 25.6 inches (65 cm)

NECK WIDTH AT NUT: 1¾ inches (4.4 cm)

NUMBER OF FRETS: 20

BRACING: G.L. Dolphin profile

FINISH: Satin

BODY DEPTH: 4²³⁄₃₂ inches (12 cm)

BODY LENGTH: 19¹¹⁄₁₆ inches (50 cm)

OVERALL LENGTH: 40⁵⁄₁₆ inches (102.5 cm)

U.S. SUGGESTED RETAIL PRICE: $5,065

Pair of Parlour L-00s

*J*oe Yanuziello's acoustic flattops are based on the Gibson L-00 of the 1930s, one of the most respected and reproduced small acoustic models of all time. The L-00 was a no-frills, Depression-era guitar, pared to essentials but offering great sound and huge projection for a modest price.

Like Gibson's coveted originals, Yanuziello's version of the guitar has radiussed, domed, X-braced tops and flat back, a combination that makes it ideal for fingerpicking. It is an extremely versatile

guitar which can also produce a huge sound when it is flatpicked. Like the Gibson original, it is a favorite of bluegrass pickers, who find that its tone and volume measure up favorably to a vintage Martin dreadnought. The all-koa version of the instrument shown here is essentially a Spanish-necked Hawaiian, with rope binding executed in short strips of contrasting holly and ebony.

Pair of Parlour L-00s, 2004 ●
Joseph Yanuziello, Yanuziello Stringed Instruments
Toronto, Canada

SPECIFICATIONS

BODY AND SIDE WOODS: Left, South American mahogany; right, curly koa

TOP WOOD: Left, Engelmann spruce; right, curly koa

BODY WIDTH, LOWER BOUT: Both, 14¾ inches (37.5 cm)

NECK WOOD: Both, South American mahogany

FRETBOARD MATERIAL: Both, ebony

FRETBOARD INLAY: Both, gold-lipped mother-of-pearl

HEADSTOCK DECORATION: Left, paddle peghead with decal logo; right, slotted with Yanuziello decal logo

SOUND HOLE INLAYS: Left, abalone; right, holly and ebony

BRIDGE: Both, modified ebony pyramid bridge

NUT AND SADDLE: Both, bone

TUNING MACHINES: Left, Waverly nickle individual tuners; right, Waverley bronze slotted peghead style

BINDING: Left, ivoroid and black and white purfling lines; right, ivoroid, holly, and ebony parallelogram purfling

SCALE LENGTH: Both, 24.75 inches (62.9 cm)

NECK WIDTH AT NUT: Both, 1¾ inches (4.4 cm)

NUMBER OF FRETS: Both, 19

BRACING: Both, 1930's L-00 style X brace

FINISH: Both, pre-catalyzed lacquer

BODY DEPTH: Both, 4¼ inches (10.8 cm)

BODY LENGTH: Both, 19½ inches (49.5 cm)

OVERALL LENGTH: Both, 39¾ inches (101 cm)

Pair of Parlour Guitars for Viscount Linley

*A*ndy Manson has been building guitars, mandolins, and other fretted instruments for more than 35 years, and has created numerous custom instruments for such prominent British musicians as Jimmy Page, John Paul Jones, Andy Summers, Mike Oldfield, and Ian Anderson and Martin Barre of Jethro Tull. He is also the author of *Talking Wood*, a diary of a year in the guitar maker's life.

This pair of instruments, one using nylon strings and the other steel, was built in the style of Romantic guitars of the early nineteenth century. They were made for the prestigious Linley Gallery in London as part of "The Craft of the Luthier," an exhibition celebrating the work of British luthiers. The exhibition was staged by Viscount David Linley (the son of England's Princess Margaret and Lord Snowdon and a furniture designer of international renown) and designer David Costa, and was presented and opened by Sir George Martin MBE, the legendary producer of the Beatles.

♠ **Pair of Parlour Guitars for Viscount Linley, 2001**
Andy Manson, Andy Manson Custom Guitars
Crediton, Devon, England

SPECIFICATIONS

BODY AND SIDE WOODS: Brazilian rosewood

TOP WOOD: European spruce

BODY WIDTH, LOWER BOUT: 12⅜ inches (31.3 cm)

NECK WOOD: Cuban mahogany

FRETBOARD MATERIAL: Ebony

BRIDGE: Brazilian rosewood

NUT AND SADDLE: Corian

TUNING MACHINES: Rodgers, handmade

BINDING: Koa

SCALE LENGTH: 25.2 inches (63 cm)

NECK WIDTH AT NUT: 1¾ inches (4.4 cm)

NUMBER OF FRETS: 18

BRACING: Steel-string, Martin style; nylon string, Fan

FINISH: Tung oil

BODY DEPTH: 3¾ inches (9.5 cm)

BODY LENGTH: 18 inches (45.8 cm)

OVERALL LENGTH: 37⅛ inches (94.3 cm)

U.S. SUGGESTED RETAIL PRICE: $10,000

M-43 Acoustic
with Offset Sound Hole

Steve Klein

The M-43 was Steve Klein's attempt to create a simpler, easier-to-build instrument that would bring his prices down into a range affordable to professional guitarists. It has a much more traditional shape than previous Kleins and a straight bridge that allowed working musicians to attach acoustic amplification systems.

Klein built M-43s with either standard center sound holes or a single offset one like this example. The idea of an offset sound hole came from Klein's studies of the theories of Dr. Michael Kasha and luthier Richard Schneider, who spent years putting Kasha's ideas into physical form. Moving the sound hole to the treble side of the upper eliminated the need for the flying brace Klein used to support the top of his center sound hole guitars and also gave the top a dynamic, asymmetrical aesthetic.

M-43 Acoustic with Offset Sound Hole, 1998 ▶
Steve Klein
Vineburg, California
Collection of Jeff Doctorow

127

SPECIFICATIONS

BODY AND SIDE WOODS: Indian rosewood

TOP WOOD: Spruce

BODY WIDTH, LOWER BOUT: 16¾ inches (42.5 cm)

NECK WOOD: Indian rosewood with carbon fiber

BRIDGE: Ebony

NECK WIDTH AT NUT: 17½ inches (44.5 cm)

FLATTOP

Experimental Guitar

*M*ichi Matsuda is one of the most original and innovative luthiers at work today. He was born and raised in Japan, and a spare Japanese aesthetic, influenced by the organic forms of nature, informs all of his work. Even his mentors find his designs remarkable. Frank Ford, with whom he worked at Gryphon Instruments, says, "Michi has a habit of showing us curves we didn't realize were there all along."

Matsuda came to America in 1997 to fulfill his long-time dream of becoming a guitar builder. He graduated from the Roberto-Venn School of Luthiery and also studied with Japanese guitar maker Taku Sakashta, whom he cites as a major influence. His primary training came during the three years he spent working as apprentice to Ervin Somogyi, whom Matsuda says showed him the meaning of craftsmanship and taught him "the subtle art of making wood sing."

◀ **Experimental Guitar, 2003**
Michihiro Matsuda, Matsuda Guitars
Oakland, California

SPECIFICATIONS

BODY AND SIDE WOODS: Indian rosewood

TOP WOOD: Sitka spruce

BODY WIDTH, LOWER BOUT: 15½ inches (39.4 cm)

NECK WOOD: Mahogany

FRETBOARD MATERIAL: Ebony

BRIDGE: Brazilian rosewood and wenge

NUT AND SADDLE: Bone

TUNING MACHINES: Gotoh 510

BINDING: Rosewood

SCALE LENGTH: 25.25 inches (64.1 cm)

NECK WIDTH AT NUT: 1¾ inches (4.4 cm)

NUMBER OF FRETS: 21

BRACING: Experimental honeycomb bracing

FINISH: Nitrocellulose lacquer

BODY DEPTH: 4¹³⁄₁₆ inches (12.2 cm)

BODY LENGTH: 19⅜ inches (49.2 cm)

OVERALL LENGTH: 41 inches (104.1 cm)

RM Deluxe

efore turning his attention to lutherie, Jack Coobs studied painting at art schools in Sarasota, Florida, and Cleveland, Ohio. He then spent nearly ten years at McSwain's Handmade Furniture, a North Carolina reproduction furniture company, before founding Coobs Inc., his own custom furniture business. But stringed instruments ultimately beckoned because, he says, they represented the ultimate woodworking challenge. "You can build a beautiful instrument," Coobs explains, "but if it doesn't sound good, you've wasted your time."

Coobs builds a variety of flattop, classical, and acoustic and electric archtop guitars as well as bouzoukis and mandolins. His years as a furniture maker also helped him master the art of traditional inlay, and many of his instruments are festooned with his own gorgeous abalone and mother-of-pearl designs.

◀ **RM Deluxe, 1999**
Jack Coobs, Coobs Guitars
Indian Trail, North Carolina

129

SPECIFICATIONS

BODY AND SIDE WOODS: Honduran rosewood

TOP WOOD: Master-grade Engelmann spruce

BODY WIDTH, LOWER BOUT: 16 inches (40.6 cm)

ELECTRONICS: LR Baggs ribbon transducer, Micro Equalizer

NECK WOOD: Mahogany

FRETBOARD MATERIAL: Ebony

FRETBOARD INLAY: Mother-of-pearl

HEADSTOCK DECORATION: Cocobolo with mother-of-pearl logo

SOUND HOLE INLAYS: Abalone and ebony

BRIDGE: Ebony

NUT AND SADDLE: Bone

TUNING MACHINES: Schaller

BINDING: Corian

SCALE LENGTH: 25.4 inches (64.5 cm)

NECK WIDTH AT NUT: 1¾ inches (4.4 cm)

NUMBER OF FRETS: 20

BRACING: Scalloped X bracing

FINISH: Nitro lacquer

BODY DEPTH: 4 inches (10.2 cm)

BODY LENGTH: 20 inches (50.8 cm)

OVERALL LENGTH: 41 inches (104.1 cm)

U.S. SUGGESTED RETAIL PRICE: $4,300

1902 00-45S Limited Edition

This custom, limited-edition guitar is a faithful reproduction of one of Martin's rarest and most beautiful turn-of-the-century creations, a special order 00-42 built in 1902. Style 42 was the top of Martin's line in 1902, but the company occasionally added even more decoration to special order instruments, a practice that led to the official introduction of Style 45 in 1904. In this case, Martin luthiers added extra pearl borders and festooned the fingerboard with an intricate vine design. The fingerboard inlay was complemented by an equally fancy pickguard, placed between the bridge and sound hole as on some of the company's bowl-back mandolins.

Only about six of these "loaded" 00-45s were made, in part because the thin layers of inlay were inevitably damaged if fretwork became necessary. Martin dubbed its reproduction 00-45S, a designation that more accurately describes the instrument's over-the-top decoration. Martin uses the "S" suffix to designate something nonstandard and/or out of the ordinary, in this case a 12-fret neck on a Style 45 instrument, for which a 14-fret neck is standard.

◀ **1902 00-45S Limited Edition, 2005**
C.F. Martin & Co.
Nazareth, Pennsylvania

SPECIFICATIONS

BODY AND SIDE WOODS: Brazilian rosewood

TOP WOOD: Adirondack spruce

BODY WIDTH, LOWER BOUT: 14⅛ inches (35.9 cm)

NECK WOOD: Genuine mahogany

FRETBOARD MATERIAL: Genuine black ebony

FRETBOARD INLAY: Tree of life in abalone pearl

HEADSTOCK DECORATION: Martin flower pot inlay in abalone pearl

SOUND HOLE INLAYS: Style 45 with abalone pearl inlay

BRIDGE: Genuine black ebony

NUT AND SADDLE: Fossil ivory

TUNING MACHINES: Waverly Sloane engraved brass #3500 side mount

BINDING: Grained ivoroid

SCALE LENGTH: 24.9 inches (63.2 cm)

NECK WIDTH AT NUT: 1⅞ inches (4.8 cm)

NUMBER OF FRETS: 19

BRACING: Martin scalloped X bracing

FINISH: Polished gloss nitrocellulose lacquer

BODY DEPTH: 4¹⁄₁₆ inches (10.3 cm)

BODY LENGTH: 19⅝ inches (49.8 cm)

OVERALL LENGTH: 37¾ inches (95.9 cm)

U.S. SUGGESTED RETAIL PRICE: $22,500

000-Echf Bellezza Nera
Limited Edition

*I*n recent years, Martin has worked with a wide variety of prominent guitarists to design signature models that reflect the artist's taste and style. The Bellezza Nera and its sister model, the all white Bellezza Blanco, are the result of a particularly unusual collaboration between legendary British guitarist Eric Clapton and Japanese trendsetter Hiroshi Fujiwara, a visionary DJ responsible for creating and introducing cutting-edge "club" music and fashions to Tokyo in the 1990s.

While best known for his electric lead work, Clapton is also a formidable acoustic player who has long favored vintage pre-World War II Martin 14-fret 000s. Appropriately,

Clapton and Martin's first joint venture was, like this guitar, a 000, the Eric Clapton 000-42EC Signature Edition, a recreation of Clapton's own 1938 000-42 that Martin released in 2000.

After working together on other projects, Clapton and Fujiwara decided to design a guitar that would combine great sound with elegant, understated design. C.F. Martin built eight custom guitars based on their concept, one of which can be seen on the cover of Clapton's Robert Johnson tribute CD, *Me and Mr. Johnson*, and Clapton, Fujiwara, and Martin were all so pleased with the completed guitars that they then decided to collaborate on a limited edition version for the public.

SPECIFICATIONS

BODY AND SIDE WOODS: East Indian rosewood

TOP WOOD: Italian alpine spruce

BODY WIDTH, LOWER BOUT: 15 inches (38.1 cm)

NECK WOOD: Genuine mahogany

FRETBOARD MATERIAL: Genuine black ebony

FRETBOARD INLAY: Style 45 snowflake inlays in abalone

HEADSTOCK DECORATION: Martin alternate torch inlay in abalone

SOUND HOLE INLAYS: Mother-of-pearl slotted squares in radial pattern

BRIDGE: Genuine black ebony

NUT AND SADDLE: Genuine bone

TUNING MACHINES: Schaller sterling silver plated M-6

BINDING: Grained ivoroid

SCALE LENGTH: 24.9 inches (63.2 cm)

NECK WIDTH AT NUT: 1¾ inches (4.4 cm)

NUMBER OF FRETS: 20

BRACING: Martin scalloped X bracing

FINISH: Polished gloss black nitrocellulose lacquer

BODY DEPTH: 4⅛ inches (10.5 cm)

BODY LENGTH: 19⅜ inches (49.2 cm)

OVERALL LENGTH: 39⅜ inches (100 cm)

U.S. SUGGESTED RETAIL PRICE: $5,999

◀ **000-Echf Bellezza Nera Limited Edition, 2004**
C.F. Martin & Co.
Nazareth, Pennsylvania

131

Lucas SJ Presentation Model

Randy Lucas began repairing, restoring, and building acoustic guitars in 1988, after working as a mechanical designer for 15 years, and he says both his experience as a designer and his early experiences a repairman have influenced his career as a luthier.

Among the hundreds of instruments he worked on were several vintage pre-war Martins and Gibsons. "I still have the notes, drawings, and photos of those fabulous instruments," he says. "I invested hundreds of hours analyzing them, because I wanted to find out why they sounded so good."

Lucas is a self-professed "nut" about materials; he cuts his own spruce and maple trees so he has control from start to finish. After ten years of building mostly traditional OMs and dreadnoughts, he has added a new line of modernized Jumbo designs; all of them feature more rigid necks and pegheads than traditional guitars and more rounded transitions to the edges where the player's hands and body meet the guitar. "A soft neck material or one-piece neck can really become an acoustic sponge," he says. Lucas therefore laminates his necks from medium-weight, book-matched curly maple; he finds the lamination is stronger and more rigid than a traditional one-piece and increases sustain on notes up the neck. The guitar also has a rosewood veneer added to the back of the peghead, which adds rigidity from the peghead

to the neck shaft, and a flatter than normal arc to the back of the neck as it transitions from the ninth fret to the heel cap. Lucas admits that the flatter arc is a tradeoff; it makes it a little harder for the player to reach for higher notes but keeps the neck from stretching with time, thus staving off the need for a neck reset as the guitar ages.

SPECIFICATIONS

BODY AND SIDE WOODS: Master-grade old-growth Brazilian rosewood and solid paua shell rear trim (The back is Brazilian 3-piece with curly maple and black border purflings separating the three panels.)

TOP WOOD: Master-grade German spruce circa 1905 and solid paua shell top trim

BODY WIDTH, LOWER BOUT: 15⅝ inches (39.7 cm)

ELECTRONICS: B-band A2.2

NECK WOOD: 2-piece book-matched curly mahogany with Brazilian rosewood center stringer strip

FRETBOARD MATERIAL: Ebony

FRETBOARD INLAY: Solid paua shell vine

HEADSTOCK DECORATION: Brazilian rosewood front and rear veneer

SOUND HOLE INLAYS: Solid paua shell and wooden purflings

BRIDGE: Ebony

NUT AND SADDLE: Fossil ivory

TUNING MACHINES: Waverly

BINDING: Curly maple binding on peghead, fingerboard, body, and heel cap with black/white wooden purflings on body and peghead veneer

SCALE LENGTH: 25.4 inches (64.5 cm)

NECK WIDTH AT NUT: 1¾ inches (4.4 cm)

NUMBER OF FRETS: 20

BRACING: X bracing

FINISH: Nitrocellulose lacquer

BODY DEPTH: 3½ to 4⅜ inches (8.9 to 11.1 cm)

BODY LENGTH: 19¾ inches (50.2 cm)

OVERALL LENGTH: 41¼ inches (104.8 cm)

U.S. SUGGESTED RETAIL PRICE: $16,000

Lucas SJ Presentation Model, 2005 ▶
Randy Lucas, Lucas Custom Instruments
Columbus, Indiana

Mitsuhiro Uchida

Dual Soundboard Guitar

Mitsuhiro Uchida apprenticed with classical luthier Toshihiko Nakade before spending four years working for Japanese manufacturers. In 1983, he took a job in Germany repairing stringed instruments for BSA, and then, in 1987, moved to Northern Ireland to work for Lowden, where he participated in the creation of custom guitars for such artists as Pierre Bensusan, Jackson Browne, Elvis Costello, Bob Dylan, David Lindley, John Renbourn, and James Taylor.

Uchida left Lowden in 1990 and returned to Japan to open his own shop. He has become one of Japan's most successful luthiers and has a ten-year waiting list for his work. He designs and builds a constantly evolving variety of guitars, ukuleles, and tiples (10-stringed, four-course instruments related to ukuleles), while his wife Izumi does the finish work. His guitars vary in size from the 41 cm (16⅛ inches) U to a tiny, soprano uke-sized piccolo guitar that measures only 20.6 cm (8⅛ inches) across the lower bout. He has built many guitars for the popular Japanese guitarist Morihiko "Mori" Yasuda, whose main instrument is a 27-string terz harp guitar by Uchida that sports an extended combination of sub-bass and treble harp strings.

Dual Soundboard Guitar, 2000 ▶
Mitsuhiro Uchida
Nagano, Japan

134

SPECIFICATIONS

BODY AND SIDE WOODS: African blackwood

TOP WOOD: Spruce

BODY WIDTH, LOWER BOUT: 15⅞₁₆ inches (39.2 cm)

NECK WOOD: Mahogany

FRETBOARD MATERIAL: Ebony

HEADSTOCK DECORATION: Mother-of-pearl

SOUND HOLE INLAYS: Mother-of-pearl and ebony

BRIDGE: Jacaranda (Brazilian rosewood)

NUT AND SADDLE: Bone

TUNING MACHINES: Rodgers

BINDING: Ebony

SCALE LENGTH: 25.6 inches (65 cm)

NECK WIDTH AT NUT: 1¹¹⁄₁₆ inches (4.3 cm)

NUMBER OF FRETS: 20

BRACING: Original

FINISH: Lacquer

BODY DEPTH: 4⅛ inches (10.5 cm)

BODY LENGTH: 19½ inches (49.5 cm)

OVERALL LENGTH: 41¾ inches (106 cm)

U.S. SUGGESTED RETAIL PRICE: $15,000

Morning Glory

arry Fleishman designed his first guitar when he was 12, built his first when he was 14, and is still going strong after more than three decades as a professional luthier.

He has built a number of harlequin acoustic guitars and basses over the years, with the tops made from contrasting pieces of wood rather than a conventional book-matched pair. This spectacular example not only has an asymmetrical body shape but also splits the sound hole into two smaller units on either side of the upper bout, with the one on the longer, bass side of the instrument slightly larger than its treble companion. Each of the sound hole rosettes includes a pair of large

inlaid morning glory flowers that echo the fingerboard decoration and extend into the negative space of the sound hole itself.

In addition to building and playing classical and acoustic guitars, as well as acoustic and electric basses, Fleishman also directs the Luthiers School International, which offers a variety of classes in steel-string and classical guitar making. According to the prospectus, students build their own instruments from scratch, "using individually selected materials of the high quality you would expect in a fine guitar." And, as he asserts and his guitars testify, "We use no kits!"

◄ **Morning Glory, 1996**
Harry Fleishman, Fleishman Instruments
Sebastopol, California
Collection of Jeff Doctorow

SPECIFICATIONS

BODY AND SIDE WOODS: Curly koa

TOP WOOD: Half redwood/half spruce

BODY WIDTH, LOWER BOUT: 15¾ inches (40 cm)

ELECTRONICS: Fleishman stereo amplification system

NECK WOOD: Mahogany

FRETBOARD MATERIAL: Ebony

FRETBOARD INLAY: Pearl and abalone morning glories

HEADSTOCK DECORATION: Pearl and abalone dragonfly

SOUND HOLE INLAYS: Pearl and abalone morning glories

BRIDGE: Ebony

NUT AND SADDLE: Antique bone

TUNING MACHINES: Schaller with handmade ebony buttons

BINDING: Rosewood

SCALE LENGTH: Multi-scale 25 to 26 inches (63.5 to 66 cm)

NECK WIDTH AT NUT: 1¹¹⁄₁₆ inches (4.3 cm)

NUMBER OF FRETS: 24

BRACING: Fleishman Y bracing

FINISH: Nitrocellulose lacquer

BODY DEPTH: Tapered from 3½ to 4¼ inches (8.9 to 10.8 cm)

U.S. SUGGESTED RETAIL PRICE: $18,000

Martin Simpson
Signature Model D

Stefan Sobell's interest in acoustic instruments began in the British folk clubs of the 1960s. "In those days of unamplified venues," he recalls, "we were all searching for instruments with good power and tone; at that time there weren't many around. I experimented with the instruments I had and soon found that with a little thought and experimentation I could make a reasonable instrument sound considerably worse; a hard way to learn, especially when the modifications were non-reversible."

Sobell did learn from his mistakes, however, and has been one of Great Britain's most respected luthiers for more than three decades. Searching for an instrument equally suited for playing traditional dance tunes and accompanying singing, he built the first modern cittern in 1973, a form that has been embraced by many players and luthiers since, and he is generally credited with developing a uniquely British acoustic guitar, with sound qualities quite different from American steel-strings.

Martin Simpson, the masterful British fingerstyle player for whom this guitar was designed, says, "Sobells have a unique sound, a combination of clarity and power, separation, and richness that I don't find in other guitars. This new guitar is a distinct variation on the Sobell theme. The treble is more bell-like than ever, and there is an added depth to the bass. Because of its clarity and tone, it's a perfect guitar for quiet slow airs, yet if I want to, I can make it absolutely roar without a suggestion of the sound breaking up: a remarkable achievement."

Martin Simpson Signature Model D, 2006
Stefan Sobell,
Stefan Sobell Musical Instruments
Hexham, England

SPECIFICATIONS

BODY AND SIDE WOODS: Old Brazilian rosewood

TOP WOOD: European spruce

BODY WIDTH, LOWER BOUT: 16⅝ inches (42.2 cm)

ELECTRONICS: Bridge pickup

NECK WOOD: Old Cuban mahogany

FRETBOARD MATERIAL: Ebony

FRETBOARD INLAY: Mother-of-pearl dots

HEADSTOCK DECORATION: Brazilian rosewood headstock veneer, matching back and sides

SOUND HOLE INLAYS: Birdsfoot trim with red and white purfling

BRIDGE: Ebony

NUT AND SADDLE: Bone

TUNING MACHINES: Gotoh 510

BINDING: Ebony with red and white purfling

SCALE LENGTH: 28.5 inches (72.5 cm)

NECK WIDTH AT NUT: 1²⁵⁄₃₂ inches (4.5 cm)

NUMBER OF FRETS: 20

BRACING: Simpson signature type Sobell X bracing

FINISH: Acid catalyst melamine

BODY DEPTH: 4¾ inches (12 cm)

BODY LENGTH: 19¼ inches (49 cm)

OVERALL LENGTH: 42¼ inches (107.3 cm)

U.S. SUGGESTED RETAIL PRICE: $15,700

McCollum Double Neck

*L*ance McCollum says he began building guitars simply because he hadn't found the sound he was looking for in something he could buy off the rack. He started playing guitar when he was 12 and almost immediately began to tinker with his instruments. Nearly 300 guitars later, he is still working to perfect the sound he seeks.

McCollum has always followed his own muse. As a teenager, he redesigned, rewelded and repainted his own and his friends' BMX bicycles, designed his own surfboards and topped them off with airbrushed artwork, designed jewelry, and, when the time came, took up auto painting.

McCollum has built a reputation for meticulous traditional craftsmanship, including dovetailed neck joints, and is known for his rosettes and his use of unusual woods, in this case walnut for the back and sides. This six/12-string double neck also features a small second sound hole on the bass side of the upper bout.

SPECIFICATIONS

BODY AND SIDE WOODS: Walnut

TOP WOOD: Sitka spruce with sunburst

BODY WIDTH, LOWER BOUT: 17¼ inches (43.8 cm)

ELECTRONICS: Baggs

NECK WOOD: Mahogany

FRETBOARD MATERIAL: Cocobolo

FRETBOARD INLAY: Celtic knot

SOUND HOLE INLAYS: Paua shell

BRIDGE: Cocobolo

NUT AND SADDLE: Bone

TUNING MACHINES: Gold

BINDING: Koa with green purfling

SCALE LENGTH: 25.5 inches (64.8 cm) on each neck

NECK WIDTH AT NUT: 1¹¹⁄₁₆ inches (4.3 cm)

NUMBER OF FRETS: 22 on each neck

FINISH: Nitrocellulose lacquer

BODY DEPTH: 5¼ inches (13.3 cm)

BODY LENGTH: 20 inches (50.8 cm)

OVERALL LENGTH: 42 inches (106.7 cm)

U.S. SUGGESTED RETAIL PRICE: $9,000

♠ **McCollum Double Neck, 2000**
Lance McCollum, McCollum Guitars
Colfax, California

137

Model R Custom
Eight-String Fan Fret

$\mathcal{M}$odel R is the second largest guitar Jeff Traugott builds, with a 15½-inch lower bout and 25.375-inch scale length when built with a standard bridge and fingerboard. When built with a standard bridge and fingerboard, this eight-string variation of the Model R adds an extra string at each side of the instrument, with the high string usually tuned to A above high E and the extra low string usually tuned to A or B below low E. The guitar also uses Ralph Novak's patented Novax Fanned-Fret system, which makes it possible to create a wide range of scale lengths, from 27¾ inches for the low A string to 23¾ inches for the highest A string.

The Novax Fanned-Fret concept evolved from luthier and repairman Ralph Novak's desire to produce an instrument with balanced tone and string tension. Novak explains that the "fanning" of the frets results from manipulating the scale length of the bass side of the neck relative to the treble side: the fret spacing is wider for the long scale and closer for the short scale.

Novak's system is particularly useful on guitars with added strings, which are notoriously difficult to keep in tune. The varied scale lengths and fanned frets of the Novax system eliminate tuning problems and allow players to take full advantage of the extra strings. San Francisco-based acoustic jazz guitarist Jack West, for example, plays a Traugott eight-string he commissioned and tunes his guitar (A),E,A,d,e,a,d',a'; or (B),E,A,d,f#,b,e',a' or (B),E,A,d,g,b',e',a'; or (B),E,A,d,f#,a,e',a'; in addition to the "standard" (A),E,A,d,g,b,e',a'.

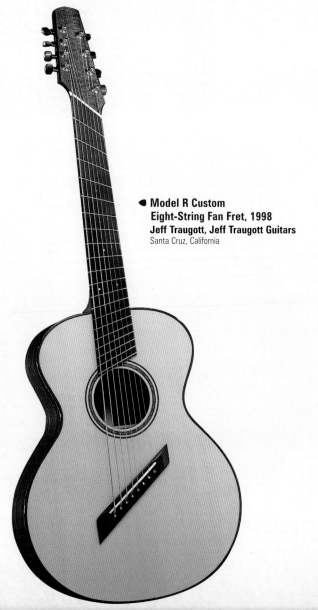

◄ **Model R Custom**
Eight-String Fan Fret, 1998
Jeff Traugott, Jeff Traugott Guitars
Santa Cruz, California

138

SPECIFICATIONS

BODY AND SIDE WOODS: Indian rosewood

TOP WOOD: German spruce

BODY WIDTH, LOWER BOUT: 15½ inches (39.4 cm)

ELECTRONICS: Custom

NECK WOOD: Mahogany

FRETBOARD MATERIAL: Ebony

FRETBOARD INLAY: Mother-of-pearl dots

HEADSTOCK DECORATION: Koa

SOUND HOLE INLAYS: Koa

BRIDGE: Ebony

NUT AND SADDLE: Bone

TUNING MACHINES: Schallers with ebony buttons

BINDING: Ebony

SCALE LENGTH: Fan fret–bass 27.75 inches (70.5 cm), treble 23.75 inches (60.3 cm)

NECK WIDTH AT NUT: 2³⁄₃₂ inches (5.3 cm)

NUMBER OF FRETS: 20

BRACING: Modified X

FINISH: Lacquer

BODY DEPTH: 4⅜ inches (11.1 cm)

BODY LENGTH: 19½ inches (49.5 cm)

Meghann 000

*L*ance McCollum builds with a wide variety
of unusual exotic and domestic tonewoods,
including beeswing, black limba, Macassar ebony,
myrtle, pau ferro, sapele, and Tasmanian blackwood,
and takes advantage of the colors and figure of the
lumber. This 000 is topped with Flamed Spanish cedar
and paired with an olive wood body and sides.

SPECIFICATIONS

BODY AND SIDE WOODS: Olive Wood

TOP WOOD: Flamed Spanish cedar

BODY WIDTH, LOWER BOUT: 15 inches (38.1 cm)

NECK WOOD: Mahogany

FRETBOARD MATERIAL: Striped ebony

SOUND HOLE INLAYS: Brown lip pearl

BRIDGE: Ebony

NUT AND SADDLE: Bone

TUNING MACHINES: Gold with ebony buttons

BINDING: Cocobolo with rippled green heart abalone

SCALE LENGTH: 25.7 inches (65.3 cm)

NECK WIDTH AT NUT: 1¾ inches (4.4 cm)

NUMBER OF FRETS: 22

BRACING: X bracing

FINISH: Nitrocellulose lacquer

BODY DEPTH: 4⅝ inches (11.7 cm)

BODY LENGTH: 19 inches (48.3 cm)

OVERALL LENGTH: 42 inches (106.7 cm)

U.S. SUGGESTED RETAIL PRICE: $6,000

♠ **Meghann 000, 2002**
Lance McCollum,
McCollum Guitars
Colfax, California

MG 4.5 Custom

McPherson guitars take advantage of three technical innovations by the company: an oddly-shaped offset sound hole in the bass side of the upper bout; a cantilevered neck that is not connected or glued to the top of the guitar; and innovative bracing that maximizes the available open, "vibrating" area on the inside of the guitar face.

The elliptical shape, size, and location of McPherson's offset sound hole are the result of exhaustive testing. Moving the sound hole "to the edge" —a very specific and crucial position on the guitar's face—effectively increases the sound-enhancing flexible surface area of the central part of the instrument.

The unconventional "no-touch" design of McPherson's neck allows the top to vibrate and resound to its fullest potential.

The patent-pending cantilevered neck also offers tremendous neck stability and thereby inhibits the potential for warpage. The company's state-of-the-art bracing expands the top's vibrating ability by minimizing the bracing connection to the underside.

McPherson offers customers a wide range of wood choices. This top-of-the-line custom sports a dramatically figured, flamed redwood top with Brazilian rosewood back and sides.

♠ **MG 4.5 Custom, 2007**
McPherson Guitars
Sparta, Wisconsin

SPECIFICATIONS

BODY AND SIDE WOODS: Brazilian rosewood

TOP WOOD: Bearclaw Sitka spruce

BODY WIDTH, LOWER BOUT: 16 inches (40.6 cm)

ELECTRONICS: LR Baggs RTS2 with discrete volume wheel inside the signature Offset Soundhole Technology

NECK WOOD: Mahogany

FRETBOARD MATERIAL: Ebony

HEADSTOCK DECORATION: Brazilian rosewood with mother-of-pearl inlay on the head cap and mother-of-pearl inlay in reverse on the IE Rosewood bridgeplate inside the guitar

SOUND HOLE INLAYS: McPherson signature Offset Soundhole Technology with flamed curly koa binding

BRIDGE: Brazilian rosewood

NUT AND SADDLE: Natural bone

TUNING MACHINES: Schaller M6GA gold finish

BINDING: Flamed curly koa

SCALE LENGTH: 25.5 inches (64.8 cm), nut to saddle

NECK WIDTH AT NUT: 1¾ inches (4.4 cm)

NUMBER OF FRETS: 20

BRACING: McPherson Guitars State of the Art bracing system (Finish: Lawrence-McFadden polyester finish)

BODY DEPTH: 4 inches (10.2 cm)

BODY LENGTH: 20 inches (50.8 cm)

OVERALL LENGTH: 41½ inches (105.4 cm)

U.S. SUGGESTED RETAIL PRICE: $8,175

Phil Green

Miranda Steel String
S-250 Travel Guitar

Miranda Steel String S-250 ▶
Travel Guitar, 2005
Phil Green, Miranda Guitars
Los Altos, California

*M*iranda Guitars was founded by Dr. Phil Green, a pioneer in ultrasonic imaging and "robotic" surgery. One of Dr. Green's dreams was to develop a full-sized guitar with the portability of a violin, and the feel, playability, and full-bodied sound of an acoustic instrument. The patented instruments he designed, the steel-stringed S-250 and its nylon-stringed cousin, the CFX-200, sound, feel, and play like traditional acoustic guitars, but can be quickly and easily disassembled to fit into a case small enough to be stowed overhead on any airplane.

The Miranda has a full-sized, full-depth ergonomic body contour and standard scale length, and its proprietary electronics deliver an acoustic sound that is so good that some professional musicians are using it on stage. It can also be played silently with the Remain Silent headphones that come with it.

142

SPECIFICATIONS

BODY AND SIDE WOODS: Unitary neck and solid core body of mahogany; acrylic side panels and heel plate

BODY WIDTH, LOWER BOUT: 15 inches (38.1 cm)

ELECTRONICS: Under-saddle pickup and Miranda proprietary preamplifier/signal processor

NECK WOOD: Mahogany

FRETBOARD MATERIAL: Rosewood

SOUND HOLE INLAYS: Decal-simulated sound hole

BRIDGE: Rosewood

NUT AND SADDLE: Corian nut; bone saddle

TUNING MACHINES: Gotoh

SCALE LENGTH: 25.6 inches (65 cm)

NECK WIDTH AT NUT: 1 11/16 inches (4.3 cm)

NUMBER OF FRETS: 20

FINISH: Clear lacquer; satin

BODY DEPTH: 3 3/8 inches (8.6 cm)

BODY LENGTH: 18 1/2 inches (47 cm)

OVERALL LENGTH: 33 7/8 inches (86.1 cm) assembled

U.S. SUGGESTED RETAIL PRICE: $1,195

Rockbridge Custom Guitar for Geoff Simpson

*I*n addition to being a master of inlay and guitar making, Brian Calhoun is also an avid basketball player who boasts that he is in the minority of luthiers who can do a 360 degree dunk. His partner, master flatpicker and luthier Randall Ray, had built about 20 guitars when he and Brian officially teamed up in 2002. Ray's guitar heroes are Clarence White, Doc Watson, and Django Reinhardt, and he claims he personally "test drives" each new Rockbridge Guitar with a medley of "Reno's Ride," "Stones Rag," and "Nuages," based on the versions played by those three legends.

Rockbridge specializes in dreadnoughts for Bluegrass flatpickers and a smaller, shallower 000-size guitar aimed at fingerpickers, and they have recently expanded their line to include a slope shoulder dreadnought, a small jumbo, and a 0 model. This Rockbridge was commissioned by a guitar-playing priest, and the inlay symbolizes his Christian testimony.

**Rockbridge Custom Guitar ▶
for Geoff Simpson, 2006
Brian Calhoun and Randall Ray,
Rockbridge Guitar Company**
Lexington, Virginia

143

SPECIFICATIONS

BODY AND SIDE WOODS: Quilted Honduran mahogany

TOP WOOD: Cedar

BODY WIDTH, LOWER BOUT: 15⅛ inches (38.4 cm)

ELECTRONICS: LR Baggs I-beam

NECK WOOD: Honduran mahogany

FRETBOARD MATERIAL: Ebony

FRETBOARD INLAY: Various shells, woods, stones, and metals

HEADSTOCK DECORATION: Abalone, mother-of-pearl

SOUND HOLE INLAYS: D-18 purfling

BRIDGE: Ebony

NUT AND SADDLE: Bone

TUNING MACHINES: Waverly

BINDING: D-18 purfling/tortoise-shell binding on body; maple/tortoise-shell binding on fingerboard and peghead

SCALE LENGTH: 25 inches (63.5 cm)

NECK WIDTH AT NUT: 1¾ inches (4.4 cm)

NUMBER OF FRETS: 21

BRACING: Adirondack spruce

FINISH: Water-based acrylic urethane

BODY DEPTH: 4⅛ inches (10.5 cm)

BODY LENGTH: 19½ inches (49.5 cm)

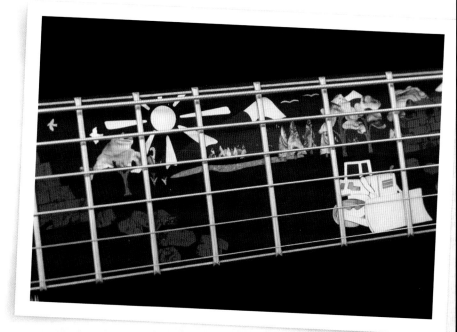

The Oracle Fingerstyle Guitar

Sheldon Schwartz's Oracle is a thoroughly modern acoustic guitar, carrying such features as a lattice-braced, carbon fiber-reinforced soundboard, double-walled side construction, a carbon fiber-reinforced, X-braced back, a bentwood-style armrest, three elliptical sound holes, a rear access panel, a five-piece laminated neck with 24 frets clear of the body, and a long, 26-inch scale.

Schwartz moved the sound holes so he could do away with the heavy bracing typical of center sound hole construction and open up this prime real estate to vibrate freely and produce sound. Moving the sound holes to the bass side of the upper bout has the added effect of making the guitar much more audible to the player, and it also created space at the end of the fingerboard for some additional frets. "Having 24 frets only makes sense if they are accessible," says Schwartz. "I've done that with the extension bevel in the cutaway. Believe it or not, this makes the 24th fret reachable while still having your thumb around the heel of the neck. The design takes up minimal air space inside the box, and the interior structure of the Oracle allows these high notes to ring true, without the characteristic 'plink' you might expect. While most guitar music does not require those notes, it is because they have not been available on an acoustic guitar up until now. I'm sure that with the Oracle someone will create music that uses them."

SPECIFICATIONS

BODY AND SIDE WOODS: East Indian rosewood

TOP WOOD: Sitka spruce

BODY WIDTH, LOWER BOUT: 16 inches (40.6 cm)

ELECTRONICS: Highlander IP-1

NECK WOOD: Mahogany

FRETBOARD MATERIAL: Ebony

FRETBOARD INLAY: Two brass rings at 12th fret

HEADSTOCK DECORATION: Schwartz guitars logo in black mother-of-pearl

SOUND HOLE INLAYS: Black cross-grain veneer in soundhole edge

BRIDGE: Ebony

NUT AND SADDLE: Black TUSQ from graph-tech

TUNING MACHINES: Gotoh 510s

SCALE LENGTH: 26 inches (66 cm)

NECK WIDTH AT NUT: 1 13/16 inches (4.6 cm)

NUMBER OF FRETS: 24

BRACING: Sitka spruce lattice reinforce with carbon fiber

FINISH: Nitrocellulose

BODY DEPTH: 4 7/16 inches (11.3 cm)

BODY LENGTH: 20 1/8 inches (51.1 cm)

OVERALL LENGTH: 41 9/16 inches (105.6 cm)

U.S. SUGGESTED RETAIL PRICE: $8,500

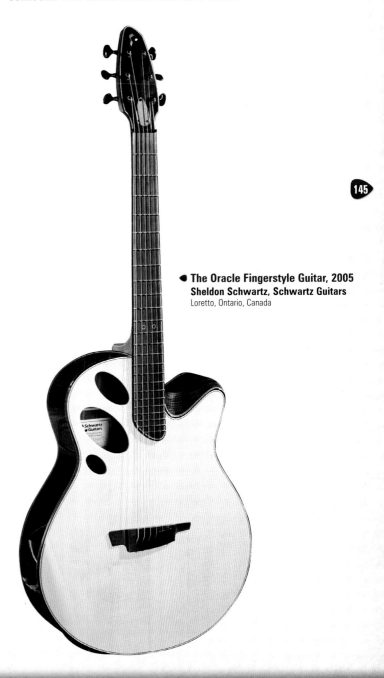

The Oracle Fingerstyle Guitar, 2005
Sheldon Schwartz, Schwartz Guitars
Loretto, Ontario, Canada

Froggy Bottom Model L Prototype

Froggy Bottom founder Michael Millard is one of many prominent luthiers who cut their teeth in the shop of the legendary Michael Gurian. Millard joined Gurian in 1970 and built his first "Froggy" in the kitchen of his Lower East Side apartment that same year. He moved to New Hampshire with the Gurian operation in 1973 and struck out on his own a year later. Andy Mueller brought his machine shop experience to Froggy Bottom when he became Millard's partner in 1994, and the company is now a five-person team (three of them working full time) that makes about 100 instruments a year.

Froggy Bottom's two Parlor models, the P-12 & P-14, are widely considered the best modern parlor guitars being made. Millard says they created this third parlor design, the smallest guitar Froggy has ever built, "to see how small we could effectively go on a six-string tuned to pitch with a scale length of full-size proportions. We also plan to use the body design with different scale lengths for a high-strung instrument and perhaps for a four-string tenor guitar. The instrument should be able to stand up in comparison to any guitar without being criticized as small."

"The materials and ornamentation of the prototype are about as fine as we do," continues Millard. "It's all handwork; we don't do most of the elaborate work with CNCs (Computer Numerical Controls). Pretty or not, it's still a guitar and the music it makes is the true bottom line."

◀ **Froggy Bottom Model L Prototype, 2006**
Michael Millard and Andrew Mueller, Froggy Bottom Guitars
Newfane, Vermont

SPECIFICATIONS

BODY AND SIDE WOODS: Spalted Brazilian rosewood

TOP WOOD: Adirondack red spruce

BODY WIDTH, LOWER BOUT: 13 inches (33 cm)

NECK WOOD: Mahogany

FRETBOARD MATERIAL: African ebony

FRETBOARD INLAY: Green abalone

HEADSTOCK DECORATION: Brazilian rosewood, abalone logo inlay

SOUND HOLE INLAYS: Paua abalone

BRIDGE: African ebony

NUT AND SADDLE: Bone

TUNING MACHINES: Waverly, side mount

BINDING: Big leaf maple, paua abalone, cellulose line purfling

SCALE LENGTH: 24.75 inches (62.9 cm)

NECK WIDTH AT NUT: 1¾ inches (4.4 cm)

NUMBER OF FRETS: 18

BRACING: Red spruce

FINISH: Nitrocellulose

BODY DEPTH: 4¼ inches (10.8 cm)

BODY LENGTH: 19 inches (48.3 cm)

OVERALL LENGTH: 38⅛ inches (96.8 cm)

U.S. SUGGESTED RETAIL PRICE: $22,000

Moonstone J-90 Eagle, Brazilian Rose #3

Steve Helgeson has been building guitars since the early 1970s. He built the first Brazilian Rose as a birthday present for himself and never intended to let it go until J.J. Cale (composer of "After Midnight," "Cocaine," and others) talked him out of it. Helgeson then had to make another for himself and was commissioned to build this third in the series by a customer on the condition that it come out better than the first two guitars.

Helgeson elaborates, "The client chose one of the best rosewood sets I had, ordered a custom fit neck width, and then I decided to add a little color to the inlay by mixing in some reconstituted stone such as red coral,

red spiney, blue river agate, and one piece of clear turquoise. I also used a finer-cut width of paua abalone for the trim on the back and sides, making it look even more delicate. I hate to get too attached to some of my guitars when I know they will be leaving me."

147

Moonstone J-90 Eagle,
Brazilian Rose #3, 2005
Steve Helgeson, Moonstone Guitars
Eureka, California

SPECIFICATIONS

BODY AND SIDE WOODS: Brazilian rosewood

TOP WOOD: Adirondack red spruce

BODY WIDTH, LOWER BOUT: 16⅝ inches (42.2 cm)

NECK WOOD: Honduran mahogany

FRETBOARD MATERIAL: African ebony

FRETBOARD INLAY: Original rosevine design of abalone, pearl, reconstituted stone

HEADSTOCK DECORATION: Abalone, pearl, reconstituted stone

SOUND HOLE INLAYS: Abalone, pearl, reconstituted stone inlaid into ebony

BRIDGE: Hand-carved eagle design in ebony

NUT AND SADDLE: Ivory

TUNING MACHINES: Schaller mini gold-plated with ebony buttons

BINDING: Curly maple, paua abalone

SCALE LENGTH: 25.5 inches (64.8 cm)

NECK WIDTH AT NUT: 1¹¹⁄₁₆ inches (4.3 cm)

NUMBER OF FRETS: 20

BRACING: Modified scalloped X bracing in red spruce

FINISH: Nitrocellulose lacquer

BODY DEPTH: 4⅝ inches (11.7 cm)

BODY LENGTH: 20⅜ inches (51.8 cm)

OVERALL LENGTH: 41¼ inches (104.8 cm)

U.S. SUGGESTED RETAIL PRICE: $16,870

Stuart Mossman
Golden Era Deluxe #4662

Flatpicker and luthier Stuart Mossman began making guitars in 1965. Seeing an opportunity to take advantage of the booming market for acoustic guitars, he expanded his business in the early 1970s and, for a few years, competed directly with Martin in the creation of high quality instruments made from the best available materials and yet offered at a competitive price. He was the first small manufacturer to expand into large scale production.

Sadly, a disastrous fire in 1975 destroyed Mossman's supply of tonewoods, including an irreplaceable stock of fine old Brazilian rosewood. Mossman then switched to East Indian rosewood, and, though plagued by

more bad business luck, he continued to craft outstanding instruments until he sold the company in 1986. The Mossman company is now located in Sulphur Springs, Texas, and still produces fine guitars, including the Golden Era model.

This Golden Era Deluxe, serial #4662, was formerly owned by the renowned fiddler and flatpicker Mark O'Connor, who won it when he became the National Flatpicking Champion in 1977. It features extensive abalone inlay on the body as well as a classic "tree-of-life" fretboard inlay inspired by the work of the Larson Brothers. Following Mossman tradition, every worker who helped build the instrument initialed the label.

◆ **Golden Era Deluxe #4662, 1977**
Designed by Stuart Mossman, S.L. Mossman Guitars
Winfield, Kansas
National Music Museum
The University of South Dakota
Bill Willroth, Sr., Photographer
Ex coll.: Mark O'Connor. Tony and Bonnie Vinatieri Family Trust, 2005

SPECIFICATIONS

BODY AND SIDE WOODS: Two-piece book-matched East Indian rosewood

TOP WOOD: Two-piece spruce

BODY WIDTH, LOWER BOUT: 15¾ inches (40 cm)

NECK WOOD: Mahogany

FRETBOARD MATERIAL: Ebony with nickel-silver frets

FRETBOARD INLAY: Ebony, abalone "Tree of Life"

HEADSTOCK DECORATION: "M" logo inlaid in abalone

BRIDGE: Ebony with curved lower edge

NUT AND SADDLE: Ivory nut; angles light brown celluloid saddle

TUNING MACHINES: Six gold-plated steel worm-gear machine tuners by Grover with convex head surfaces and enclosed worm-gear mechanisms

BINDING: White celluloid; top trim comprised of abalone surrounded on each side by three-ply, thin black-light-black hardwood purfling strips; floral abalone inlay with "M" logo

NECK WIDTH AT NUT: 1⅝ inches (4.1 cm)

NUMBER OF FRETS: 20

BRACING: Spruce X bracing, top; six spruce back braces

FINISH: Clear; matte finish on neck

BODY LENGTH: 20³⁄₃₂ inches (51 cm)

OVERALL LENGTH: 40¾ inches (103.5 cm)

148

Four-String Plectrum Guitar

Steve Parks

Four-stringed plectrum banjos, so-called because they were intended to be played with a pick, first appeared in the early twentieth century. Typically tuned C, G, B, D, they were favored by jazz players who liked their long scale necks—usually 26 inches (66 cm)—and big sound, which enabled them to hold their own with the other solo instruments in a jazz band.

Plectrum guitars are the guitar-bodied equivalents of the plectrum banjos, and, like tenor guitars, they were adopted by many banjoists in the 1920s, as guitars took over the banjo's preciously dominant role as a rhythm and melody instrument in jazz. Their most famous proponent was Albert "Eddie" Condon, who worked with Red Nichols's

Five Pennies in the late 1920s and also recorded with Louis Armstrong. Condon played a Gibson L-7 plectrum guitar throughout his long career.

While the majority of early plectrum guitars were little more than a six-string body with a long skinny neck attached, Steve Parks's instruments are specifically designed as plectrum guitars. Parks is a professional musician who also builds and plays octave mandolins (also called Irish bouzoukis or citterns), mountain dulcimers, and tenor guitars.

Parks has been obsessed with traditional American music since he was a teenager and says that by his mid-thirties, after trying several professions (including building fine, custom Queen Anne-style furniture) while playing music on the side, "I realized this was what I should have been doing all along. So, with lots of support from my long-suffering wife, I dove back into instrument making and performing whenever I wasn't chasing the kids around." Now, he adds, "Life is good."

SPECIFICATIONS

BODY AND SIDE WOODS: Indian rosewood

TOP WOOD: Sitka spruce

BODY WIDTH, LOWER BOUT: 15 inches (38.1 cm)

ELECTRONICS: Fishman acoustic matrix

NECK WOOD: Curly maple

FRETBOARD MATERIAL: Ebony

FRETBOARD INLAY: Scrollwork in white mother-of-pearl

HEADSTOCK DECORATION: Rose in white mother-of-pearl and silver wire

SOUND HOLE INLAYS: White mother-of-pearl ring

BRIDGE: Indian rosewood

NUT AND SADDLE: Bone

TUNING MACHINES: Gold Gotoh minis

BINDING: Curly maple

SCALE LENGTH: 26.2 inches (66.5 cm)

NECK WIDTH AT NUT: 1 5/16 inches (3.3 cm)

NUMBER OF FRETS: 22

BRACING: X bracing

FINISH: Oil varnish

BODY DEPTH: 4 inches (10.2 cm)

BODY LENGTH: 19 1/2 inches (49.5 cm)

OVERALL LENGTH: 40 inches (101.6 cm)

U.S. SUGGESTED RETAIL PRICE: $3,000

Four-String Plectrum Guitar, 2006 ▶
Steve Parks
Dayton, Virginia

Presentation Model

This spectacular parlor instrument, with a lower bout less than a foot wide, is a reproduction of an 1830's "Presentation" guitar built by Christian Frederick Martin Sr., the founder of the Martin guitar company. Martin immigrated to America from his native Saxony in 1833 and established a music store in New York City. He moved the operation to Nazareth, Pennsylvania, in 1838, and the Martin company has set the standards for flattop acoustics ever since.

Presentation guitars were the boutique instruments of their day and were made to appeal to the eye as well as the ear. They had marvelous features such as scroll headstocks, staggered and mortised tuners, veneered and inlaid necks and heels, cantilevered fingerboards, and extensive inlays. They were time-consuming and complex to build.

Martin's original had an ivory fingerboard and headplate, which Spodaryk replicated with a thermoset composite material originally developed in the 1890s. He also had to design an approximation of the original's complex and obsolete Viennese tuners, which he fashioned with the help of a skilled machinist. He made sure the guitar sounds as good as it looks, adding modern X bracing to support steel strings that give it a surprisingly vibrant sound for such a tiny body. Finally, he built a custom period walnut "coffin" case to complete the authentic package.

In addition to Stauffer and C.F. Martin, Steve Spodaryk cites legendary craftsmen James Krenov, George Nakashima, and David Pye as inspirations. He honed his craft under the tutelage of furniture builder John Reed Fox and master luthier Julius Borges. "I worked side by side with Julius for nearly three years," he says, "learning every step of his building process—working my way from 'elf' to 'shop foreman.'" This guitar shows he has become a master in his own right.

SPECIFICATIONS

BODY AND SIDE WOODS: Bolivian rosewood/pau ferro

TOP WOOD: Red spruce

BODY WIDTH, LOWER BOUT: 11 9/16 inches (29.4 cm)

NECK WOOD: Ebonized mahogany

FRETBOARD MATERIAL: White linen micarta

FRETBOARD INLAY: Mother-of-pearl dots

HEADSTOCK DECORATION: Scroll headstock, micarta headplate

SOUND HOLE INLAYS: Paua abalone, mother-of-pearl

BRIDGE: Ivory

NUT AND SADDLE: Bone

TUNING MACHINES: Heavily customized Waverlys, brass cover plate

BINDING: Plastic

SCALE LENGTH: 24 inches (61 cm)

NECK WIDTH AT NUT: 1 3/4 inches (4.4 cm)

NUMBER OF FRETS: 21

BRACING: X braced; red spruce

FINISH: Nitrocellulose lacquer

BODY DEPTH: 3 1/2 inches (8.9 cm) tapering to 4 1/16 inches (10.3 cm)

BODY LENGTH: 17 inches (43.2 cm)

OVERALL LENGTH: 36 inches (91.4 cm)

U.S. SUGGESTED RETAIL PRICE: $13,500

♠ Presentation Model, 2005
Stephen Spodaryk, Spodaryk Guitars
Somerville, Massachusetts

Tenor Guitar using the Novax Fanned-Fret System

*I*nvented around the turn of the twentieth century, four-stringed tenor guitars were most popular in the 1920s and early 1930s, during the period of transition between the banjo and the guitar as the primary rhythm instrument in small ensembles. The tenor guitar is traditionally tuned in fifths like a tenor banjo or mandola (C, G, D, A), making it easy for players of those instruments to move to guitar.

Martin began building tenors in 1927 and is the only major manufacturer that still has a tenor model in its line. The instrument is also associated with Nick Reynolds of the Kingston Trio, whose playing of a Martin tenor gave it renewed popularity during the folk boom of the late 1950s and early 1960s.

With a 14¾-inch wide lower bout, the bodies of Steve Parks's tenors are slightly larger than Martin's highly regarded instruments. The extra width adds more warmth and bass response—"a lovely sound," says Parks.

The tenor's scale length of almost 23 inches gives it a good guitar sound, but is quite long for the high C, G, D, A tuning. "The D and A strings are too tense," says Parks. "Just about everyone is constantly breaking their A string." To solve this problem, Parks applied the Novax Fanned Fret system to the tenor. "The scale gets shorter as you get to the treble side," explains Parks, "giving all the strings an appropriate length. It works great, sounds great, and is actually easier to play than a standard instrument!"

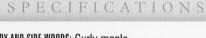

SPECIFICATIONS

BODY AND SIDE WOODS: Curly maple

TOP WOOD: Sitka spruce

BODY WIDTH, LOWER BOUT: 14¾ inches (37.5 cm)

ELECTRONICS: Pickup the World brand #57 with internal preamp

NECK WOOD: Curly maple

FRETBOARD MATERIAL: Ebony

FRETBOARD INLAY: Knotwork in white mother-of-pearl, Chinese calligraphy for "harmony" at 12th fret

HEADSTOCK DECORATION: Dragon with pearl, white and black mother-of-pearl

SOUND HOLE INLAYS: Feng Shui bagua in black mother-of-pearl

BRIDGE: Indian rosewood

NUT AND SADDLE: Bone

TUNING MACHINES: Gold Gotoh minis

BINDING: Indian rosewood

SCALE LENGTH: Bass side - 22.56 inches (57.3 cm), treble - 21.75 inches (55.2 cm)

NECK WIDTH AT NUT: 1⁵⁄₁₆ inches (3.3 cm)

NUMBER OF FRETS: 22

BRACING: X bracing

FINISH: Water-based lacquer (KTM 9)

♠ **Tenor Guitar using the Novax Fanned-Fret System, 2006**
Steve Parks
Dayton, Virginia

152

Prairie State Jumbo

*R*alph Bown is one of Britain's foremost luthiers. His guitars are played by such prominent and idiosyncratic musicians as Martin Simpson, John Renbourn, Henry Kaiser, and Peter Rowan. He works in a small workshop in the heart of ancient York, where he builds a wide range of acoustic guitars and related instruments, including tiples and harp guitars. Bown freely admits he has never been very good at working with one eye on the clock. "I'm not sure how far one can do this," he says. "I try to, but I'm still a time and motion man's nightmare."

This Bown Jumbo is based on one of the Larson Brothers' Prairie State models from the 1930s. The Chicago-based Larson brothers were among the first luthiers to build instruments intentionally braced for steel strings, and their estimated production of 10,000 to 12,000 instruments, small only in comparison to Gibson, Martin, and other large manufacturers, is remarkable for its consistent quality and variety. In addition to flattop guitars that ranged from 12-inch (30.5 cm) parlor instruments to a monster with a 21-inch (53.3 cm) lower bout, they also crafted harp guitars, a full line of mandolin family instruments, the occasional tiple and uke, and three prototype electric guitars that were custom-ordered by Les Paul in 1934.

153

♠ **Prairie State Jumbo, 2002**
Ralph S. Bown, Bown Guitars
York, England

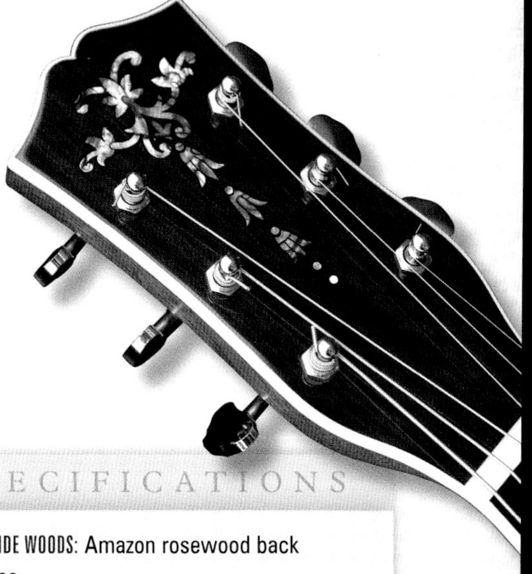

SPECIFICATIONS

BODY AND SIDE WOODS: Amazon rosewood back and sides

TOP WOOD: German spruce

BODY WIDTH, LOWER BOUT: 17 inches (43.2 cm)

NECK WIDTH AT NUT: 1 13/16 inches (4.6 cm)

BRACING: Laminated

BODY DEPTH: 3¼ inches (8.3 cm) tapering to 4 inches (10.2 cm)

Size E Custom Cutaway

𝒶 lthough Judy Threet holds a PhD in philosophy from Stanford University, she switched careers soon after building her first guitar. In 1987, while teaching at the University of Calgary, she joined a local folk-swing band, where she met the highly respected luthier Michael Heiden. In no time, she placed an order for a guitar. Though still teaching, she spent many hours at Michael's shop and by 1989 asked him to teach her the principles of inlay "as a diversion," she claims. A year later, Heiden oversaw the building of her first guitar, and by 1991 she had quit teaching and opened her own shop.

Threet, who has a reputation as one of the most fastidious luthiers around, closed her waiting list in 2005, after it had grown to three years. Frank Ford of Gryphon Instruments calls Threet "one of the old guard" in the current luthier revival. "She does all her own work, including inlays and finishing, with no CNC (Computer Numerical Controls)," says Ford with admiration. "Last time I spoke with her, she was moving in quite the opposite direction from most modern builders, doing more work by hand than ever before."

◄ **Size E Custom Cutaway, 2005**
Judy Threet, Threet Guitars
Calgary, Alberta, Canada

SPECIFICATIONS

BODY AND SIDE WOODS: Cocobolo

TOP WOOD: Sitka spruce

BODY WIDTH, LOWER BOUT: 15⅝ inches (39.7 cm)

NECK WOOD: Mahogany

FRETBOARD MATERIAL: Ebony

FRETBOARD INLAY: White mother-of-pearl slotted diamonds, gold mother-of-pearl goose eggs, and an abalone maple leaf

HEADSTOCK DECORATION: Light koa, white and black mother-of-pearl, ebony, gold mother-of-pearl, and dark koa

SOUND HOLE INLAYS: Cocobolo

BRIDGE: Rosewood

NUT AND SADDLE: Bone

TUNING MACHINES: Gotoh 510s, gold with black knobs

BINDING: Koa

SCALE LENGTH: 25.4 inches (64.5 cm)

NECK WIDTH AT NUT: 1¾ inches (4.4 cm)

NUMBER OF FRETS: 21

BRACING: X with asymmetric lower tone bars

FINISH: Nitrocellulose lacquer

BODY DEPTH: 4½ inches (11.4 cm) at tailblock

BODY LENGTH: 20 inches (50.8 cm)

OVERALL LENGTH: 40½ inches (102.9 cm)

U.S. SUGGESTED RETAIL PRICE: $10,000

The Presentation LC6 Limited Edition

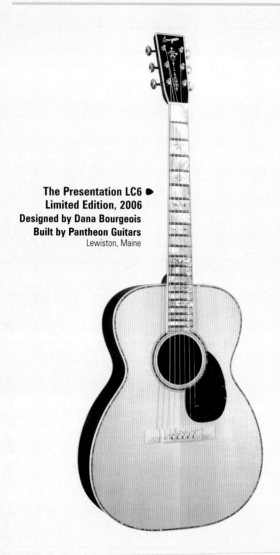

**The Presentation LC6 ▶
Limited Edition, 2006
Designed by Dana Bourgeois
Built by Pantheon Guitars**
Lewiston, Maine

The Presentation LC6 is a slope-shouldered dreadnought based on a guitar Dana Bourgeois originally designed for Ricky Skaggs. Skaggs asked Bourgeois to make him "...an awards ceremony guitar—you know, something I can play while I'm wearing a tux," telling him he wanted a guitar that not only required a tux, but sunglasses as well.

Bourgeois says The Presentation LC6, made in a limited edition of just 10 guitars, "is pretty close to Ricky's guitar." The certified fossil mammoth ivory used on this guitar is "almost as expensive as the Brazilian rosewood," Bourgeois elaborates, "and the fretboard is real mother-of-pearl, inlaid with abalone. It's the same as on Ricky's guitar, and it's the part he needs sunglasses for."

This guitar's ornate decoration harkens back to the flash of late nineteenth- and early twentieth-century instruments made by the Chicago-based Washburn company, whose fanciest model also featured a pearl fretboard.

SPECIFICATIONS

BODY AND SIDE WOODS: Brazilian rosewood

TOP WOOD: Eastern red Adirondack spruce

BODY WIDTH, LOWER BOUT: 15 1/16 inches (38.3 cm)

NECK WOOD: Mahogany

FRETBOARD MATERIAL: Ebony

FRETBOARD INLAY: Mother-of-pearl deco block inlaid with abalone floral pattern

HEADSTOCK DECORATION: Brazilian rosewood veneer with presentation abalone headstock inlay and mother-of-pearl Bourgeois headstock inlay

SOUND HOLE INLAYS: 3 ring with abalone

BRIDGE: Certified mammoth ivory pyramid bridge with fossil walrus pins

NUT AND SADDLE: Bone

TUNING MACHINES: Gold engraved Waverly tuners

BINDING: Grained ivoroid

SCALE LENGTH: 25.5 inches (64.8 cm)

NECK WIDTH AT NUT: 1 3/4 inches (4.4 cm)

NUMBER OF FRETS: 20

BRACING: Modified X bracing

FINISH: Catalyzed urethane

BODY DEPTH: 4 3/16 inches (10.6 cm) at tailblock, 3 5/16 inches (8.4 cm) at neck

BODY LENGTH: 19 5/16 inches (49.1 cm)

OVERALL LENGTH: 39 9/16 inches (100.5 cm)

SJ Guitar with African Faces

*B*alazs Prohaszka is a Hungarian luthier who is currently living in Northern Ireland. He studied building and repairing methods and the theoretical background of the guitar, violin, and lute-type musical instruments at a Hungarian school of luthiery. After graduation, he worked first for a violin maker and then in a double-bass workshop, where he restored and built double-basses, an experience he says has been incredibly useful in guitar building. He set up his own workshop in 2000 and built mainly archtop guitars until 2003 when he moved to Northern Ireland to work as a senior craftsman for Lowden Guitars. Lowden has since become Avalon Guitars, where Prohaszka is responsible for custom projects and inlays, while making six or seven of his own original designs on the side each year.

Prohaszka says his main influence in guitar building is nature itself, "mirrored in my ornamentation and exploiting the beauty of the wood not only in appearance but in sound, too."

SJ Guitar with African Faces, 2005 ▶
Balazs Prohaszka
Newtownards, Ireland

157

SPECIFICATIONS

BODY AND SIDE WOODS: Indian rosewood

TOP WOOD: Trade secret

BODY WIDTH, LOWER BOUT: 16½ inches (41.2 cm)

NECK WOOD: Honduran mahogany

FRETBOARD MATERIAL: Ziricote

SOUND HOLE INLAYS: Indian and Brazilian rosewood, koa, mahogany, mother-of-pearl, abalone, tagua nut, ebony

BRIDGE: Brazilian rosewood

NUT AND SADDLE: Ox bone

TUNING MACHINES: Steinberger tuners

BINDING: Australian blackwood

SCALE LENGTH: 25.92 inches (64.8 cm)

NECK WIDTH AT NUT: 1¾ inches (4.4 cm)

NUMBER OF FRETS: 21

BRACING: Scalloped X bracing

FINISH: Satin

BODY DEPTH: 4⅝ inches (11.6 cm)

BODY LENGTH: 19⅝ inches (49.2 cm)

U.S. SUGGESTED RETAIL PRICE: $6,000

Collectors Series Brazilian Cedar SJ

*L*uthier and toolmaker Jim Olson has been building acoustic flattop guitars since 1977. His instruments began getting national attention in the mid-1980s, after the rising acoustic guitarist, singer, and songwriter Phil Keaggy commissioned the first cedar-topped Olson SJ guitar and began playing Olson guitars almost exclusively on his albums and in concert. In 1989, James Taylor bought three Olson guitars, and through his visibility and advocacy, Olsons became known to acoustic players around the world. In turn, Olson Guitars' new high profile sparked interest in handcrafted, non-factory guitars and opened doors that many other skilled acoustic builders were able to walk through. More than a few credit Jim Olson with making their careers possible.

Olson has also been highly influential as a toolmaker. He has designed and manufactured dozens of jigs and specialized tools that enable him to build 40 or more high-quality guitars each year, and his highly customized tooling has influenced many other luthiers' working habits.

159

◄ **Collectors Series Brazilian Cedar SJ, 2006**
James A. Olson, Olson Guitars
Circle Plains, Minnesota

SPECIFICATIONS

BODY AND SIDE WOODS: Brazilian rosewood

TOP WOOD: Cedar

BODY WIDTH, LOWER BOUT: 15 inches (38.1 cm)

NECK WOOD: Mahogany, maple, and Indian rosewood

FRETBOARD MATERIAL: Ebony

FRETBOARD INLAY: Paua shell

HEADSTOCK DECORATION: Paua shell

SOUND HOLE INLAYS: Paua shell and Brazilian rosewood

BRIDGE: Ebony

NUT AND SADDLE: Bone

TUNING MACHINES: Gotoh 510

BINDING: Brazilian rosewood

SCALE LENGTH: 25.4 inches (64.5 cm)

NECK WIDTH AT NUT: 1¾ inches (4.4 cm)

NUMBER OF FRETS: 20

BRACING: X braced

FINISH: Polyester UV cured

BODY DEPTH: 4¾ inches (12.1 cm)

BODY LENGTH: 19⅜ inches (49.2 cm)

OVERALL LENGTH: 40½ inches (102.9 cm)

U.S. SUGGESTED RETAIL PRICE: $25,000

Model 1, Grand Auditorium

Dennis Scannell is an MIT graduate and master woodworker who has played and worked on guitars since the early 1970s. He established True North Guitars in 1994, initially focusing on high quality steel-string guitars for fingerstyle players who favor altered tunings but eventually expanding his offerings to also include guitars suitable for flatpicking.

Before turning to luthiery full-time, Scannell worked in custom cabinetry and design, and for several years ran a crew of talented finish carpenters for a custom design/build company specializing in unique high-end passive solar homes. He also has more than 15 years experience as a product engineer and product manager for a semiconductor equipment company and in both product management and program management for a renewable energy company.

As his background suggests, Scannell's work is elegant, meticulous, and mathematically precise; his instruments feature pure, graceful lines and a unified design sensibility. His typically detailed list of True North appointments includes ergonomic side-tapered bodies based on Linda Manzer's Wedge concept, optional Venetian cutaways, hand-voiced radiussed soundboards with hand-scalloped braces and sculpted X-braced joints, graphite-reinforced necks, bound fingerboards with semi-hemispherical frets, asymmetrical headstocks, and select Green Heart abalone trim and rosette inlay.

SPECIFICATIONS

BODY AND SIDE WOODS: Madagascar rosewood

TOP WOOD: Salvaged "LS" redwood

BODY WIDTH, LOWER BOUT: 16 inches (40.6 cm)

NECK WOOD: Mahogany

FRETBOARD MATERIAL: Ebony

FRETBOARD INLAY: Chinese character 12th fret inlay

HEADSTOCK DECORATION: Ebony headplate with True North logo

SOUND HOLE INLAYS: Two-ring rosette with select green abalone inlay

BRIDGE: Ebony

NUT AND SADDLE: Unbleached "vintage" bone

TUNING MACHINES: Violet-chrome Gotoh 510 supertuners with ebony buttons

BINDING: Macassar ebony

SCALE LENGTH: 25.8 inches (65.5 cm)

NECK WIDTH AT NUT: 1¾ inches (4.4 cm)

NUMBER OF FRETS: 20

BRACING: Hand-carved and voiced red spruce (soundboard) and Sitka spruce (back), with basswood side braces

FINISH: Nitrocellulose lacquer

BODY DEPTH: 4⅜ inches (11.1 cm) at end block, 4¹³⁄₁₆ inches (12.2 cm) at far side of lower bout due to side-tapered body

BODY LENGTH: 20⅛ inches (51.1 cm)

OVERALL LENGTH: 41⅝ inches (105.7 cm)

U.S. SUGGESTED RETAIL PRICE: $10,755

♠ **Model 1, Grand Auditorium, 2006**
Dennis Scannell, True North Guitars
Waterbury, Vermont

T. J. Thompson

OM 45 Deluxe

*A*lthough he is neither well known nor prolific, T.J. Thompson is a luthier's luthier who many sophisticated musicians and fellow artisans think builds flattops that rank with the best ever made by Martin. Thompson, who began his career as a luthier in 1983, has also built a reputation for his meticulous and sometimes miraculous repair work on pre-World War II Martins. He apprenticed with Dana Bourgeois, and then led a five-man team at Elderly Instruments in Lansing, Michigan, for several years before opening his own shop in 1993. His clients have included Eric Clapton, Keith Richards, Paul Simon, and Sting.

Thompson still spends a considerable amount of his time working on vintage Martins and only builds about five guitars a year. He is a perfectionist who believes that great guitars are the result of a combination of a luthier's experiences and personality. He told Allen St. John, author of *Clapton's Guitar*, that when people ask him how to build a better guitar, "I always think and sometimes say, 'Be a better person.' You can't keep your personality out of the work. It's impossible."

SPECIFICATIONS

BODY AND SIDE WOODS: Brazilian

TOP WOOD: Adirondack spruce

BODY WIDTH, LOWER BOUT: 15⅛ inches (38.4 cm)

NECK WOOD: Mahogany

FRETBOARD MATERIAL: Ebony

FRETBOARD INLAY: Pearl

HEADSTOCK DECORATION: Variation on traditional torch

SOUND HOLE INLAYS: Abalone

BRIDGE: Ebony

NUT AND SADDLE: Bone

TUNING MACHINES: Waverly

BINDING: Ivoroid

SCALE LENGTH: 25.4 inches (64.5 cm)

NECK WIDTH AT NUT: 1¾ inches (4.4 cm)

NUMBER OF FRETS: 19

BRACING: Adirondack spruce

FINISH: Nitrocellulose

BODY DEPTH: 4 inches (10.2 cm)

BODY LENGTH: 19 inches (48.3 cm)

OVERALL LENGTH: 40 inches (101.6 cm)

♠ OM 45 Deluxe
T.J. Thompson
West Concord, Massachusetts

161

Matthew Mustapick
Deep Baritone Steel-String Guitar #33

Matthew Mustapick's Deep Baritone can be tuned either a fourth lower than a normal six-string (B to B), or a fifth lower (A to A), using either standard tuning intervals between strings, or any alternative tuning the player desires, brought down into the baritone range. For example, D, A, D, G, A, D players can tune down to A, E, A, D, E, A and use the same chord forms they are familiar with.

The D, A, D, G, A, D tuning was invented by the little known but incredibly influential British guitarist Davey Graham and has been adopted by such other master fingerstyle players as Pierre Bensusan, Dick Gaughan, Bert Jansch, and Richard Thompson. Because it allows the use of moving chord shapes with droning open strings, it has proved particularly suited to traditional Celtic music. Irish guitarists Mícheál Ó Domhnaill and Dáithi Sproule both championed it, and it was also used by Jimmy Page on Led Zeppelin's "Black Mountain Side" and "Kashmir."

The Deep Baritone uses heavier and longer strings than a standard acoustic guitars (having a 28.9-inch scale length), and so its design does not rely on looser-than-normal string tension to play in this low range. Unlike acoustic basses, which can sound thin without amplification, the slightly higher range and deep, rich resonance of the baritone guitar are fully supported by a somewhat smaller than the largest jumbo guitars. While the baritone sounds great when simply strummed with open chords, it also opens up new challenges for sophisticated players, inviting them to rethink their playing and discover new voicings and approaches that take advantage of the instrument's lower frequency range.

The back and sides of this example are zebrawood, a hard, heavy exotic West African lumber named for its bold light-and-dark striped pattern.

● Deep Baritone Steel-String Guitar #33, 2006
Matthew Mustapick, Mustapick Guitars
Soquel, California

SPECIFICATIONS

BODY AND SIDE WOODS: Cocobolo

TOP WOOD: Bearclaw German spruce

BODY WIDTH, LOWER BOUT: 16 inches (40.6 cm)

FRETBOARD MATERIAL: Cocobolo

HEADSTOCK DECORATION: Curly koa

BRIDGE: Cocobolo

NUT AND SADDLE: Bone

TUNING MACHINES: Gotoh 510

BINDING: Curly koa

SCALE LENGTH: 28.9 inches (73.4 cm)

NECK WIDTH AT NUT: 1 7/8 inches (4.8 cm)

NUMBER OF FRETS: 20

BRACING: X braced

FINISH: Nitrocellulose lacquer applied by Addam Stark

BODY DEPTH: 4 5/8 inches (11.7 cm)

BODY LENGTH: 20 3/16 inches (51.3 cm)

OVERALL LENGTH: 43 1/4 inches (109.9 cm)

U.S. SUGGESTED RETAIL PRICE: $4,300

163

FLATTOP

Schoenberg Soloist

*E*ric Schoenberg, who pioneered the translating of Scott Joplin piano rags to fingerstyle guitar, has been a champion of the Martin OM since he first encountered one in the 1960s. As much as he loved the original OM model, however, Schoenberg always dreamed of a cutaway version that would allow him to reach higher up the fingerboard.

Working with luthier Dana Bourgeois, Schoenberg designed a modern 14-fret bodied OM cutaway they dubbed The Schoenberg Soloist, and in 1987 they began a seven-year collaboration with Martin that resulted in the creation of about 300 instruments. The prospectus for the Soloist described it as a "unique instrument [which] combines the size, balance, and playability of the legendary Martin OM of the 1930s with a master luthier's attention to construction." Working at his shop in Maine, Bourgeois says he built the guitars in runs of 10, 15, or 20 at a time. "I selected all of the

materials, made up most of the parts in my shop, and essentially sent guitar kits to Martin to assemble for us. During construction, I went to the Martin plant and voiced each soundboard, making minute gradations based upon what I heard."

The collaboration with Martin ended when Bourgeois moved on to work for Paul Reed Smith, but Schoenberg has continued to produce the Soloist and several other models over the years, with the help of some of America's most skilled luthiers including T.J. Thompson, John Slobod, Bruce Sexauer, and Robert Anderson.

Martin company spokesman and historian Dick Boak has said, "Martin owes a great thanks to Eric Schoenberg for almost single-handedly bringing back the OM. ...Eric raised everyone's understanding of the value of Martin's old guitars."

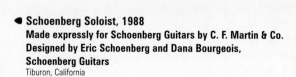

◀ **Schoenberg Soloist, 1988**
Made expressly for Schoenberg Guitars by C. F. Martin & Co.
Designed by Eric Schoenberg and Dana Bourgeois,
Schoenberg Guitars
Tiburon, California

SPECIFICATIONS

BODY AND SIDE WOODS: Brazilian rosewood

TOP WOOD: European spruce

BODY WIDTH, LOWER BOUT: 15 inches (38.1 cm)

NECK WOOD: Mahogany

FRETBOARD MATERIAL: Ebony

FRETBOARD INLAY: Pearl

SOUND HOLE INLAYS: Maple and ebony

BRIDGE: Ebony

NUT AND SADDLE: Bone

SCALE LENGTH: 25.4 inches (64.5 cm)

NECK WIDTH AT NUT: 1 13/16 inches (4.6 cm)

NUMBER OF FRETS: 14 to the body

BRACING: Scalloped X

FINISH: Nitrocellulose lacquer

BODY DEPTH: 4 inches (10.2 cm)

BODY LENGTH: 19 inches (48.3 cm)

OVERALL LENGTH: 39 5/16 inches (99.9 cm)

Madrigal Grand Auditorium with Venetian Cutaway

erald Sheppard has played guitar since he was a kid, and has been repairing, refinishing, and building guitars for 25 years. Sheppard holds a degree in Industrial Technology, and spent most of his professional life in the engineering division of a large manufacturing company where he incorporated quality management methodology into industrial and management processes. He changed careers in 1993 and now builds 14 to 18 guitars a year as a full-time occupation.

Sheppard prefers to keep his instruments relatively unadorned so that the beauty of the many soundboard and tonewoods he uses can take precedence over flashy inlay. He has built a number of guitars with rare

African blackwood backs and sides and, in addition to the gorgeous cocobolo seen here, also builds bodies of Brazilian rosewood, flamed acacia, striped Macassar ebony, flamed and figured koa, Indian rosewood, ziricote, bubinga, and flamed Claro walnut, and topping his guitars with Adirondack, Sitka, Bosnian, and Engelmann spruce, koa, and Western red cedar.

The richly appointed Madrigal is the middle of the three models Sheppard builds, and he offers all three styles in five different body shapes, ranging from the 15-inch (38.1 cm) Grand Concert to a 16½-inch (41.9 cm) Jumbo.

SPECIFICATIONS

BODY AND SIDE WOODS: Cocobolo rosewood

TOP WOOD: Master-grade Engelmann spruce with dyed maple purfling

BODY WIDTH, LOWER BOUT: 15¾ inches (40 cm)

NECK WOOD: Mahogany

FRETBOARD MATERIAL: Ebony

FRETBOARD INLAY: Paua pearl side dots

HEADSTOCK DECORATION: Mother-of-pearl "S" logo

SOUND HOLE INLAYS: Dyed maple lines, paua heart abalone pearl

BRIDGE: Ebony

NUT AND SADDLE: Mammoth ivory

TUNING MACHINES: Gotoh super 510 with black composite buttons

BINDING: African blackwood and black/white/black/white maple side purfling

SCALE LENGTH: 25.4 inches (64.5 cm)

NECK WIDTH AT NUT: 1¹³⁄₁₆ inches (4.6 cm)

NUMBER OF FRETS: 20

BRACING: X-style top bracing

FINISH: Waterborne polymer spray lacquer

BODY DEPTH: 3½ to 4½ inches (8.9 to 11.4 cm)

BODY LENGTH: 19⅜ inches (49.2 cm)

OVERALL LENGTH: 39⅝ inches (100.6 cm)

U.S. SUGGESTED RETAIL PRICE: $6,555

◀ **Madrigal Grand Auditorium with Venetian Cutaway, 2006**
Gerald Sheppard
Kingsport, Tennessee

Kathy Wingert
Concert Muse Elite with Cutaway

Kathy Wingert began making guitars in 1996 and has built a strong reputation for her focused craftsmanship. Wingert builds her necks of choice mahogany, laminated with fine veneers for rigidity, strength, and structure. She joins the body and neck with traditional dovetail construction, using hardwood or graphite reinforcements in addition to a double-acting truss rod. She does not offer a standard neck size or shape; instead, each instrument is custom made to meet the client's specific needs.

Wingert says that one of the parts she likes best about building guitars is working one-on-one with a client. "I love knowing the background, and playing style, and the name of the spouse and kids. It makes the whole process so personal, and I love that. I love thinking that each guitar might be the one I get to keep, but like the proverbial shoemaker, I do without. My Elite series allows me to follow my own muse, to do with certain chosen materials what I want to do. Sometimes the runs are very short, perhaps as small as three, and I know they will never be longer than 10. So I get to build for me and keep the bills paid."

Wingert says her Model CM, which is a favorite with fingerstyle players, has a sweetness and clarity to the tone "that will invite your muse to show up and deliver inspiration." Despite its small comfortable body size, it also has impressive bass response. This example's hand-cut paua rosette was designed and executed by Wingert's talented daughter Jimmi, who does all the inlay work on her mother's instruments.

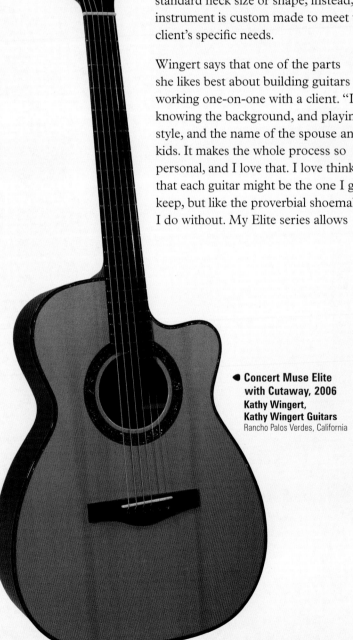

◄ **Concert Muse Elite
with Cutaway, 2006
Kathy Wingert,
Kathy Wingert Guitars**
Rancho Palos Verdes, California

SPECIFICATIONS

BODY AND SIDE WOODS: Brazilian rosewood

TOP WOOD: Italian spruce

BODY WIDTH, LOWER BOUT: 14½ inches (36.8 cm)

NECK WOOD: Mahogany

FRETBOARD MATERIAL: Ebony

HEADSTOCK DECORATION: Signature

SOUND HOLE INLAYS: Jimmi Wingert

BRIDGE: Ebony

NUT AND SADDLE: Bone

TUNING MACHINES: Gotoh 510

BINDING: Ebony

SCALE LENGTH: 25.4 inches (64.5 cm)

NECK WIDTH AT NUT: 1 25/32 inches (4.5 cm)

NUMBER OF FRETS: 20 + 2 (partial)

BRACING: Adirondack X

FINISH: Nitrocellulose lacquer

BODY DEPTH: 4¼ inches (10.8 cm)

BODY LENGTH: 19 inches (48.3 cm)

OVERALL LENGTH: 40½ inches (102.9 cm)

U.S. SUGGESTED RETAIL PRICE: $15,500

166

Concert Model Koa

$\mathcal{T}$he late John Zeidler was one of the few luthiers recognized as a master of both archtop and flattop building. While he was best known for his superb archtops, including one built for Scott Chinery's Blue Guitar project, he also produced a limited number of extraordinary acoustic steel-string flattops, and these rare instruments are much sought-after by players and collectors.

Zeidler was 15 when he built his first dulcimers and banjos. He went on to build more than 100 guitars, about 30 mandolins, and many other stringed instruments before his untimely death from leukemia in 2002. He was renowned for his attention to detail and fine craftsmanship, and greatly respected by his peers in the archtop world, who collaborated on a guitar to defray his medical expenses after he was diagnosed with cancer.

167

♠ **Concert Model Koa, 1993**
John Zeidler, J.R. Zeidler Guitars
Philadelphia, Pennsylvania

SPECIFICATIONS

BODY AND SIDE WOODS: Figured koa

TOP WOOD: Sitka spruce

BODY WIDTH, LOWER BOUT: 15 inches (38.1 cm)

NECK WOOD: Mahogany

FRETBOARD MATERIAL: Ebony

HEADSTOCK DECORATION: Zeidler logo, pearl truss rod cover

BRIDGE: Ebony

TUNING MACHINES: Gold Waverly tuners

BINDING: Turtoise

NECK WIDTH AT NUT: 1¹¹⁄₁₆ inches (4.3 cm)

BRACING: Scallop

FLATTOP

HARP

Harp guitars, which first appeared in the early nineteenth century, combine a guitar neck with several added open, unfretted "harp" strings to extend the range of the conventional six-string guitar. In most cases, the added strings are bass notes, but some harp guitars also add a number of treble strings tuned above the normal high E. Because harp strings are unfretted, they also ring in sympathy with notes plucked or struck on other strings, further adding to the richness of the instrument's sound.

Harp guitars reached the height of their popularity in the first two decades of the twentieth century, when Gibson promoted its two steel-strung models as an integral part of community mandolin orchestras. Other acoustic guitar manufacturers, including Martin, Regal, Washburn, and Lyon & Healy offered variations as well, but the most inventive early

twentieth century harp guitars were created by independent luthiers Chris Knutsen and Carl and August Larson, whose wildly inventive instruments are highly sought after by collectors and musicians.

Harp guitars have enjoyed a resurgence in popularity in recent years, with players such as Muriel Anderson, Stephen Bennett, and John Doan exploring new ways to use the instrument, and a handful of intrepid luthiers, including Fred Carlson, Mike Doolin, William Eaton, and Jeffrey Elliott, reinvigorating and expanding the possibilities of the extremely malleable form.

Big Red, 38-String Harp-Sympitar

Big Red was commissioned by Athens, Georgia–based composer and musician Erik Hinds, who describes his music as "Appalachian-trance-metal." Hinds saw Carlson's previous harp-sympitar, which took a year to build and, though he knew he couldn't afford it, wanted one like it. "When Erik told me [what he could afford]," says Carlson, "I thought about it for a minute and then asked him, 'Well, would you let me make it out of papier-mâché, with the back and sides cast as a shell?' Erik's eyes got wide, and he said, 'Would you?'"

Big Red's 38 strings are comprised of 6 nylon, main playing strings on a fretted neck; 5 nylon (bronze-wound on nylon fiber core) unfretted sub-bass harp strings on a "harp frame" on the bass side of the neck; 15 steel supertreble harp strings running parallel to the main strings on the treble side of the body; and 12 steel internal sympathetic resonating strings that run inside the neck and body of the instrument.

What does Big Red sound like? It's hard to describe, but Carlson offers this attempt. "All of the strings resonate acoustically, separately and together, to provide an amazing range of sonic possibilities. In addition to this rich acoustic potential, each set of strings also has an electronic pickup system and the separate outputs of each can be mixed and processed. The main strings, sub-bass harp strings and supertreble harp strings each have a pickup made from piezo cable material. The sympathetic strings have a piezo film material laminated into their bridge. All the pickups have onboard Bartolini pre-amp/buffers, and each has its own separate output jack at the butt of the instrument."

SPECIFICATIONS

BODY AND SIDE WOODS: Alirecel

TOP WOOD: Salvaged old-growth redwood

BODY WIDTH, LOWER BOUT: 18⅛ inches (46 cm)

ELECTRONICS: 4 separate custom piezo pickups with internal Bartolini preamps and separate output jacks; one for each set of strings

NECK WOOD: Flamed big leaf maple

FRETBOARD MATERIAL: Maple and brass

HEADSTOCK DECORATION: Black and white wood veneer sandwich with relief carving

SOUND HOLE INLAYS: Acrylic paints, maple sound-hole binding

BRIDGE: Big leaf maple

NUT AND SADDLE: Black water buffalo horn, ebony

TUNING MACHINES: Main strings: sloane leaf pattern bronze with ebony buttons; sympathetic strings: schaller mini gold with ebony buttons, Steinberger gearless black; sub-bass harp strings: gotoh mini bass black; supertreble harp strings: zither pins and Wittner uni-midget violin fine tuners

BINDING: Acrylic paints

SCALE LENGTH: 27.4 inches (69.5 cm) (main strings)

NECK WIDTH AT NUT: 1¹⁵⁄₁₆ inches (4.9 cm)

NUMBER OF FRETS: 24

BRACING: Modified fan-type

FINISH: Shellac over raw wood or acrylic paint; oil varnish on neck and heads

BODY DEPTH: 5½ inches (14 cm) at deepest

BODY LENGTH: 28 inches (71.1 cm)

OVERALL LENGTH: 52 inches (132.1 cm)

U.S. SUGGESTED RETAIL PRICE: $65,000

◆ **Big Red, 38-String Harp-Sympitar, 2005**
Fred Carlson, Beyond the Trees
Santa Cruz, California

Kali, 14-String Guitar

F red Carlson, who may be the most original luthier at work today, asks us to "imagine a world full of wondrous guitars, singing songs of the trees to the sky and the stars." His instruments are indeed wondrous, and this typically imaginative example of his work provides ample evidence why he has been called a living national treasure.

Kali is essentially a 12-string guitar with two added sub-bass strings, which run parallel to but not over the fingerboard. The sub-bass strings function like the added strings on a conventional harp guitar, but instead of

extending over a second neck, they are attached to an unusual elevated peghead extension, while extra large holes and bridge-pins at the bridge end allow for the use of acoustic bass guitar strings.

Kali's owner tunes the lowest sub-bass string to a low D, an octave and a second below the low E string. Carlson describes the instrument's voice as "a big, 'shimmery' sound that sparkles above the dark, piano-like ring of the sub-basses."

SPECIFICATIONS

BODY AND SIDE WOODS: Black acacia

TOP WOOD: Sitka spruce

BODY WIDTH, LOWER BOUT: 15½ inches (39.4 cm)

NECK WOOD: Black walnut

FRETBOARD MATERIAL: Ebony

FRETBOARD INLAY: Maple

HEADSTOCK DECORATION: Carving; maple
   veneer strip

SOUND HOLE INLAYS: Sound hole binding–
   black dyed maple

BRIDGE: Ebony

NUT AND SADDLE: Bone

TUNING MACHINES: Schaller nylon-bodied
   mini with ebony button

BINDING: Flamed koa

SCALE LENGTH: 24.8 inches (63.1 cm)

NECK WIDTH AT NUT: 1⅞ inches (4.8 cm)

NUMBER OF FRETS: 24

BRACING: Modified X with radial elements

FINISH: Top–waterborne polymer; back and sides–
   oil and wax

BODY DEPTH: 4³⁄₁₆ to 4¹⁵⁄₁₆ inches
   (10.6 to 12.5 cm)

BODY LENGTH: 20 inches (50.8 cm)

OVERALL LENGTH: 44⅜ inches (112.7 cm)

U.S. SUGGESTED RETAIL PRICE: $14,000

Kali, 14-String Guitar, 2000 ▶
Fred Carlson, Beyond the Trees
Santa Cruz, California

The Scherzer 10-String Harp Guitar

Guitars with added unfretted contrabass "harp" strings were first made in the late 1700s, and many nineteenth-century Romantic guitarists played and composed for the instrument. The four to six added strings were supported by a second neck running parallel to the fretboard and were attached either to the same bridge as the guitar's main strings or to a separate bridge extension; they not only provided deep open bass notes but also sounded in sympathy to the fretted strings.

Like C.F. Martin Sr., Johann Gottfried Scherzer apprenticed with the renowned Austrian luthier Johann Stauffer, but, while Martin moved to America, Scherzer remained in Vienna and eventually took over his master's business. Although he is less well-known today, Scherzer was considered a master during his lifetime, and his instruments were owned by such well-known guitarist-composers as Johann Kaspar Mertz and Nikolai Makarov. Makarov, a wealthy Russian nobleman, sponsored a luthiers' contest in Brussels in 1852, at which the Scherzer 10-String took the first prize.

Luthier Gary Southwell thinks very highly of Scherzer's work. "Although there are few surviving instruments," says Southwell, "his reputation is due for re-examination. Having had the pleasure of studying many of the known examples of his work, I feel he should be regarded amongst the very finest guitar makers of all time."

Southwell's reproduction Scherzer has two necks, with six strings on the fretted fingerboard and four bass strings that run over the second neck. The unfretted contrabass strings are tuned to a sequence of natural notes, that is, A, B, C, D, while the six fretted strings are tuned normally, E, A, D, G, B, E. Southwell says, "The guitar is heavy. It is also big by nineteenth-century standards, and it sounds amazing." Classical guitarist and lutenist Robert Trent, who is an expert on nineteenth-century guitar performance practices, often performs on a Southwell Scherzer 10-String, as does the historian, musicologist, and music publisher Matanya Ophee.

172

SPECIFICATIONS

BODY AND SIDE WOODS: Maple and Brazilian rosewood laminate

TOP WOOD: European spruce

BODY WIDTH, LOWER BOUT: 13½ inches (38.4 cm)

NECK WOOD: Maple veneered in ebony

FRETBOARD MATERIAL: Ebony

HEADSTOCK DECORATION: Maple veneered in ebony

SOUND HOLE INLAYS: Rosewood/maple/ebony lines

BRIDGE: Ebony

NUT AND SADDLE: Ivory

TUNING MACHINES: Rodgers

BINDING: Rosewood

SCALE LENGTH: 25.25 inches (64 cm)

NECK WIDTH AT NUT: 1⅞ inches (4.6 cm)

NUMBER OF FRETS: 24

BRACING: Transverse bars

FINISH: Oil varnish

BODY DEPTH: 3½ inches (8.8 cm)

BODY LENGTH: 18½ inches (47 cm)

OVERALL LENGTH: 39¼ inches (99 cm)

● **The Scherzer 10-String Harp Guitar, 1997**
Gary Southwell, Southwell Guitars
Nottingham, England

Concert 20-String Steel Harp Guitar

This is a prototype harp guitar built for the master harp guitarist John Doan, who currently is an Associate Professor of Music at Willamette University in Salem, Oregon. Doan was very clear about what he wanted—a concert harp guitar with an extended range of 20 strings, including the normal six sub-basses and six fretted strings but with an additional eight treble harp strings running from the top of the treble side of the upper bout to the bridge. He wanted the instrument to sound steel-string at its core but with the balance, evenness, and tonal range more typical of a classical guitar. He expected to compose and perform using extra-light string tension (300 lbs. with all 20 strings fully tightened), and he wanted to play with classical guitar technique using his nails and fingertips instead of picks.

Jeffrey Elliott collaborated on the project with John Sullivan, another Portland-based luthier and violin maker whom Doan describes as a virtuoso woodworker. Before they began to work on their own design, Elliott and Sullivan looked at several older harp guitars and discovered that many were "under built," which had led to major structural problems, "like collapsing tops, and the neck and the bass arm going off in different directions. So," explains Elliott, "one of the design features of this guitar is a one-piece neck with a Spanish heel and a common head for the sub-bass strings."

Twenty years after its completion, Elliott proudly asserts that the instrument "has withstood the test of time, the rigors of international travel and constant performance, and the scrutiny of the recording studio; and it also has served as the model for many other harp guitars."

SPECIFICATIONS

BODY AND SIDE WOODS: African blackwood rosewood

TOP WOOD: Sitka spruce

BODY WIDTH, LOWER BOUT: 15⅝ inches (39.7 cm)

NECK WOOD: One-piece mahogany neck

FRETBOARD MATERIAL: African ebony

FRETBOARD INLAY: Mother-of-pearl dot inlays

HEADSTOCK DECORATION: African blackwood rosewood veneer

SOUND HOLE INLAYS: Blackwood and abalone

BRIDGE: Brazilian rosewood

NUT AND SADDLE: Bone

TUNING MACHINES: Schaller mini tuners for standard guitar and sub-basses; Schaller 5th string banjo tuners for treble strings; all tuners have custom-made African blackwood rosewood buttons

BINDING: Lemonwood

SCALE LENGTH: 25.7 to 25.9 inches (65.2 to 65.7 cm)

NECK WIDTH AT NUT: 1⅞ inches (4.8 cm)

NUMBER OF FRETS: 21

BRACING: Elliott hybrid X and fan pattern

FINISH: Traditional French polish

BODY DEPTH: 3⅜ inches (8.6 cm) at heel; 4¼ inches (10.9 cm) at end

BODY LENGTH: 20⁹⁄₁₆ inches (52.2 cm)

OVERALL LENGTH: 40¼ inches (102.3 cm)

▲ **Concert 20-String Steel Harp Guitar, 1986**
Designed by Jeffrey Elliott and John Sullivan, built by John Sullivan
Portland, Oregon

Harp Guitar

om Davis is one of several contemporary luthiers who have tried their hand at harp guitars based on the designs of harp guitar pioneers Chris Knutsen and the Larson Brothers. This example was commissioned by noted solo acoustic guitarist and composer Bill Dutcher and was built over a two-and-a-half-year period. Davis based the body and bracing on his own six-string guitar design. According to Dutcher, his harp design is not intended to be a vintage replica, but rather to keep the concept the same while building something more technically up-to-date.

Most players agree that the Larson Brothers "Symphony" harp guitars, which were marketed by W.J. Dyer & Bros., are the most successful and playable of all early twentieth-century models. Based on recent research by Gregg

Miner, Bob Hartman, and other harp guitar enthusiasts, it appears that the Larsons' guitar was actually based on 1890s designs by the wildly innovative Washington-state-based luthier Chris Knutsen. Knutsen's original concepts include the hollow harp arm with its own sound hole and the bent bridge, which accommodates the harp strings' longer scale lengths.

Davis began building guitars in the mid-1970s while pursuing a degree in music. His other clients include Pierre Bensusan, Arlo Guthrie, James Hetfield of Metallica, Leo Kottke, Manus Lunny of Capercaillie, and the Indigo Girls' Amy Ray.

◀ **Harp Guitar, 2002**
J. Thomas Davis,
J. Thomas Davis Guitar Maker
Columbus, Ohio

SPECIFICATIONS

BODY AND SIDE WOODS: Claro walnut

TOP WOOD: Engelmann spruce

BODY WIDTH, LOWER BOUT: 16⅝ inches (42.2 cm)

ELECTRONICS: Under saddle pickups

NECK WOOD: Claro walnut

FRETBOARD MATERIAL: Ziricote

FRETBOARD INLAY: Pearl

SOUND HOLE INLAYS: Assorted wood veneers

BRIDGE: Ziricote

NUT AND SADDLE: Bone

TUNING MACHINES: Waverly tuners on guitar side; Schaller banjo tuners on harp side

BINDING: Walnut and maple purfling, sycamore binding

SCALE LENGTH: 25.6 inches (65 cm)

NECK WIDTH AT NUT: 1¹³⁄₁₆ inches (4.6 cm)

NUMBER OF FRETS: 20

BRACING: X bracing

FINISH: Acrylic-urethane

BODY DEPTH: 4¹³⁄₁₆ inches (12.2 cm)

BODY LENGTH: 20⅝ inches (52.4 cm) on guitar side, 33½ inches (85.1 cm) on harp side

OVERALL LENGTH: 42⅜ inches (107.6 cm)

U.S. SUGGESTED RETAIL PRICE: $8,950

William Eaton

Double Neck Harp Guitar

SPECIFICATIONS

BODY AND SIDE WOODS: Structural frame is one-piece poplar with sculptural overlays; Brazilian satinwood and purple heart back (with vermillion circle caps); vermillion sides

TOP WOOD: Redwood

BODY WIDTH, LOWER BOUT: 13⅜ inches (34 cm)

ELECTRONICS: Acoustic neck, RMC piezo pickups with RMC pre-amp for synth controller; harp strings, Pick-up the World, piezo transducer and pre-amp; electric neck, EMG pickups

NECK WOOD: Laminated–vermillion, bloodwood, Brazilian satinwood

FRETBOARD MATERIAL: Ebony

FRETBOARD INLAY: Turquose and spiny oyster shell

HEADSTOCK DECORATION: Laminated with vermillion (paduk), purple heart

SOUND HOLE INLAYS: Trimmed with ebony, Brazilian satinwood, vermillion, and purple heart

BRIDGE: Acoustic bridge (for acoustic neck and harp string attachment), ebony with vermillion overlay and trimmed with Brazilian satinwood and vermillion; string anchor for harp strings made from ebony glued on top of thin Brazilian satinwood laminate

NUT AND SADDLE: Bone nut and RMC piezo pickups, acoustic neck; bone saddle, harp strings; locking nut–graphite, electric neck

TUNING MACHINES: Schaller banjo tuners

BINDING: Ebony, vermillion, Brazillian satinwood, purple heart

SCALE LENGTH: 24.75 inches (62.9 cm), both necks

NECK WIDTH AT NUT: Acoustic neck 1¾ inches (4.4 cm), electric neck 1¹¹⁄₁₆ inches (4.3 cm)

NUMBER OF FRETS: Acoustic neck, 20; electric neck, 21

BRACING: Ebony laminate plate support under acoustic bridge

FINISH: French polish (shellac)

BODY DEPTH: 3 inches (7.6 cm)

BODY LENGTH: 18 inches (45.7 cm)

OVERALL LENGTH: 42⅞ inches (108.9 cm)

William Eaton is a luthier, performer, and teacher who has specialized in one-of-a-kind multi-stringed instruments since 1976. A co-founder and the current director of the Roberto-Venn School of Luthiery in Phoenix, he also has recorded 16 albums, several of which have been nominated for GRAMMY awards.

This instrument, the seventh in a series of bow harps that Eaton has created, began with the idea of combining thin-line acoustic and solid-body electric guitars with harp strings attached to a "bowed" extension.

Eaton's bow harps draw inspiration from ancient shamans' bows and hunters' singing bows, which he contends "represent the first traces of the evolution of all of the stringed instrument families." This instrument is the most sophisticated and complex of Eaton's harp designs and combines the resonance of ancient traditions with cutting edge technology.

As he worked on the design, Eaton imagined being able to access both acoustic and electric tones, as well as the mid-range pitches of the harp strings. He could switch back and forth between the acoustic and electric necks during a composition to access different tunings, and also use a capo on the electric neck to create higher pitched trebles.

The guitar employs a Transperformance tuning system on the electric neck and individual bridge-mounted RMC piezo pickups for the six-string acoustic neck. Eaton explains that the Transperformance tuning system uses a small computer, mounted inside of the guitar, to control six servomotors that adjust the tension of each string. Dozens of alternate tunings can be programmed into the computer and changed instantaneously, opening up a host of tuning possibilities, chord voicings, and compositional effects to the performer.

◄ **Double Neck Harp Guitar, 1996–2006**
William Eaton
Tempe, Arizona

Arch Harp Guitar

Alan Perlman

*A*lan Perlman is a musician and luthier who has built a wide variety of classical and steel-string guitars, including instruments with 11 and 13 strings.

This new form, built for fingerstyle guitarist James Kline, is a combination of an 11-string arch guitar and a removable harp attachment that adds six treble harp strings to the guitar. The separate harp body, which was Kline's idea, has several advantages. First, Kline did not want to significantly modify the arch guitar itself, which he wanted to be able to play by itself. As a professional musician, he also travels a great deal, and being able to break the instrument in two makes travel easier. The arch guitar is small enough to be a carry-on item for air travel, while the harp can be carried in a fitted attaché case. The form also gave Perlman the opportunity to optimize tone and balance; he could leave the arch guitar's sound chamber undisturbed and create a suitably small one for the harp, which is tuned from B above the high E string to an octave above. All the harp strings have sharping levers and the bridges are pinless.

Perlman has also crafted a steel-string arch harp guitar for Kline that combines an X brace with full fan bracing. The hybrid bracing pattern necessitated a pinless-bridge design because pins would have penetrated the fan braces.

♠ **Arch Harp Guitar, 2003**
Alan Perlman, Perlman Guitars
San Francisco, California

SPECIFICATIONS

BODY AND SIDE WOODS: East Indian rosewood

TOP WOOD: Swiss spruce

BODY WIDTH, LOWER BOUT: 11⅝ inches (29.5 cm), 16⅞ inches (42.9 cm) with harp

ELECTRONICS: Highlander IP2 in the 11 string; Highlander IP1 in the harp, both with internal preamps

NECK WOOD: Honduran mahogany

FRETBOARD MATERIAL: Gabon ebony

HEADSTOCK DECORATION: Ebony faceplate with holly and dyed maple under-veneers, shaped to echo baroque motifs

SOUND HOLE INLAYS: Wood banding composed of curly maple, ebony, and holly veneers

BRIDGE: Ebony, shaped to echo baroque motifs

NUT AND SADDLE: Bone

TUNING MACHINES: Waverly V-2 planetary geared

BINDING: Curly maple with purfling composed of curly maple, ebony, and holly veneers

SCALE LENGTH: 25.2 inches (63 cm)

NECK WIDTH AT NUT: 2⁹⁄₁₆ inches (6.5 cm)

NUMBER OF FRETS: 19

BRACING: Hybrid fan brace with X brace overlay

FINISH: Thinly applied nitrocellulose lacquer, hand rubbed

BODY DEPTH: 3¹⁄₁₆ inches (7.8 cm) at heel, tapering to 3⁷⁄₁₆ (8.7 cm) inches at tail

BODY LENGTH: 17¾ inches (45.1 cm)

OVERALL LENGTH: 37⅛ inches (94.3 cm)

U.S. SUGGESTED RETAIL PRICE: $9,750

ACOUSTIC BASS

Acoustic bass guitars (ABGs) are large-bodied, long-necked instruments made to assume the role of an upright bass fiddle in accompanying standard acoustic guitars. The ABG is a late twentieth-century invention, inspired by the massive guitarróns used to play the bass part in Mexican mariachi bands. Guitarróns, which developed not from guitars but from a sixteenth-century Spanish instrument called the *bajo de uña*, are fretless six-stringed instruments with extremely deep bodies and short necks.

The ABG concept was first pursued by custom string entrepreneur Ernie Ball, who says he simply thought that if there were electric bass guitars to go with electric guitars, "then you ought to have acoustic bass guitars to go with acoustic guitars." Ball's friend, the legendary George Fullerton of Fender, built the prototype in 1972.

Although Ball and Fullerton's Earthwood bass was nearly as big as a guitarrón and proved too awkward for most players, the ABG concept has been taken up and refined by a critical mass of players and luthiers in the past 25 years and, while they have vocal critics, ABGs are now a well-established and generally accepted acoustic guitar form.

Bluejay Model Acoustic Bass Guitar

*J*ay Hargreaves has played electric bass guitar since he was in high school, so building his own acoustic bass guitar was a natural progression.

Hargreaves studied acoustic guitar building with Anthony Huvard and from him learned about the radical designs that Richard Schneider was building. Hargreaves worked with Schneider for 10 years, learning the intricacies of Dr. Michael Kasha's principles, and how to apply them to the acoustic bass. All three men were pleasantly surprised with the resulting guitar's rich, full-bodied sound. "It almost sounds like an upright bass," says Hargreaves, "but easier to cart around!"

Kasha bracing is intended to allow the top of a guitar to move freely, like the diaphragm in a speaker. Both the tops and backs of Hargreaves's large-bodied Bluejay basses are built of spruce and braced with similar Kasha bracing so that the back moves with the top, which results in longer sustain, warmer sound, and more volume.

SPECIFICATIONS

BODY AND SIDE WOODS: Western flame maple

TOP WOOD: Sitka spruce

BODY WIDTH, LOWER BOUT: 18 inches (45.7 cm)

ELECTRONICS: Countryman internal microphone

NECK WOOD: Eastern maple

FRETBOARD MATERIAL: Ebony

HEADSTOCK DECORATION: Abalone

SOUND HOLE INLAYS: Brazilian rosewood

BRIDGE: Maple and walnut, painted matte black

NUT AND SADDLE: Ivory nut, corian saddles

TUNING MACHINES: Schaller

BINDING: Brazilian rosewood

SCALE LENGTH: 30.5 inches (77.5 cm)

NECK WIDTH AT NUT: 1¾ inches (4.4 cm)

NUMBER OF FRETS: Fretless/24

BRACING: Kasha/Schneider

FINISH: Oil finished top, tinted lacquer sides, back, and neck

BODY DEPTH: 5 inches (12.7 cm)

BODY LENGTH: 24⁵⁄₁₆ inches (61.8 cm)

OVERALL LENGTH: 47½ inches (120.7 cm)

U.S. SUGGESTED RETAIL PRICE: $10,000

♠ **Bluejay Model Acoustic Bass Guitar, 1995**
Jay Hargreaves, J.T. Hargreaves Basses & Guitars
Des Moines, Washington

Smoothtalker Acoustic Bass Model SNB3

*M*erv Davis comes by his craft naturally; both his father and grandfather were amateur violin makers and his father built a mandolin while imprisoned during the Second World War.

For more than 20 years, Davis has been perfecting a completely new approach to acoustic guitar design that he calls the Smoothtalker. The body shape of a Smoothtalker is similar to that of a banjo, but, instead of a skin head, it has a round, fan-braced Engelmann spruce top. A space between the top of the soundboard and the neck serves as a "breather," which facilitates the movement of air both outside and within the guitar. The design is largely modular, bolted together with steel cap screws, so the whole instrument can be disassembled easily. Davis says his removable soundboard concept afforded him the opportunity to perform hundreds of tests and changes that would have been impossible in conventional guitars.

"Playability was the main criteria when I developed the Smoothtalker," explains Davis. "The playing action is low and the sound 'jumps at you.' The left hand has undisturbed access to the highest frets on the fingerboard, which makes it an excellent instrument to learn to play on." And, because Davis's design almost completely eliminates the left upper bout and leaves just the skeleton of the right upper bout to help orient the player, the instrument is considerably lighter than a conventional instrument.

SPECIFICATIONS

BODY AND SIDE WOODS: African kiaat

TOP WOOD: Russian pine

BODY WIDTH, LOWER BOUT: 17¾ inches (45 cm)

ELECTRONICS: L.R. Baggs element active

NECK WOOD: African kiaat

FRETBOARD MATERIAL: African blackwood

FRETBOARD INLAY: Pearl dots on side

HEADSTOCK DECORATION: Panga panga veneer with kiaat crown

BRIDGE: Russian pine

NUT AND SADDLE: Warthog ivory nut, African blackwood saddle

TUNING MACHINES: Hipshot

BINDING: African blackwood

SCALE LENGTH: 33.7 inches (85 cm)

NECK WIDTH AT NUT: 2¹⁄₁₆ inches (5.3 cm)

NUMBER OF FRETS: 24

BRACING: Parallel (5)

FINISH: Penetrating wax

BODY DEPTH: 2¾ inches (7 cm)

BODY LENGTH: 22⁷⁄₁₆ inches (57 cm)

OVERALL LENGTH: 49³⁄₁₆ inches (125 cm)

U.S. SUGGESTED RETAIL PRICE: $3,500

♠ **Smoothtalker Acoustic Bass Model SNB3, 2005**
Mervyn Davis
Broederstroon, South Africa

180

Custom Acoustic Bass Guitar

*M*ike Doolin is a skilled bass player himself, and this is his personal guitar. The bass incorporates a number of Doolin's favorite design concepts, including a deep and uniquely shaped double cutaway that allows the player to reach every fret on the instrument and a small offset sound hole that Doolin says "tunes the body down" into the bass register for a full bass sound. Doolin builds both standard four-string acoustic bass guitars and a five-string with an added high C.

He emphasizes that while his designs may be very contemporary, when it comes to craft, he is a traditionalist. "I'm not a factory," he says, "I'm a luthier, working alone. There is only one pair of hands at Doolin Guitars—mine."

181

SPECIFICATIONS

BODY AND SIDE WOODS: Quilted sapele

TOP WOOD: Sitka spruce

BODY WIDTH, LOWER BOUT: 18 inches (45.7 cm)

ELECTRONICS: B-Band AZ

NECK WOOD: Quilted sapele, boxwood

FRETBOARD MATERIAL: Ebony

FRETBOARD INLAY: Gray plastic for fret lines

HEADSTOCK DECORATION: Pearl logo

SOUND HOLE INLAYS: Spalted maple

BRIDGE: Macassar ebony

NUT AND SADDLE: Bone nut, corian saddle

TUNING MACHINES: Gotoh

BINDING: Boxwood

SCALE LENGTH: 34 inches (86.4 cm)

NECK WIDTH AT NUT: 1⅝ inches (4.1 cm)

NUMBER OF FRETS: 24

BRACING: Kasha

FINISH: Polyester

BODY DEPTH: 5½ inches (14 cm)

BODY LENGTH: 24 inches (61 cm)

OVERALL LENGTH: 51 inches (129.5 cm)

U.S. SUGGESTED RETAIL PRICE: $5,750

♠ **Custom Acoustic Bass Guitar, 2006**
Michael Doolin, Doolin Guitars
Portland, Oregon

Kingslight K-18 Acoustic Bass Guitar (Fretless)

John Kingslight points out that Portage, Michigan, where he currently lives and works, is right next door to Kalamazoo, the site of the original Gibson company. "Seems like a good place to make guitars," he says.

With a 19½ inch wide lower bout and an overall length over 50 inches (127 cm), Kingslight's ABG dwarfs even a jumbo-sized guitar and produces a powerful acoustic thump that he describes as "more like upright basses—not like jumbos with bass strings." The bass is fretless but has maple reference lines set into the fingerboard where the frets would be to help players orient themselves. The body and sides are African padauk (*Pterocarpus soyauxii*), a hard, dense, and heavy wood that is becoming popular as a substitute for rosewood. Commonly called "coral" or "vermillion" because its heartwood can be bright orange, purple-red, or almost crimson when freshly cut, padauk oxidizes and eventually mellows to a rich purple-brown over time.

♠ **Kingslight K-18 Acoustic Bass Guitar (fretless), 2005**
John Kingslight, Kingslight Guitars
Portage, Michigan

SPECIFICATIONS

BODY AND SIDE WOODS: Padauk

TOP WOOD: Sitka

BODY WIDTH, LOWER BOUT: 19½ inches (49.5 cm)

ELECTRONICS: K&K passive western for bass

NECK WOOD: Honduran mahogany

FRETBOARD MATERIAL: Ebony

FRETBOARD INLAY: Maple inlaid fretlines

HEADSTOCK DECORATION: Kingslight heart-sun logo

SOUND HOLE INLAYS: Abalone rosette

BRIDGE: Ebony

NUT AND SADDLE: Bone

TUNING MACHINES: Chrome Schaller bass tuners

BINDING: Flamed maple

SCALE LENGTH: 34 inches (86.4 cm)

NECK WIDTH AT NUT: 1¹¹⁄₁₆ inches (4.3 cm)

NUMBER OF FRETS: 0

BRACING: X bracing

FINISH: KTM-9 high gloss waterborne lacquer

BODY DEPTH: 6 inches (15.2 cm) tapering to 5 inches (12.7 cm)

BODY LENGTH: 23 inches (58.4 cm)

OVERALL LENGTH: 50¼ inches (127.6 cm)

U.S. SUGGESTED RETAIL PRICE: $2,845

Acoustic Bass Guitar Prototype

*T*his remarkable acoustic bass guitar is a prototype for a production instrument developed by luthiers Steve Klein and Bob Taylor of Taylor Guitars for the Taylor company. Noticing that Taylor did not have an acoustic bass guitar in its line, Klein asked company president Bob Taylor if he would be interested in working on one together. Taylor jumped at the chance to work with Klein, and the two immediately began to draw up plans on a computer. "We did the body shape head to head," Klein remembers, "The lower bout is Klein, and the upper bout is Taylor. We designed a cutaway we both liked that was very Maccaferri-like, and the whole process was challenging and fun."

The Taylor AB-1 was introduced in 1995 and quickly found favor with Stanley Clarke, Billy Sheehan, Sting, and other prominent rock and jazz bassists.

♠ **Acoustic Bass Guitar Prototype, 1992**
Designed by Steve Klein and Bob Taylor
Built by Steve Klein and Steve Kauffman
Vineburg, California
Collection of Jeff Doctorow

Into the Woods
Five-String Bass Guitar

This one-of-a-kind acoustic bass guitar was commissioned by a Stephen Sondheim fan who asked Grit Laskin to design the headstock inlay based on Sondheim's then brand-new play, "Into the Woods." The play weaves characters from classic fairy tales into the story of a childless couple who are trying to lift a curse that prevents them from becoming pregnant, and it promised to offer Laskin a host of visual choices. A Toronto production was about to open, so he talked the producers into lending him some rehearsal stills to work from. The inlay he designed depicts Little Red Riding Hood in the grip of the Wolf, with a portrait of Sondheim himself watching his characters from above. The bass also features Laskin's trademark armrest bevel on the bass side of the lower bout.

Laskin describes himself as a "tailor" who customizes guitars in ways particular to each player. "It is a role that gives me great pleasure," he explains. "Acoustics, playability, physical shapes, ergonomic issues, rare materials, aesthetic appointments, inlay art—all are topics for discussion until details are confirmed to each of our satisfactions. Since my clients live around the globe, you can imagine my phone bills!"

◆ **Into the Woods Five-String Bass Guitar, 1996**
William "Grit" Laskin
Toronto, Ontario

SPECIFICATIONS

BODY AND SIDE WOODS: Flamed koa

TOP WOOD: Sitka spruce

BODY WIDTH, LOWER BOUT: 16⅝ inches (42.2 cm)

NECK WOOD: Mahogany

FRETBOARD MATERIAL: Ebony

FRETBOARD INLAY: Engraved shell and stone

HEADSTOCK DECORATION: Engraved shell and stone

SOUND HOLE INLAYS: Abalone, rosewood, and dyed veneer

BRIDGE: Ebony

NUT AND SADDLE: Bone

TUNING MACHINES: Schaller

BINDING: Ebony

SCALE LENGTH: 34 inches (86.4 cm)

NUMBER OF FRETS: 20

BRACING: Spruce

FINISH: Lacquer

BODY DEPTH: 5½ inches (14 cm)

BODY LENGTH: 20⁹⁄₁₆ inches (52.3 cm)

OVERALL LENGTH: 86¹³⁄₁₆ inches (220.5 cm)

U.S. SUGGESTED RETAIL PRICE: $15,000

ACOUSTIC BASS

Four-String Fretless Acoustic Bass

Dave Maize has built acoustic bass guitars for the likes of Jeff Ament of Pearl Jam, Jack Casady, Adam Clayton, and Phil Lesh. Lesh calls his Maize bass "the easiest to play and best-sounding acoustic instrument I've ever owned."

From the beginning of his guitar-making career in 1990, Maize has utilized both reclaimed and sustainably harvested tonewoods for his own instruments and supplied these earth-friendly woods to other builders. "I made this decision after seeing the diminishing supply of traditional luthiery woods such as mahogany, ebony, spruce, and rosewood," he explains. "I discovered that there is a wealth of both reclaimed traditional tonewoods and underutilized woods, which can produce a superb instrument and help to stretch the supply of these precious materials."

Among the woods Maize likes to build with most are Claro walnut, which he salvages from urban tree removals, redwood (from building demolition), bay laurel (from driftwood logs), Sitka and Englemann spruce (from blowdowns or bug-killed trees), and red and Port Orford cedar (from fire-killed trees).

SPECIFICATIONS

BODY AND SIDE WOODS: Figured claro walnut

TOP WOOD: Reclaimed redwood

BODY WIDTH, LOWER BOUT: 18 inches (45.7 cm)

NECK WOOD: Claro walnut

FRETBOARD MATERIAL: Black phenolic

HEADSTOCK DECORATION: Madrone burl, black-dyed poplar lines, brass ring

SOUND HOLE INLAYS: Walnut, dyed black maple rings, maple rings

BRIDGE: Katalox

NUT AND SADDLE: Graph-tech trem nut; black phenolic saddle

TUNING MACHINES: Sperzel black locking bass tuners

BINDING: Dyed black maple, maple purflings, bloodwood binding

SCALE LENGTH: 34 inches (86.4 cm)

NECK WIDTH AT NUT: 1 9/16 inches (4 cm)

NUMBER OF FRETS: Fretless

BRACING: Modified X bracing

FINISH: Water-base urethane with amber tint

BODY DEPTH: 5¾ inches (14.6 cm)

BODY LENGTH: 21¼ inches (54 cm)

OVERALL LENGTH: 48½ inches (123.2 cm)

U.S. SUGGESTED RETAIL PRICE: $4,500

Four-String Fretless Acoustic Bass, 1995 ▶
Dave Maize, Dave Maize Acoustic Guitars
Cave Junction, Oregon

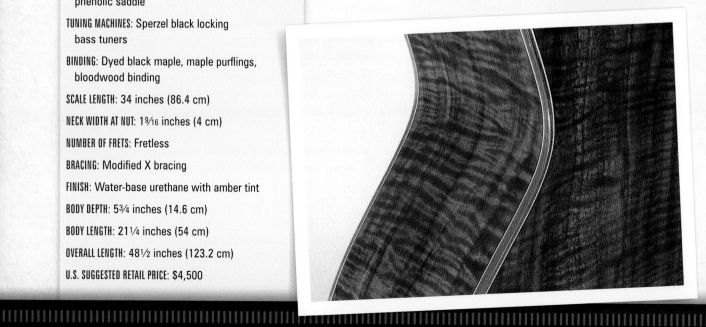

Pathmaker Acoustic Bass
Model 9400

*A*be Wechter built a prototype of his innovative Pathmaker double cutaway acoustic guitar in 1994 and soon realized that the design could have application far beyond the high price range in which he was working as a custom builder. As much as he enjoyed building unique custom guitars, Wechter wanted to bring the Pathmaker design to professional and amateur guitar players who could not afford such expensive instruments, so he decided to set up a manufacturing facility in his hometown of Paw Paw, Michigan.

Applying the Pathmaker concept to the acoustic bass seemed "the perfect combination" to Wechter. The Pathmaker bass combines steel-string-style X bracing with modified classical-style fan bracing below the bridge. All the braces are hand carved, and the top stiffness is adjusted on each bass after the body is built, a process that allows Wechter and his team to build for the best possible acoustic and amplified tone.

Among the special features of the Pathmaker Bass is an elevated wooden thumbrest that attaches near the headblock with a single screw and allows the player to anchor his thumb along almost 6 inches (15.2 cm) of elevated support without dampening the top vibration.

SPECIFICATIONS

BODY AND SIDE WOODS: Curly maple

TOP WOOD: Sitka spruce

BODY WIDTH, LOWER BOUT: 17¼ inches (43.8 cm)

ELECTRONICS: Fishman custom

NECK WOOD: Curly maple

FRETBOARD MATERIAL: Ebony

FRETBOARD INLAY: Abalone dot

HEADSTOCK DECORATION: Inlaid logo

SOUND HOLE INLAYS: Abalone

BRIDGE: Walnut/ebony

NUT AND SADDLE: Bone

TUNING MACHINES: Gotoh

BINDING: Rosewood

SCALE LENGTH: 34 inches (86.4 cm)

NECK WIDTH AT NUT: 1⅝ inches (4.1 cm)

NUMBER OF FRETS: 24

BRACING: Wechter

FINISH: Urethane gloss, cremona brown sides, back, and neck, natural top

BODY DEPTH: 5½ inches (14 cm)

BODY LENGTH: 21 inches (53.3 cm)

OVERALL LENGTH: 49½ inches (125.7 cm)

U.S. SUGGESTED RETAIL PRICE: $4,250

♠ **Pathmaker Acoustic Bass, Model 9400, 2005**
Abe Wechter, Wechter Guitars
Paw Paw, Michigan

B-95 Acoustic Bass

*S*elf-taught California luthier Steve Helgeson has been building a wide range of acoustic, electric, and bass guitars since 1972. His business grew to a peak of production in the '80s, with a team of luthiers building more than 1,000 guitars a year. An arsonist torched Moonstone's factory in the late '80s, but Helgeson was able to salvage most of the equipment and went back to working alone.

The huge, 20-inch lower bout of the B-95 Acoustic Bass gives it a voice that can be heard when accompanying two or more acoustic guitars. Helgeson builds it with either four or five strings and a choice of a rounded Venetian or pointed Florentine cutaway.

◆ **B-95 Acoustic Bass, 2003**
Steve Helgeson, Moonstone Guitars
Eureka, California

SPECIFICATIONS

BODY AND SIDE WOODS: African wenge

TOP WOOD: Sitka spruce

BODY WIDTH, LOWER BOUT: 20¼ inches (51.4 cm)

ELECTRONICS: Fishman transducer

NECK WOOD: Wenge

FRETBOARD MATERIAL: Ebony

FRETBOARD INLAY: Abalone-filled pearl ovals

HEADSTOCK DECORATION: Pearl logo and crescent moon in abalone

SOUND HOLE INLAYS: Maple and ebony rifling pattern

BRIDGE: Ebony

NUT AND SADDLE: Bone

TUNING MACHINES: Gold Schallers

BINDING: Ivoroid

SCALE LENGTH: 34 inches (86.4 cm)

NECK WIDTH AT NUT: 1¹⁹⁄₃₂ inches (4 cm)

NUMBER OF FRETS: 20

BRACING: Modified X brace Sitka spruce

FINISH: Nitrocellulose lacquer

BODY DEPTH: 5 inches (12.7 cm)

BODY LENGTH: 23⅜ inches (59.4 cm)

OVERALL LENGTH: 49 inches (124.5 cm)

U.S. SUGGESTED RETAIL PRICE: $5,700

Bobby Vega Halfling Bass

$\mathcal{T}$he Halfling is a unique proprietary design that combines the flat bass side of a steel-string or classical guitar with the carved treble side of an archtop. The result is an instrument that is capable of a large, full, fundamental bass response and a clear separation of notes ringing together in a complex chord. In addition to the Halfling Bass, a Halfling Jazz Guitar is now available as well.

Tom Ribbecke explains, "We combined the best of both worlds for the contemporary guitarist, whose literature now crosses over into both [flattop and archtop] worlds. This is the logical conclusion of years of research and development…melding flattop and archtop concepts in one instrument."

Ribbecke and guitarist/entrepreneur Paul Szmanda founded a new company, the Ribbecke Guitar Corporation, to offer less expensive, domestically built instruments crafted on a production basis under Ribbecke's supervision. He also hand-builds Halflings to customer specs at a substantially higher price point. His own Halflings are hand-voiced and "fussed over as are all my private practice instruments!"

189

SPECIFICATIONS

BODY AND SIDE WOODS: Myrtle

TOP WOOD: Cedar

BODY WIDTH, LOWER BOUT: 17 inches (43.2 cm)

ELECTRONICS: Timberline

NECK WOOD: Birdseye maple

FRETBOARD MATERIAL: Ebony

HEADSTOCK DECORATION: Pearl

SOUND HOLE INLAYS: Ebony

BRIDGE: Ebony

TUNING MACHINES: Hipshot

BINDING: Ebony

SCALE LENGTH: 34 inches (86.4 cm)

NECK WIDTH AT NUT: 1½ inches (3.8 cm)

BRACING: X bracing

BODY DEPTH: 4⅞ inches (12.4 cm)

BODY LENGTH: 21 inches (53.3 cm)

OVERALL LENGTH: 46 inches (116.9 cm)

U.S. SUGGESTED RETAIL PRICE: $15,000

♠ **Bobby Vega Halfling Bass, 2003**
Tom Ribbecke, Ribbecke Guitar Corporation
Healdsburg, California

ARCHTOP & OTHER JAZZ

Archtop guitars are steel-stringed instruments named for their slightly convex, hand-carved tops, similar to those of violins and cellos. The carved-top guitar was the brainchild of Orville Gibson, a mandolin maker who built the first such instruments in the 1890s. Gibson's archtop concept was refined in the early 1920s by Lloyd Loar, a sound engineer and designer for Gibson who is best known today for his unparalleled F-5 mandolin. Loar's highly influential L-5 guitar, introduced in 1922 along with the F-5, added paired, F-shaped, violin-style sound holes to the arched top and remains the standard by which other archtops are judged. The L-5 was adopted by both country and jazz musicians, including Maybelle Carter and Eddie Lang, and it became the dominant rhythm guitar of the big band era.

Among those who were inspired by the L-5 was John D'Angelico, a Manhattan-based builder who brought his own sophisticated design sense and Old World craftsmanship to the archtop in the 1930s. His protégé, James D'Aquisto, kept the form alive after his master's death in 1964, and it was taken up by a number of skilled younger luthiers in the 1970s and '80s, who in recent years have brought the archtop to new heights of artistry and craftsmanship.

A separate jazz guitar tradition developed in France, where the virtuoso Gypsy guitarist Django Reinhardt teamed with suave violinist Stéphane Grappelli and popularized a hot swinging sound that featured guitar and violin as lead instruments. "Gypsy jazz" has been revived in recent years, and a number of luthiers are making guitars similar to the one Reinhardt played, while other makers and jazz musicians are experimenting with nylon-stringed guitars and other variations.

The Gold Standard

*a*fter studying guitar making at the Roberto-Venn School of Luthiery and apprenticing with Nick Kukich at Franklin Guitars, Steve Andersen built his initial reputation for his F-5 style mandolins. After moving to Seattle in 1986, he worked on a number of D'Angelico, Gibson, and Stromberg archtops and became fascinated by the form. He found many similarities between carved-top guitars and mandolins—(Orville Gibson was also a mandolin builder before he turned his attention to guitars, and Lloyd Loar was the designer of both the Gibson F-5 and the L-5 guitar, the first "modern" archtop)—and felt his experience gave him a leg up as he began to concentrate on designing and building archtops. He is now considered one of the most skilled and innovative archtop artisans in the world.

The Gold Standard, 2005 ▶
Steve Andersen, Andersen Stringed Instruments
Seattle, Washington

The Gold Standard is Andersen's top-of-the-line archtop, punningly named for its use of 14-karat gold wire inlay, which divides the deep black ebony and striped Macassar ebony in the peghead, fingerboard, and tailpiece, and also borders the Macassar ebony pickguard. This example is in Andersen's violin finish, a rich blend of red and amber coloring under high gloss lacquer.

SPECIFICATIONS

BODY AND SIDE WOODS: European maple

TOP WOOD: European spruce

BODY WIDTH, LOWER BOUT: 17 inches (43.2 cm)

NECK WOOD: American maple

FRETBOARD MATERIAL: Ebony, Macassar ebony

FRETBOARD INLAY: 14-karat gold wire

HEADSTOCK DECORATION: 14-karat gold wire

BRIDGE: Macassar ebony

NUT AND SADDLE: Micarta nut, ebony saddle

BINDING: White celluloid

SCALE LENGTH: 25.4 inches (64.5 cm)

NECK WIDTH AT NUT: 1 11/16 inches (4.3 cm)

NUMBER OF FRETS: 21

BRACING: X bracing

FINISH: Nitrocellulose lacquer

BODY DEPTH: 3 inches (7.6 cm)

BODY LENGTH: 21 inches (53.3 cm)

OVERALL LENGTH: 43 inches (109.2 cm)

U.S. SUGGESTED RETAIL PRICE: $16,500

James D'Aquisto

New Yorker Classic

More than a few experts consider James D'Aquisto (1935–1995) the greatest guitar maker of all time. D'Aquisto, an aspiring jazz guitarist, served as apprentice to the legendary John D'Angelico from 1952 until D'Angelico's death in 1964, absorbing the old master's techniques and stylistic approaches as they worked side by side in his small shop in lower Manhattan.

After D'Angelico's death, D'Aquisto continued making the Excel and the New Yorker, the archtop guitar forms designed and made famous by his mentor. Over the years, he added a number of subtle refinements of his own to D'Angelico's designs, including ebony bridges, slimmer pickguards, wider and less angular f-holes, and a semi-circular pediment on the headstock, eventually creating guitars with an utterly distinctive look. D'Aquisto also moved away from his master's extensive use of inlay and other decorative elements, choosing a "less is more" approach to decoration and allowing the quality of his woods and craftsmanship to stand on their own.

This instrument is crafted entirely of wood, substituting ebony for parts other luthiers often made from metal or plastic. In addition to the ebony tailpiece, bridge, and binding, even the knobs of the tuning machines are carved from ebony. The guitar's resulting spare, clean look is made even more striking by the lack of fingerboard inlay.

◀ **New Yorker Classic, 1987**
James D'Aquisto
Farmingdale, New York

Ultrafox "Abyssinian Dreams"

SPECIFICATIONS

BODY AND SIDE WOODS: 1 satinwood side; 1 ebony side; ebony, padauk, satinwood, and ironwood, back

TOP WOOD: Sitka spruce and Douglas fir

BODY WIDTH, LOWER BOUT: 16⅛ inches (41 cm)

NECK WOOD: Honduran mahogany

FRETBOARD MATERIAL: Ebony

FRETBOARD INLAY: White dots

HEADSTOCK DECORATION: Satinwood, padauk, ironwood, and ebony

SOUND HOLE INLAYS: Stained strips

BRIDGE: Ebony and satinwood

NUT AND SADDLE: Bone nut

TUNING MACHINES: Sperzel with custom colors

BINDING: Ebony

SCALE LENGTH: 26.4 inches (67 cm)

NECK WIDTH AT NUT: 1¹³⁄₁₆ inches (4.6 cm)

NUMBER OF FRETS: 21

BRACING: Lateral

FINISH: Water lacquer

BODY DEPTH: 4¹⁄₁₆ inches (10.4 cm)

BODY LENGTH: 18½ inches (47 cm)

OVERALL LENGTH: 39¾ inches (101 cm)

*A*lthough he specializes in hand building custom Maccaferri- and Selmer-style gypsy guitars, Michael Dunn has also built and played archtops, Weissenborn- and Knutsen-style Hawaiian guitars, harp-guitars, Knutsen-style harp-ukeleles, and even an African kora. The music and instruments of Django Reinhardt have been his biggest inspiration over the years, and he has designed and built more gypsy guitar models than any other luthier.

The Mystery Pacific and Ultrafox are his two most advanced models. Dunn modeled the Mystery Pacific after the Mario Maccaferri original, patented 1930 design. Like Maccaferri's instrument, it is fitted with an internal soundbox and reflector that act as a sort of resonator, giving it tremendous projection. Dunn calls the Mystery Pacific, "a lead guitarist's dream," explaining that the higher up on the instrument's fingerboard a musician plays, the more the volume increases.

The Ultrafox represents Dunn's latest refinement of Maccaferri's concepts. "If the original interior soundbox design by Maccaferri could be called 'stage one,'" he says, "and my Mystery Pacific soundbox, which is very different, called 'stage two,' then this would be a 'stage three' design, making this instrument the most sophisticated gypsy guitar design on the planet."

◆ **Ultrafox "Abyssinian Dreams," 2006**
Michael Dunn, Michael Dunn Art Guitars
New Westminster, British Columbia, Canada

Mystery Pacific
"The Translucent Harlequin"

SPECIFICATIONS

BODY AND SIDE WOODS: Ebony and Mediterranean cypress

TOP WOOD: Western red cedar

BODY WIDTH, LOWER BOUT: 16⅛ inches (41 cm)

NECK WOOD: Honduran mahogany

FRETBOARD MATERIAL: Ebony

HEADSTOCK DECORATION: Cypress with holly and ebony squares

SOUND HOLE INLAYS: Wood strips - reflector 72 pieces of ebony and holly

BRIDGE: Ebony and bone

NUT AND SADDLE: Bone

TUNING MACHINES: Grover

BINDING: Boxwood and ebony

SCALE LENGTH: 25.2 inches (64 cm)

NECK WIDTH AT NUT: 1¹³⁄₁₆ inches (4.6 cm)

NUMBER OF FRETS: 21

BRACING: Lateral with interior soundbox

FINISH: French polish

BODY DEPTH: 4¹⁄₁₆ inches (10.4 cm)

BODY LENGTH: 1¹³⁄₁₆ inches (47 cm)

OVERALL LENGTH: 39¾ inches (101 cm)

U.S. SUGGESTED RETAIL PRICE: $6,000

♦ **Mystery Pacific "The Translucent Harlequin," 2006**
Michael Dunn, Michael Dunn Art Guitars
New Westminster, British Columbia, Canada

Ted Megas
Apollo Custom Oval Hole

a s a young man, Ted Megas played rock, blues, and jazz fusion, and for a time combined a day job as a fine cabinetmaker with nights on the bandstand. Perhaps because of his own varied musical background, he believes that archtops are too often pigeonholed as strictly jazz instruments, and that they are capable of working well in a variety of musical forms, particularly if builders and players work closely together on design.

"I think we're still discovering what the range of an archtop guitar is," says Megas. "Depending on how it's built, an archtop can move more toward the open, sustained sound of a flattop guitar, or retain more of the traditional soft, warm quality, which flattops can't do. It's important to understand, though, that it's a question of balance: the more you strive for one quality, the more likely it is you'll lose something of the others."

♠ **Apollo Custom Oval Hole, 2005**
Ted Megas, Megas Guitars
Portland, Oregon

196

SPECIFICATIONS

BODY AND SIDE WOODS: Curly maple

TOP WOOD: Spruce

BODY WIDTH, LOWER BOUT: 17 inches (43.2 cm)

ELECTRONICS: PUTW under bridge, ribbon pickup

NECK WOOD: Curly maple

FRETBOARD MATERIAL: Ebony

HEADSTOCK DECORATION: Ebony with mother-of-pearl logo

BRIDGE: Ebony

NUT AND SADDLE: Mother-of-pearl nut

TUNING MACHINES: Gold Schaller/ebony buttons

BINDING: Curly maple

SCALE LENGTH: 25.25 inches (64.1 cm)

NECK WIDTH AT NUT: 1 11/16 inches (4.3 cm)

NUMBER OF FRETS: 21

BRACING: Parallel

FINISH: Dark amber-burst nitro-lacquer

BODY DEPTH: 3 inches (7.6 cm)

BODY LENGTH: 20¾ inches (52.7 cm)

OVERALL LENGTH: 42½ inches (108 cm)

U.S. SUGGESTED RETAIL PRICE: $7,800

16-Inch Archtop

Mario Beauregard attended the Roberto-Venn School of Luthiery under a grant from the Quebec Council of Arts and Letters. There he met Ervin Somogyi, who invited Beauregard to apprentice with him. "During the week I would work and study with Ervin and during the weekend I would drive up to Taku Sakashta's shop to learn about archtops," recalls Beauregard, who also cites such masters as James D'Aquisto, Steve Klein, Ted Megas, John Monteleone, and Steve Grimes as influences and sources of inspiration for his work.

Beauregard builds every type of guitar he studied with his mentors—acoustic and electric archtops and nylon- and steel-string acoustics—and he has established a reputation for his elegant design and superb craftsmanship that rivals those of his teachers. The sensuous but still classical lines of this archtop are typical of his subtle and distinctive touch.

SPECIFICATIONS

BODY AND SIDE WOODS: Quilt maple

TOP WOOD: European spruce

BODY WIDTH, LOWER BOUT: 16 inches (40.6 cm)

ELECTRONICS: Ken Armstrong

NECK WOOD: Hardrock maple

FRETBOARD MATERIAL: Ebony

FRETBOARD INLAY: Purflings

HEADSTOCK DECORATION: Pearl/abalone logo, snakewood bindings with purflings

BRIDGE: Ebony bridge and saddle and ebony carved tailpiece

NUT AND SADDLE: Bone nut

TUNING MACHINES: Alessis with snakewood buttons

BINDING: Snakewood

SCALE LENGTH: 25 inches (63.5 cm)

NECK WIDTH AT NUT: 1¹¹⁄₁₆ inches (4.3 cm)

NUMBER OF FRETS: 22

BRACING: Parallel

BODY DEPTH: 3 inches (7.6 cm)

U.S. SUGGESTED RETAIL PRICE: $12,500

◆ **16-Inch Archtop, 2006**
Mario Beauregard, Beauregard Guitars
Saint-Denis-sur-Richelieu, Quebec, Canada

Jazz Nylon

Mario Beauregard designed the Jazz Nylon for jazz and flattop players who want to feel at home on an easy-to-amplify nylon-string guitar. Beauregard also wanted to create an instrument with distinctive tonal qualities, "a little more restricted in the overtone aspect, more percussive, and not as boomy as a classical guitar."

The Jazz Nylon is built very differently from a typical classical guitar, incorporating elements more common to archtops. The neck is narrower, shaped to feel comfortable to a non-classical player, while the top of the neck has three radii at 12, 10, and 9 inches (30.5, 25.4, and 22.9 cm), and supports an elevated fingerboard (an idea borrowed from classical builder Thomas Humphrey). The back is a hand-carved arched with a "recurve" near the edge that Beauregard feels is key to the instrument's sound. This example also features back and sides of beautifully figured curly maple instead of the Brazilian rosewood favored by traditionalists.

● **Jazz Nylon, 2006**
Mario Beauregard,
Beauregard Guitars
Saint-Denis-sur-Richelieu,
Quebec, Canada

198

SPECIFICATIONS

BODY AND SIDE WOODS: Carved back European maple

TOP WOOD: European spruce

ELECTRONICS: K & K Trinity System

NECK WOOD: Mahogany

FRETBOARD MATERIAL: Madagascar rosewood

FRETBOARD INLAY: Purflings

HEADSTOCK DECORATION: Hand-carved recessed headplate with Madrone veneer on back

SOUND HOLE INLAYS: Spalted maple

BRIDGE: Brazilian rosewood

NUT AND SADDLE: Bone nut

TUNING MACHINES: Irving Sloane

BINDING: Brazilian rosewood

SCALE LENGTH: 25.6 inches (65 cm)

NECK WIDTH AT NUT: 1⅞ inches (4.7 cm)

NUMBER OF FRETS: 21

BRACING: Radial

U.S. SUGGESTED RETAIL PRICE: $8,700

Big Sound Model B Hole

*B*ecause the Gypsy jazz guitar originated in Europe and the majority of contemporary players live there, many of the leading builders of the style are also European. Dutch luthier Gerrit van Bergeijk builds three gypsy guitars, all inspired by the Selmer-Maccaferri tradition but incorporating his own ideas.

The Big Sound is based on Maccaferri principles but it is at once smaller and heavier than the instruments played by Django Reinhardt. Van Bergeijk also gave the guitar a wider sound hole than the original, which he believes creates a more balanced sound. The back and sides are very stiff, constructed of solid rosewood sandwiched between pieces of cedar and balsa and reinforced with small braces.

Van Bergeijk says he doesn't see any advantage in building lightweight guitars. He says the top and related parts have to be very light, and all other parts need to be stiff. "The result," he says, "is a very loud, excellently balanced instrument with a great projection."

◀ **Big Sound Model B Hole, 2005**
Gerrit van Bergeijk
Noordwijkerhout, The Netherlands

SPECIFICATIONS

BODY AND SIDE WOODS: Indian rosewood, rosewood, balsa, and cedar

TOP WOOD: 25-year-old European spruce

BODY WIDTH, LOWER BOUT: 15½ inches (39.5 cm)

NECK WOOD: Honduran mahogany

FRETBOARD MATERIAL: Ebony

FRETBOARD INLAY: Small sidemarks

HEADSTOCK DECORATION: Selmer tradition

SOUND HOLE INLAYS: Abalone

BRIDGE: Rosewood

TUNING MACHINES: Gotoh gold machine heads

BINDING: Natural wood

SCALE LENGTH: 26.18 inches (66.5 cm)

NUMBER OF FRETS: 24

BRACING: Lightly braced bridge

FINISH: Modern varnish

BODY DEPTH: 3¾ inches (9.5 cm)

BODY LENGTH: 18½ inches (47 cm)

OVERALL LENGTH: 39⅜ inches (100 cm)

The Vinodetto

*N*apa Valley vintner David Miner, the president and co-owner of Miner Family Vineyards, is also a guitar player and collector, so it was natural for him to collaborate with Bob Benedetto on two projects—a guitar and a wine bottling. Miner commissioned Benedetto to make an oval-holed archtop with "wine-stained" maple sides and back, and the two men also bottled an elegant, limited-production 2002 Cabernet Sauvignon.

Benedetto created the dark red stain for the guitar with fermented Cabernet Sauvignon drawn from oak barrels stored in the vineyard's mountainside caves. The instrument also features a hand-cut grapevine inlay motif worked in abalone and mother-of-pearl, tortoise-shell binding with fine-line purfling, and the Miner family logo on the rear of the headstock.

Miner and Benedetto see a number of parallels between making wine and building archtop guitars: both endeavors rely on the passion of an experienced artisan who controls development but never loses sight of his intended audience; both require special relationships with suppliers to guarantee the best available raw materials; both depend on balancing the chemistry of the materials with the artistry of the maker; and both products develop more complexity and structure with careful aging.

● **The Vinodetto, 2005**
Robert Benedetto, Benedetto Guitars
Savannah, Georgia

SPECIFICATIONS

BODY AND SIDE WOODS: European flamed maple

TOP WOOD: European spruce

BODY WIDTH, LOWER BOUT: 16 inches (40.6 cm)

NECK WOOD: Mahogany

FRETBOARD MATERIAL: Ebony

FRETBOARD INLAY: Hand-cut grapevine inlay in abalone and mother-of-pearl

HEADSTOCK DECORATION: Hand-cut grapevine inlay in abalone and mother-of-pearl

SOUND HOLE INLAYS: Fine-lined purfling and tortoise-shell binding

BRIDGE: Ebony two-piece adjustable

NUT AND SADDLE: Ebony nut

TUNING MACHINES: Schaller M6 minis with ebony buttons

BINDING: Fine-lined purfling and tortoise-shell binding

SCALE LENGTH: 25.5 inches (64.8 cm)

NECK WIDTH AT NUT: 1 11/16 inches (4.3 cm)

NUMBER OF FRETS: 21

BRACING: Parallel

FINISH: Stained with Miner Wines' Benedetto Signature Cabernet; nitrocellulose lacquer topcoat

BODY DEPTH: 3 inches (7.6 cm)

BODY LENGTH: 20 3/16 inches (51.3 cm)

OVERALL LENGTH: 41 11/16 inches (105.9 cm)

U.S. SUGGESTED RETAIL PRICE: $125,000

201

The 35th Anniversary Guitar

*B*ob Benedetto, one of the world's most admired archtop guitar makers, says that the two things he has cared about since he was a little boy are music and wood. "Guitars were all I thought about," he admits. "I played guitar on weekends in a local band, and I would pour over Gibson and Gretsch guitar catalogs and knew exactly which archtop model and its endorsers were on each page."

Benedetto learned fine woodworking from his father, who was a master cabinetmaker, and built his first guitar in 1968. His world renowned archtops have been played by such masterful jazzmen as Howard Alden, Jimmy Bruno, Kenny Burrell, John and Bucky Pizzarelli, Johnny Smith, Andy Summers, Martin Taylor, and Chuck Wayne. He is also the author of the definitive instruction book, *Making an Archtop Guitar.*

This one-of-a-kind custom creation was commissioned by Ratthakrai Sirisook in 2003 to celebrate Benedetto's 35 years as an acoustic archtop guitar maker. Completed in January 2006, the guitar's appointments include custom, carved floral-shaped sound holes in the upper left and lower right bouts, elegant abalone inlays, and a 14-karat gold inlay at the twelfth fret.

SPECIFICATIONS

BODY AND SIDE WOODS: Aged European flamed maple

TOP WOOD: Aged European spruce

BODY WIDTH, LOWER BOUT: 17 inches (43.2 cm)

NECK WOOD: One-piece American flamed maple

FRETBOARD MATERIAL: Ebony

FRETBOARD INLAY: 14-karat gold floral inlay on 12th fret

HEADSTOCK DECORATION: Custom hand-cut ribbon and floral inlay of mother-of-pearl and abalone

SOUND HOLE INLAYS: Custom floral-shaped sound openings

BRIDGE: Two-piece ebony adjustable with exotic burl veneer

NUT AND SADDLE: Ebony nut

TUNING MACHINES: Gold Schaller M6 minis with ebony buttons veneered with exotic burl

BINDING: Curly koa wood binding and fine-lined black and white wood purfling

SCALE LENGTH: 25 inches (63.5 cm)

NECK WIDTH AT NUT: 1¾ inches (4.4 cm)

NUMBER OF FRETS: 21

BRACING: X bracing

FINISH: Aged honey blonde nitrocellulose lacquer

BODY DEPTH: 3 inches (7.6 cm)

BODY LENGTH: 20¾ inches (52.7 cm)

OVERALL LENGTH: 42⅜ inches (107.6 cm)

U.S. SUGGESTED RETAIL PRICE: $175,000

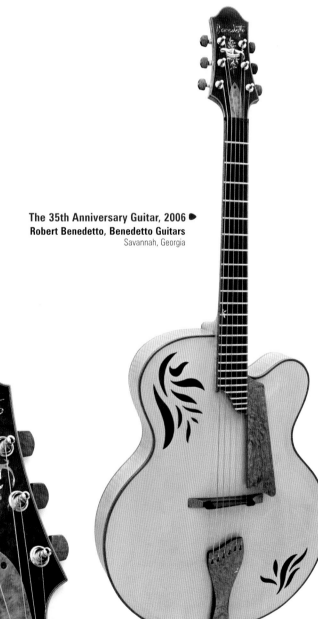

The 35th Anniversary Guitar, 2006 ▶
Robert Benedetto, Benedetto Guitars
Savannah, Georgia

Millennium Guitar

*J*ohn Buscarino studied classical guitar, apprenticed with the master American-born classical luthier Augustino LoPrinzi, and worked with the renowned archtop builder Robert Benedetto for two years before setting out on this own in 1981. He built solid- and hollow-bodied electric guitars for a dozen years before he returned to his original training in classical and archtop instruments, for which he is now internationally known.

The Millennium Guitar was inspired by news coverage of fireworks displays held around the world to celebrate the arrival of the new millennium. Buscarino was particularly struck by the fireworks erupting from the Eiffel Tower, which were recreated on the headstock by master inlay artist, Paul Bordeaux of Malone, New York. Bordeaux recalls, "John asked me to do a replica of the Eiffel Tower on the headstock with fireworks behind it. It was 3½ inches (8.9 cm) tall in gold mother-of-pearl, and I engraved every girder. I also cut out sixty or seventy tiny arcs of fireworks coming off it."

Buscarino also decided to use this guitar to pay tribute to the archtop tradition and to illustrate how far archtop building had come since the first Gibson. The block inlays on the fingerboard are engraved with important events in the history of the archtop.

The Millennium Guitar is one of 14 Buscarino guitars owned by John Ferolito, the owner of AriZona Iced Tea, who collects vintage and one-of-a-kind instruments.

204

SPECIFICATIONS

BODY AND SIDE WOODS: Aged select East Indian rosewood

TOP WOOD: Master-grade western cedar

BODY WIDTH, LOWER BOUT: 17 inches (43.2 cm)

ELECTRONICS: Buscarino signature floating humbucker made by Kent Armstrong

NECK WOOD: Quarter-sawn highly figured rock maple

FRETBOARD MATERIAL: Madagascar ebony

FRETBOARD INLAY: Mother-of-pearl blocks with pau shell borders by Tom Ellis, engraving by Ron Chancey with important moments in the history of guitar building

HEADSTOCK DECORATION: Inlay by Paul Bordeaux, replica of Eiffel Tower as seen on New Year's Eve with fireworks erupting from it to celebrate the millennium

SOUND HOLE INLAYS: Ebony with red dyed pearwood purfling

BRIDGE: Madagascar ebony

▲ **Millennium Guitar, 2000**
John Buscarino, Buscarino Guitars
Franklin, North Carolina

Cameo

ark Campellone's life has revolved around guitars and music since he was a kid. He started playing guitar when he was 10, studied at the prestigious Berklee College of Music in Boston, and was working as a professional musician when he began repairing and building guitars in the mid-1970s.

The first decent guitar he owned was a Gibson, and Campellone cites Gibson archtops as his main influence as a builder. He worked on several top-quality Gibson archtops before he built his first archtop in 1988, and taking them apart and putting them back together provided a great education in what made them tick. His studies paid off so well that guitar historian and dealer George Gruhn, who has handled more than a few great Gibsons in his time, has said, "His workmanship is, if anything, better than some of the (famous) Gibsons of the 1950s."

The Cameo is Campellone's top-of-the-line model and features a host of decorative detailing, including multiple bindings on the top, back, fingerboard, peghead, pickguard, and holes; abalone "filigree" position markers on the fingerboard; and oval cameo inlays on both sides of the peghead.

Cameo, 2002 ▶
Mark Campellone,
M.Campellone Guitars
Greenville, Rhode Island

SPECIFICATIONS

BODY AND SIDE WOODS: Western big leaf flame maple

TOP WOOD: Sitka spruce

BODY WIDTH, LOWER BOUT: 17 inches (43.2 cm)

ELECTRONICS: Kent Armstrong floating pickup with volume control

NECK WOOD: Eastern flame maple

FRETBOARD MATERIAL: Ebony

FRETBOARD INLAY: Abalone

HEADSTOCK DECORATION: Abalone and mother-of-pearl

BRIDGE: Ebony

TUNING MACHINES: Grover rotomatic with solid pearl buttons

BINDING: ABS plastic

SCALE LENGTH: 25 inches (63.5 cm)

NECK WIDTH AT NUT: 1¾ inches (4.4 cm)

NUMBER OF FRETS: 20

BRACING: X bracing

FINISH: Nitrocellulose lacquer

BODY DEPTH: 3 inches (7.6 cm)

BODY LENGTH: 20½ inches (52.1 cm)

OVERALL LENGTH: 41⅝ inches (105.7 cm)

U.S. SUGGESTED RETAIL PRICE: $10,500

Rocket Convertible

Rocket Convertible, 1996 ▶
John Monteleone
Islip, New York

*N*ot long after Jimmy D'Aquisto's untimely death in 1995, the late collector extraordinaire Scott Chinery commissioned 22 master luthiers from the United States, Canada, and Europe to build blue guitars in his honor. D'Aquisto's blue Centura Deluxe, which Chinery had also commissioned, was the inspiration. Chinery specified only that each guitar be 18 inches across the lower bout and have the same blue finish that he had asked D'Aquisto to use, a blue lacquer obtainable from a single manufacturer in Amsterdam, New York. Everything else was left up to the individual luthier's imagination.

Chinery explained the genesis of the Blue Guitars this way, "I had often thought that it would be neat to get all the great portrait painters together to interpret the same subject and then see the differences among them. So that's what I set out to do with the Blue Guitars. All of these great luthiers saw this as a friendly competition, and as a result they went beyond anything they'd ever done. We ended up with a collection of the greatest archtop guitars ever made."

These photos show D'Aquisto's original Blue Centura Deluxe (far right) with the Blue Guitars of the two greatest archtop builders of the succeeding generation, John Monteleone and Bob Benedetto.

SPECIFICATIONS

BODY AND SIDE WOODS: European curly maple

TOP WOOD: European spruce

BODY WIDTH, LOWER BOUT: 18 inches (45.7 cm)

NECK WOOD: American curly maple

FRETBOARD MATERIAL: Ebony

FRETBOARD INLAY: Original 12th fret floral abalone inlay

HEADSTOCK DECORATION: Exotic burl veneer with floral abalone inlay

SOUND HOLE INLAYS: Original floral sound openings

BRIDGE: Ebony/adjustable

NUT AND SADDLE: Ebony

TUNING MACHINES: Schaller with ebony buttons

SCALE LENGTH: 25 inches (63.5 cm)

NECK WIDTH AT NUT: 1⅞ inches (4.8 cm)

La Cremona Azzurra

Centura Deluxe, 1994 ◗
James D'Aquisto
New York City, New York

◀ **La Cremona Azzurra, 1996**
Robert Benedetto, Benedetto Guitars
Savannah, Georgia

207

SPECIFICATIONS

BODY AND SIDE WOODS: Curly tiger maple

TOP WOOD: Adirondack red spruce

BODY WIDTH, LOWER BOUT: 18 inches (45.7 cm)

NECK WOOD: Curly tiger maple

FRETBOARD MATERIAL: Macassar ebony

FRETBOARD INLAY: No inlay. Use of natural inclusion pattern of the ebony showing a quarter moon at first fret with vapor trail below

HEADSTOCK DECORATION: Convex carved with inlaid truss rod cover surrounded by piano key ivory

SOUND HOLE INLAYS: Carved ebony rings, sculpted from solid ebony blocks. (Among the first applications of sound holes on the side of an instrument. Later trademarked as "Side Sound.")

BRIDGE: Gaboon ebony

NUT AND SADDLE: Ivory nut

TUNING MACHINES: Schallers fitted with handmade letter "M" tuning buttons, nickel plated

BINDING: Curly red tiger maple

SCALE LENGTH: 25.4 inches (64.5 cm)

NECK WIDTH AT NUT: 1 13/16 inches (4.6 cm)

NUMBER OF FRETS: 24

BRACING: Simple X braces

FINISH: Nitrocellulose, blue shading

BODY DEPTH: 3 inches (7.6 cm)

ClassiCool

$\mathcal{M}$ark Blanchard calls his ClassiCool a "contemporary nylon-string guitar," meaning that it is aimed at jazz and steel-string players who want to take advantage of the warm, rich tone of nylon strings. The guitar has a narrower neck than a traditional classical guitar, and its radiused fingerboard and modified body shape also help give it a feel similar to a steel-string guitar.

This example of the ClassiCool features extremely rare and dramatic spalted Brazilian rosewood on the back, headstock, and rosette, ebony knobs on the tuning pegs, and an ebony armrest on the lower bout.

Blanchard is a versatile builder whose immaculately clean craftsmanship is highly respected by clients and fellow luthiers alike. In addition to the ClassiCool and a traditional classical model, he also makes acoustic steel-strings in seven different body sizes and added a classic 17-inch acoustic archtop to his line in 2001.

SPECIFICATIONS

BODY AND SIDE WOODS: Spalted Brazilian rosewood

TOP WOOD: Engelmann spruce

BODY WIDTH, LOWER BOUT: 14⅝ inches (37.1 cm)

ELECTRONICS: Pick-up the World dynamic duo

NECK WOOD: Honduran mahogany

FRETBOARD MATERIAL: Ebony

HEADSTOCK DECORATION: Spalted Brazilian rosewood

SOUND HOLE INLAYS: Brazilian rosewood and spalted Brazilian rosewood

BRIDGE: Madagascar rosewood

NUT AND SADDLE: Bone

TUNING MACHINES: Sloane, bronze with ebony knobs

BINDING: Macassar ebony

SCALE LENGTH: 25.6 inches (65 cm)

NECK WIDTH AT NUT: 1⅞ inches (4.8 cm)

NUMBER OF FRETS: 19

BRACING: Torres-style fan bracing

FINISH: Nitrocellulose lacquer

BODY DEPTH: 4 inches (10.2 cm) at tail

BODY LENGTH: 19¼ inches (48.9 cm)

OVERALL LENGTH: 38⅜ inches (97.5 cm)

U.S. SUGGESTED RETAIL PRICE: $8,700

♠ **ClassiCool, 2005**
Mark Blanchard, Mark Blanchard Guitars
Eureka, Montana

The Vanguard

anadian luthier Michael Greenfield emphasizes that he is a traditional hand builder. While he is by no means averse to incorporating contemporary techniques and design features—some of his own invention—into his instruments, he does not believe in reinventing the wheel. He assembles his guitars with hot, animal hide glue and makes no bones about insisting that "building non-cookie-cutter, individually tailored instruments demands and emphasizes the skillful use of simple hand tools. [My] braces are shaped and plates voiced using knives, gouges, and chisels," he elaborates. "Fingerboards are leveled with hand planes. Necks are individually carved using draw knives, spoke shaves, rasps, files, scrapers, and lots of hand sanding. Archtop plates are carved and graduated using palm and then finger planes."

The Vanguard, a traditional 17-inch acoustic model, is the biggest of three archtop models that Greenfield builds. As an option to the standard "thumbwheel" bridge, Greenfield offers his customers his own "full contact bridge," designed to transfer the maximum amount of string energy to the top of the guitar. The necks of his archtops are also unconventional, fitted with carbon graphite truss rods that extend into the neck extension and run the entire length of the neck, into the peghead. "Carbon graphite has a higher stiffness-to-weight ratio than steel," says Greenfield, "and it's extremely light, adding very little weight to the instrument. This makes for an extremely true and stable neck, which is also very energy efficient, virtually eliminating 'dead spots.'"

◄ **The Vanguard, 2004**
Michael Greenfield, Greenfield Guitars
Montreal, Quebec, Canada

209

SPECIFICATIONS

BODY AND SIDE WOODS: European maple

TOP WOOD: Alpine spruce

BODY WIDTH, LOWER BOUT: 17 inches (43.2 cm)

ELECTRONICS: Kent Armstrong

NECK WOOD: Red maple

FRETBOARD MATERIAL: Ebony

HEADSTOCK DECORATION: Mother-of-pearl "g" logo

BRIDGE: Macassar ebony

NUT AND SADDLE: Bone nut, macassar ebony saddle

TUNING MACHINES: Waverly

BINDING: Koa

SCALE LENGTH: 25 inches (63.5 cm)

NECK WIDTH AT NUT: 1¾ inches (4.4 cm)

NUMBER OF FRETS: 21

BRACING: Parallel

FINISH: Lacquer

BODY DEPTH: 3⅛ inches (7.9 cm)

BODY LENGTH: 20¾ inches (52.7 cm)

OVERALL LENGTH: 41½ inches (105.4 cm)

U.S. SUGGESTED RETAIL PRICE: $16,000

John Bolin
Arched Top Guitar

*J*ohn Bolin's archtop, which is modeled after Jimmy D'Aquisto's Solo model, pays homage to the D'Angelico/D'Aquisto tradition. The Solo, with its distinctive split sound holes, was one of D'Aqusito "Futuristic Series," a group of designs that moved decisively away from the classic archtop look and sound, codified in part by his mentor John D'Angelico. The Solo and other Futuristic models have a more open sound than traditional archtops and were intended to be used in a variety of musical settings, instead of being restricted to jazz alone.

Unlike D'Aquisto, who eschewed inlaid decoration of any kind on his later instruments, Bolin chose to inlay single flowers on the headstock, tailpiece, and lower fingerboard, below where it meets the body at the 14th fret. The three inlays are carefully spaced, so they lead the eye through the center of the instrument from head to tail. The fingerboard inlay provides a strong central focus at the apex of the triangle suggested by the inward-facing sound holes.

◄ **Arched Top Guitar, 1993**
John Bolin, Bolin Guitars
Boise, Idaho

SPECIFICATIONS

BODY AND SIDE WOODS: European silver flame maple

TOP WOOD: European spruce

BODY WIDTH, LOWER BOUT: 17 inches (43.2 cm)

NECK WOOD: European silver flame maple

FRETBOARD MATERIAL: Ebony

FRETBOARD INLAY: Mother-of-pearl handcut tiger family

HEADSTOCK DECORATION: Mother-of-pearl handcut tiger family

BRIDGE: Ebony James D'Aquisto design

NUT AND SADDLE: Bone

TUNING MACHINES: Schaller

BINDING: European maple/ebony lim

SCALE LENGTH: 25.5 inches (64.8 cm)

NECK WIDTH AT NUT: 1¾ inches (4.4 cm)

NUMBER OF FRETS: 22

BRACING: X style

FINISH: Lacquer nitro

BODY DEPTH: 4 inches (10.2 cm)

BODY LENGTH: 21 inches (53.3 cm)

OVERALL LENGTH: 44 inches (111.8 cm)

U.S. SUGGESTED RETAIL PRICE: $17,000

The Jazz Laureate

*B*efore turning to guitar making, Steve Grimes studied with a violin maker and built a reputation for his carved-top mandolins. However, because he is a guitarist himself, he began building archtop guitars in 1974, and eventually added unique flattop and electric designs to his repertoire.

Grimes's archtops combine innovative design and traditional styling; he utilizes the latest advances in acoustical technology while retaining "Old World" quality and craftsmanship. Grimes is a student of instrument acoustics who has presented several papers at the Guild of American Luthiers' convention. He is also a stickler about wood who tests hundreds of samples of master-grade wood for lightness, stiffness, sustain, and purity of tone. His acuity in both areas allows him to build in the precise, individual tonal character desired by each of his clients.

The Jazz Laureate is Grimes's top-of-the-line archtop model and represents one of the pinnacles of today's traditional archtop guitar design and sound reproduction. To ensure visual and tonal continuity, Grimes uses only the best of the best of his woods for this model and cuts the backs and sides of the guitar from the same billet of old cello wood. In addition to tonal quality, Grimes also looks for wood with the kind of striking figure that gives the deep, "3-D" appearance seen here.

◀ **The Jazz Laureate, 1988**
Steve Grimes, Grimes Guitars
Kula, Hawaii

SPECIFICATIONS

BODY AND SIDE WOODS: Western, sugar, or German maple; curly koa

TOP WOOD: German, red, Engelmann, or Carpathian spruce

BODY WIDTH, LOWER BOUT: 16, 16½, 17, 18 inches (40.6, 41.9, 43.2, 45.7 cm)

TUNING MACHINES: Gotoh 510 Special or Schaller

SCALE LENGTH: 25.5 inches (64.8 cm)

NECK WIDTH AT NUT: 1¹¹⁄₁₆ or 1¾ inches (4.3 or 4.4 cm)

NUMBER OF FRETS: 21 to 24

BRACING: European or Carpathian spruce

FINISH: Nitrocellulose lacquer

BODY DEPTH: 16, 16½-inch (40.6, 41.9 cm) models: 2⅞ inches (7.3 cm); 17 and 18-inch (43.2 and 45.7 cm) models: 3 inches (7.6 cm)

BODY LENGTH: 16, 16½-inch (40.6, 41.9 cm) models: 20½ inches (52.1 cm); 17-inch (43.2 cm) model: 21 inches (53.3 cm); 18-inch (45.7 cm) model: 21½ inches (54.6 cm)

OVERALL LENGTH: 42½ inches (108 cm)

U.S. SUGGESTED RETAIL PRICE: $16,000

The Frame Modern Classic Fretless Midi Guitar

*T*he Frame is a professional-quality travel guitar that is being used by a wide variety of jazz, pop, and rock musicians, including Gilberto Gil, Mick Goodrick, Pat Metheny, and Caetano Veloso.

Luthier Frank Krocker says the Frame concept started more or less by chance in 1995, when a customer asked for a compact, high-quality classical guitar for performing and traveling. What Krocker came up with was a radical, minimalist guitar consisting of a hand-shaped, headless mahogany neck/body and a pair of foam rubber covered resonance tubes that attach to steel pins on the body to simulate the size and feel of a "regular" guitar. The Frame's headstock sits at the bottom of the neck and allows easy access to the machine heads for precise tuning, while strings are attached to a tieblock/tailpiece located at the top end of the fingerboard.

◀ **The Frame Modern Classic Fretless Midi Guitar, 2005**
Frank Krocker, Frame Works Guitars
Mehring, Germany

213

SPECIFICATIONS

BODY AND SIDE WOODS: Form rubber-covered resonance tubes

BODY WIDTH, LOWER BOUT: 14 9/16 inches (37 cm)

ELECTRONICS: Onboard polyphonic preamp by RMCO

NECK WOOD: Mahogany

FRETBOARD MATERIAL: Ebony

BRIDGE: Ebony

TUNING MACHINES: Customized Schaller mini

SCALE LENGTH: 25.6 inches (65 cm)

NECK WIDTH AT NUT: 1 7/8 inches (4.8 cm)

FINISH: Hard-rubbed satin gloss varnish

BODY LENGTH: 17 1/2 inches (44.5 cm)

OVERALL LENGTH: 32 11/16 inches (83 cm)

16-Inch Archtop

*B*ill Collings has been building steel-string acoustic guitars since the mid-1970s. He founded Collings Guitars in 1989, with two employees and a 1,000-square-foot workspace. The company has grown steadily over the years, and today, Collings employs 50 full-time staff who work in a brand new 22,000-square-foot shop.

While his company is best known for high quality flattops and mandolins, Collings himself is also a master of the archtop. He was one of the elite group of luthiers chosen by the late Scott Chinery to build a Blue Guitar (see page 206), and his work is highly respected by his peers. This 16-inch sunburst archtop, which looks back to Lloyd Loar's seminal Gibson L-5 for its inspiration, showcases Collings's considerable skills as a designer and builder.

215

16-Inch Archtop, 2007 ▶
Bill Collings, Collings Guitars and Mandolins
Austin, Texas

SPECIFICATIONS

BODY AND SIDE WOODS: Western maple

TOP WOOD: Italian red spruce

BODY WIDTH, LOWER BOUT: 16 inches (40.6 cm)

NUT AND SADDLE: Bone

TUNING MACHINES: Waverly

SCALE LENGTH: 25.5 inches (64.8 cm)

NECK WIDTH AT NUT: 1¹¹⁄₁₆ inches (4.3 cm)

Kunkel Jazz Deco Archtop

The Jazz Deco is Bruce Kunkel's take on the classic Art Deco-influenced archtop designs of the 1930s. Kunkel's added features include a carved armrest, boldly stylized f-holes that terminate in half-heart shapes, and interchangeable pickguards, one equipped with a pair of floating humbucking pickups for electric playing, and one without pickups for totally acoustic playing.

Kunkel studied painting and sculpture at the School of Visual Arts in New York, and struggled for a few years as a painter before teaming with his father in building reproductions of eighteenth-century furniture. He moved to Nashville in 1992 to pursue music and instrument making—he is also an accomplished songwriter who plays banjo and guitar—and soon after was hired by Gibson to produce one-of-a-kind art pieces for their Custom Shop.

During his tenure at Gibson, Kunkel created a string of unique instruments, including tributes to Elvis, Chet Atkins, and B.B. King, a series of Art Deco archtops, and Kix Brooks's Les Paul Gator Guitar. He was also key in the design and creation of several limited production instruments, including the Old Hickory and Indian Motorcycle Les Pauls.

Kunkel left Gibson in January 2003 to pursue his own guitar designs, which also include several acoustic flattop models with heart- shaped sound holes. He continues to create art pieces for Gibson on a contract basis.

SPECIFICATIONS

BODY AND SIDE WOODS: Big leaf curly maple

TOP WOOD: Adirondack spruce or Sitka spruce

BODY WIDTH, LOWER BOUT: 17 inches (43.2 cm)

ELECTRONICS: EMG passive humbuckers, convertible to acoustic. Designed by D.R. Auten.

NECK WOOD: Five-piece hard rock maple (curly) and walnut verneer laminate

FRETBOARD MATERIAL: Ebony

FRETBOARD INLAY: Kunkel Jazz Deco motif in hand-cut white mother-of-pearl

HEADSTOCK DECORATION: Kunkel white pearl banner/ Kunkel gold mother-of-pearl lion holding red abalone heart

SOUND HOLE INLAYS: Kunkel half-heart "F" hole

BRIDGE: Ebony handmade adjustable

NUT AND SADDLE: Bone nut, ebony saddle

TUNING MACHINES: Grover Imperials, gold plated

BINDING: W/B/W/B abs binding

SCALE LENGTH: 25.4 inches (64.5 cm)

NECK WIDTH AT NUT: 1¾ inches (4.4 cm)

NUMBER OF FRETS: 21

BRACING: Hand-scalloped X-braced top

FINISH: Nitrocellulose 12+ coats, wet sanded and buffed

BODY DEPTH: 3 inches (7.6 cm) at rim; 4½ inches (11.4 cm) top-back with arch

BODY LENGTH: 21 inches (53.3 cm)

OVERALL LENGTH: 43 inches (109.2 cm)

U.S. SUGGESTED RETAIL PRICE: $15,000

216

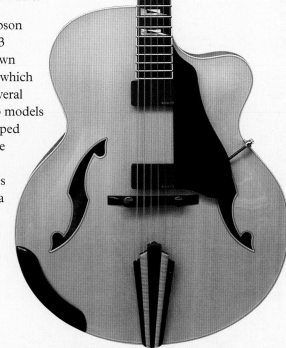

◆ **Kunkel Jazz Deco Archtop, 2004**
Bruce J. Kunkel, Kunkel Guitars
Nashville, Tennessee

ASAST

◀ ASAST, 2005
Chris Larkin, Chris Larkin Custom Guitars
Castlegregory, Ireland

*W*orking alone in his shop beside the beach on the west coast of Ireland, Chris Larkin builds a wide range of acoustic and electric guitars, including 15- and 17-inch archtops. This traditional 17-inch was his first with a "pointy" Venetian cutaway. Rather than following the standard practice of applying the same finish to both body and neck after they are joined, Larkin finished the contrasting parts separately and then glued them together. To complete the dramatic contrasts of wood and finish, Larkin also fashioned the pickguard, headstock veneer, and top-loading tailpiece of clear, finished birdseye maple.

Although he has been building guitars full time for more than 20 years, Larkin freely and happily admits, "The more I learn, the more I know I have to learn." He adds, "There is no Holy Grail in guitar making. There are too many variables in hand making an instrument to be sure of anything. The traditional 'rules' are there to be tested. At this stage, working with wood has become largely intuitive for me. And I am a wood junkie!"

SPECIFICATIONS

BODY AND SIDE WOODS: Flamed maple

TOP WOOD: Sitka spruce

BODY WIDTH, LOWER BOUT: 17 inches (43.2 cm)

ELECTRONICS: Single volume control, Kent Armstrong, custom-made humbucker

NECK WOOD: Flamed maple laminate with walnut veneer details

FRETBOARD MATERIAL: Ebony bound with grained ivoroid

FRETBOARD INLAY: Mother-of-pearl

HEADSTOCK DECORATION: Mother-of-pearl inlaid in birdseye maple

BRIDGE: Ebony

NUT AND SADDLE: Micarta nut, ebony saddle

TUNING MACHINES: Schaller vintage gold

BINDING: Grained ivoroid with maple/black fiber purfling

SCALE LENGTH: 25.6 inches (65 cm)

NECK WIDTH AT NUT: 1¹¹⁄₁₆ inches (4.3 cm)

NUMBER OF FRETS: 20 Dunlop 6230

BRACING: 2x parallel spruce bars

FINISH: Gloss 2 pack acid-catalyzed, acid-cured melamine

BODY DEPTH: 2¹⁵⁄₁₆ inches (7.5 cm)

BODY LENGTH: 20¹³⁄₁₆ inches (53 cm)

OVERALL LENGTH: 42½ inches (108 cm)

U.S. SUGGESTED RETAIL PRICE: Approximately $5,000

Renaissance Archtop

*B*ill Comins started playing guitars as a kid and majored in "Jazz Guitar Performance" at Temple University. He taught private guitar lessons and played in wedding bands to make ends meet, but says that by the late 1980s, he was anxious to retire his "out-dated, poorly fitting, well-worn tuxedo" and concentrate on luthiery.

He worked in a violin shop for several years and also maintained his own repair business. After building several instruments on his own, he sought out master archtop luthier Robert Benedetto and, under his tutelage, built his first archtop guitar in 1992. He opened his own shop in 1994, and got his first big break a couple of years later when the late Scott Chinery invited him to build one of the Blue Guitars (see page 206) In 2000, Comins moved his shop to a wooded setting just outside of Philadelphia. "Here," he says, "surrounded by tall oak, maple, poplar, and birch trees, I found a tranquil backdrop that not only facilitates a deeper clarity of practice and purpose, [but also] makes for an excellent meeting spot for late night poker games."

The Renaissance is one of Comins's original takes on the archtop form. He offers a variety of sound-hole treatments to his clients. This example has small, unusually shaped recessed sound holes set in frames that echo their form.

◀ **Renaissance Archtop, 1998**
William B. Comins, Comins Guitars
Willow Grove, Pennsylvania

SPECIFICATIONS

BODY AND SIDE WOODS: Flamed maple

TOP WOOD: European spruce

BODY WIDTH, LOWER BOUT: 17 inches (43.2 cm)

NECK WOOD: Flamed maple with fine lines of cherry and walnut

FRETBOARD MATERIAL: Ebony

HEADSTOCK DECORATION: Flamed koa face with fine violin purfling

SOUND HOLE INLAYS: Ebony handles on baffles

BRIDGE: Carved ebony with gold plated inserts and posts

NUT AND SADDLE: Ebony nut

TUNING MACHINES: Gold plated Schaller tuners with ebony buttons

BINDING: Flamed koa with fine violin purfling

SCALE LENGTH: 25 inches (63.5 cm)

NECK WIDTH AT NUT: 1¾ inches (4.4 cm)

NUMBER OF FRETS: 22

BRACING: X-braced

FINISH: Natural nitrocellulose lacquer

BODY DEPTH: 3⅛ inches (7.9 cm)

BODY LENGTH: 21 inches (53.3 cm)

OVERALL LENGTH: 43 inches (109.2 cm)

U.S. SUGGESTED RETAIL PRICE: $15,000

Dream Feather

ichael Lewis's elegant Dream Feather was built on a commission arranged by Richard Glick of Fine Guitar Consultants. The basis for the guitar was Lewis's 17-inch carved archtop cutaway D'Angelico Excel, which Lewis says "evolved from there to this physical manifestation of images, ideas, dreams, and visions."

The unique instrument combines a hand-carved top of golden-brown bear claw-figured Sitka spruce with a back, sides, and neck of cream-colored European maple. To blend the colors of the unusual combination of woods,

Lewis chose a binding of dark red-brown koa. The fingerboard, finger rest, and tailpiece are black ebony, and the bridge is very dark Brazilian rosewood. Lewis's vivid feather motif appears on the headstock, fingerboard, and tailpiece, where it is repeated in black on black, and the sound holes also echo the shape. The position markers along the bass side of the fingerboard are gold circles filled with malachite, a beautiful green mineral that contrasts perfectly with the red-brown of the koa binding.

"The woods of this guitar play beautifully in reflected light," Lewis says proudly. "There is just enough runout in the top and back to show the 'harlequin' effect so opposing areas light up as the instrument moves. The bear claw figure jumps to life then recedes as the light changes on it. The dreamlike figure of the back lights up as it is rolled in the light and disappears as if into a fog at the edges."

SPECIFICATIONS

BODY AND SIDE WOODS: European maple

TOP WOOD: Sitka spruce with bear claw figure

BODY WIDTH, LOWER BOUT: 17 inches (43.2 cm)

ELECTRONICS: Bartolini 5J7 7 string pickup with volume and tone controls

NECK WOOD: European maple

FRETBOARD MATERIAL: Ebony

FRETBOARD INLAY: Simplified feather in silver

HEADSTOCK DECORATION: Pearl and gold feather inlaid into maple and ebony veneers

SOUND HOLE INLAYS: Koa binding and multiple black/white purfling

BRIDGE: Very dark Brazilian rosewood

NUT AND SADDLE: Walrus ivory

TUNING MACHINES: Waverly 4071-G with snakewood buttons

BINDING: Dark koa with black, white, and light koa purfling

SCALE LENGTH: 25.4 inches (64.5 cm)

NECK WIDTH AT NUT: 2 1/16 inches (5.2 cm)

NUMBER OF FRETS: 22

BRACING: X bracing

FINISH: Clear nitro lacquer, oil finished neck

BODY DEPTH: 3 1/4 inches (8.3 cm)

BODY LENGTH: 20 1/4 inches (51.4 cm)

OVERALL LENGTH: 42 3/4 inches (108.6 cm)

U.S. SUGGESTED RETAIL PRICE: $30,000

220

♠ **Dream Feather, 2005**
Michael A. Lewis, Michael Lewis Instruments
Grass Valley, California

Linda Manzer

12-String Archtop

$\mathcal{W}$ hile most archtops have six strings, some luthiers build seven- or even eight-string models that offer players added bass notes and a wider range of fingering and voicing possibilities. But a 12-string archtop is a rara avis.

Into the vacuum stepped the intrepid Linda Manzer, to whom 12-strings are just a beginning. In addition to her two multi-necked, 42-stringed Pikasso guitars, Manzer also includes an acoustic flattop 12-string in her line, which shares the same open carved headstock design used on this archtop.

Manzer studied archtop building with James D'Aquisto and his influence can be seen in the simple lines, gentle curves, and spare ornamentation of this archtop. Like D'Aquisto's later work, this guitar's pickguard and tailpiece are carved wood rather than the metal favored by earlier masters such as D'Angelico, Epiphone, Gibson, and Stromberg.

◀ **12-String Archtop**
Linda Manzer
Toronto, Ontario, Canada
Courtesy of the Collection of Jeff Doctorow

SPECIFICATIONS

BODY AND SIDE WOODS: Curly koa

TOP WOOD: German spruce

NECK WOOD: South American mahogany

FRETBOARD MATERIAL: Ebony bound with ebony and abalone

FRETBOARD INLAY: Side dots (Abalone fingerboard optional)

BRIDGE: Ebony

ARCHTOP & OTHER JAZZ

Moderne

Dutch luthier Frans Elferink has a degree in electronic engineering and works part time as an acoustical and electrical engineer. A specialist in archtops, he is a meticulous craftsman who is noted for using carefully aged tonewoods more often reserved for concert-grade cellos than guitars. His instruments are played by a host of professional European jazz guitarists and have found their way into the hands of several American players as well.

Elferink's Moderne model takes its name and form from one of the four innovative "modern" archtop models that the legendary James D'Aquisto designed and built in his last years. Elferink offers his Moderne in both 17-inch (43.2 cm) and 18-inch (45.7 cm) sizes.

Moderne, 2006 ▶
Frans Elferink, Elferink Guitars
Noordwijkerhout, The Netherlands

SPECIFICATIONS

BODY AND SIDE WOODS: Flamed big leaf maple

TOP WOOD: Bear claw Sitka spruce

BODY WIDTH, LOWER BOUT: 18 inches (45.7 cm)

ELECTRONICS: Condensor microphone (internal), pickup (magnetic) integrated in fingerboard

NECK WOOD: One-piece flamed big leaf maple

FRETBOARD MATERIAL: African ebony

FRETBOARD INLAY: Fairy

HEADSTOCK DECORATION: Fairy

SOUND HOLE INLAYS: Flamed maple

BRIDGE: Macassar ebony

NUT AND SADDLE: Graphtech

TUNING MACHINES: Schaller gold with ebony buttons

BINDING: Flamed maple

SCALE LENGTH: 25.5 inches (64.8 cm)

NECK WIDTH AT NUT: 1 11/16 inches (4.3 cm)

NUMBER OF FRETS: 19

BRACING: X bracing

FINISH: Nitrocellulose

BODY DEPTH: 3½ inches (8.9 cm)

BODY LENGTH: 21 inches (53.3 cm)

OVERALL LENGTH: 44½ inches (113 cm)

U.S. SUGGESTED RETAIL PRICE: $5,900

223

Mark Whitfield Archtop

Stephen Marchione has been jazz guitarist Mark Whitfield's luthier since 1999, and the pair has collaborated on five guitars. Since beginning his professional career in New York in 1987, Whitfield has performed and recorded with such legendary artists as George Benson, Art Blakey, Betty Carter, Dizzy Gillespie, Herbie Hancock, Quincy Jones, B.B. King, Jimmy Smith, Clark Terry, McCoy Tyner, and Joe Williams, and such stalwarts of the current scene as Terence Blanchard, Mary J. Blige, D'Angelo, Branford and Wynton Marsalis, and The Roots.

Marchione is a versatile musician and luthier who plays jazz, blues, classical, and flamenco styles, makes a wide variety of electric and acoustic instruments, and also says he "adores" crafting violins on the patterns of Stradivari and Guarnieri.

◄ **Mark Whitfield Archtop, 2003**
Stephen Marchione,
Marchione Guitars
Houston, Texas

224

SPECIFICATIONS

BODY AND SIDE WOODS: Sugar maple

TOP WOOD: Engelmann spruce

BODY WIDTH, LOWER BOUT: 17 inches (43.2 cm)

ELECTRONICS: Proprietary Marchione electronics

NECK WOOD: Sugar maple

FRETBOARD MATERIAL: African ebony

HEADSTOCK DECORATION: Marchione logo

SOUND HOLE INLAYS: Marchione modern f-holes

BRIDGE: African ebony

NUT AND SADDLE: Black ivory

TUNING MACHINES: Custom Sperzel

BINDING: African ebony

SCALE LENGTH: 25.5 inches (64.8 cm)

NECK WIDTH AT NUT: 1¾ inches (4.4 cm)

NUMBER OF FRETS: 22

BRACING: Marchione rule of 7

FINISH: French polish and lacquer

BODY DEPTH: 2⅞ inches (7.3 cm)

BODY LENGTH: 21¼ inches (54 cm)

OVERALL LENGTH: 43½ inches (110.5 cm)

U.S. SUGGESTED RETAIL PRICE: $22,000

The Bear

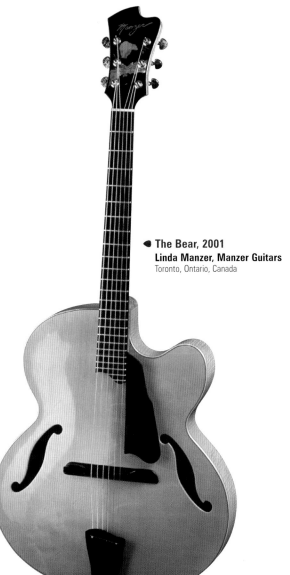

◀ **The Bear, 2001**
Linda Manzer, Manzer Guitars
Toronto, Ontario, Canada

𝓛 inda Manzer designed and built The Bear to celebrate her 25th anniversary as a luthier. The inspiration for the guitar came from a unique piece of German bear claw spruce in Manzer's collection of woods. She carved the top from the piece of bear claw, which gets its name from the rare and distinctive figure that makes the wood look as if it has been gouged by the claws of a bear.

The guitar's intricate inlay celebrates the life of bears in their natural habitat. Manzer explains, "The bears depicted are rare Kermode bears (pronounced ker-mode-ee). While Kermodes resemble polar bears (or albinos), they are actually a variety of black bear found only in northern British Columbia. [I created] the inlaid illustration using mother-of-pearl, gold pearl, and wood burl bordered by a purple heart and curly maple beveled veneer."

Manzer also hand carved the heel of the guitar to depict a bear's paw reaching for some berries among the leaves and included her "sliding panel" sound port on the top side, which allows the player to hear the sound that normally projects forward and also to create a variety of tonal expression that can be heard by both the player and the audience.

SPECIFICATIONS

BODY AND SIDE WOODS: European maple

TOP WOOD: German bear claw spruce

BODY WIDTH, LOWER BOUT: 17¼ inches (43.8 cm)

NECK WOOD: One-piece hard curly maple

FRETBOARD MATERIAL: Ebony

BRIDGE: Ebony

TUNING MACHINES: Waverly

BINDING: Maple

SCALE LENGTH: 25.4 inches (64.5 cm)

NECK WIDTH AT NUT: 1¾ inches (4.4 cm)

BODY DEPTH: 3¼ inches (8.3 cm)

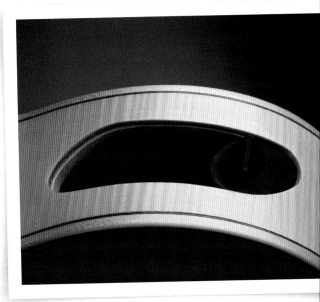

Archtop

$\mathcal{P}$aul Gudelsky (1963–1996) studied sculpture before embarking on a career in luthiery. He began his studies at the Roberto-Venn School of Luthiery in Phoenix, and then in 1990 apprenticed with James D'Aquisto. After D'Aquisto's untimely death in 1995, Gudelsky inherited the bench and tools with which D'Aquisto and his mentor, John D'Angelico, had worked. Gudelsky was tragically murdered the following year, and his family ultimately donated the workshop to the National Music Museum at the University of South Dakota. In addition to archtops by D'Angelico, Gibson, and Elmer Stromberg, the museum also owns a Fender/ D'Aquisto Ultra model and one of the two surviving guitars built by legendary luthier Antonio Stradivari.

Like his mentor, Gudelsky was committed to modernizing the archtop form, creating instruments that would appeal to contemporary players and assure the survival of the tradition. This guitar's elongated sound holes and the echoing lines of its open headstock are examples of his design ideas.

226

◀ **Archtop, 1995**
Harris Paul Gudelsky
Vista, California
Courtesy of Louise Palazola and the Collection of Jeff Doctorow

SPECIFICATIONS

BODY AND SIDE WOODS: German maple

TOP WOOD: Engelmann spruce

NECK WOOD: Maple, one piece

FRETBOARD MATERIAL: Ebony

HEADSTOCK DECORATION: Gudelsky Guitar inlay mother-of-pearl

BRIDGE: Ebony

The Pikasso

This four-necked, 42-stringed acoustic electric instrument was created for jazz guitarist Pat Metheny after he jokingly asked Manzer how many strings she could put on a guitar. She and Metheny collaborated on the design, which she estimates took about 1,000 hours over a two-year period to build.

The Pikasso weighs 14¾ pounds (6.7 kg), and its 42 strings put the instrument under a massive pressure of approximately 1,000 pounds (453.6 kg). Manzer specifically designed a special trademarked body shape she calls the Wedge for this instrument. The side closest to the player is thinner than the side that rests on the player's knee, so the top back leans towards the player and all the necks and strings can be easily seen. Manzer says the Wedge is also more comfortable under the player's arm, and she now offers it as an option on all her acoustic guitars. Because of its weight and multiple necks, the Pikasso can also be played mounted on a stand attached to its bottom side, allowing the player to move freely from neck to neck.

♠ **The Pikasso, 1984**
Linda Manzer, commissioned by Pat Metheny
Toronto, Ontario, Canada

227

SPECIFICATIONS

BODY AND SIDE WOODS: Indian rosewood

TOP WOOD: German spruce

NECK WOOD: Mahogany

FRETBOARD MATERIAL: Ebony

BRIDGE: Ebony

Gibson L-5 "Auburn" Archtop

This is the third in a series of extraordinary archtop guitars created for Gibson by master luthier Bruce J. Kunkel as tributes to the Art Deco era. The guitar pays tribute to the Auburn Automobile Company's Boattail Speedster, one of the most admired classic American car designs of the Art Deco era. The top features painted radiating bands, while the back is hand-cut marquetry of a 1934 Auburn Boattail and is crafted from more than 200 pieces of a dozen or so exotic woods and aluminum. Kunkel also deeply carved the heel of the guitar, one of his trademark touches.

Auburn grew out of the Eckhart Carriage Company in Auburn, Indiana. Although the company was bought and then merged with Cord and Duesenberg in the mid-1920s, the Auburn brand name continued to grace a remarkable line of cars until the Depression killed the market for high-end autos.

Kunkel's work on these special guitars for Gibson would not have been possible without strong support from many in the company, most notably Rick Gembar and Mike McGuire.

Gibson L-5 "Auburn" Archtop, 2001 ♠
Built by Bruce J. Kunkel
Gibson Guitar Corporation, Custom, Art & Historic Division
Nashville, Tennessee

SPECIFICATIONS

BODY AND SIDE WOODS: Maple

TOP WOOD: Spruce

BODY WIDTH, LOWER BOUT: 17 inches (43.2 cm)

ELECTRONICS: Gibson Charlie Christian pickups

NECK WOOD: Maple

FRETBOARD MATERIAL: Ebony

FRETBOARD INLAY: Mother-of-pearl

HEADSTOCK DECORATION: Custom truss rod cover

BRIDGE: Rosewood

NUT AND SADDLE: Bone

TUNING MACHINES: Schaller with Art Deco mother-of-pearl knobs

BINDING: Traditional B/W/B

NECK WIDTH AT NUT: 1 13/16 inches (4.6 cm)

NUMBER OF FRETS: 20

BRACING: Traditional parallel spruce

FINISH: Nitrocellulose lacquer

BODY DEPTH: 3 inches (7.6 cm)

Jazz Moderne Acoustic

$\mathcal{C}$ ris Mirabella was 11 when got his first "good" guitar, a 1979 Fender Strat that was seriously in need of attention. A friend told him he should take it to a local vintage guitar shop, and so he rode over on his bike, balancing the guitar as he went. Mirabella felt as if he had walked into a candy shop and told *Just Jazz Guitar* magazine that when he laid his guitar on the counter, he said, "I need a setup and I want a job here, sweeping floors, anything." After his mother intervened, the owner finally relented, and he's been in a guitar shop ever since.

As he learned more about guitar building and began to do repair work, Mirabella became fascinated with archtops and built a reputation for his ability with handmade pickguards. Living on Long Island was also fortuitous because he was able to meet his hero Jimmy D'Aquisto and spend time at his shop. He says that despite having a reputation for impatience, D'Aquisto always answered his questions and never told him to "go away, kid." He set out on his own in 1996 and now builds custom guitars and mandolins in addition to making pickguards and doing repair work.

Mirabella's Moderne is based on D'Aquisto's model of the same name, which divided a crescent-moon-shaped f-hole into one large and two short segments on each side of the top. Mirabella's version exaggerates the relative sizes even more than D'Aquisto did. He builds every part of the guitar except the tuners and frets and uses his own proprietary asymmetrical X bracing.

SPECIFICATIONS

BODY AND SIDE WOODS: European flame maple, cello wood, air dried

TOP WOOD: Well-aged, air-dried German spruce

BODY WIDTH, LOWER BOUT: 17 inches (43.2 cm)

ELECTRONICS: Additional guard with floating Kent Armstrong pickup

NECK WOOD: One-piece European highly flamed maple

FRETBOARD MATERIAL: Madagascar ebony

HEADSTOCK DECORATION: Signature Mirabella truss rod cover

BRIDGE: Macassar ebony, wedge bridge

NUT AND SADDLE: Ivory nut

TUNING MACHINES: Schallers, gold with ebony buttons

BINDING: European flamed maple and Madagascar ebony

SCALE LENGTH: 25 inches (63.5 cm)

NECK WIDTH AT NUT: 1¾ inches (4.4 cm)

NUMBER OF FRETS: 24

BRACING: C. Mirabella-designed asymmetrical X bracing

FINISH: Natural blonde, nitrocellulose lacquer

BODY DEPTH: 2⅞ inches (7.3 cm)

BODY LENGTH: 20⅜ inches (51.8 cm)

OVERALL LENGTH: 42½ inches (108 cm)

U.S. SUGGESTED RETAIL PRICE: $10,500

♠ **Jazz Moderne Acoustic, 2006**
Cristian Mirabella, Mirabella Guitars
Babylon, New York

The Wildwood

The Wildwood, 2003
Linda Manzer
Toronto, Canada
Courtesy of the Collection of Jeff Doctorow

This stunning Linda Manzer one-off is named for the wildly spalted European maple that covers half of its back. Manzer complemented the maple with equally striking flamed koa binding. The front of the guitar is as quiet and elegant as the back is flamboyant, with a hand-carved ebony pickguard and tailpiece contrasting with the creamy European spruce top.

Paul Heumiller of Dream Guitars says the name Wildwood also seems to fit because the guitar has attitude. "It is the loudest and most responsive archtop we've seen," he explains, "with volume and projection more like a flattop. But the tone is pure maple and spruce magic….There is clarity throughout the fingerboard and this guitar is also content playing Freddie Green or Joe Pass."

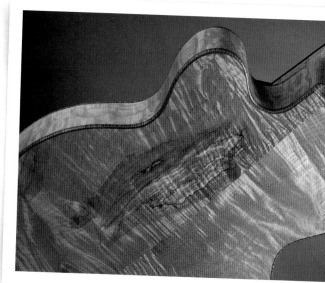

SPECIFICATIONS

BODY AND SIDE WOODS: European maple

TOP WOOD: European spruce

NECK WOOD: Mahogany

BRIDGE: Ebony

TUNING MACHINES: Gold Gotoh

BINDING: Flamed koa

Michael Dunn

The Air Mail Special

*T*his guitar was named after jazz guitar legend Charlie Christian's tune, "Good Enough to Keep (Air Mail Special)," recorded by the Benny Goodman Sextet in 1941.

Luthier Michael Dunn says he wanted to evoke the insouciant spirit of the Roaring Twenties, when airmail was a new phenomenon (The U.S. Post Office initiated airmail service in 1918.), so he inlaid stylized Art Deco images of planes on the guitar's back. He also inlaid fretboard silhouettes of Charles Lindbergh's "Spirit of St. Louis," the plane Lucky Lindy used to make the first nonstop, trans-Atlantic flight in 1929.

Charlie Christian was one of the first great solo jazz guitarists and a pioneer of the electric guitar. In addition to his work with Goodman, Christian also jammed after hours with Dizzy Gillespie, tenor saxist Don Byas, drummer Kenny Clarke, and a then little-known pianist named Thelonious Monk in ad-libbed sessions that marked the beginning of bebop. Tragically, Christian died of tuberculosis in 1942, just three years after Columbia

Records producer John Hammond—who first brought Bessie Smith, Billie Holiday, Count Basie, Robert Johnson, Aretha Franklin, Bob Dylan, and Bruce Springsteen to the attention of the world—introduced him to Goodman.

Even though Christian was only 25 at the time of his passing, his playing has influenced virtually every electric guitarist who has come after him.

◀ **The Air Mail Special, 2004**
Michael Dunn, Michael Dunn Art Guitars
New Westminster, British Columbia, Canada

232

SPECIFICATIONS

BODY AND SIDE WOODS: Broadleaf flamed maple

TOP WOOD: Douglas fir

BODY WIDTH, LOWER BOUT: 17⁵⁄₁₆ inches (44 cm)

NECK WOOD: Stained maple

FRETBOARD MATERIAL: Ebony

FRETBOARD INLAY: Mother-of-pearl "Spirit of St. Louis" taking off

HEADSTOCK DECORATION: Engine-turned brass with ebony frame

BRIDGE: Ebony

NUT AND SADDLE: Bone nut

TUNING MACHINES: Grover

BINDING: Ebony with rope purfling

SCALE LENGTH: 25.2 inches (64 cm)

NECK WIDTH AT NUT: 1¹³⁄₁₆ inches (4.6 cm)

NUMBER OF FRETS: 24

BRACING: Tone bars

FINISH: Water-based lacquer

BODY DEPTH: 3¼ inches (8.3 cm)

BODY LENGTH: 20½ inches (52 cm)

OVERALL LENGTH: 42⅛ inches (107 cm)

Pagelli
Archtop Guitar for Louis Christ

♠ **Archtop Guitar for Louis Christ, 1997**
Designed by Claudia and Claudio Pagelli,
built by Claudio Pagelli, Pagelli Guitars
Chur, Switzerland

234

rchtop master Robert Benedetto has called this remarkable instrument "the most beautiful guitar I've ever seen, built by the most creative guitar builder I've ever met." The guitar was created for and designed in cooperation with the Swiss jazz guitarist and pianist Louis Christ and was built in the form of a stylized woman's body. It has both f-holes and a half circle central sound hole and comes with a novel wooden sound hole cover that allows the instrument to be converted from an open acoustic sound to a compressed f-hole jazz tonality.

Claudio Pagelli, a former professional guitarist, producer, and recording engineer, is one of the most innovative luthiers at work today. In addition to archtops, one of which he covered with 60,000 Swarovski glass crystals, he has built unique acoustic flattops, gypsy jazz guitars, electrics, and electric bass guitars. Pagelli's wife Claudia is an equal partner in the family business who plays a major role in designing most of the 10 custom instruments Claudio builds each year.

SPECIFICATIONS

BODY AND SIDE WOODS: Highly flamed European maple

TOP WOOD: Swiss mountain spruce

BODY WIDTH, LOWER BOUT: 17 inches (43.2 cm)

ELECTRONICS: Schertler blue stick

NECK WOOD: Pear with ebony layers

FRETBOARD MATERIAL: Ebony, floating over the top

HEADSTOCK DECORATION: Ebony

SOUND HOLE INLAYS: Walnut veneer decoration on spruce top

BRIDGE: Ebony with walnut veneer

NUT AND SADDLE: Ebony

TUNING MACHINES: LSR

BINDING: Ebony

SCALE LENGTH: 25.6 inches (65 cm)

NECK WIDTH AT NUT: 1¾ inches (4.4 cm)

NUMBER OF FRETS: 18

BRACING: X bracing

FINISH: Nitrocellulose

Virtuoso

Mark Lacey

Mark Lacey was born in Great Britain and studied Musical Instrument Technology at The London College of Furniture & Interior Design. He spent two years there building Renaissance and Baroque lutes, guitars, citterns, and viols, and then, during his final year at college, building modern fretted guitars. After graduation, he migrated to job opportunities in Norway, Nashville, Los Angeles, and Rhode Island, building and repairing instruments for others before setting up his own shop in Los Angeles and ultimately returning to Nashville. Over the years, Lacey has built and repaired instruments for a diverse group of musicians that includes Jackson Browne, Herb Ellis, John Fogerty, Leo Kottke, Paul McCartney, Terje Rypdal, Rod Stewart, Sting, Tiny Tim, and Stevie Ray Vaughan.

Lacey cites John D'Angelico, James D'Aquisto, and Gibson as his main influences, and his work reflects his respect for traditional designs and hand-building methods. "Having done a great deal of repairs over the years," says Lacey, "one learns how *not* to build a guitar. I've had to deal with just about every type of repair situation, both acoustic and electric. My main objective, besides building guitars that sound good, is to build guitars that will last."

The Virtuoso is his top-of-the-line archtop, which he builds in both 17-inch and 18-inch (45.7 cm) body sizes. Both are decorated with a hand-engraved, soap-pierced, gold-plated tailpiece and intricately engraved mother-of-pearl inlay. Lacey built a blue, 18-inch (45.7 cm) Virtuoso for the late Scott Chinery's Blue Guitars collection (see page 206).

SPECIFICATIONS

BODY AND SIDE WOODS: Quilted maple

TOP WOOD: Sitka spruce

BODY WIDTH, LOWER BOUT: 17 inches (43.2 cm)

ELECTRONICS: Volume/tone and Gibson floating pick-up

NECK WOOD: Fiddleback maple and ebony

FRETBOARD MATERIAL: Ebony

FRETBOARD INLAY: Mother-of-pearl

HEADSTOCK DECORATION: Mother-of-pearl

BRIDGE: Ebony

NUT AND SADDLE: Bone

TUNING MACHINES: Grover Imperials

BINDING: Ivoroid

SCALE LENGTH: 25 inches (63.5 cm)

NECK WIDTH AT NUT: 1¹¹⁄₁₆ inches (4.3 cm)

NUMBER OF FRETS: 22

BRACING: X bracing

FINISH: Nitrocellulose lacquer

BODY DEPTH: 3¼ inches (8.3 cm)

BODY LENGTH: 20½ inches (52.1 cm)

OVERALL LENGTH: 42 inches (106.7 cm)

U.S. SUGGESTED RETAIL PRICE: $25,000

Virtuoso, 2004 ▶
Mark Lacey, Lacey Guitars
Kingston Springs, Tennessee

235

Gibson 20th Century Tribute Guitar

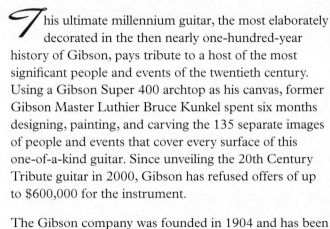

*T*his ultimate millennium guitar, the most elaborately decorated in the then nearly one-hundred-year history of Gibson, pays tribute to a host of the most significant people and events of the twentieth century. Using a Gibson Super 400 archtop as his canvas, former Gibson Master Luthier Bruce Kunkel spent six months designing, painting, and carving the 135 separate images of people and events that cover every surface of this one-of-a-kind guitar. Since unveiling the 20th Century Tribute guitar in 2000, Gibson has refused offers of up to $600,000 for the instrument.

The Gibson company was founded in 1904 and has been an industry leader ever since, producing some of the finest and most influential fretted, stringed instruments of all time, including such icons as the F-5 mandolin, L-5 archtop guitar, Granada five-string banjo, and the Les Paul and Flying V electric guitars.

◀ **Gibson 20th Century Tribute Guitar, 1999–2000**
Bruce J. Kunkel
Gibson Guitar Corporation, Custom, Art & Historic Division
Nashville, Tennessee
Collection of the Gibson Guitar Corporation

236

SPECIFICATIONS

BODY AND SIDE WOODS: Curly maple

TOP WOOD: Sitka spruce

BODY WIDTH, LOWER BOUT: 18 inches (45.7 cm)

NECK WOOD: Maple

FRETBOARD MATERIAL: Ebony

FRETBOARD INLAY: 14-karat white gold

HEADSTOCK DECORATION: 14-karat white gold, turquoise, mother-of-pearl

SOUND HOLE INLAYS: Bound F holes

BRIDGE: Ebony

NUT AND SADDLE: Bone

TUNING MACHINES: Gold Kluson, Art Deco mother-of-pearl knobs

BINDING: B/W/B ABS

NECK WIDTH AT NUT: 1 13/16 inches (4.6 cm)

NUMBER OF FRETS: 20

FINISH: Nitrocellulose lacquer

The Little Archie (Model 14 Oval Hole)

🔹 **The Little Archie (Model 14 Oval Hole), 1996**
Steve Andersen, Andersen Stringed Instruments
Seattle, Washington

This guitar design arose from conversations Steve Andersen had with renowned jazz guitarist Bill Frisell, who wanted an archtop he could travel with. He built the first Little Archie for Frisell in 1996, who was thrilled with it. Although the Little Archie's lower bout is only 14 inches wide and its body only two inches deep, the guitar is "full-sized" in the areas that really count: scale length, neck size and shape, and bridge and soundboard design. Andersen placed the Little Archie's single sound hole on the bass side of the upper bout to compensate for any bass response lost by its small body size.

Frisell says, "I travel a lot, and finally, with this guitar, I'm able to carry it on an airplane (which is a serious problem with the larger instruments). The Model 14 is not a travel guitar—it's a full-blown archtop. The combination of the smaller body and the added bass from the oval sound hole makes for an incredibly balanced sound. The acoustic properties weren't compromised with the smaller size. I'm so excited to finally be able to start taking a guitar like this with me wherever I go."

SPECIFICATIONS

BODY AND SIDE WOODS: Western maple

TOP WOOD: Engelmann spruce

BODY WIDTH, LOWER BOUT: 14 inches (35.6 cm)

ELECTRONICS: Bartolini pickup

NECK WOOD: Eastern maple

FRETBOARD MATERIAL: Ebony

HEADSTOCK DECORATION: Andersen mother-of-pearl logo

BRIDGE: Ebony

NUT AND SADDLE: Micarta nut, ebony saddle

TUNING MACHINES: Waverly

BINDING: Ivoroid

SCALE LENGTH: 25.4 inches (64.5 cm)

NECK WIDTH AT NUT: 1 11/16 inches (4.3 cm)

NUMBER OF FRETS: 21

BRACING: X bracing

FINISH: Nitrocellulose lacquer

BODY DEPTH: 2 inches (5 cm)

U.S. SUGGESTED RETAIL PRICE: $7,000

Tom Ribbecke

Chinery "Blue Mingione"

*O*ne of the "Blue Guitars" commissioned by the late Scott Chinery, Tom Ribbecke's Blue Mingione is named for an obscure, old-time jazz player named Andy Mingione.

Rather than building one of his standard archtops for Chinery, Ribbecke decided to make his Blue Guitar a clear homage to Jimmy D'Aquisto, whose work he says has been the primary influence on his own building. The Blue Mingione's asymmetrical body, large A-shaped sound holes, and wooden pickguard and tailpiece are all nods in D'Aquisto's direction.

Chinery asked some of the builders to add sound ports to their guitars, small sound holes in the player side of the guitar intended to direct sound up toward the musician rather than out toward other listeners. Although Ribbecke was not specifically asked to build a side port, he came up with perhaps the most unusual approach to the concept among the Blue Guitar luthiers (page 206). He added an ebony sound port to the side of the upper bout into which the player can insert a carved ebony sound horn, allowing an even more focused redirection of sound up toward the player's left ear.

SPECIFICATIONS

BODY AND SIDE WOODS: Quilted big leaf maple

TOP WOOD: Sitka spruce

BODY WIDTH, LOWER BOUT: 18 inches (45.7 cm)

NECK WOOD: Birdseye maple

FRETBOARD MATERIAL: Ebony

HEADSTOCK DECORATION: Abalone mother-of-pearl

SOUND HOLE INLAYS: Koa

BRIDGE: Gaboon and Macassar ebony

TUNING MACHINES: Schaller M6

BINDING: Koa

SCALE LENGTH: 25 inches (63.5 cm)

NECK WIDTH AT NUT: 1⅞ inches (4.8 cm)

BRACING: X bracing

FINISH: Nitro lacquer

BODY DEPTH: 3¼ inches (8.3 cm)

BODY LENGTH: 21 inches (53.3 cm)

U.S. SUGGESTED RETAIL PRICE: $30,000

♠ **Chinery "Blue Mingione," 1994**
Tom Ribbecke, Ribbecke Guitars
Healdsburg, California
Courtesy of the Chinery Collection

Modele Elan 14 Non-Cutaway and Left-Handed Modele Encore

Shelley Park is one of the world's most accomplished builders of Gypsy jazz guitars similar to those associated with the Belgian jazz guitarist Django Reinhardt. Reinhardt was one of the most original jazz stylists of all time, and his sound, at once lyrical, romantic, and rhythmically complex, is the holy grail of all subsequent proponents of what is now called "Gypsy jazz." Working with his musical partner, the suave violinist Stéphane Grappelli, Reinhardt forged the first uniquely European jazz style, and most jazz historians consider their Quintette of the Hot Club of France the greatest of all European jazz bands.

The guitar most commonly associated with Gypsy jazz was actually designed by a classical guitarist named Mario Maccaferri, who knew neither Reinhardt nor his music. He devised an instrument with a large D-shaped sound hole and an interior resonator, a small wooden box glued to the top of the guitar and intended to act as a second sound chamber, considerably changing the tone of the guitar. What is now known as the Selmer/Maccaferri guitar was produced in 1932–33 by the Selmer company in France under Maccaferri's supervision, but the resonator proved problematic and very few were ever made.

240

♠ **Modele Elan 14 Non-Cutaway and Left-Handed Modele Encore, 2001**
Shelley D. Park, Shelley D. Park Guitars
Vancouver, British Columbia, Canada
Elan 14 Non-Cutaway (left)
Left-Handed Modele (right)

SPECIFICATIONS

BODY AND SIDE WOODS: Elan, big leaf maple; Encore, Indian rosewood

TOP WOOD: Elan, western red cedar; Encore, Sitka spruce

BODY WIDTH, LOWER BOUT: 15⅞ inches (40.3 cm)

NECK WOOD: Honduran mahogany

FRETBOARD MATERIAL: Ebony

FRETBOARD INLAY: Encore, mother-of-pearl position markers

BRIDGE: Indian rosewood

TUNING MACHINES: Schaller 3-on-plate

BINDING: Elan, big leaf maple; Encore, Indian rosewood

SCALE LENGTH: Elan, 25.2 inches (64 cm); Encore, 26.4 inches (67 cm)

NECK WIDTH AT NUT: 1¾ inches (4.5 cm)

NUMBER OF FRETS: Elan, 24; Encore, 21

BRACING: Lateral bracing

FINISH: Catalyzed polyester varnish

BODY DEPTH: 4⅛ inches (10.5 cm)

BODY LENGTH: 18¾ inches (47.6 cm)

OVERALL LENGTH: Elan, 38 inches (96.5 cm); Encore, 40 inches (101.6 cm)

U.S. SUGGESTED RETAIL PRICE: $4,000

Ken Parker

The Olive Branch

Although he is best known as the inventor of the revolutionary Parker Fly electric guitar, Ken Parker began his career as an archtop builder. He has long believed that the acoustic archtop form offers huge potential that has been largely unexplored. "Many factory-built archtops," says Parker, "and many others built by hand in the style, are much too heavy and stiff to be responsive and fun to play. The acoustic archtop guitar has not been optimized with respect to the selection of materials and the proportions of stiffness, tuning, and damping, although a prodigious amount of energy has been spent embellishing them!"

The Olive Branch, the first of Parker's new archtop designs, represents as thorough a rethinking of the acoustic archtop as the Parker Fly did of the electric guitar. To begin with, this is a full sized archtop (16½ inches across the lower bout) that weighs a mere 3½ pounds! The guitar has a big, open voice with excellent clarity, sustain, and separation, and Parker says it is so light, alive, and responsive that playing it "feels like getting a belly massage." The string height can be adjusted by the player with a simple hidden screw that elevates the neck, adjusting the action without the need to retune. The tailpiece is anodized aluminum and is also adjustable for height, while the tuning pegs are 16:1 ratio planetary gears with specially designed Pernambuco knobs. And, adds Parker, "a small red olive is inlaid in the back in case you get hungry."

"This guitar has been a long time coming, but will soon be followed by siblings and cousins," promises Parker.

The Olive Branch, 2006 ▶
Ken Parker, Parker Guitars
Garnerville, New York

SPECIFICATIONS

BODY AND SIDE WOODS: Koa

TOP WOOD: Red spruce

BODY WIDTH, LOWER BOUT: 16½ inches (41.9 cm)

NECK WOOD: Koa, Douglas fir

FRETBOARD MATERIAL: Pernambuco

BRIDGE: Spruce, Pernambuco

NUT AND SADDLE: Pernambuco

TUNING MACHINES: Herin/Parker

BINDING: Purfling 5-ply BWBWB

SCALE LENGTH: 25.5 inches (64.8 cm)

NECK WIDTH AT NUT: 1¹¹⁄₁₆ inches (4.3 cm)

NUMBER OF FRETS: 22

BRACING: Interrupted X

FINISH: Varnish

BODY DEPTH: 2½ inches (6.4 cm)

BODY LENGTH: 21 inches (53.3 cm)

OVERALL LENGTH: 42¼ inches (107.3 cm)

U.S. SUGGESTED RETAIL PRICE: $30,000

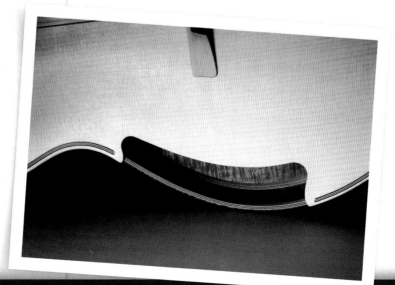

241

Moderna

Ric McCurdy, who has been building custom guitars since 1983, studied archtop luthiery with Bob Benedetto and specializes in acoustic and electric archtops which are designed to bring the D'Angelico sound to modern players. McCurdy's highly regarded archtops are played by such renowned jazz artists as John Abercrombie, Joe Beck, and Matt Munisteri, as well as members of The Blue Man Group.

As its name suggests, the Moderna is the most modern looking archtop in McCurdy's line and the one showing the most influence of Jimmy D'Aquisto's groundbreaking later work. Like D'Aquisto's progressive archtop models of the 1980s and 1990s, McCurdy's Moderna has distinctive, non-traditionally shaped sound holes, a carved wooden pickguard and tail piece, and no ornamentation at all on the fingerboard or head. The subtle, restrained design puts emphasis on the guitar's understated lines and carefully balanced choices of wood rather than on added ornamentation.

242

♠ **Moderna, 2003**
Ric McCurdy, McCurdy Guitars
New York, New York
Courtesy of the Collection of Jeff Doctorow

SPECIFICATIONS

BODY AND SIDE WOODS: Curly European maple

TOP WOOD: European spruce

BODY WIDTH, LOWER BOUT: 17 inches (43.2 cm)

ELECTRONICS: Volume and tone thumbwheel pots, mounted on pickguard edge; Kent Armstrong custom pickup for bronze strings

NECK WOOD: Hard curly maple

FRETBOARD MATERIAL: Black Brazilian rosewood

FRETBOARD INLAY: Abalone dots at 12th fret

HEADSTOCK DECORATION: Abalone name

SOUND HOLE INLAYS: Maple, ebony

BRIDGE: Solid ebony full-contact bridge

NUT AND SADDLE: Unbleached bone/rosewood

TUNING MACHINES: Gotoh SG-36 with abalone buttons

BINDING: 5-ply maple binding

SCALE LENGTH: 25.5 inches (64.8 cm)

NECK WIDTH AT NUT: 1¾ inches (4.4 cm)

NUMBER OF FRETS: 24

BRACING: Hand-tuned X brace

FINISH: Clear nitrocellulose

BODY DEPTH: 3 inches (7.6 cm)

BODY LENGTH: 20¾ inches (52.7 cm)

OVERALL LENGTH: 43 inches (109.2 cm)

U.S. SUGGESTED RETAIL PRICE: $9,000

Version R Electric Archtop

♠ **Version R Electric Archtop, 2005**
Taku Sakashta, Taku Sakashta Guitars
Petaluma, California

*T*aku Sakashta created the Version R to overcome the limitations he and many modern players find in traditional amplified archtop guitars—severely restricted attack, no sustain, and feedback problems—and to support a wide variety of playing styles.

He noticed the sustained tones that solid-body guitars produce when they are played unplugged, and that those tones disappear when the instruments are plugged in. "I thought about this over and over," he says, "realizing the need to capture these lost sustained tones which clearly support current playing styles and music."

His answer was to add rounded, hand-carved side rims to the body of his standard archtop models. According to Sakashta, the side rims create "first response with sustain, plus carry reproduction of full overtones even with thin, clear amplifier settings. Sounds so generated," he adds, "have natural overdrive—full, clear tone." The Version R's reduced internal volume efficiently turns limited electric guitar picking energy into clear, undistorted overdrive, without distortion or feedback.

SPECIFICATIONS

BODY AND SIDE WOODS: Maple

TOP WOOD: Spruce

BODY WIDTH, LOWER BOUT: 15 inches (38.1 cm)

ELECTRONICS: Bartoliny

NECK WOOD: Maple

FRETBOARD MATERIAL: Ebony

BRIDGE: Ebony

NUT AND SADDLE: Scalloped tempered bone nut

TUNING MACHINES: Schaller

BINDING: Wood

SCALE LENGTH: 24.75 inches (62.9 cm)

NECK WIDTH AT NUT: 1 11/16 inches (4.3 cm)

NUMBER OF FRETS: 22

BRACING: X braced

FINISH: Nitrocellulose lacquer finish

The Turquoise Archtop

Takahiro Shimo

*T*akahiro Shimo is an original and extremely versatile luthier and musician who builds and plays a wide range of acoustic and electric guitars and ukeleles. He came to the United States in 1980 to study luthiery at the Roberto-Venn School of Luthiery in Phoenix and opened his own shop in Tokyo in 1982. Shimo is a seemingly fearless artisan who will try anything once, including double necks—he has even built a double-necked acoustic guitar/uke—and harp guitars, lap steels, electric bass guitars, and resonators.

This 18-inch archtop represents yet another facet of Shimo's talents as a designer and builder. The Turquoise combines a unique finish color with exaggerated lightning bolt-shaped sound holes, an ebony fingerboard with turquoise position markers, and a tall, distinctively shaped headstock.

♠ **The Turquoise Archtop, 2000**
Takahiro Shimo, Shimo Guitars
Tokyo, Japan

SPECIFICATIONS

BODY AND SIDE WOODS: Curly European maple

TOP WOOD: German spruce

BODY WIDTH, LOWER BOUT: 18 inches (45.7 cm)

NECK WOOD: Curly European maple

FRETBOARD MATERIAL: Indian ebony

FRETBOARD INLAY: Turquoise

HEADSTOCK DECORATION: Mother-of-pearl logo inlay on Brazilian rosewood

BRIDGE: Brazilian rosewood

NUT AND SADDLE: Ivory nut

TUNING MACHINES: Schaller M6 gold with mother-of-pearl button

BINDING: Curly European maple

SCALE LENGTH: 25 inches (63.5 cm)

NECK WIDTH AT NUT: 1 11/16 inches (4.3 cm)

NUMBER OF FRETS: 22

BRACING: X bracing

FINISH: See-through turquoise blue/lacquer

BODY DEPTH: 3 inches (7.6 cm)

BODY LENGTH: 20½ inches (52.1 cm)

OVERALL LENGTH: 42¾ inches (108.6 cm)

U.S. SUGGESTED RETAIL PRICE: $12,500

Seven-String Bolt-On Neck Archtop

*G*ary Rizzolo has played guitar professionally since the mid-1960s and built and repaired guitars since 1976. An accomplished furniture maker as well as a luthier, he has a Diploma in Crafts as well as a Bachelor of Fine Arts in Design in Wood from the University of Tasmania.

In addition to archtops, Rizzolo builds acoustic flattops and solid-bodied electric guitars and basses. Living in Tasmania, he has direct access to the region's unique exotic tonewoods and particularly likes to work with figured blackwood and Tasmanian oak, finding the latter particularly well suited for the bodies of electric instruments.

He makes archtops with six, seven, or eight strings; this seven-string features an unusual sound hole treatment in which the smaller modified f-holes are mirror images of their larger companions. The mirroring pairs of sound holes create an illusion of movement and almost appear to be wriggling up the body of the guitar.

♠ **Seven-String Bolt-On Neck Archtop, 2001**
Gary Rizzolo, Rizzolo Guitar Company
Sandy Bay, Tasmania, Australia

SPECIFICATIONS

BODY AND SIDE WOODS: European maple

TOP WOOD: European spruce

BODY WIDTH, LOWER BOUT: 14⅛ inches (36 cm)

ELECTRONICS: Kent Armstrong custom seven-string Fishman Prefix Pro with custom piezo under saddle pickup

NECK WOOD: Three-piece rock maple with Macassar ebony veneers

FRETBOARD MATERIAL: African ebony

FRETBOARD INLAY: Mother-of-pearl leaves at 12th fret

HEADSTOCK DECORATION: Birdseye maple with African black ebony inlay front, Macassar ebony back

SOUND HOLE INLAYS: Unbound leaf holes

BRIDGE: African ebony

NUT AND SADDLE: African black ebony

TUNING MACHINES: Gold Schaller rear locking with ebony buttons

BINDING: Queensland walnut and rock maple veneers

SCALE LENGTH: 25.4 inches (64.5 cm)

NECK WIDTH AT NUT: 2⅛ inches (5.4 cm)

NUMBER OF FRETS: 19 frets

BRACING: European spruce X bracing

FINISH: Nitrocellulose lacquer

BODY DEPTH: 3⅛ inches (8 cm)

BODY LENGTH: 19⅝ inches (50 cm)

OVERALL LENGTH: 41 inches (104 cm)

U.S. SUGGESTED RETAIL PRICE: $9,000

Jazz Harp Guitar

Mike Doolin had made several acoustic harp guitars for other musicians before he decided to build one for himself. Since his musical background is playing jazz and R&B on electric guitar, he decided an electric archtop would be most comfortable for him. Next he thought, "If I was going to try to play jazz on this thing, it had to be a fully chromatic instrument, capable of playing in all keys." Whereas most harp guitars have five to seven sub-bass strings, which are tuned diatonically in one key, Doolin wanted an instrument with all 12 notes of the chromatic scale in the sub-basses. To keep the right hand stretch reasonable, he decided the low E on the neck could be the starting E, which left him with 11 sub-basses, tuned in descending half steps down to F.

To make dealing with so many sub-bass strings easier, Doolin blackened all the sharps, so the sub-basses look like the familiar black and white pattern of a piano keyboard. He put a stock Gibson humbucking pickup in the neck position "for that familiar dark jazz tone" and a piezo pickup in the sub-bass headstock which runs through an FET pre-amp mounted under the pickguard. "The two signals go out separately through a stereo output jack," he explains, "so I can add effects to the neck while keeping the sub-basses dry."

Since finishing the guitar, Doolin has been "woodshedding" and says he's got one Leni Stern tune pretty well down and is working on another by Pat Metheny. "I'm also thinking of Monk's 'Round Midnight' and Billie Holiday's 'God Bless the Child,'" he adds. "Ultimately, the goal is to be able to improvise over changes while keeping the bass line going. Wish me luck."

♠ Jazz Harp Guitar, 2006
Michael Doolin, Doolin Guitars
Portland, Oregon

SPECIFICATIONS

BODY AND SIDE WOODS: Birdseye maple

TOP WOOD: Sitka spruce

BODY WIDTH, LOWER BOUT: 17 inches (43.2 cm)

ELECTRONICS: Duncan '59 humbucker for neck, piezo film in harp head for subs with FET pre-amp

NECK WOOD: Birdseye maple

FRETBOARD MATERIAL: Ebony

FRETBOARD INLAY: Pearl side dots

HEADSTOCK DECORATION: Pearl logo

SOUND HOLE INLAYS: Bound in boxwood

BRIDGES: Ebony

NUT AND SADDLE: Bone nut

TUNING MACHINES: Gotoh

BINDING: Boxwood

SCALE LENGTH: 25.5 inches (64.8 cm) for neck, 26 to 34 inches (66 to 86.4 cm) for subs

NECK WIDTH AT NUT: 1 11/16 inches (4.3 cm)

NUMBER OF FRETS: 20

BRACING: X braced

FINISH: Polyester

BODY DEPTH: 4 inches (10.2 cm)

BODY LENGTH: 35 inches (88.9 cm)

OVERALL LENGTH: 42 inches (106.7 cm)

247

Grand Artist Deluxe Triport

*J*ohn Monteleone smashed his first guitar to bits against a lally column in his basement. He remembers it as "a horrible excuse for a guitar, with three or four of the blackest, rustiest, nastiest strings ever seen," and says his experiment probably produced the best sound the guitar ever made. It also left a pile of interesting splinters of spruce and maple and revealed the cheap old guitar's guts to the curious 12 year old. "I then realized that there was a reason for all of these things and that it was somehow important to the sound of any guitar," Monteleone deadpans. "This was enlightening."

Monteleone is now recognized as one of the preeminent builders of archtop guitars in the world. This one-of-a-kind custom built archtop includes one of his many innovations—additional sound holes on the left side of the guitar which project sound up toward the player rather than out toward listeners and thus make it easier for the musician to hear himself.

♠ **Grand Artist Deluxe Triport, 1999**
John Monteleone
Islip, New York

SPECIFICATIONS

BODY AND SIDE WOODS: Quartersawn big leaf maple from Oregon

TOP WOOD: Alpine spruce from Switzerland/Austria

BODY WIDTH, LOWER BOUT: 18 inches (45.7 cm)

NECK WOOD: Big leaf maple

FRETBOARD MATERIAL: Macassar ebony

FRETBOARD INLAY: Mother-of-pearl and red coral stone

HEADSTOCK DECORATION: Mother-of-pearl with red coral stone

SOUND HOLE INLAYS: Single ring of ebony

BRIDGE: Movable, adjustable Macassar ebony

NUT AND SADDLE: Mother-of-pearl nut, ebony saddle

TUNING MACHINES: Schaller with custom cast letter "M" buttons

BINDING: Curly red maple

SCALE LENGTH: 25.4 inches (64.5 cm)

NECK WIDTH AT NUT: 1¾ inches (4.4 cm)

NUMBER OF FRETS: 24

BRACING: X brace

FINISH: Natural nitrocellulose

BODY DEPTH: 2⅞ inches (7.3 cm)

BODY LENGTH: 23½ inches (59.7 cm)

OVERALL LENGTH: 45 inches (114.3 cm)

U.S. SUGGESTED RETAIL PRICE: $65,000

The Royale Premiere

Artist and musician Ian Schneller began using Specimen Products as a name for his sculptures in 1981 while he was an undergraduate at the Memphis Academy of Art. "It was the anonymity of the words 'Specimen' and 'Products' that appealed to me," he laughs. "It also seemed a funny little ruse—pretending to be a company instead of myself." After Schneller moved on to graduate studies at the School of the Art Institute of Chicago in 1984, Specimen Products expanded into a music- and instrument-making endeavor—first to fulfill his own personal needs, and then for his friends, band mates, and other musicians.

This recent Specimen guitar design is a unique take on the archtop tradition defined by luthiers like John D'Angelico and James D'Aquisto that has been brewing in Schneller's mind for many years. "The headstock and body are inspired by the sinewy horror of a praying mantis," he says, "while the pastels mimic natural color themes found somewhere between chlorophyll and entomology." The pickup ring, trapeze, and finial are handcrafted from solid billets of aluminum, and the bridge is carved from one piece of ebony. Both the D and G strings have banjo tuners that can be used for special drop-tuning effects. This particular Royale model also features a single neck pickup format, which lets the guitar resonate to its fullest extent. The pickup is a Lindy Fralin humbucker which Schneller says sounds "very good indeed—robust, full spectrum, and cooperative."

SPECIFICATIONS

BODY AND SIDE WOODS: Linden

TOP WOOD: Linden

BODY WIDTH, LOWER BOUT: 15¾ inches (40 cm)

ELECTRONICS: Volume, tone, Lindy Fralin humbucker

NECK WOOD: Mahogany

FRETBOARD MATERIAL: Ebony

FRETBOARD INLAY: Mother-of-pearl with colored mastic

HEADSTOCK DECORATION: Diver's helmet finial sculpted from aluminum billet

BRIDGE: One-piece floating, ebony

NUT AND SADDLE: Bone

TUNING MACHINES: Four Grover Imperials and two Schaller banjo tuners

BINDING: White/yellow/white

SCALE LENGTH: 24.5 inches (62.2 cm)

NECK WIDTH AT NUT: 1¾ inches (4.4 cm)

NUMBER OF FRETS: 21

BRACING: Internally carved from the body billets

FINISH: Pale blue nitrocellulose

BODY DEPTH: 3½ inches (8.9 cm)

BODY LENGTH: 19 inches (48.3 cm)

OVERALL LENGTH: 42 inches (106.7 cm)

U.S. SUGGESTED RETAIL PRICE: $6,500

The Royale Premiere, 2001 ▶
Ian Schneller, Specimen Guitar Shop
Chicago, Illinois

Stochelo Rosenberg Signature Model

*L*eo Eimers, who plays rhythm guitar in a band called Mojo Swing and the For Fellows Big Band at Parisian venue The Hot Club, describes himself as a true fan of gypsy music and Django Reinhardt in particular. Reinhardt's music drew him to the gypsy guitars of Maccaferri, Selmer, Busato, Favino, and other luthiers who developed the form prior to World War II. He cut his teeth repairing vintage guitars by the greats and learning about their choices of wood as well as their construction and finishing techniques.

Eimers has specialized in building Selmer/Maccaferri-style guitars for more than 15 years. He offers one of the widest ranges of models currently available, including an acoustic bass, an archtop, and the reduced-size Mini Mac, designed for children and as a travel guitar for adults.

Stochelo Rosenberg is Holland's leading gypsy guitarist. He and his cousins Nous'che and Nonnie Rosenberg grew up in an extended musical family and have been playing together since they were kids. As the Rosenberg Trio, they have recorded many albums, performed around the world, and were invited by Django's legendary musical partner Stéphane Grappelli to play with him at Carnegie Hall in a celebration of his 85th birthday.

Although Stochelo Rosenberg is the proud owner of Selmer guitar serial #504 (Django Reinhardt owned #503), he thought highly enough of Leo Eimers's work to collaborate with him on this Signature Model. That is high praise indeed.

SPECIFICATIONS

BODY AND SIDE WOODS: Palisander, poplar, and mahogany veneers

TOP WOOD: German spruce

BODY WIDTH, LOWER BOUT: 10¼ inches (26 cm)

ELECTRONICS: Passive Big Tone piezo pickup

NECK WOOD: French walnut; three-part neck

FRETBOARD MATERIAL: Ebony

FRETBOARD INLAY: Mother-of-pearl position dots on top of neck

HEADSTOCK DECORATION: Engraved Eimers logo and name of Stochelo Rosenberg filled with gold wax

SOUND HOLE INLAYS: Black and white bands of veneers

BRIDGE: Ebony or palisander

NUT AND SADDLE: Bone

TUNING MACHINES: Brass, replica Selmer tuners (SR stamped in each of the six casings)

BINDING: Black/white/black/white veneer purfling with an outer palisander binding

SCALE LENGTH: 26.4 inches (67 cm)

NECK WIDTH AT NUT: 1²⁵/₃₂ inches (4.5 cm)

NUMBER OF FRETS: 21

BRACING: Five parallel braces as in original Selmer models

FINISH: Nitrocellulose lacquer; top lacquer is pigmented and called vintage-orange finish

BODY DEPTH: 3⁹/₁₆ to 4⅛ inches (9 to 10.5 cm)

BODY LENGTH: 18½ inches (47 cm)

OVERALL LENGTH: 39⅜ inches (100 cm)

U.S. SUGGESTED RETAIL PRICE: Approximately $4,400

♠ **Stochelo Rosenberg Signature Model, 2001**
Leo T. Eimers, Eimers Guitars
Almere, The Netherlands

The Vienna Sunset

Theo Scharpach

Theo Scharpach is a contradiction—a forward looking, old school luthier who says he has never understood why other makers narrow their product lines so much. "This is not in the tradition of the art of instrument making," he asserts. "The craftsmen of the eighteenth and nineteenth centuries were much more versatile. A violin maker often makes cellos as well. Even Stradivari made guitars and other instruments but this is often not known."

Scharpach's new Vienna Sunset archtop builds on the fine art of violin or cello making, using similar acoustical design principles and starting points as Stradivari did for his top carving, while adapting them to guitar acoustics. The unusual open headstock features countersunk machine heads that Scharpach says tune more precisely than others. The guitar also features a bicolor, partially gold-plated titanium tailpiece designed by Scharpach, who believes a massive metal tailpiece does a much better acoustic job than an ebony tailpiece. "Even the wheel and thread in the adjustable bridge are made of titanium for reducing weight and lending a faster response time to the bridge," he adds.

Scharpach carves the Vienna Sunset from roughly pre-cut tops he bought more than 15 years from the widow of Artur Lang, a well-known German guitar maker who died in 1975. Although some of the topwood has minor visual flaws, Lang bought it when the supply of high quality wood was plentiful, and it is acoustically far superior to almost anything available today.

SPECIFICATIONS

BODY AND SIDE WOODS: Figured German maple

TOP WOOD: Spruce

BODY WIDTH, LOWER BOUT: 17¹³⁄₁₆ inches (45.2 cm)

ELECTRONICS: Floating custom humbucker on request

NECK WOOD: Figured German maple

FRETBOARD MATERIAL: Ebony

FRETBOARD INLAY: Mother-of-pearl dots on side only

HEADSTOCK DECORATION: Sterling silver machine covers, maple veneered headplate with black/white/black veneers

SOUND HOLE INLAYS: F-hole inlay—wooden purfling black/white/black and maple binding

BRIDGE: Ebony

NUT AND SADDLE: Mammoth; saddle, ebony

TUNING MACHINES: Custom-designed Scharpach

BINDING: Wooden purfling black/white/black and maple binding

SCALE LENGTH: 25.3 inches (64.3 cm)

NECK WIDTH AT NUT: 1¾ to 1⅞ inches (4.4 to 4.8 cm)

NUMBER OF FRETS: 24

BRACING: X bracing

FINISH: Custom

BODY DEPTH: 3¼ inches (8.2 cm)

BODY LENGTH: 21⅝ inches (55 cm)

OVERALL LENGTH: 42⅛ inches (107 cm)

♠ **The Vienna Sunset, 2005**
Theo Scharpach, Scharpach Guitars
Groessen, The Netherlands

Three Archtops

𝒶 born inventor and tinkerer, Woody Phifer had begun building go-carts, bicycles, kites, and remote control gliders by the time he was six. He majored in electronics and built wood sculptures in college and, inspired by Jimi Hendrix, took up the guitar as well. His curiosity about how things work soon led him in another direction. "I borrowed a friend's Fender, took it apart, and put it back together again," he says matter-of-factly. Based on his investigation, he started to build his own electric and, during a school break, took the train into New York to buy pickups for it. As fate would have it, he got off at the wrong stop and ended up in luthier Charlie LoBue's Guitar Lab. LoBue was looking for an intern and Phifer ended up working with him for five years.

Phifer's motto is, "If you don't have a Woody, you just have a guitar," and his instruments are decidedly different from other archtops. First and foremost, Phifer carves the back and sides of his instruments from a single piece of wood! He designed his own tailpiece and fully adjustable bridge as well as unique internal sound chambers that enhance the guitar's tone. He shapes his instruments with the human body in mind; the carved back of a Phifer hugs the body. The offset cutaways offer greater access to the fretboard, and the body is so well balanced in either a standing or seated playing position that a Phifer guitar will sit in a musician's lap or rest on his knee without support.

♠ **Three Archtops, 2000**
Sherwood "Woody" Phifer, Phifer Designs & Concepts
Garnerville, New York

252

SPECIFICATIONS

BODY AND SIDE WOODS: Maple

TOP WOOD: Sitka spruce

BODY WIDTH, LOWER BOUT: 15¾ and 17 inches (40 and 43.2 cm)

NECK WOOD: Maple

BRIDGE: Ebony

NUT AND SADDLE: Bone

TUNING MACHINES: Sperzel

BINDING: African ribbon mahogany

SCALE LENGTH: 25 or 25.5 inches (63.5 or 64.8 cm)

NECK WIDTH AT NUT: 1¾ inches (4.4 cm)

BODY DEPTH: 3⅜ inches (8.6 cm)

The Zeidler Project Archtop

When the late archtop builder John Zeidler was diagnosed with the acute myelogenous leukemia to which he ultimately succumbed, a who's who of his peers decided to build a special guitar to help defray his medical expenses and assist his family.

The project was coordinated by Linda Manzer. Details of the guitar's design were worked out by the entire group of 14 luthiers, who sought to pay tribute to Zeidler's style and preferences. The guitar traveled from shop to shop across North America, as each builder added his/her own touch before passing it on to the next luthier.

John Monteleone carved the soundboard from Adirondack red spruce chosen by Zeidler at the beginning of the project. Tom Ribbecke carved the back from maple also provided by Zeidler, and Steve Andersen

bent and attached the sides. Steve Grimes made and installed the koa binding, while John Buscarino, Bob Benedetto, and several others contributed to the neck. Mark Campellone detailed the headstock and added binding to the fingerboard and headstock, and Ted Megas installed the frets. Bill Comins provided the fingerboard and made and designed the tailpiece, using a hinge supplied by Buscarino. Bill Collings made the pickguard, while the truss rod cover, "Z" inlay, and nut were made by Mark Lacey. Linda Manzer made the bridge, and Tom Cerletti applied a special gilding to the headstock that was specially requested by Zeidler. The guitar was finished by Richard Hoover of Santa Cruz Guitars with assistance from Addam Stark and Stephen Strahm, and Al Williams of Calton Case Company donated a professional-quality case for the guitar.

"It's kind of an impossibility that this could happen," says John Monteleone. "Just the concept of pulling all these people together, [people] who had the highest regard for each other and for John. We all felt very close to him, very attached to his sense of style and his natural abilities."

SPECIFICATIONS

BODY AND SIDE WOODS: Quilted maple

TOP WOOD: Adirondack

BODY WIDTH, LOWER BOUT: 18⅛ inches (46 cm)

NECK WOOD: 5-ply maple/ebony/maple/ebony/maple

FRETBOARD MATERIAL: Ebony

HEADSTOCK DECORATION: Tom Cerletti variegated metallic headplate

BRIDGE: Two-piece ebony adjustable bridge

NUT AND SADDLE: Bone nut

TUNING MACHINES: Ebony button large Schaller

BINDING: Flamed koa

SCALE LENGTH: 25.5 inches (64.8 cm)

NECK WIDTH AT NUT: 1¾ inches (4.4 cm)

NUMBER OF FRETS: 22

BRACING: X bracing

FINISH: Natural

BODY DEPTH: 3⅛ inches (7.9 cm)

BODY LENGTH: 21¾ inches (55.2 cm)

OVERALL LENGTH: 43¼ inches (109.9 cm) including tailpin

U.S. SUGGESTED RETAIL PRICE: $100,000

▲ **The Zeidler Project Archtop, 2004–2005**
Steve Andersen, Robert Benedetto, John Buscarino, Mark Campellone, Tom Cerletti, Bill Collings, Bill Comins, Steve Grimes, Richard Hoover, Mark Lacey, John Monteleone, Linda Manzer, Ted Megas, and Tom Ribbecke
Courtesy of Stan Jay, Mandolin Brothers
Staten Island, New York

White Lightning

Dale Unger grew up in Nazareth, Pennsylvania, the home of C.F. Martin & Co., so he could hardly escape the spell of handcrafted guitars. Having such easy access to some to the world's finest craftsmen inspired him both to play guitars and then to build them. In the late 1970s, he collaborated on his first flattop guitar with long-time Martin employee Dick Boak (later to become head of Artist Relations and Publicity for the company). He began an apprenticeship with master archtop builder Bob Benedetto in 1993 and worked with him for three years before establishing his own archtop business. Unger has recently brought his career full circle, collaborating with Martin on an affordable archtop model built at the Martin factory under his supervision.

The White Lightning is a one-off that shows Unger at his best, firmly rooted in the Benedetto tradition, but clearly his own man, brewing his own potent concoctions.

◀ **White Lightning, 2002**
Dale Unger, American Archtop Guitars
Stroudsburg, Pennsylvania

255

SPECIFICATIONS

BODY AND SIDE WOODS: European flamed maple

TOP WOOD: German spruce

BODY WIDTH, LOWER BOUT: 16 inches (40.6 cm)

ELECTRONICS: Kent Armstrong floating pickup

NECK WOOD: Maple

FRETBOARD MATERIAL: Ebony

HEADSTOCK DECORATION: American archtop mother-of-pearl logo

BRIDGE: Ebony

NUT AND SADDLE: Ebony

TUNING MACHINES: Schaller with ebony knobs

SCALE LENGTH: 25 inches (63.5 cm)

NECK WIDTH AT NUT: 1¾ inches (4.4 cm)

NUMBER OF FRETS: 21

BRACING: X bracing

FINISH: Nitrocellulose lacquer

BODY DEPTH: 3 inches (7.6 cm)

BODY LENGTH: 20¼ inches (51.4 cm)

OVERALL LENGTH: 42 inches (106.7 cm)

U.S. SUGGESTED RETAIL PRICE: $8,000

ARCHTOP & OTHER JAZZ

Prelude #7

Otto D'Ambrosio repaired instruments at Mandolin Brothers, apprenticed for a time with John Monteleone, and then worked in the Guild factory in Westerly, Rhode Island, before striking out on his own in 1997. Recalling the many highly skilled older luthiers he worked with at Guild, a company that he characterizes as "possessed of tremendous amounts of old-world skill," D'Ambrosio says simply, "We grew sad, realizing that CNCs (computer numerical control machines) and cheap labor would soon displace years of tradition."

As a hand builder, D'Ambrosio wanted to continue working with the challenges of archtops and, over the past decade, he has built a reputation as an innovator. This thin-bodied Prelude is the result

of his search for sonic alternatives to the sound of traditional archtops. The guitar's shallow neck angle lessens stress on the body and allows D'Ambrosio to greatly reduce the thickness of the top, bracing, and back plates. Those changes gave him the deeper and more complex tonal range he was looking for, and, he adds with pride, "I believe my instruments are the first archtops that successfully produce the enhanced clarity of a flattop instrument."

SPECIFICATIONS

BODY AND SIDE WOODS: Premium grade figured big leaf maple

TOP WOOD: Sitka spruce

BODY WIDTH, LOWER BOUT: 17 inches (43.2 cm)

ELECTRONICS: Vintage DeArmond with volume and tone mounted on floating finger-rest

NECK WOOD: One-piece figured big leaf maple

FRETBOARD MATERIAL: Cocobolo

FRETBOARD INLAY: Stainless steel ring position and side markers

HEADSTOCK DECORATION: Laser cut stainless steel logo in ebony oval with pearl accents

BRIDGE: Carved cocobolo bridge base with thumbwheel action adjustment

NUT AND SADDLE: Fossilized ivory nut, carved ebony compensated saddle

TUNING MACHINES: Gotoh with pearloid buttons

BINDING: Cocobolo edge trim with ebony/maple/ebony purfling

SCALE LENGTH: 25 inches (63.5 cm)

NECK WIDTH AT NUT: 1 11/16 inches (4.3 cm)

NUMBER OF FRETS: 21

BRACING: Parallel braced

FINISH: Antique red burst

BODY DEPTH: 2 7/8 inches (7.3 cm)

BODY LENGTH: 21 inches (53.3 cm)

OVERALL LENGTH: 43 inches (109.2 cm)

♠ **Prelude #7, 2006**
Matt "Otto" D'Ambrosio
D'Ambrosio Archtop Guitars
Providence, Rhode Island

HAWAIIAN & RESONATOR

Hawaiian music, the first world music craze, was all the rage from 1910 through the 1930s. Along with the ukulele, the Hawaiian steel guitar, fretted with a steel bar and played lying flat on the player's knees, defined the music's sound. While the first Hawaiian guitars were simply standard acoustic steel-strings with a converter nut slipped in to raise the strings above the frets, guitars designed specifically for Hawaiian-style playing were introduced by luthiers Chris Knutsen and Hermann Weissenborn soon after the Hawaiian craze hit mainland America, and their designs remain the standard today,

The resonator guitar, invented in the late 1920s by a Czech immigrant named John Dopyera, incorporated metal resonator cones into the body of the instrument to increase volume. The original National resonator guitars had cast metal bodies, while a wooden-bodied resonator guitar,

dubbed the Dobro, was introduced soon after. The Dobro, now a registered trademark of Gibson, is a square-necked instrument that can only be played with a slide, while National's metal-bodied guitars were offered in both square-neck and standard round Spanish-neck versions.

Although they declined precipitously in popularity after the introduction of the electric guitar in the 1930s, Hawaiian and resonator guitars were rediscovered in the 1960s along with the blues, country, and Hawaiian music they made possible in the 1920s and '30s. Today, dozens of luthiers specialize in these once forgotten instruments, allowing players to revive and build upon the great traditions of Hawaiian and resonator music.

Old Crippled Charles

his unique custom eight-string, square-neck resonator is built entirely from marbled Macassar ebony complemented with gold-plated hardware.

Marbled Macassar ebony is an outstanding tonewood from East Indonesia that has striking alternating bands of black and light tan. The guitar's body is asymmetrical, one inch (2.5 cm) thicker at the neck than at the heel block. "It's so subtle and well-executed,

nobody even notices until I point it out," says the owner, Charles Fisher. "The shape allows me to play for a much longer time without shoulder pain. The headstock is elegant, shaped for low weight, and besides, Mr. Benoit and I just really like alligators."

Eight or more strings are not uncommon since the strings are fretted with a slide. The extra strings extend the guitar's range and open up the variety of note positions and combinations available to the player.

Old Crippled Charles, 2003 ▶
Carroll Benoit, Benoit Resonator Guitars
Mauriceville, Texas

SPECIFICATIONS

BODY AND SIDE WOODS: Macassar ebony

TOP WOOD: Macassar ebony

BODY WIDTH, LOWER BOUT: 14¼ inches (36.2 cm)

NECK WOOD: Curly maple

FRETBOARD MATERIAL: Ebony

FRETBOARD INLAY: Half moon position markers with inlaid mother-of-pearl frets

HEADSTOCK DECORATION: Slotted headstock, Benoit with Bethlehem star logo

SOUND HOLE INLAYS: Sound hole screens, coverplate, and tailpiece engraved by Steffan Baker, 24-karat gold plated

BRIDGE: Hard rock maple

NUT AND SADDLE: Bone

TUNING MACHINES: #4065 gold Waverly with ebony knobs

BINDING: Ebony with w/b strips

SCALE LENGTH: 22.9 inches (58.1 cm)

NECK WIDTH AT NUT: 2⅞ inches (7.3 cm)

NUMBER OF FRETS: 20

BRACING: Soundwell

FINISH: Nitrocellulose lacquer

BODY DEPTH: 4¼ inches (10.8 cm) at neck, 3¼ inches (8.3 cm) at heel

BODY LENGTH: 18½ inches (47 cm)

OVERALL LENGTH: 38 inches (96.5 cm)

U.S. SUGGESTED RETAIL PRICE: $4,200

Large Body Koa Resonator

*T*odd Clinesmith, who freely admits he is "an all-around Dobro fanatic," builds resonator and Hawaiian guitars and plays reso in a Bluegrass band and steel guitar in what he describes as a "Western swing/real country band."

Clinesmith builds six-, seven-, or eight-string models and uses a unique sound post/baffle construction instead of the plywood "soundwell" found in traditional resonator guitars. "With sound posts transferring sound from the top to the back and baffles optimizing projection," he explains, "the entire body of the guitar—along with the resonator chamber—contributes to the sound, producing superior volume and bass, and a brighter, fuller tone that grows as the instrument ages."

This is Clinesmith's personal guitar.

♠ Large Body Koa Resonator, 2005
Todd Clinesmith, Clinesmith Instruments
Glide, Oregon

SPECIFICATIONS

BODY AND SIDE WOODS: Curly koa

TOP WOOD: Curly koa

BODY WIDTH, LOWER BOUT: 14¼ inches (36.2 cm)

NECK WOOD: Curly koa

FRETBOARD MATERIAL: Ziricote

FRETBOARD INLAY: Abalone dots, mother-of-pearl script

HEADSTOCK DECORATION: Ziricote

NUT AND SADDLE: Bone nut

TUNING MACHINES: Waverly

BINDING: Curly koa

SCALE LENGTH: 25 inches (63.5 cm)

NECK WIDTH AT NUT: 1⅞ inches (4.8 cm)

NUMBER OF FRETS: 19

BRACING: Sitka spruce

FINISH: Hand-rubbed hard oil

BODY DEPTH: 4 inches (10.2 cm)

BODY LENGTH: 19⅞ inches (50.5 cm)

U.S. SUGGESTED RETAIL PRICE: $4,200

261

Randy Allen
Squareneck Resonator

hile Randy Allen's resonator guitars have a body shape that is based on a late 1920s Dobro, they differ from traditional instruments in many ways.

Early resonators were ruggedly built and heavily braced, often with inexpensive wood, but like several other contemporary luthiers, Allen builds his deep-bodied instruments from high-grade solid woods such as flamed maple, myrtle, mahogany, and walnut and embellishes them with fine hardware, exotic wood bindings, intricate purflings and inlays, and elegant hand-engraved hardware.

Allen also takes an alternative approach to the resonator itself, using a baffleless structure held up by sound posts that transfer the load off the top to the back, which is braced to resist the load. He bolts the coverplate into the top with machine-threaded inserts. "The traditional method," Allen explains, "is to attach the coverplate with wood screws that usually strip out over time. The extra work and expense is more than justified by creating greater structural integrity where it is needed. When you make a hole this big in a guitar, it will definitely need some strengthening! Who knows," he adds, "this instrument may have gotten its start by [someone] trying to fix that screwed-up sound hole rosette purfling!"

SPECIFICATIONS

BODY AND SIDE WOODS: Koa

TOP WOOD: German spruce

NECK WOOD: Mahogany

FRETBOARD MATERIAL: Ebony

FRETBOARD INLAY: Mother-of-pearl, green abalone, and paua shell

HEADSTOCK DECORATION: Mother-of-pearl and paua shell

SOUND HOLE INLAYS: Paua

BRIDGE: Spider

NUT AND SADDLE: Bone and maple

TUNING MACHINES: Imperial

BINDING: Curly koa

SCALE LENGTH: 25.5 inches (64.8 cm)

NECK WIDTH AT NUT: 1¾ inches (4.4 cm)

FINISH: Lacquer

U.S. SUGGESTED RETAIL PRICE: $7,900

♠ **Squareneck Resonator, 2003**
Randy Allen, Allen Guitar & Luthier Supplies
Colfax, California

Maalaea Artist Series

Richard Mermer Jr.

$\mathcal{R}$ich Mermer Jr. studied luthiery at the Roberto-Venn School of Luthiery in Phoenix. One of Mermer's instructors at Roberto-Venn was musician and master craftsman William Eaton, who is best known for his highly original harp guitars. Eaton's example gave Mermer permission to move beyond building "clones" of popular designs and follow his own muse.

While the shape of Mermer's Maalaea acoustic lap steel guitar was inspired by the classic Weissenborn Hawaiian guitars of the 1920s, its construction is considerably different. Mermer modified the internal bracing pattern to take full advantage of the guitar's large resonating cavity and added offset sound holes and "trap door" access at the butt. The opening at the butt allows easy access to the inside of the guitar and can also serve as a gateway and platform for any electronics the player wants to add.

SPECIFICATIONS

BODY AND SIDE WOODS: All figured koa

TOP WOOD: Figured koa

BODY WIDTH, LOWER BOUT: 15¼ inches (38.7 cm)

FRETBOARD MATERIAL: Ebony, bound in ebony

FRETBOARD INLAY: Koa and pearl "M" at 12th fret, pearl dots, maple fret lines

HEADSTOCK DECORATION: Koa overlay with koa binding and b-w-b purfling, koa underlay

SOUND HOLE INLAYS: Koa and pearl weave set in ebony

BRIDGE: Ebony

NUT AND SADDLE: Bone

TUNING MACHINES: Gold Schallers with ebony buttons

BINDING: Koa with b-w-b purfling

SCALE LENGTH: 28 inches (71.1 cm)

NECK WIDTH AT NUT: 2⅛ inches (5.4 cm)

NUMBER OF FRETS: 20

BRACING: X with modifications in the upper bout

FINISH: Nitrocellulose lacquer

BODY DEPTH: 2⅛ to 3⅞ inches (5.4 to 9.8 cm)

BODY LENGTH: 34½ inches (87.6 cm)

OVERALL LENGTH: 40¾ inches (103.5 cm)

U.S. SUGGESTED RETAIL PRICE: $4,975

♠ **Maalaea Artist Series**
Richard Mermer Jr., Mermer Guitars
Sebastian, Florida

263

Paul Beard

Chancellorsville Square-Neck & Gods and Generals Round-Neck Resonators with Artwork by Rick Parks

These two extraordinary guitars pay tribute to some of the heroes of the pivotal Civil War battles of Chancellorsville, which took place May 1 through 5, 1863, and Gettysburg, which was fought July 1 through 3 of the same year.

Chancellorsville, a resounding Confederate victory that opened the way to the Army of Northern Virginia's invasion of the North, is regarded as Robert E. Lee's greatest strategic battle. It was a bittersweet victory for the South, however, because among the 30,000 Union and Confederate casualties was Lee's "right arm," Thomas "Stonewall" Jackson, who was mortally wounded by friendly fire on

May 3. Lee appears on the headstock of the Chancellorsville guitar, while Jackson is depicted on the treble side of the Gods and Generals guitar. The South's Major General J.E.B. (James Ewell Brown) Stuart, who took over Jackson's command after he was shot, and his lieutenant, the legendary partisan raider John Singleton Mosby, face each other on the upper bout of the Chancellorsville guitar, while Jackson is paired with the only Yankee on the guitars, Colonel Joshua Lawrence Chamberlain, commander of the 20th Maine, which successfully held the Union left at Little Round Top on the first day of the battle of Gettysburg.

The flamboyant, heavily bearded Stuart, who rode to battle wearing a red-lined gray cape, a yellow sash, and a cocked hat festooned with a peacock feather, was the South's greatest cavalry officer. Mosby, by contrast, specialized in not being noticed; known as the "Gray Ghost," he lead daring, lightning fast raids behind Union lines and then dismayed his pursuers by seemingly disappearing into thin air. Stuart was killed in May 1864, but Mosby fought on to the war's end. He never formally surrendered and lived until 1916.

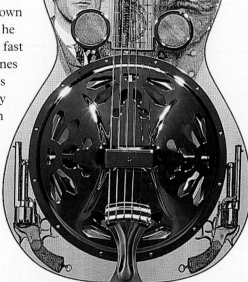

♦ **Chancellorsville Square-Neck Resonator, Artwork by Rick Parks, 1999**
Paul Beard, Beard Guitars
Hagerstown, Maryland

SPECIFICATIONS

BODY AND SIDE WOODS: Wenge

TOP WOOD: Sitka spruce

BODY WIDTH, LOWER BOUT: 14¼ inches (36.2 cm)

NECK WOOD: Mahogany

FRETBOARD MATERIAL: Zebrawood

FRETBOARD INLAY: Drawn artwork

HEADSTOCK DECORATION: Drawn artwork

BRIDGE: Ebony-capped maple

NUT AND SADDLE: Bone nut

TUNING MACHINES: Grover

BINDING: Ivoroid

SCALE LENGTH: 25 inches (63.5 cm)

NECK WIDTH AT NUT: 1⅞ inches (4.8 cm)

NUMBER OF FRETS: 24 abalone frets

BRACING: Soundwell construction

FINISH: Lacquer

BODY DEPTH: 3⅝ inches (9.2 cm)

BODY LENGTH: 19½ inches (49.5 cm)

OVERALL LENGTH: 39 inches (99.1 cm)

U.S. SUGGESTED RETAIL PRICE: $9,500

264

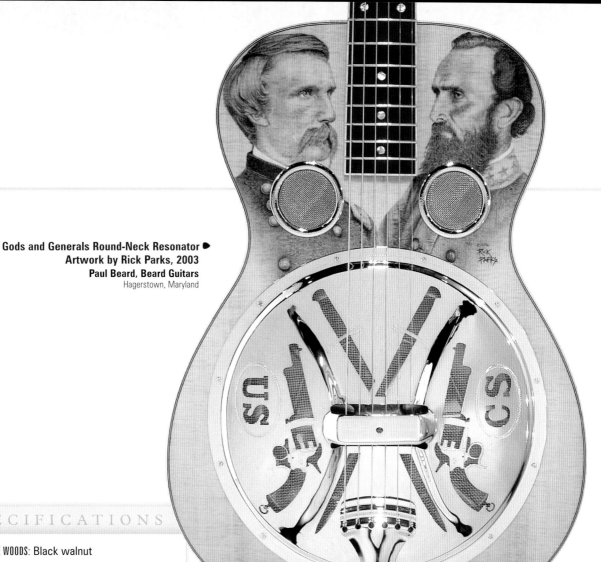

Gods and Generals Round-Neck Resonator ▶
Artwork by Rick Parks, 2003
Paul Beard, Beard Guitars
Hagerstown, Maryland

SPECIFICATIONS

BODY AND SIDE WOODS: Black walnut

TOP WOOD: Sitka spruce

BODY WIDTH, LOWER BOUT: 14¼ inches (36.2 cm)

NECK WOOD: Mahogany

FRETBOARD MATERIAL: Ebony

FRETBOARD INLAY: Abalone dots

HEADSTOCK DECORATION: Abalone logo and truss rod cover

BRIDGE: Ebony-capped maple

NUT AND SADDLE: Bone nut

TUNING MACHINES: Schaller

BINDING: Curly maple

SCALE LENGTH: 25 inches (63.5 cm)

NECK WIDTH AT NUT: 1¾ inches (4.4 cm)

NUMBER OF FRETS: 19

BRACING: Soundwell

FINISH: Poly

BODY DEPTH: 3⅝ inches (9.2 cm)

BODY LENGTH: 19½ inches (49.5 cm)

OVERALL LENGTH: 38½ inches (97.8 cm)

U.S. SUGGESTED RETAIL PRICE: $19,500

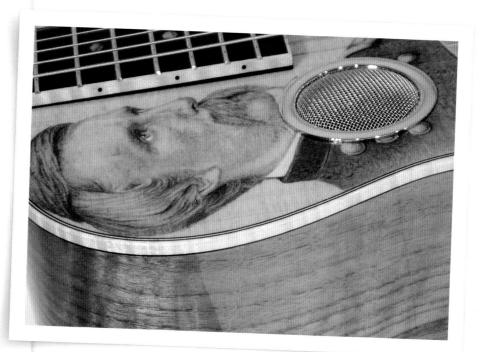

Terraplane, Arlen Roth
Signature Model Serial #1

*B*uild me a guitar with a coverplate that resembles the hubcap of my 1930's Hudson Terraplane car. Call it the Terraplane." So said the great slide guitarist Arlen Roth to his friend and luthier Mark Simon. The two worked together on the design, which includes a patent-pending string-anchoring system. The system puts greater string tension against the bridge saddle for increased tone and volume, and, unlike other resonators, does not have a tailpiece, which would vibrate and rattle against the coverplate. The guitar is also available with magnetic pickups custom designed by Jason Lollar and a unique pickup raising/lowering system and mute (patent pending) that allow the instrument to be used in either an acoustic or electric mode.

SPECIFICATIONS

BODY AND SIDES: Nickel-plated brass

TOP WOOD: Brass, spun brass coverplate, spun resonator cone, cast aluminum spider, hammer-formed logo indentation, bridge cover and string cover

BODY WIDTH, LOWER BOUT: 14½ inches (36.8 cm)

ELECTRONICS: Two Jason Lollar Chicago Steels magnetic pickups

NECK WOOD: Mahogany

FRETBOARD MATERIAL: Ebony

FRETBOARD INLAY: Ivory

HEADSTOCK DECORATION: Pearl acetate, hand-engraved borders, decal

BRIDGE: Maple on aluminum cast spider

NUT AND SADDLE: Ivory nut, maple compensated saddle

TUNING MACHINES: Kluson strip

BINDING: Rolled wired edge, hand formed, single white celluloid on fingerboard

SCALE LENGTH: 24.75 inches (62.9 cm)

NECK WIDTH AT NUT: 1⅞ inches (4.8 cm)

NUMBER OF FRETS: 19

FINISH: Nickel-plated brass

BODY DEPTH: 3½ inches (8.9 cm)

BODY LENGTH: 18¾ inches (47.6 cm)

OVERALL LENGTH: 38¼ inches (97.2 cm)

U.S. SUGGESTED RETAIL PRICE: $10,000

Terraplane, Arlen Roth ♦
Signature Model Serial #1, 1994
**Designed by Mark Simon and Arlen Roth,
built by Mark Simon, Mark Simon Guitars**
Bridgewater, New Jersey

Dart Style–4 Hawaiian Guitar

David Dart specializes in Hawaiian slide guitars made in the traditional style of early twentieth-century instruments by Kona, Chris Knutsen, and Hermann Weissenborn. Their guitars, which were made to be played lying flat in the player's lap, have hollow necks that give them incredible volume and sustain. In effect, the sides of the guitars narrow and continue up to the headstock, creating a single enormous sound chamber, with a result that has often been compared to a piano. Since they are always played with a slide, the strings are raised well above the fingerboard to avoid fret noise from metal hitting metal.

Although Dart grew up in a musical family, he is largely self-taught as a luthier. He built his first instrument, a mountain dulcimer, when he was 14, and has gone on to make a wide range of acoustic instruments including mandolins, violins, a variety of guitars, Middle Eastern sazes and ouds (built for L.A. studio wizard David Lindley), and lutes and other Renaissance instruments. Dart's "museum-style lutes" were one of the inspirations for a unique bowl-back Hawaiian guitar he designed for slide master Ben Harper. While his Hawaiian guitars are inspired by early examples, Dart insists that his instruments are by no means slavish copies. "My guitars are built with both top and back radiussed and the braces voiced to produce the best acoustic response and the most stability," he explains.

SPECIFICATIONS

BODY AND SIDE WOODS: Honduran mahogany

TOP WOOD: Honduran mahogany

BODY WIDTH, LOWER BOUT: 15 inches (38.1 cm)

NECK WOOD: Honduran mahogany

FRETBOARD MATERIAL: Ebony

FRETBOARD INLAY: Sea otters of ivory (old piano keys); abalone, mother-of-pearl; silver frets

HEADSTOCK DECORATION: Owl is abalone heart on mother-of-pearl

SOUND HOLE INLAYS: Abalone with black and white rings

BRIDGE: Ebony with abalone inlay

NUT AND SADDLE: Bone

TUNING MACHINES: Waverly

BINDING: Abalone purfling with ebony edge binding

SCALE LENGTH: 25 inches (63.5 cm)

NECK WIDTH AT NUT: 2¹⁄₁₆ inches (5.2 cm)

NUMBER OF FRETS: 19

BRACING: Elongated X

FINISH: Lacquer

BODY DEPTH: 3 inches (7.6 cm) at end to 1½ inches (3.8 cm) at head

BODY LENGTH: 31 inches (78.7 cm)

OVERALL LENGTH: 39 inches (99.1 cm)

U.S. SUGGESTED RETAIL PRICE: $6,000

267

🌢 **Dart Style–4 Hawaiian Guitar, 2001**
David L. Dart, Dart Instruments
Philo, California

Mecano Tricone Style 3, Ivy Engraved

Like National's top-of-the-line originals, this contemporary triplate has a nickel-plated German silver body and a triple resonator, with three aluminum cones arranged in a triangle. Two of the cones are set on the bass side of the guitar, one on the treble, and all three are connected to a T-shaped aluminum bridge that sits under a wooden saddle. When the strings are plucked or strummed, the vibrations travel through the saddle to the bridge and finally on to the three resonator cones.

German silver is actually not silver at all, but a silver-colored alloy of nickel, copper, and zinc that has been used to make inexpensive jewelry and household utensils since the mid-1800s.

◄ **Mecano Tricone Style 3, Ivy Engraved, 1990**
Mike Lewis and Pierre Avocat, Fine Resophonic
Vitry-sur-Seine, France

SPECIFICATIONS

BODY AND SIDE WOODS: Nickel-plated brass

BODY WIDTH, LOWER BOUT: 14⅛ inches (36 cm)

NECK WOOD: Flamed maple

FRETBOARD MATERIAL: Ebony

FRETBOARD INLAY: Pearl and abalone

HEADSTOCK DECORATION: Pearloid and abalone

BRIDGE: Maple biscuit

NUT AND SADDLE: Bone nut

TUNING MACHINES: Kluson

BINDING: Ivoroid

SCALE LENGTH: 25.3 inches (64.3 cm)

NECK WIDTH AT NUT: 1²⁵⁄₃₂ inches (4.5 cm)

NUMBER OF FRETS: 19

FINISH: Nickel plating

BODY DEPTH: 2¹⁵⁄₁₆ inches (7.5 cm) front; 3⁵⁄₁₆ inches (8.5 cm) back

BODY LENGTH: 19¹¹⁄₁₆ inches (50 cm)

OVERALL LENGTH: 38³⁄₁₆ inches (97 cm)

U.S. SUGGESTED RETAIL PRICE: Approximately $8,000

Forbidden Fruit
12-String Snake

Forbidden Fruit 12-String Snake, 2001 ▶
Paul Norman, Forbidden Fruit Guitars
Cambridge, Massachusetts

SPECIFICATIONS

BODY AND SIDE WOODS: Rope and straight-grain cherry

TOP WOOD: Rope and straight-grain cherry

BODY WIDTH, LOWER BOUT: 17 inches (43.2 cm)

NECK WOOD: Walnut and maple

FRETBOARD MATERIAL: Ebony

FRETBOARD INLAY: Gold mother-of-pearl diamonds

HEADSTOCK DECORATION: Apple—cocobolo, ebony, walnut, blue mahoe

SOUND HOLE INLAYS: Snake—treated (darkened) lacewood background, curly and burled maple diamonds, tiger eye (snake's eyes)

BRIDGE: Carbon fiber biscuit bridge

NUT AND SADDLE: Bone nut

TUNING MACHINES: Gold Waverly open back

BINDING: Walnut

SCALE LENGTH: 23.6 inches (60 cm)

NECK WIDTH AT NUT: 2⅛ inches (5.4 cm)

NUMBER OF FRETS: 12 to body, 18 overall

BRACING: Laminate cone well

FINISH: Hand-applied varnish

BODY DEPTH: 4 inches (10.2 cm) lower bout, 3½ inches (8.9 cm) at heel

BODY LENGTH: 20¾ inches (52.7 cm)

OVERALL LENGTH: 43⅜ inches (110.2 cm)

U.S. SUGGESTED RETAIL PRICE: $7,000

270

𝒫aul Norman studied guitar making with the accomplished Canadian luthier Alan Carruth, and his unusual focus as a builder grew out of a friendly rivalry between the two men. Norman and Carruth challenged each other to see who could build the wildest possible instrument. Norman continues the story: "I said, 'How about a 12-string resonator, hah!' Al said, 'Build it!' Thus was born Forbidden Fruit Guitars."

Somewhat to his surprise, Norman's guitar turned out to be a perfect guitar for a performing musician, with a big, bluesy sound easily able to cut through the din of the loudest bar without amplification. Norman proudly sums up his experiment this way: "This is the largest, loudest, and most outrageous resonator guitar you can find. If snakes were this loud and clear, nobody would ever get bit."

Pasifika Tricone Lap Guitar

eltona grew from the efforts of a pair of British resonator fanatics, luthier Steve Evans and engineer Bill Johnson, who set out to produce a couple of instruments for themselves. No one else was making metal-bodied resonator guitars at the time and demand for their high quality, handcrafted metal instruments, which replicated the best features of the originals but also made adjustments and improvements where they were needed, grew their efforts into a business.

Although they started handcrafting metal-bodied resonators in the style of classic National steel guitars of the 1920s and '30s, Beltona has made only carbon and glass fiber instruments since 2002. Building with space age materials was originally undertaken as a way to cut down on production costs and time, but, in addition to greatly increasing the ease and speed of production, the new materials also projected sound better than the originals and were lighter and stronger than metal to boot.

Like the original Nationals it is patterned after, the Beltona Pasifika Tricone has a square, hollow neck and is intended solely for lap-style slide playing. The body is made of molded-glass fiber-reinforced resin, and the neck and the piece that connects the three interior resonators are carbon fiber.

271

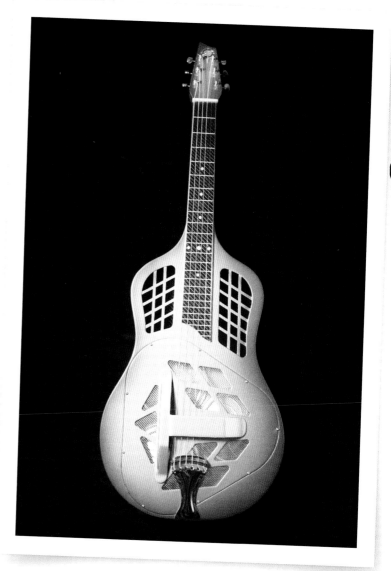

◄ **Pasifika Tricone Lap Guitar, 2004**
Steve Evans, Beltona Resonator Instruments
Whangarei, New Zealand

SPECIFICATIONS

BODY AND SIDE WOODS: Fiberglass

TOP WOOD: Carbon fiber

BODY WIDTH, LOWER BOUT: 14 inches (35.6 cm)

NECK WOOD: Hollow construction

FRETBOARD MATERIAL: Carbon fiber

FRETBOARD INLAY: Printed

HEADSTOCK DECORATION: Carbon fiber

BRIDGE: Aluminum T-piece with boxwood saddle

TUNING MACHINES: Gotoh

NECK WIDTH AT NUT: 1⅞ inches (4.8 cm)

NUMBER OF FRETS: 24

FINISH: Auto paint

BODY DEPTH: 3⅛ inches (7.9 cm)

BODY LENGTH: 19 inches (48.3 cm)

OVERALL LENGTH: 38⅜ inches (97.5 cm)

Resonator Guitar for Gregg Miner

Multi-instrumentalist and collector Gregg Miner, who managed to play all of the then-100 instruments in his Miner Museum of Vintage, Exotic, and Just Plain Unusual Instruments on a pair of Christmas CDs he recorded in 1995, commissioned the versatile luthier and repairman Kerry Char to build this unique all-koa resonator guitar.

The two men met through Miner's passionate interest in vintage harp guitars, several of which Char has repaired. After hearing one of Char's koa resonators with its special, custom internal baffling system, Miner said he "had to have one." He designed the headstock inlay and chose the "Violette" pattern (named for a special Dobro presentation model made for Rudy Dopyera's niece around 1929) for the resonator. All the hardware

on Dopyera's guitar was gold-plated, so Miner was delighted when he met master-engraver David Giulietti and was able to add his engraved, gold-plated hardware to the guitar a few months after Char completed it.

In addition to his specialty of building and repairing harp guitars, Kerry Char also crafts classical, flamenco, and acoustic flattop guitars. He says that working with Gregg Miner allowed him to make connections with a whole network of people "involved in cool old instruments" and eventually to quit his 16-year stint as a baggage handler for Continental Airlines. "Even if I were a successful builder, I probably would still want to do some repair work, at least the restoration part," says Char. "That's the fun stuff. People send me stuff from all over the place," he says. "I love getting boxes in the mail. It's always something interesting."

◀ **Resonator Guitar
for Gregg Miner, 1997
Kerry Char, Kerry Char Lutheries**
Portland, Oregon

SPECIFICATIONS

BODY AND SIDE WOODS: Koa

TOP WOOD: Koa

BODY WIDTH, LOWER BOUT: 14 inches (35.6 cm)

FRETBOARD MATERIAL: Ebony

FRETBOARD INLAY: Abalone

HEADSTOCK DECORATION: Pearl caricature of owner (Gregg Miner)

NUT AND SADDLE: Bone

SCALE LENGTH: 25 inches (63.5 cm)

NECK WIDTH AT NUT: 1⅞ inches (4.8 cm)

FINISH: Lacquer

BODY DEPTH: 3½ inches (8.9 cm)

BODY LENGTH: 20 inches (50.8 cm)

OVERALL LENGTH: 38½ inches (97.8 cm)

U.S. SUGGESTED RETAIL PRICE: $3,600

Style O Single Resonator

The original National guitars—metal-bodied instruments with internal resonators that amplified their sound—were produced by the National String Instrument Corporation, founded in 1927 by a Czech immigrant named John Dopyera. Three to five times louder than a conventional guitar, they satisfied the need of guitarists to be heard over the horns in a jazz band, the din in a bar, or the ruckus of a street corner. The guitars, which produced an extremely loud, brash, and (not surprisingly) metallic sound, were offered with either a square "Hawaiian" neck for lap-style slide playing or a conventional rounded "Spanish" neck, and they became the favored instrument of many Hawaiian, blues, and early country musicians.

Resonator guitars went out of favor after the first electric guitars appeared in the mid-1930s, and by end of the decade, they had become obsolete. The resurgence of interest in early blues and Hawaiian guitar playing in the 1970s and '80s drove prices of vintage Nationals up and convinced Don Young and McGregor Gaines that there was a market for new instruments. They founded National Reso-Phonic in 1989, and the company now produces an extensive line of single and triple "Tricone" resonator instruments that replicate and extend the National tradition.

♠ **Style O Single Resonator, 2006**
National Reso-Phonic Guitars
San Luis Obispo, California

SPECIFICATIONS

BODY AND SIDE WOODS: Etched, nickel-plated polished brass

TOP WOOD: Etched, nickel-plated polished brass

BODY WIDTH, LOWER BOUT: 14 inches (35.6 cm)

NECK WOOD: Hard rock maple

FRETBOARD MATERIAL: Ebony bound in cross-grain ivoroid

BRIDGE: Brass

NUT AND SADDLE: Bone

TUNING MACHINES: Three-on-a-plate vintage style open gear

SCALE LENGTH: 25 inches (63.5 cm)

NECK WIDTH AT NUT: 1 13/16 inches (4.6 cm)

BODY DEPTH: 3 1/8 inches (7.9 cm)

273

Rustbucket Tricone

When Don Morrison first got interested in metal-bodied resonator guitars, they just weren't available in South Australia. He decided to try to make his own, but, because there also were no books on the subject, he had to start from scratch and recalls that his first efforts involved the steel from the door of an old Volvo car! "I soon realized it was way too heavy," he recalls. "I would lay awake at night thinking of ways to overcome difficulties and eventually got one guitar made well enough to string it up. I made another, better one and then one for a friend, and now, seven years later, I don't have time to do very much else."

Morrison now makes a variety of wood and steel-bodied single and tricone guitars as well as resonator ukes and mandolins. Like many of his steel guitars, this one is built from salvaged Galvo, the galvanized steel sheets from which Aussies made millions of houses, sheds, water tanks, and fences because wood was in short supply in many areas of the country. Morrison complements the naturally weathered and corroded Galvo with an artificially rusted cone and sound holes. He induces rust with vinegar and peroxide and then lacquers the steel when it has reached the right look to halt the process and preserve the wonderfully grungy surface.

◀ **Rustbucket Tricone, 2006**
Don Morrison, Donmo Resonator Guitars
Klemzig, Australia

SPECIFICATIONS

BODY AND SIDES: Reclaimed corrugated iron, rolled flat

BODY WIDTH, LOWER BOUT: 13¾ inches (35 cm)

ELECTRONICS: Donmo tricone pickup

FRETBOARD MATERIAL: Reclaimed jarrah (from the floor joists of a demolished house)

BRIDGE: Maple

NUT AND SADDLE: Bone nut

SCALE LENGTH: 25.5 inches (64.8 cm)

NECK WIDTH AT NUT: 1⅞ inches (4.8 cm)

NUMBER OF FRETS: 19

BODY DEPTH: 3⁵⁄₁₆ inches (8.5 cm)

BODY LENGTH: 19¹¹⁄₁₆ inches (50 cm)

OVERALL LENGTH: 39¾ inches (101 cm)

Round Neck Resophonic Cutaway

*J*oseph Yanuziello studied painting and sculpture at art college and then, like many people, did something completely different when he graduated. He made his first guitar in 1979 and says "building instruments combines a lot of my interests: design, engineering, fabrication, and last but not least, playing and listening to music."

Yanuziello makes a wide variety of guitars, including solid- and hollow-bodied electric guitars, solid-bodied electric mandolins, mandolas, and mandocellos, acoustic flattops, acoustic and electric Hawaiian steels, cutaway and non-cutaway resonators, and even a komungo, an ancient Korean instrument related to the Chinese ch'in and Japanese koto. Describing his resonators, Yanuziello says, "These guitars have a clear tone with full bass and treble response and enough volume to wake up the neighbors."

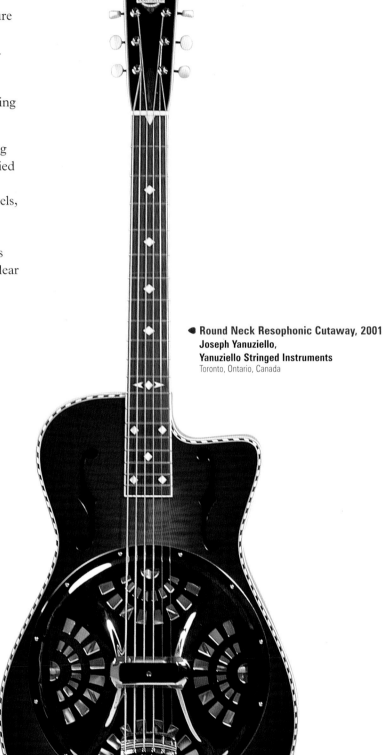

◀ **Round Neck Resophonic Cutaway, 2001**
Joseph Yanuziello,
Yanuziello Stringed Instruments
Toronto, Ontario, Canada

SPECIFICATIONS

BODY AND SIDE WOODS: Curly maple

TOP WOOD: Curly maple

BODY WIDTH, LOWER BOUT: 14⅛ inches (35.9 cm)

NECK WOOD: Curly maple

FRETBOARD MATERIAL: Ebony

FRETBOARD INLAY: Corian diamonds and arrows

HEADSTOCK DECORATION: Yanuziello decal logo

BRIDGE: Spider and maple saddle inserts

NUT AND SADDLE: Bone nut, hard maple saddle

TUNING MACHINES: Gotoh Kluson style

BINDING: Ivoroid, holly, and ebony parallelogram purfling

SCALE LENGTH: 25 inches (63.5 cm)

NECK WIDTH AT NUT: 1¾ inches (4.4 cm)

NUMBER OF FRETS: 19

FINISH: Sunburst, pre-catalyzed lacquer

BODY DEPTH: 3¼ inches (8.3 cm) to 3½ inches (8.9 cm) at end pin

BODY LENGTH: 19⅞ inches (50.5 cm)

OVERALL LENGTH: 39 inches (99.1 cm)

U.S. SUGGESTED RETAIL PRICE: $4,200

ELECTRIC GUITARS

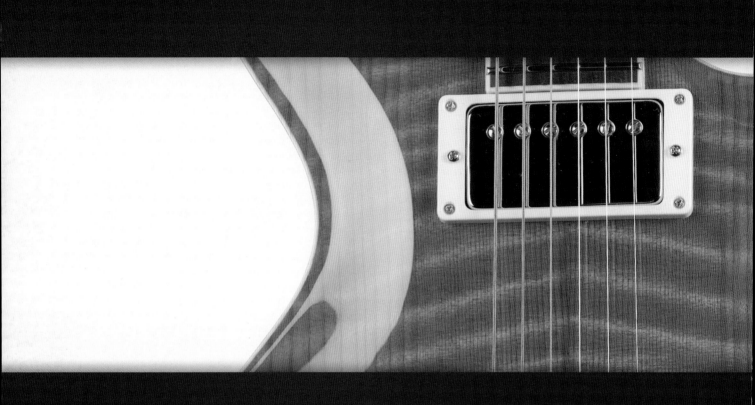

HOLLOW & SOLID BODIED ELECTRICS

The first viable electric guitars appeared in the early 1930s, and while sales were initially slow, the concept began to take hold after Gibson and National introduced their first electrics in the middle of the decade. Although a few builders, including guitarist and inventor Les Paul, experimented with solid-bodied instruments, the electric guitar remained basically a hollow-bodied acoustic with added magnetic pickups throughout the 1930s and '40s, with Gibson's increasingly sophisticated instruments dominating the market during those years.

Leo Fender, who has often been called the Henry Ford of the electric guitar, introduced the first commercially successful solid-bodied electric guitar, the bare bones Telecaster, in 1950 and followed with the comparatively sleek and feature-laden Stratocaster in 1954. Gibson responded quickly, bringing out its first solid-bodied electric, the carved-top Les Paul Model,

in 1952. The looks and sounds of these three guitars have defined the genre ever since and inspired thousands of copies and imitations over the years.

Beginning with Alembic in the early 1970s, a generation of young designers and builders who had "cut their teeth" on Fenders and Gibsons began to work with the electric guitar, improving its electronics and experimenting with form and materials. Today, while Fender and Gibson remain industry leaders, many smaller companies and independent builders continue to refine and improve the founding fathers' original designs as well as to create original instruments with strikingly new looks and sonic capabilities.

Fender

1956 Stratocaster Relic Ltd.

The Fender Stratocaster, conceived and introduced by Leo Fender in 1954, is the most imitated guitar of all time and a recognized masterpiece of twentieth century industrial design. Dozens, if not hundreds, of manufacturers and individual luthiers around the world have copied Fender's design as closely as patent laws allow, and Fender itself has issued spot-on copies of coveted early models like this 1956 Taos Turquoise in response to the demand for rare and expensive originals.

The Strat was intended to serve as a refined, upscale complement to the Telecaster. It retailed for $324 when it was introduced in 1954, more than twice the price of a Tele. It was the first double cutaway electric solid body, with a horned, contoured body form, three pickups, and a unique vibrato system that Fender called a "tremolo bar."

The 1956 Strat is one of the most coveted and collectible of all Fenders, and since the gorgeous Taos Turquoise finish was only available as a custom order in 1956, originals in this color are few and far between. This reproduction, made in a limited run of 100 instruments, is part of Fender's Relic series and features all original detailing built from original tooling, including a 10/'56 "Boat Neck" shape and a reverse wound/reverse polarity middle pickup. Fender also recreated tooling holes and marks made during the original production process and applied its Relic treatment to imitate "years of natural wear and tear, with nicks, scratches, worn finish, rusty hardware, and aged plastic parts."

1956 Stratocaster Relic Ltd. (Taos Turquoise), 2006 ▶
Fender Custom Shop,
Fender Musical Instruments Corporation
Corona, California

279

SPECIFICATIONS

BODY AND SIDE WOODS: Select swamp ash

TOP WOOD: Select swamp ash

BODY WIDTH, LOWER BOUT: 12¾ inches (32.4 cm)

Fender

'50s Telecaster Relic Ltd.
with Custom Artwork by Shepard Fairey

*T*he Telecaster has been in constant production and demand since its official introduction in 1951, and Fender has created myriad special- and limited-edition variations of the basic design over the years. Each one of this limited custom-shop edition of 13 guitars is decorated with a unique collage by graphic artist Shepard Fairey, whose purposefully contradictory work straddles the worlds of street art, propaganda, and commercial advertising. Fairey first gained notoriety when his "Andre the Giant has a Posse" poster hit a nerve and mysteriously began appearing in public spaces all over the world. Since then, his art has evolved into a business/campaign called "Obey Giant," which bills itself as "manufacturing quality dissent since 1989." Fairey, who describes himself as a "capitalism-embracing entrepreneur" but also feels compelled to illegally paste up his posters wherever he goes, told *Inc.* magazine, "People make this very black-and-white delineation. But I say, 'How would you feel about it if it were a little more ambiguous? If all companies had marketing materials that didn't insult the consumer? That were somewhat creative and intelligent and almost like an art piece with a product behind it?'"

The Tele, which produces a distinctive, piercing treble tone, has been particularly popular with blues, country, and soul guitarists. Among the diverse group of guitarists who have been identified with the Tele are Jimmy Bryant, Roy Buchanan, James Burton (who plays a 1968 pink paisley model), Albert Collins, Steve Cropper, Danny Gatton, Merle Haggard, Albert Lee, Roy Nichols, Buck Owens (and his long-time lead guitarist Don Rich), Keith Richards, Robbie Robertson, Bruce Springsteen (who plays a modified Esquire he bought in a pawn shop on the Jersey shore), Joe Strummer, Andy Summers, Muddy Waters, and Clarence White.

◄ **'50s Telecaster Relic Ltd.**
with Custom Artwork by Shepard Fairey, 2005
Fender Custom Shop,
Fender Musical Instruments Corporation
Corona, California

SPECIFICATIONS

BODY AND SIDE WOODS: Select alder

TOP WOOD: Select alder

BODY WIDTH, LOWER BOUT: 12¾ inches (32.4 cm)

Tom Anderson
Crowdster Plus Acoustic

*A*nderson's Crowdster acoustic guitar was designed to be plugged into a PA system, making live acoustic playing possible in the largest venues. The guitar's L.R. Baggs piezo pickup system gives it a rich, woody acoustic voice, and its sealed hollow body makes it impervious to the feedback that plagues amplified acoustic instruments.

The Crowdster Plus adds a specially designed Anderson electric guitar pickup to the original acoustic model, allowing the player to blend electric and acoustic guitar sounds. Since the Crowdster is strung with bronze strings, like a conventional acoustic guitar, the electric pickup was designed to capture the distinctive timbre and nuances of bronze strings and still balance output into a genuine electric guitar sound. In mono mode the guitar's piezo and electric outputs are sent to a single amp, while its stereo mode allows acoustic signal to be sent to the PA or an acoustic amp while the electric signal runs to an electric guitar amp.

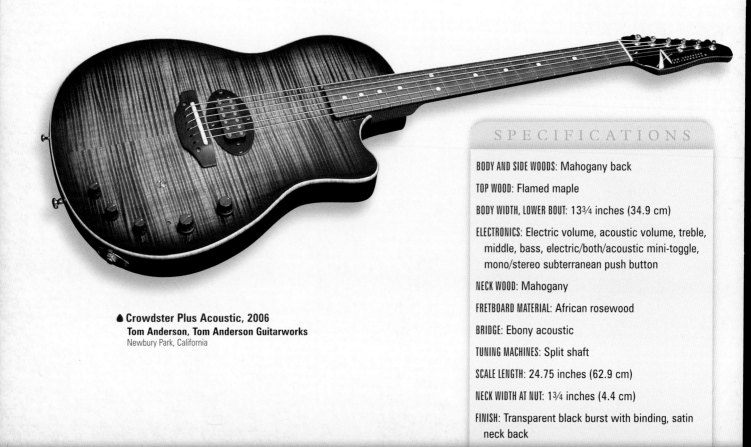

● **Crowdster Plus Acoustic, 2006**
Tom Anderson, Tom Anderson Guitarworks
Newbury Park, California

SPECIFICATIONS

BODY AND SIDE WOODS: Mahogany back

TOP WOOD: Flamed maple

BODY WIDTH, LOWER BOUT: 13¾ inches (34.9 cm)

ELECTRONICS: Electric volume, acoustic volume, treble, middle, bass, electric/both/acoustic mini-toggle, mono/stereo subterranean push button

NECK WOOD: Mahogany

FRETBOARD MATERIAL: African rosewood

BRIDGE: Ebony acoustic

TUNING MACHINES: Split shaft

SCALE LENGTH: 24.75 inches (62.9 cm)

NECK WIDTH AT NUT: 1¾ inches (4.4 cm)

FINISH: Transparent black burst with binding, satin neck back

Hollow Drop Top Classic

rop Top guitars are made by laminating a ⅛ inch (3 mm) thick skin of book-matched exotic wood such as quilted maple, koa, or zebrawood onto a standard solid or hollow body. The process allows luthiers to create electrics with purely decorative, highly figured tops that do not change the core sound of the instrument. Demand is such that companies such as Warmoth Guitar Products produce unfinished "replacement" Strat- and Tele-style drop top bodies and necks (along with pickups, paint, pickguards, and other parts) for do-it-yourselfers who want to assemble their own unique instruments, while Tom Anderson and other electric luthiers build high quality drop tops from the ground up.

Anderson has been building guitars for more than 30 years. He offers customers an extremely wide range of body, top, and neck woods and combinations because he believes both the wood and the player's own hands and playing style produce unique tones. "Very basically," Anderson explains, "your hands produce either a clear, articulate sound or a rich, thick sound. The clear, articulate sound might best be complemented by a wood tone that has a thick, rich midrange. Hands that have a rich, thick, smooth tone usually sound best with a wood that produces a clear and sparkling sound. And, each type of wood, even though it falls into one of these two categories, also has its own timbre or sonic personality."

This maple-on-alder Drop Top Classic is finished in Anderson's "Deep Bora Bora Blue" color, one of a wide variety of choices the company offers. Like all Drop Top Classics, it comes with a vintage looking pickguard. Anderson includes the pickguard for aesthetic reasons, but points out that the pickguard is also an essential component in creating a classic-sounding guitar, adding more overtones to the sound while at the same time reducing the fundamental.

♠ **Hollow Drop Top Classic, 2006**
Tom Anderson, Tom Anderson
Guitarworks
Newbury Park, California

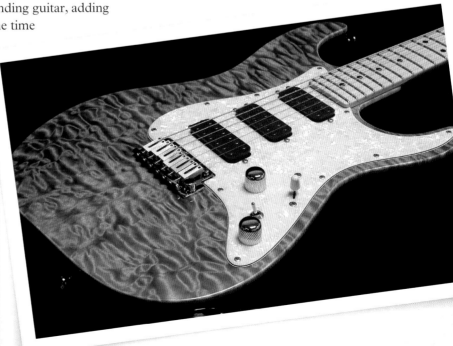

SPECIFICATIONS

BODY AND SIDE WOODS: Alder back

TOP WOOD: Quilted maple

BODY WIDTH, LOWER BOUT: 12½ inches (31.8 cm)

ELECTRONICS: 5-way with bridge splitter switch and add-bridge push/pull for 10 sounds

NECK WOOD: Maple

BRIDGE: Vintage Tremolo

TUNING MACHINES: Locking

SCALE LENGTH: 25.5 inches (64.8 cm)

NECK WIDTH AT NUT: 1¹¹⁄₁₆ inches (4.3 cm)

FINISH: Deep bora bora blue with binding

Soloway Swan LN6 Original

Jim Soloway's long-necked, semi-hollow-bodied Swan guitars all feature an unusual extended 27-inch scale length. Scale length, the distance from the nut to the bridge, is one of the critical design elements of any guitar because it determines the tonal parameters of the instrument. Gibsons typically have a 24.75-inch (62.9 cm) scale length and Fenders 25.5-inch (64.8 cm), while Paul Reed Smith's 25-inch (63.5 cm) scale length provided the tonal compromise between Gibson and Fender that he was looking for. Soloway says the 27-inch scale length of his Swan "produces a level of clarity, presence, and articulation that most guitarists have never experienced. Notes just seem to jump off the guitar."

The extended scale length also enhances bass response, giving the guitar a big, full bottom end. ("Long necks and big bottoms" is the catch line for the Swan.) Soloway is known for his seven-string guitars—his quest for the perfect seven-string first led him to the 27-inch scale length—and he offers a Swan seven, with an added low B string, as well as a conventional six. Although the Swan is intended to be tuned normally, some players find dropping the pitch to D takes the best advantage of the instrument's strengths.

♦ Soloway Swan LN6 Original, 2006
Jim Soloway, Soloway Guitars
Portland, Oregon

SPECIFICATIONS

BODY AND SIDE WOODS: Lightweight swamp ash

TOP WOOD: Figured bubinga

BODY WIDTH, LOWER BOUT: 12¾ inches (32.4 cm)

ELECTRONICS: Dual humbucker pickups, tone and volume controls

NECK WOOD: Maple

FRETBOARD MATERIAL: Pau ferro

FRETBOARD INLAY: Sea snail with brass surrounding ring

HEADSTOCK DECORATION: Mother-of-pearl truss rod cover with swan inlay

BRIDGE: Gold-plated milled brass

NUT AND SADDLE: Bone nut, brass saddles

TUNING MACHINES: Open-back Sperzel Sound Lock

BINDING: 3-ply tortoise celluloid with black and white purfling

SCALE LENGTH: 27 inches (68.6 cm)

NECK WIDTH AT NUT: 1¹¹⁄₁₆ inches (4.3 cm)

NUMBER OF FRETS: 22

FINISH: Nitrocellulose

BODY DEPTH: 2 inches (5 cm)

BODY LENGTH: 17¾ inches (45.1 cm)

OVERALL LENGTH: 38 inches (96.5 cm)

U.S. SUGGESTED RETAIL PRICE: $3,000

Ben Harper Model Series II Limited Edition

SPECIFICATIONS

BODY AND SIDE WOODS: Mahogany

TOP WOOD: Curly maple

BODY WIDTH, LOWER BOUT: 13½ inches (34.3 cm)

ELECTRONICS: Passive, CTS pots

NECK WOOD: Mahogany

FRETBOARD MATERIAL: Koa

FRETBOARD INLAY: Mother-of-pearl

HEADSTOCK DECORATION: Black lacquer with gold logos

BRIDGE: Tone pros

NUT AND SADDLE: Bone nut

TUNING MACHINES: Tone pros/Kluson

BINDING: Cream

SCALE LENGTH: 25 inches (63.5 cm)

NECK WIDTH AT NUT: 2⅛ inches (5.4 cm)

NUMBER OF FRETS: 22

FINISH: Nitrocellulose

BODY DEPTH: 1¾ inches (4.4 cm)

BODY LENGTH: 19 inches (48.3 cm)

OVERALL LENGTH: 37¼ inches (94.6 cm)

U.S. SUGGESTED RETAIL PRICE: $2,800

*L*uthier Bill Asher and slide master Ben Harper collaborated on a lap steel design in 1998, creating an instrument that combined more sustain and greater tonal variation than traditional lap steels by offering pickup options much like those of modern electric guitars. This follow-up, a limited-edition run of 100 instruments, draws inspiration from the classic '59 Gibson Les Paul and features a flame maple top with cherry sunburst finish and a pair of Seymour Duncan custom shop '59-style humbuckers.

Asher built his first guitar, a copy of a Fender Strat, in his high school wood shop class, a project that helped him land an apprenticeship at a Los Angeles guitar making and repair shop in 1982. He ran his own shop in the mid-1980s, building a reputation for his repair and restoration talents, and also did work for such highly respected luthiers as Rick Turner and Mark Lacey. Along the way Asher built a long and diverse client list that includes such stars as the Black Crowes, Jackson Browne, Lindsey Buckingham, T-Bone Burnett, Tracy Chapman, Ry Cooder, David Crosby, Cindy Cashdollar, Donovan, John Fogerty, Robben Ford, P.J. Harvey, Los Lobos, Bonnie Raitt, Axl Rose, Brian Setzer, and Stephen Stills.

Ben Harper has played lap steel guitar since he was a kid, and his best-selling albums have brought new attention to both acoustic and electric steel playing in recent years.

◀ **Ben Harper Model Series II Limited Edition, 2006**
Bill Asher, Asher Guitars & Lap Steels
Venice, California

Bar Rashi Electric Guitar

$\mathcal{M}$usician, composer, inventor, poet, photographer, and film editor Allan Gittler, who died in 2000, was a major innovator in New York's underground jazz/art scene during the 1960s and '70s. He recorded with Elvin Jones, Gil Evans, flutist Lloyd McNeill, and many others, and invented the bare bones Gittler Electric Guitar, one of only two musical instruments ever to become part of the collection of the Museum of Modern Art.

Gittler later changed his name to Avraham Bar Rashi and moved to Israel, where he continued to play jazz and build minimalist electric guitars. This wide-necked solid oak example, with fishline frets and 12 pieces of identical hardware that serve as nut, bridge, and tuner, was used by Bar Rashi on his 1998 CD, *Deep Hip*. A photograph of him playing the instrument appears on the record's cover. Reportedly, Bar Rashi built five of these instruments, but this is the only example currently known to be extant.

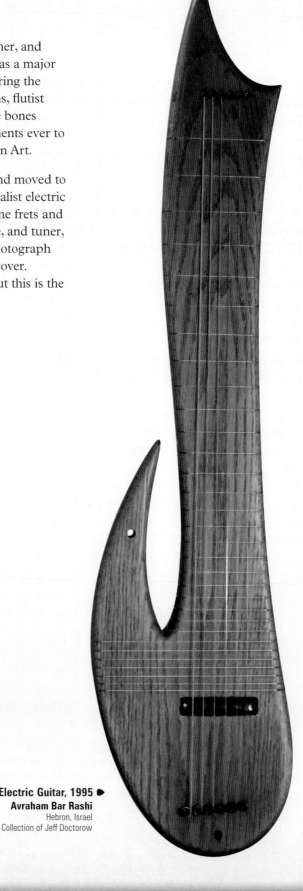

Bar Rashi Electric Guitar, 1995 ►
Avraham Bar Rashi
Hebron, Israel
Collection of Jeff Doctorow

SPECIFICATIONS

BODY AND SIDE WOODS: Solid oak

TOP WOOD: Solid oak

BODY WIDTH, LOWER BOUT: 7¹⁄₁₆ inches (18 cm)

NECK WIDTH AT NUT: 3¹⁵⁄₁₆ inches (10 cm)

NUMBER OF FRETS: 38

BODY DEPTH: 1⅛ inches (3.5 cm)

OVERALL LENGTH: 32¼ inches (82 cm)

Gene Baker
b3 Six-String

Gene Baker started playing guitar at 11, built his first guitar at 13, and nearly 30 years later is still obsessed with both playing and building. He graduated from the Guitar Institute of Technology in 1986, tried and failed to become a rock star, and spent the '90s working first alongside Roger Giffin in Gibson's West Coast custom shop and then for six years in Fender's custom shop. All along, he built his own guitars on the side before going out on his own with Baker Guitars in 1997.

Baker's latest venture, the b3, comes in five "flavors"—Earth, a flattop model; Fire, a carved-top solid body; Wood models with chambered-to-hollow bodies; carved top/carved back hollow Water models; and neck through Metal models. Combinations of elements such as an Earth/Wood model, a flattop with a hollow body, or a Fire/Metal carved top neck through are also possible. Baker says his new company is focused on raising the bar on quality and expectations as high as it can possibly go. Fine Tuned Instruments LLC is a company, says Baker, "devoted to embracing technology and advancement throughout the industry with a vintage heart and soul—the passion of music itself being the primary driving force behind our pursuit of life, liberty, happiness, and business."

♠ b3 Six-String, 2006
Gene Baker, Fine Tuned Instruments
Arroyo Grande, California

287

SPECIFICATIONS

BODY AND SIDE WOODS: Solid body mahogany

TOP WOOD: Carved maple, 5A quilted maple

BODY WIDTH, LOWER BOUT: 13¼ inches (33.7 cm)

ELECTRONICS: Seymour Duncan or DiMazio pickups, P90s, or Humbuckers

NECK WOOD: Mahogany

FRETBOARD MATERIAL: Ebony

FRETBOARD INLAY: Diamond blocks

HEADSTOCK DECORATION: Ebony overlay with inlaid b3 logo

BRIDGE: TonePros double-locking bridge and tailpiece

NUT AND SADDLE: Buzz Feiten bone logo nut

TUNING MACHINES: Buzz Feiten tuning system; Sperzel lock

BINDING: Creme, white, multiple WBWBW, tortoise, or natural maple

SCALE LENGTH: 24.6 inches (62.5 cm)

NECK WIDTH AT NUT: 1⅝ inches (4.1 cm)

NUMBER OF FRETS: 22

Albert King Magenta Metal Flake

Albert King, who died in 1992, was one of the most important bluesmen of the post-war era and a major influence on such younger players as Mike Bloomfield, Eric Clapton, Peter Green, Jimi Hendrix, and Stevie Ray Vaughn, who called him "Daddy." Bloomfield once said, "Albert can take four notes and write a volume. He can say more with fewer notes than anyone I've ever known." Clapton's admiration was such that his solo on "Strange Brew," from the 1968 Cream album *Disraeli Gears*, is a nearly note for note copy of King's solo on his "Oh, Pretty Woman," recorded a year before for Stax.

Clapton has also admitted that he took the riff for "Layla" directly from King's "As the Years Go Passing By," another of his Stax recordings.

King was left-handed but usually played right-handed guitars flipped over and upside-down so the low E-string was on the bottom. In later years he played a custom-made guitar that was basically left-handed, but had the strings reversed (as he was used to playing).

The Gibson Flying V was King's signature guitar; he played one he called "Lucy" for years. John Bolin's flamboyant take on the shape, built on commission for King, adds outrageous color to an audacious form.

◀ **Albert King Magenta Metal Flake**
John Bolin, Bolin Guitars
Boise, Idaho

SPECIFICATIONS

BODY AND SIDE WOODS: Mahogany

TOP WOOD: Maple

ELECTRONICS: Seymour Duncan

NECK WOOD: Mahogany

FRETBOARD MATERIAL: Rosewood

FRETBOARD INLAY: Silver metal flake paint, custom font

HEADSTOCK DECORATION: Silver metal flake paint

BRIDGE: T.O.M. custom V tailpiece

NUT AND SADDLE: Bone

TUNING MACHINES: Schaller

BINDING: Silver metal flake

SCALE LENGTH: 24.6 inches (62.5 cm)

NECK WIDTH AT NUT: 1 11/16 inches (4.3 cm)

NUMBER OF FRETS: 22

FINISH: Lacquer

BODY DEPTH: 1 1/2 inches (3.8 cm)

BODY LENGTH: 28 inches (71.1 cm)

OVERALL LENGTH: 48 inches (121.9 cm)

U.S. SUGGESTED RETAIL PRICE: $7,500

The Butternut Guitar
Sound Block Design

Thomas Lieber is one of the most creative luthiers at work today, and the elegant Butternut Guitar is the latest example of his visually stunning and masterfully crafted instruments.

Lieber started designing and building guitars in 1971, and over the years, has designed and produced one-of-a-kind instruments for the likes of Jerry Garcia and Phil Lesh of The Grateful Dead, Chris Stein of Blondie, jazz great Stanley Clarke, Sir Paul McCartney, and singer-songwriter Iris DeMent. In the process, he has redesigned nearly every part of the guitar and patented unique bridges, tailpieces, necks, and pickups.

Lieber loves to work with artists, combining their ideas with his innovative ingenuity. He says, "I got started working directly with artists while I was working with Doug Irwin who is best known for the incredible custom guitars he built for Jerry Garcia. In 1975, I designed and built a custom bass for Pete Sears of Jefferson Starship

and held several design sessions with Pete to work out details of the instrument he had in mind. Many good things came as a result of those sessions: Pete had a beautiful bass; Pete and I became good friends; and I realized if I really listened to artists' needs, I could build them an instrument they loved, and, at the same time, I could push the envelope of guitar building a little further. From that point on, the company began its long run of patented innovations."

290

SPECIFICATIONS

BODY AND SIDE WOODS: Butternut (white walnut)

BODY WIDTH, LOWER BOUT: 12 inches (30.5 cm)

ELECTRONICS: EMG or any other humbucker design

NECK WOOD ASSEMBLY: Bubinga (African rosewood)

FRETBOARD MATERIAL: Gaboon ebony

FRETBOARD INLAY: Mother-of-pearl dots

HEADSTOCK DECORATION: Compound radius mother-of-pearl

BRIDGE: Original Lieber design, gold-plated solid machined brass

NUT AND SADDLE: Sperzel gold-plated XL

TUNING MACHINES: Steinberger

SCALE LENGTH: 25.5 inches (64.8 cm)

NECK WIDTH AT NUT: 1⅝ inches (4.1 cm)

NUMBER OF FRETS: 21

FINISH: Catalyzed varnish

BODY DEPTH: 1¾ inches (4.4 cm)

BODY LENGTH: 16½ inches (41.9 cm)

OVERALL LENGTH: 39½ inches (100.3 cm)

U.S. SUGGESTED RETAIL PRICE: $6,200

◆ The Butternut Guitar, Sound Block Design, 1996
Thomas Lieber, Lieber Instruments
Fly Creek, New York

Retro-Phonic Lightning Bolt

*P*aul Beard became fascinated with resonator guitars when he was 18, about the same time he started repairing stringed instruments, and has been building resonator guitars full time since 1985. As a working musician, Beard grew frustrated with the quality of available resonator guitars and decided to focus his skills on the design and construction of a next-generation instrument, a guitar that in Beard's words would "take advantage of new technologies and techniques while honoring the tradition of the Dopyera family." Today, Beard and his small team of skilled hand craftsmen build 14 square-neck and round-neck resonator models, and Beard resonators are played by such renowned masters of the instrument as Mike Auldridge, LeRoy Mack, and Tim Graves.

Beard's Art Deco-influenced Retro-Phonic electric resonator combines a rear-loaded, specially treated resonator assembly with a P-90 magnetic pickup and Fishman Resonator pickup. The signals for each pickup are discrete even though they are brought out through a single jack, allowing the player to control the range of sounds from what Beard describes as "a rich, mellow, fat, and warm guitar to a screaming, bluesy, resonant slide guitar" or any combination of the two.

◀ **Retro-Phonic Lightning Bolt, 2003**
Paul Beard, Beard Guitars
Hagerstown, Maryland

SPECIFICATIONS

BODY AND SIDE WOODS: Curly maple

TOP WOOD: Curly maple

BODY WIDTH, LOWER BOUT: 14½ inches (36.8 cm)

ELECTRONICS: P-90, Fishman passive with blend and master volume controls

NECK WOOD: Mahogany

FRETBOARD MATERIAL: Ebony

FRETBOARD INLAY: Abalone dots

HEADSTOCK DECORATION: Beard logo

BRIDGE: Aluminum

NUT AND SADDLE: Bone nut

TUNING MACHINES: Schaller

BINDING: Plastic

SCALE LENGTH: 25 inches (63.5 cm)

NECK WIDTH AT NUT: 1¾ inches (4.4 cm)

NUMBER OF FRETS: 19

BRACING: Graphite, wood

FINISH: Poly

BODY DEPTH: 3⅝ inches (9.2 cm)

BODY LENGTH: 19½ inches (49.5 cm)

OVERALL LENGTH: 39⅞ inches (101.3 cm)

U.S. SUGGESTED RETAIL PRICE: $3,900

Fatline TV

$\mathscr{M}$aster archtop luthier Tom Ribbecke says Bill Chapin knows more about the relationship between acoustic and electric instruments than anyone he has ever met. Chapin, who has been building fine quality instruments for more than 20 years, focuses on process rather than outcome and says his approach revolves around the instrument "as an individual voice. There are many variations of any given type of tone, each with its own charms and nuances that make it unique and special. This 'magic' lies in the synergy between the design (including the execution of the design) and the materials. Over the many years that I've been building instruments. I've learned how to 'read' the wood and carefully craft it so that, at every stage, the elements of design further the tonal goal instead of contradicting it. This involves incorporating the classic tonal heritage of the past but also reinterpreting it, building on the precise tonal strengths of the exact materials involved," Chapin says.

Chapin's Fatline TV, a vaulted internal brace design, semi-hollow electric with a tremolo was named not for the silver screen, but for guitarist, composer, arranger, and record producer Tim Volpicella.

◄ **Fatline TV, 1994**
William Chapin, Chapin Guitars
Canby, Oregon

SPECIFICATIONS

BODY AND SIDE WOODS: Honduran mahogany

TOP WOOD: Flamed maple

BODY WIDTH, LOWER BOUT: 12¾ inches (32.4 cm)

ELECTRONICS: 5 single-coil velvet hammer pickups, piezo saddles with volume and blend, master volume and tone, push/pull split for linked singles, push/pull bridge p.v. added

NECK WOOD: Flamed maple

FRETBOARD MATERIAL: Brazilian rosewood

FRETBOARD INLAY: Abalone dots with ivory TV set at 5th fret and abalone shades at 12th fret

HEADSTOCK DECORATION: Figured koa half overlay

BRIDGE: Six-screw Tremolo with piezo saddles

NUT AND SADDLE: Documented legal walrus ivory

TUNING MACHINES: Sperzel

SCALE LENGTH: 24.75 inches (62.9 cm)

NECK WIDTH AT NUT: 1¹¹⁄₁₆ inches (4.3 cm)

NUMBER OF FRETS: 24

BRACING: Coupling braces tying top and back

FINISH: Sunburst nitrocellulose lacquer

BODY DEPTH: 2¼ inches (5.7 cm)

BODY LENGTH: 16 inches (40.6 cm)

OVERALL LENGTH: 37¾ inches (95.9 cm)

293

Michael DeTemple

Barrie Eames '56

◀ Barrie Eames '56, 2005
Michael DeTemple, DeTemple Guitars
Sherman Oaks, California

294

SPECIFICATIONS

BODY AND SIDE WOODS: Featherweight swamp ash

TOP WOOD: Featherweight swamp ash

BODY WIDTH, LOWER BOUT: 12¾ inches (32.4 cm)

ELECTRONICS: Custom wiring, DeTemple SweetSpot S-series pickups

NECK WOOD: Northeastern, quartersawn, flame maple/bocote skunk stripe

FRETBOARD MATERIAL: Northeastern, quartersawn, flame maple/bocote skunk stripe

FRETBOARD INLAY: Black mother-of-pearl

HEADSTOCK DECORATION: Hand-carved fossilized mastadon string tree

BRIDGE: DeTemple FS-11 titanium

NUT AND SADDLE: Hand-carved mastodon ivory nut, titanium saddles

TUNING MACHINES: Custom Gotoh open-back

SCALE LENGTH: 25.5 inches (64.8 cm)

NECK WIDTH AT NUT: 1¹¹⁄₁₆ inches (4.3 cm)

NUMBER OF FRETS: 21

FINISH: Hand-applied and rubbed nitrocellulose

U.S. SUGGESTED RETAIL PRICE: $5,617

Michael DeTemple is a professional guitarist, vintage instrument collector, and luthier who builds what he calls "vintage-design solid-body electrics." Rick Turner, himself one of the masters of electric guitar building, is more specific when he calls the DeTemple '56 "the one out of 5,000, the top one-half of one percent of these types of guitars, the dream Strat-style guitar that everybody's chasing after."

After years of touring and working as a session guitarist, DeTemple built a reputation as a crack repairman and guitar tech who could return, restore, or setup any guitar to peak performance. In the mid-1990s, when the great vintage electric guitars he liked to collect and play began to become too pricey to use on a regular basis, he decided to build his own. His goal was, and remains to be, to recreate the magic of the best 1950s Fender Stratocasters, Esquires, and Telecasters. Drawing on his vast knowledge of the small but critical nuances that set one instrument apart from another, he developed a host of proprietary methods and tone-improving techniques which he incorporated into his own Spirit Series guitars.

DeTemple is a fastidious builder, whose guitars are handcrafted to order with an absolutely minimum use of machinery. He insists on tightly controlling every aspect of construction in consultation with his clients, and the specs often change from order to order. He even hand builds his own SweetSpot pickups. All this hand work comes at a price—a DeTemple '56 has a base price of about $5,500—but with vintage Fenders selling for three or more times that, his guitars can almost seem like a bargain.

Custom Jimi Hendrix Memorial Monterey Pop Stratocaster

*A*lthough he used several other guitars during his all too brief life, Jimi Hendrix's main axe was a Fender Stratocaster, and his identification with the instrument has helped make it the world's best known electric guitar. This Fender custom-shop limited edition recreates the hand-painted Strat that Hendrix played and set on fire during his legendary appearance at the 1967 Monterey Pop Festival.

Like surf guitar king Dick Dale, Hendrix was left handed but almost always played a standard right-handed Strat strung backwards. More than any other player before or since, he defined the electric guitar as the instrument of rock-and-roll. Jimi Hendrix was the high priest of what the late rock critic Robert Palmer called "the church of the sonic guitar." He made the electric guitar an entirely modern instrument, bringing its roots in black blues together with a previously unimagined array of electronically generated feedback, distortion, and noise, seemingly combining the instrument's past and future into a whole that was greater than the sum of its many parts.

Nearly 40 years after his death, Hendrix remains the most influential guitarist in rock history. After a *Rolling Stone* poll ranked Hendrix the greatest guitarist of all time, The Who's Pete Townshend wrote in the magazine, "I didn't have any envy. I never had any sense that I could ever come close. Once—I think it was at a gig Jimi played at the Scotch of St. James—Eric [Clapton] and I found ourselves holding each other's hands. You know, what we were watching was so profoundly powerful. He made the electric guitar beautiful."

♠ **Custom Jimi Hendrix Memorial Monterey Pop Stratocaster, 1997**
Fender Custom Shop, Fender Musical Instruments Corporation
Corona, California

Crazy Cowboy Bass and Guitar

▶ **Crazy Cowboy Bass and Guitar, 1990**
John Bolin, Bolin Guitars
Boise, Idaho
Top, Crazy Cowboy Bass
Bottom, Crazy Cowboy Guitar

John Bolin is a renowned custom guitar builder whose clients have included Albert King, Steve Miller, Jimmy Page, Joe Perry, Lou Reed, Doc Watson, and Keith Richards and Ronnie Wood of the Rolling Stones.

Bolin started building guitars in 1978, and his company has grown to fill a manufacturing facility of more than 6,500 square feet. Production manager Andrew Jones, formerly with Patrick Eggle Guitars in England, oversees a staff of five, which includes John Bolin's son Jake. Although the company is best known for its custom guitars, Bolin Guitars also produces two lines of production instruments: the Bolin NS Guitar and Bass, designed by Ned Steinberger, and the Bolin Classic, which features a carved top and back.

Bolin made this flamboyant pair of guitars for Billy Gibbons and Dusty Hill of ZZ Top. Gibbons and Bolin have collaborated to create well over 100 guitars through the years. The two constantly challenge one another to create some of the wildest looking guitars of all time, including instruments covered with fur and glowing with neon. However outrageous his guitars look, Bolin is adamant that "it's about the music," and, as his client list testifies, the quality of his instruments is second to none.

SPECIFICATIONS

BODY AND SIDE WOODS: Maple, both

TOP WOOD: Maple, both

BODY WIDTH, LOWER BOUT: 18 inches (45.7 cm), both

ELECTRONICS: Dimarzio, top; Seymour Duncan, bottom

NECK WOOD: Mahogany, both

FRETBOARD MATERIAL: Maple, both

HEADSTOCK DECORATION: Mississippi River, both

SOUND HOLE INLAYS: Balls, both

BRIDGE: Baddass, top; T.O.M. stop, bottom

NUT AND SADDLE: Bone, both

TUNING MACHINES: Schaller, both

BINDING: Painted, both

SCALE LENGTH: 34 inches (86.4 cm), top; 24.6 inches (62.5 cm), bottom

NECK WIDTH AT NUT: 1½ inches (3.8 cm), top; 1¹¹/₁₆ inches (4.3 cm), bottom

NUMBER OF FRETS: 22, both

FINISH: Bright green and pink, both

BODY DEPTH: 3 inches (7.6 cm), both

BODY LENGTH: 23 inches (58.4 cm), both

OVERALL LENGTH: 50 inches (127 cm), top; 46 inches (116.9 cm), bottom

U.S. SUGGESTED RETAIL PRICE: $19,000 top; $10,000 bottom

Kevin Chilcott

Custom Royal Electra MK II

*K*evin Chilcott's Electra was one of the most innovative and influential "Super Strat" designs of the late 1980s. Jokingly dubbed the "Cheese" guitar due to the routed holes in its solid mahogany body, the Electra also featured prominent v-shaped mother-of-pearl fingerboard inlay and a reverse headstock. Among Chilcott's other innovative ideas were those of inserting the pickup selector through a slot in the body and setting the bridge humbucker pickup at an angle, which added to the design's already rakish look and also gave the guitar a unique tone.

A number of later builders produced guitars with routed holes, including B.C. Rich, Wayne Charvel, and Jeff Abel, whose solid aluminum-bodied Abel Axe probably represents the most refined development of the concept.

Custom Royal Electra MK II, 1989 ▶
Kevin Chilcott, Royal Guitars
Carms, Wales

SPECIFICATIONS

BODY AND SIDE WOODS: Mahogany

TOP WOOD: Mahogany

BODY WIDTH, LOWER BOUT: 12½ inches (31.8 cm)

ELECTRONICS: EMG active pickups powered by a 9V battery; 81(b) and 60(n), volume, tone, and 3-way mini toggle switch

NECK WOOD: Mahogany

FRETBOARD MATERIAL: Ebony

FRETBOARD INLAY: Hand-cut mother-of-pearl offset V's and name

HEADSTOCK DECORATION: Hand-cut mother-of-pearl logo: "Royal" in script and a crown

BRIDGE: Kahler pro in black-chromed steel

NUT AND SADDLE: Bone nut, roller saddles in black-chromed steel

TUNING MACHINES: Black-chromed mini Schallers

BINDING: White 1/16 inch (1.6 mm) on neck and headstock

SCALE LENGTH: 24.75 inches (62.9 cm)

NECK WIDTH AT NUT: 1 11/16 inches (4.3 cm)

NUMBER OF FRETS: 24

FINISH: Special flexible 2-pac to allow maximum resonance, clear basecoats, black color, and clear topcoats

BODY DEPTH: 1¾ inches (4.4 cm)

BODY LENGTH: 18 inches (45.7 cm)

OVERALL LENGTH: 39 inches (99.1 cm)

U.S. SUGGESTED RETAIL PRICE: $2,000

Apollo Artist Reserve Stock

● **Apollo Artist Reserve Stock, 2006**
Jack Briggs, Briggs Guitars
Raleigh, North Carolina

*J*ack Briggs, who began building guitars full time in 1999 after 20 odd years as a working musician and repairman, jokes that he works with a staff of three—"me, myself, and I." A meticulous craftsman, Briggs creates his carved-top instruments from a variety of choice, exotic tonewoods, the best and rarest of which make up his "Reserve Stock."

Briggs built two unique Reserve Stock guitars for the 2006 NAMM International Music Products Association show, the oldest and biggest musical instrument and products trade show in the world. The Apollo, a semi-hollow single cutaway, is his latest model. It has a set-neck, chambered body, bound fingerboard, and Jason Lollar pickups. (Lollar is the recognized master of handmade, boutique pickups; he made a special pair of low-wind Imperial humbuckers for the Apollo.)

SPECIFICATIONS

GUITAR SHAPE/STYLE: Single cutaway semi-hollow-body set-neck electric handmade instrument

BODY AND SIDE WOODS: 75-year-old air-dried Honduran mahogany back

TOP WOOD: 100-year-old air-dried spalted sycamore

NECK WOOD: Air-dried fiddleback big leaf maple

FRETBOARD MATERIAL: Air-dried Yucatan ziricote

FRETBOARD INLAY: Paua abalone side dot markers

HEADSTOCK DECORATION: Ziricote with grain-matched truss rod cover

BINDING: Fiddleback 35-year-old air-dried Hawaiian koa with multi-ply black/white purfling on headstock, fingerboard, body, and pickguard

BRIDGE: Tune-o-matic adjustable, gold-plated

NUT AND SADDLE: Vintage, unbleached bone nut

TUNING MACHINES: Grover rotomatic; custom handmade ziricote buttons

RECOMMENDED STRINGS: Everly B52 alloy .010–.046

SCALE LENGTH: 25 inches (63.5 cm)

TRUSS ROD: Vintage compression single piece

NECK WIDTH AT NUT: 1 11/16 inches (4.3 cm)

NUMBER OF FRETS: 22

FINISH: Natural nitrocellulose lacquer

ELECTRONICS: Lollar low-wind imperial PAF, 3-way switch, volume, tone, SlimFat™ control proprietary design variable coil-cut control on dual humbucking pickup layout

BODY WIDTH, LOWER BOUT: 13 inches (33 cm)

BODY DEPTH: 2½ inches (6.4 cm)

BODY LENGTH: 17¼ inches (43.8 cm)

OVERALL LENGTH: 38½ inches (97.8 cm)

CASE: Form-fitted hard shell with environmental controls

U.S. SUGGESTED RETAIL PRICE: $12,195

Leo Fender Commemorative Broadcaster

**◀ Leo Fender Commemorative
Broadcaster, 1999
Fender Custom Shop, Fender
Musical Instruments Corporation**
Corona, California

Clarence Leonidas Fender (1909–1991) didn't invent the solid-bodied electric guitar, but his brilliantly simple guitar and bass designs and streamlined production methods changed the face of both guitar manufacturing and popular music in the 1950s. Leo Fender's aim was to create an electric guitar that could be mass produced from component parts and sold at a price the average musician could afford, and he succeeded beyond his or anyone else's wildest dreams. As Doc Kauffman, his business partner from 1945 through 1946, ruefully put it years later, "I didn't see much of a future for electric guitars. I guess I was wrong."

Fender designed a prototype for a slab-bodied "electric Spanish guitar" in 1949, and his upstart company introduced a single pickup version called the Esquire the following year. Only about 50 Esquires were made before Fender began manufacturing an "improved" two pickup version of his design. Fender dubbed this first mass-produced solid-body electric guitar Broadcaster, but was soon forced to stop using the name because the long-established Fred Gretsch company had already trademarked "Broadkaster" for one of its lines of drums. Instead of halting production while he dreamed up a new name, Fender simply cut Broadcaster out of the label decal, leaving just the Fender logo. Those rare, nameless guitars have come to be called Nocasters by collectors. By early 1951, Fender's revolutionary guitar had been renamed "Telecaster," as the model has been known ever since.

This custom-shop, limited edition of 50 numbered guitars is based on Leo Fender's original specs. Other than the signature on the peghead, the main difference between it and the original is the price tag; the Broadcaster retailed for $140 in 1950, while this edition, complete with its own Plexiglas display case, listed at $10,000 and quickly sold out.

SPECIFICATIONS

BODY AND SIDE WOODS: Solid ash

TOP WOOD: Solid ash

BODY WIDTH, LOWER BOUT: 12¾ inches (32.4 cm)

ELECTRONICS: 2 Custom Shop single-coil pickups

NECK WOOD: Highly flamed maple

BRIDGE: 3 Barrel Bridge

NECK WIDTH AT NUT: 1⅝ inches (4.1 cm)

FINISH: Butterscotch blonde

Hybrid AAE

S. B. MacDonald's custom guitars are made strictly on special order. He designs each instrument around the needs, spirit, and personality of his customers, combining function, balance, and tonal flavor to create an instrument that is an extension of the player. "I insist on getting to know as much about each customer and their music as I can before design and construction begin," he says. "In the end, an instrument as unique as its owner is born."

This hybrid of archtop, acoustic, and electric (hence the AAE) technology was custom built for Brendan Brown of the multi-platinum band Wheatus, and according to MacDonald, it produces a "fat, yet tight and powerful punch that is equally appropriate for rock, blues, jazz, and rockabilly." And, even though you sure can't tell through all that key lime green paint, the Hybrid AAE's small, parlor-guitar-sized body is made from top grade Indian rosewood with a master-grade Sitka spruce top.

301

SPECIFICATIONS

BODY AND SIDE WOODS: Indian rosewood

TOP WOOD: Sitka spruce

BODY WIDTH, LOWER BOUT: 14¾ inches (37.5 cm)

ELECTRONICS: Rio Grande blues bar in neck position, Fishman saddle transducer

NECK WOOD: Mahogany

FRETBOARD MATERIAL: Ebony

FRETBOARD INLAY: Mother-of-pearl

HEADSTOCK DECORATION: Pearloid overlay

BRIDGE: Color-matched lacquered ebony

NUT AND SADDLE: Bone

TUNING MACHINES: Grover mini-rotomatics

SCALE LENGTH: 24.9 inches (63.2 cm)

NECK WIDTH AT NUT: 1¹¹⁄₁₆ inches (4.3 cm)

NUMBER OF FRETS: 22

BRACING: X braced

FINISH: Lacquer

BODY DEPTH: 4 inches (10.2 cm)

BODY LENGTH: 16½ inches (41.9 cm)

OVERALL LENGTH: 39 inches (99.1 cm)

U.S. SUGGESTED RETAIL PRICE: $4,000

♠ **Hybrid AAE, 2003**
S.B. MacDonald,
S.B. MacDonald Custom Instruments
Huntington, New York

Custom Guitar for Rick Nielsen

First Act manufactures a wide variety of instruments from inexpensive guitars, drums, and band instruments for children to limited-edition guitars for professional musicians. The company's Studio for Artists builds one-of-a-kind guitars, basses, and violins, and has created unique guitars for many rockers, including Depeche Mode, Nine Inch Nails, System of a Down, Franz Ferdinand, Aerosmith, and the Yeah Yeah Yeahs.

This angular, pink-trimmed custom was built for Rick Nielsen of Cheap Trick who, like Billy Gibbons of ZZ Top, is known as much for his outlandish stage guitars as his superb skills as a player. Like Gibbons, Nielsen is also one of the rock world's most passionate guitar collectors, with a massive and ever-expanding collection of vintage and commissioned instruments.

303

◄ **Custom Guitar for Rick Nielsen, 2004**
First Act Guitars
Boston, Massachusetts

SPECIFICATIONS

BODY AND SIDE WOODS: Mahogany

TOP WOOD: Mahogany

BODY WIDTH, LOWER BOUT: 16 inches (40.6 cm)

ELECTRONICS: (6) K.A. lipsticks, (6) volume, (6) tone, (6) on/off switches

NECK WOOD: Mahogany

FRETBOARD MATERIAL: Ebony

FRETBOARD INLAY: Pink polymer resin dots

HEADSTOCK DECORATION: First Act 6-in-line

BRIDGE: Hipshot hardtail

NUT AND SADDLE: Corian

BINDING: Pink

SCALE LENGTH: 25 inches (63.5 cm)

NECK WIDTH AT NUT: 1 21/32 inches (4.2 cm)

FINISH: Black opaque

BODY DEPTH: 1 1/2 inches (3.8 cm)

BODY LENGTH: 19 inches (48.3 cm)

OVERALL LENGTH: 44 inches (111.8 cm)

U.S. SUGGESTED RETAIL PRICE: $3,500

Etavonni
GT-1

$\mathcal{T}$he Etavonni GT-1 has an ebony fingerboard, but that's the only part of the guitar made from wood. The rest of the instrument is aluminum and carbon fiber, materials which, unlike wood, are consistent, predictable, and very controllable.

By using these non-traditional materials, the Etavonni team claims it can mathematically work out the exact tone of an instrument before building it. The GT-1's aluminum body shell is machined out of a single piece of billet and has four distinct hollow sound chambers that are formed when the top carbon fiber panels are bonded into the body shell. The neck and back are also carbon fiber, and when the back is bolted on, the body chambers are closed except for a few ported holes. These ported sound chambers are tuned to specific frequencies that resonate in response to string vibration. Etavonni also claims that because the resonant frequencies can be precisely set, the wolf tones and feedback problems that plague hollow-bodied wooden instruments can be eliminated entirely.

GT-1, 2006 ▶
Etavonni Instruments Inc.
Kentwood, Michigan

SPECIFICATIONS

BODY AND SIDE WOODS: 6061-T6 CNC'd aluminum

TOP WOOD: Carbon fiber

BODY WIDTH, LOWER BOUT: 12½ inches (31.8 cm)

ELECTRONICS: Seymour Duncan, custom-custom trem bucker/hot stack for strat "N"

NECK WOOD: Carbon fiber/maple core

FRETBOARD MATERIAL: Ebony

HEADSTOCK DECORATION: Brushed aluminum logo over carbon fiber

BRIDGE: Hipshot hardtail, chrome

NUT AND SADDLE: Graphtech nut

TUNING MACHINES: Planet Waves, auto trim, locking, chrome, in-line 6

SCALE LENGTH: 25.5 inches (64.8 cm)

NECK WIDTH AT NUT: 1¹¹⁄₁₆ inches (4.3 cm)

NUMBER OF FRETS: 22

BRACING: Aluminum (machined, scalloped)

FINISH: Bead blasted and anodized/natural carbon fiber

BODY DEPTH: 1½ inches (3.8 cm)

BODY LENGTH: 15¾ inches (40 cm)

OVERALL LENGTH: 39 inches (99.1 cm)

U.S. SUGGESTED RETAIL PRICE: $7,200

Günter Eyb

10-String Electric Sitar

*E*ver since Ravi Shankar brought the sound of the Indian sitar to world audiences in the mid-1960s, guitarists have attempted to recreate its characteristic buzzing, droning sound, modal scales, and intricate melodic structures on their own instruments. George Harrison went so far as to study sitar with Shankar and play the instrument on the Beatles' *Revolver* and *Sergeant Pepper* LPs. Roger McGuinn combined John Coltrane's phrasing with the keening sound of his Rickenbacker 12-string on the Byrd's "Eight Miles High," and Mike Bloomfield played long modal jams on the Butterfield Blues Band's epochal "East-West." Players since that time have experimented with

many ways of approximating a sitar sound, primarily with effects pedals or by stuffing paper or paper clips under the strings at the bridge.

Günter Eyb's 10-string electric sitar goes another direction, using a proprietary bridge and tailpiece that can also be purchased separately and installed to retrofit a standard electric guitar. The bridge/tailpiece approximates the distinctive buzz of a traditional Indian acoustic sitar and brings that complex and difficult instrument's sounds within reach of a skilled electric guitarist.

SPECIFICATIONS

BODY AND SIDE WOODS: Alder

TOP WOOD: Maple

BODY WIDTH, LOWER BOUT: 14⅜ inches (36 cm)

ELECTRONICS: Custom magnetic pickups by Häussel and B-Band piezo

NECK WOOD: Maple

FRETBOARD MATERIAL: Maple

FRETBOARD INLAY: Leds

HEADSTOCK DECORATION: Silk print

SOUND HOLE INLAYS: Maple

BRIDGE: Eyb sitar

NUT AND SADDLE: Bone nut

TUNING MACHINES: ABM headless tuner

SCALE LENGTH: 29.1 inches (72.7 cm)

NECK WIDTH AT NUT: 2¾ inches (7 cm)

NUMBER OF FRETS: 24

FINISH: White high gloss polyurethane

BODY DEPTH: 1¾ inches (4.5 cm)

BODY LENGTH: 19¾ inches (50 cm)

OVERALL LENGTH: 39½ inches (100 cm)

U.S. SUGGESTED RETAIL PRICE: $3,200

◆ **10-String Electric Sitar, 2000**
Günter Eyb, Eyb Guitars
Leonberg, Germany

The King and Queen

First Act's Studio for Artists is a custom shop that builds one-of-a kind instruments for rock guitarists; their clients have included Henry and JoJo Garza (Los Lonely Boys), Martin Gore (Depeche Mode), David Hidalgo (Los Lobos), Adam Levine (Maroon 5), Nick McCarthy (Franz Ferdinand), Rick Nielsen (Cheap Trick), Todd Rundgren, Serj Tankian (System of a Down), Paul Westerberg (The Replacements), Brad Whitford (Aerosmith), and Nick Zinner (The Yeah Yeah Yeahs).

Inspired by a classic deck of cards, the King and Queen guitar is intricately hand painted with playing card motifs on every surface. A king peers regally from the front, while the back is "bedecked" with a rose-clutching queen. Black and red card suit symbols run along the pearl fret markers and sides. Scrolls based on traditional playing card designs festoon the back of the neck, and the back of the headstock carries a jack in profile.

With their tongues planted firmly in their cheeks, First Act boasts, "Gold hardware adds the Midas touch. Not only does this guitar rock in all the right places, it just might make the competition fold."

● The King and Queen, 2004
First Act Guitars
Boston, Massachusetts

SPECIFICATIONS

BODY AND SIDE WOODS: Mahogany

TOP WOOD: Mahogany

BODY WIDTH, LOWER BOUT: 13½ inches (34.3 cm)

ELECTRONICS: (2) K.A. P900 pickups, 2 volume and 2 tone controls, 3-way toggle switch

NECK WOOD: Mahogany

FRETBOARD MATERIAL: Rosewood

FRETBOARD INLAY: Pearl blocks with card suits

HEADSTOCK DECORATION: 3 x 3 F.A. Pompadour

BRIDGE: Hipshot

NUT AND SADDLE: Corian

BINDING: White Plastic

SCALE LENGTH: 25 inches (63.5 cm)

NECK WIDTH AT NUT: 1¹¹⁄₁₆ inches (4.3 cm)

FINISH: Top: white with custom king, back: white with custom queen, neck: dark blue/red stripe design, rims: black and red card suits

BODY DEPTH: 1⅝ inches (4.1 cm)

BODY LENGTH: 16⅛ inches (41 cm)

OVERALL LENGTH: 38¾ inches (98.4 cm)

U.S. SUGGESTED RETAIL PRICE: $6,000

Roger Giffin

Giffin Standard Six-String Hollow Body

$\mathcal{R}$oger Giffin has been building high-quality electric guitars and basses since the late 1960s, when he opened a workshop in London that was frequented by the likes of Eric Clapton, John Entwistle, David Gilmour, Mark Knopfler, Andy Summers, and Pete Townshend.

He moved to Los Angeles in 1988 to head Gibson's custom shop and West Coast repair operation, where he built a wide range of custom guitars, including a replica of Jimmy Page's 1958 Les Paul commissioned as a backup to that famous instrument. After leaving Gibson in 1993, when the company decided to move all its operations to Nashville, Giffin re-opened Giffin Guitars, where he continues to emphasize extensive hand work and close interaction with clients.

Giffin says he first came up with the Giffin Standard guitar in the late '70s at the request of a customer who wanted a "Strat meets Les Paul" type of instrument. "The body shape that I ended up using evolved from guitars I had been building since back in the early '70s," he explains. "It's not surprising to see that many other builders hit upon this type of design at about the same time. It was a very logical guitar that needed to be invented."

307

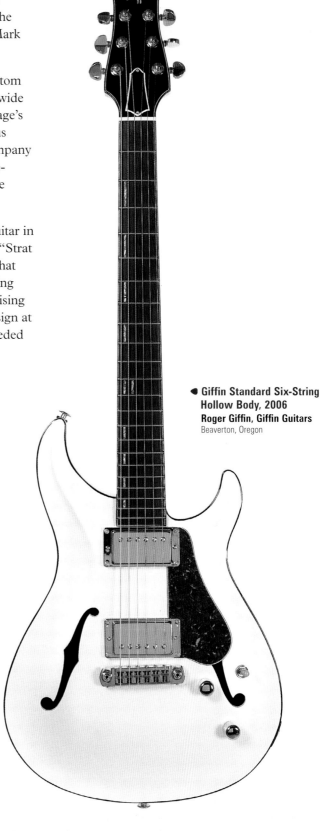

◀ **Giffin Standard Six-String Hollow Body, 2006**
Roger Giffin, Giffin Guitars
Beaverton, Oregon

SPECIFICATIONS

BODY AND SIDE WOODS: Honduran mahogany

TOP WOOD: Eastern hard rock maple

BODY WIDTH, LOWER BOUT: 13 inches (33 cm)

ELECTRONICS: Wolfetone "Greywolf" humbuckers

NECK WOOD: Honduran mahogany, maple laminate

FRETBOARD MATERIAL: Brazilian rosewood

FRETBOARD INLAY: Abalone lines

BRIDGE: Pigtail aluminum wraparound

NUT AND SADDLE: Bone

TUNING MACHINES: Grover Rotomatic

BINDING: Tortoise-shell and black/white

SCALE LENGTH: 24.75 inches (62.9 cm)

NECK WIDTH AT NUT: 1¹¹⁄₁₆ inches (4.3 cm)

NUMBER OF FRETS: 22

FINISH: Pearlescent white urethane

BODY DEPTH: 2 inches (5 cm)

BODY LENGTH: 18 inches (45.7 cm)

OVERALL LENGTH: 37 inches (94 cm)

U.S. SUGGESTED RETAIL PRICE: $4,130

ELECTRIC

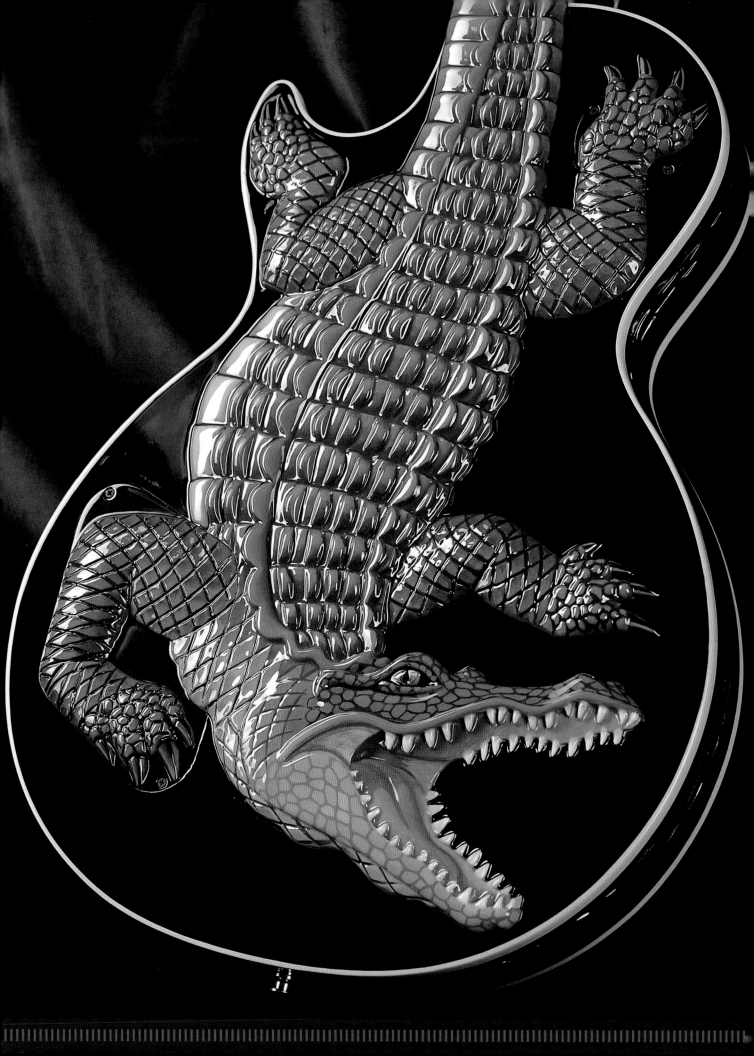

Gibson "Gator" Les Paul

This literally wild one-off custom Les Paul was built for country music star, Louisiana native, and alligator lover Kix Brooks of Brooks and Dunn.

After Brooks brought the idea of an alligator guitar to Gibson, he and master luthier Bruce Kunkel worked out the design, and then the multi-talented Kunkel spent nearly 300 hours carving, inlaying, and painting to bring the concept to life.

The hand-painted, relief-carved gator on the top of the guitar has his jaws wide open, ready to chomp down on one of the four carved frogs that serve as knobs for the tone and volume controls. The head, body, and tail of another alligator, inlaid in pearl on the fingerboard, dip in and out of the pitch black ebony "swamp" while a fifth frog, which is also inlaid in pearl, dances on the headstock, above the head of the lurking, partially-hidden gator. The back of the guitar is completely covered by a third, even larger carved alligator, whose tail extends the full length of the neck. As finishing touches, Kunkel inlaid Brooks's initials into the back of the headstock, above the tip of the gator's tail, and also carved the rims of the guitar to simulate alligator skin.

Gibson "Gator" Les Paul, 1997 ►
Built by Bruce J. Kunkel
Gibson Guitar Corporation, Custom, Art &
Historic Division
Nashville, Tennessee

SPECIFICATIONS

BODY AND SIDE WOODS: Mahogany

TOP WOOD: Mahogany

BODY WIDTH, LOWER BOUT: 14 inches (35.6 cm)

ELECTRONICS: Dual humbuckers

NECK WOOD: Mahogany

FRETBOARD MATERIAL: Ebony

FRETBOARD INLAY: 350 pieces of abalone and black pearl, image of partially submerged alligator

HEADSTOCK DECORATION: Abalone frog

BRIDGE: Nashville TOM/gold-plated

NUT AND SADDLE: Bone

TUNING MACHINES: Gold Grover rotomatics

BINDING: Traditional B/W/B

NECK WIDTH AT NUT: 1¹³⁄₁₆ inches (4.6 cm)

NUMBER OF FRETS: 22

FINISH: Nitrocellulose lacquer

309

ELECTRIC

Gretsch
G6138 Bo Diddley

Bo Diddley built his first "square" guitar around 1958 by marrying the neck and electronics from a Gretsch guitar to a body he had made himself. He commissioned Gretsch to build a second for him the following year, and that guitar became his signature instrument, which he played until he wore it out.

Diddley, who was born Otha Ellas Bates, picked up the "Bo Diddley" moniker in vocational high school. Although he has said he has no idea what it means, the most likely explanation is that Bo Diddley is simply slang for "nothing at all" as in "It don't mean bo diddley." Diddley studied violin for many years before he began playing guitar and explained that the violin was "the railroad track, or lifeline, to me playing a guitar...I used the bow licks with the guitar pick, and that's the reason for the weird sounds. That was my way of imitating the bow on the violin strings, and that was the closest I could get to it."

Whatever its origin, Bo Diddley's primal, eponymous "shave and a haircut" beat is one of the cornerstones of rock-and-roll, imitated by everyone from Buddy Holly to the Rolling Stones, The Who, Bruce Springsteen, and U2. As Tom Petty has put it, "Elvis may be King, but Diddley is Daddy."

◀ **G6138 Bo Diddley, 2004**
Gretsch Guitars
Scottsdale, Arizona

SPECIFICATIONS

BODY AND SIDE WOODS: Semi-hollow alder body

TOP WOOD: Laminated maple

BODY WIDTH, LOWER BOUT: 9¼ inches (23.5 cm)

NECK WOOD: 3-piece rock maple

FRETBOARD MATERIAL: Ebony

HEADSTOCK DECORATION: Inlaid Gretsch logo

BRIDGE: Rosewood-based Adjusto-Matic bridge

BINDING: Body binding

NECK WIDTH AT NUT: 1¹¹⁄₁₆ inches (4.3 cm)

NUMBER OF FRETS: 22

FINISH: Gloss urethane

Gretsch

G6199 "Billy Bo" Jupiter Thunderbird

*T*his outrageous guitar unites two of rock's most original and flamboyant showmen, rock-and-roll founding father Bo Diddley and ZZ Top frontman Billy F. Gibbons.

The original Jupiter Thunderbird, on which this new model is based, was a one-off 1959 collaboration between Diddley and Gretsch. Years later, Diddley gave the guitar to Gibbons, his only equal in designing and playing purposefully wild-looking stage guitars. (Diddley also had Gretsch build him guitars covered with leather and fur, to name just two of his other ideas.) Gibbons added Diddley's "science experiment gone wrong" to his vast stash of vintage and custom guitars, where it remained buried until one day, during a ZZ Top recording session, "the engineering crew and I snaked through the guitar vault searching for that 'certain-something' guitar and there it was! We didn't risk subjecting such a rare instrument to the rigors of the road, so this new, reproduction model was recreated with some BFG Mojo thrown in for good measure."

Although he may be better known for his two-foot beard and ever-present Ray Bans, Billy Gibbons is one of the Lone Star State's greatest bluesmen, and his "Little Ole Band from Texas" is one of rock's enduring joys.

G6199 "Billy Bo" Jupiter Thunderbird, 2006 ▶
Gretsch Guitars
Scottsdale, Arizona

SPECIFICATIONS

BODY AND SIDE WOODS: Laminated maple

TOP WOOD: Laminated maple

BODY WIDTH, LOWER BOUT: 11½ inches (29.2 cm)

NECK WOOD: One-piece mahogany

FRETBOARD MATERIAL: Rosewood

BRIDGE: Pinned Adjusto-Matic bridge

BINDING: Aged body bindings

NECK WIDTH AT NUT: 1¹¹⁄₁₆ inches (4.3 cm)

NUMBER OF FRETS: 22

FINISH: Gloss urethane

Guitarmst

*C*artoonist and musician Robert Armstrong is the creator of the crude, sleazy, and opportunistic '70s t-shirt icon and comic book anti-hero Mickey Rat, the owner of the Couch Potato trademark, the co-author of *The Couch Potato Guide to Life*, and, with fellow cartoonist Robert Crumb, a founding member of The Cheap Suit Serenaders, a band of passionate collectors of old 78s who recreate the old-timey blues, hokum, jazz, folk, string-band, Hawaiian, and ragtime music they love. In addition to comics and album covers, Armstrong also has designed and painted a number of guitars and ukes over the years, including a series of five limited-edition painted Cowboy guitars for C.F. Martin, and his virtuoso musical saw graced the title track of the *One Flew Over the Cuckoo's Nest* soundtrack.

This decidedly loopy but fully functional guitar was a joint venture with luthier and Fanned-Fret inventor Ralph Novak, who helped bring Armstrong's wonderfully off-center design to life. Guitarmst is simply a mash-up of guitar and Armstrong.

Guitarmst, 1999
Designed, hand built, and painted by
Robert Armstrong, in collaboration
with Ralph Novak of Novax Guitars
Winters, California

SPECIFICATIONS

BODY AND SIDE WOODS: Alder

TOP WOOD: Alder

BODY WIDTH, LOWER BOUT: 14 inches (35.6 cm)

ELECTRONICS: 2 pickups

NECK WOOD: Maple

FRETBOARD MATERIAL: Rosewood

FRETBOARD INLAY: Red and yellow plastic

HEADSTOCK DECORATION: Paint, carving with inlaid wooden ball plus black plastic overlay

BRIDGE: Purple heart

NUT AND SADDLE: Bone

TUNING MACHINES: Red Schallers

SCALE LENGTH: 24.75 to 26 inches (62.9 to 66 cm)

NECK WIDTH AT NUT: 1⅝ inches (4.1 cm)

NUMBER OF FRETS: 22

FINISH: Clear lacquer over paint

BODY DEPTH: 1¾ inches (4.4 cm)

BODY LENGTH: 17 inches (43.2 cm)

OVERALL LENGTH: 39 inches (99.1 cm)

Johan Gustavsson
JG Bluesmaster '59 Custom

*J*ohan Gustavsson built his first guitar while he was apprenticing in a furniture workshop. Necessity was the mother of invention; he couldn't afford an expensive name brand instrument, so he decided to see if he could build a guitar on his own, using the wood and machinery that was right in front of him. That first guitar won first prize in a contest sponsored by *HiFi & Music* magazine, and his course was set.

Gustavsson, who has been a professional touring and session guitarist for more than two decades, says that his experience repairing and restoring "the most coveted vintage guitars that Fullerton and Kalamazoo ever produced" forms the basis of his aesthetic. His Bluesmaster models are intended to recreate the sound and feel of classic Gibson Les Pauls, and include Goldtop, Custom '59, and Thinline variations. They are interpretations rather than copies, however, incorporating a variety of Gustavsson's own design concepts, including hand-built wrap-around bridges. He also offers his clients a wide array of options, including their choice of pickup configurations and scale lengths of 25.75, 25, and 25.5 inches (65.4, 63.5, and 64.8 cm). "My instruments are completely built with both passion and precision," he says. "The satisfaction of each individual client is job one. Simple as that!"

JG Bluesmaster '59 Custom, 2006 ▶
Johan Gustavsson, JG Guitars
Malmö, Sweden

313

SPECIFICATIONS

BODY AND SIDE WOODS: Old-growth Honduran mahogany

TOP WOOD: Eastern maple

ELECTRONICS: Wolfetone legends

NECK WOOD: Old growth Honduran mahogany

FRETBOARD MATERIAL: Old growth Brazilian rosewood

FRETBOARD INLAY: Celluloid

HEADSTOCK DECORATION: Holly veneer with mother-of-pearl inlay

BRIDGE: JG intonatabe wraparound

NUT AND SADDLE: Bone

TUNING MACHINES: Gotoh Kluson style

BINDING: Celluloid

SCALE LENGTH: 24.6 inches (62.5 cm)

NECK WIDTH AT NUT: 1 11/16 inches (4.3 cm)

NUMBER OF FRETS: 22

FINISH: Faded cherry burst, nitrocellulose lacquer

1959 Les Paul Standard Vintage Original Specs

The Les Paul Standard ranks with the Fender Stratocaster as the most influential and enduring electric guitar design of all time, and the 1959 Standard is by general consensus, the one to have, provided you can find or afford one. As longtime Nashville guitar dealer and author George Gruhn has put it, "the 1959 Gibson Les Paul Standard represents the pinnacle of electric solid-body guitar design—the point where aesthetics and functionality peaked at the same time."

The carved maple-topped sunburst 1958 through 1960 Les Paul Standard model came to prominence in the hands of a string of 1960s guitar gods, including Eric Clapton, Peter Green, Mick Taylor, Jimmy Page, Mike Bloomfield, and Duane Allman, all of whom took advantage of the fat tone and sustain of its now legendary "PAF" (Patent Applied For) humbucking pickups and its wide, fat frets, which made dramatic string bends possible.

Since a '59 in untouched condition can easily cost more than $100,000, Gibson has released a number of custom-shop Les Paul reissues in recent years, including a Jimmy Page Signature model and recreation of the '59s original specs.

♠ **1959 Les Paul Standard Vintage Original Specs, 2006**
Gibson Guitar Corporation, Custom, Art & Historic Division
Nashville, Tennessee

SPECIFICATIONS

BODY AND SIDE WOODS: Mahogany

TOP WOOD: Maple

NECK WOOD: Mahogany

FRETBOARD MATERIAL: Rosewood

FRETBOARD INLAY: Acrylic trapezoid inlay

HEADSTOCK DECORATION: Holly headstock veneer

BRIDGE: ABR-1 bridge

TUNING MACHINES: Vintage tulip tuners

BINDING: Single-ply cream binding

SCALE LENGTH: 24.75 inches (62.9 cm)

NECK WIDTH AT NUT: 1¹¹⁄₁₆ inches (4.3 cm)

Langcaster

Joh Lang

Joh Lang's Langcaster guitars are made from stunning ancient swamp kauri and fitted with his own innovative Ultimate Lo low-impedance pickups.

Both the guitar and the pickups resulted from Lang's frustrations in the recording studio. "When digital recording came," he explains, "we all had problems recording direct into a mixing desk without the cursed hum coming mainly from monitors. It took hours of expensive studio time to control sustain and distortion."

The body came first. Remembering beautiful tables made of 35,000-year-old kauri swamp roots by a Dutch friend, Jaap Tediek of Kauricraft, Lang enlisted his help in using kauri for the body of his new guitar. After six months of trial and error, they succeeded, and Lang moved on to the search for noiseless pickups and controllable sustain. After a year of work, he finally created a pickup with an unheard-of resistance of only +/-100 ohms (6,500 is normal for high impedance pickups), eight magnetic poles to eliminate signal loss when strings are bent, and built-in overdrive with adjustable gain. The pickups are virtually noiseless and allow players to use chords as long as 300 feet (91 m) without any signal or frequency loss. Lang says proudly, "I love to see a guitar player's big smile when using my 35,000-year-old guitar with the most futuristic pickups ever devised."

Langcaster, 2005 ▶
Joh Lang, Langcaster Guitars
Auckland, New Zealand

SPECIFICATIONS

BODY AND SIDE WOODS: 35,000 year-old swamp New Zealand kauri with kauri gum/amber inside

BODY WIDTH, LOWER BOUT: 13 inches (33 cm)

ELECTRONICS: Langcaster active low-impedance pickups and overdrive and LED, handmade switch plate and chrome pickup rings

NECK WOOD: Hard rock maple

FRETBOARD MATERIAL: Ebony

FRETBOARD INLAY: Paua dots

HEADSTOCK DECORATION: Carved New Zealand Maori design handmade string trees with jade or paua inlay, paua inlay logo

BRIDGE: Schaller 3D

NUT AND SADDLE: Earvana graphite nut

TUNING MACHINES: Schaller locking tuners 1:16 ratio

SCALE LENGTH: 25.5 inches (64.8 cm) and 12-inch (30.5 cm) radius

NECK WIDTH AT NUT: 1^{11}/16 inches (4.3 cm)

NUMBER OF FRETS: 22

FINISH: Two-pot lacquer DeBeer

BODY DEPTH: 1¾ inches (4.4 cm)

BODY LENGTH: 18 inches (45.7 cm)

OVERALL LENGTH: 40 inches (101.6 cm)

U.S. SUGGESTED RETAIL PRICE: $2,950

Nik Huber

Redwood

ounded in 1996, Nik Huber Guitars grew slowly but steadily as it gained a worldwide reputation for its high-quality electric guitars. Today, a team of five highly skilled specialists is building around 120 handcrafted instruments a year.

"Basically," says Nik Huber, "what we do is turn beautiful pieces of wood into excellent guitars. Building guitars with your own hands, as good as possible—and beyond—is nothing a career counselor suggests in high school. Guitar making is more a calling than a profession. It can be addictive. It has to be, in a certain way. But it is not about 'more, more.' Our constant craving is 'better, better, better.'"

The Redwood has a semi-hollow, chambered mahogany body and a spectacular carved curly redwood top. Like Huber's other guitars, it combines many of the best elements of classic "Les Pauls" (carved top, humbucker pickups) and "Strats" (25.5-inch scale length) with a number of modern design features, including Huber's carved aluminum wrapover bridge. The guitar can produce an extremely wide range of tones, from warm jazz to stinging blues.

Redwood, 2004 ▶
Nik Huber, Nik Huber Guitars
Rodgau, Germany

SPECIFICATIONS

BODY AND SIDE WOODS: South American mahogany

TOP WOOD: Curly redwood

ELECTRONICS: Passiv (master volume, mastertone, push pot for coil tap)

NECK WOOD: South American mahogany

FRETBOARD MATERIAL: Ebony

FRETBOARD INLAY: Nik Huber dolphin inlays

HEADSTOCK DECORATION: Ebony, Dolphin logo

BRIDGE: Nik Huber stoptail bridge (aluminum)

NUT AND SADDLE: TremNut by GraphTech

TUNING MACHINES: Custom Schaller "mini"/ebony buttons

BINDING: Scraped "fake" binding at body

SCALE LENGTH: 25.5 inches (64.8 cm)

NECK WIDTH AT NUT: 1 11/16 inches (4.3 cm)

NUMBER OF FRETS: 22

FINISH: Polyurethane

BODY DEPTH: 2 1/16 inches (5.2 cm)

BODY LENGTH: 15 15/16 inches (40.5 cm)

OVERALL LENGTH: 38 inches (96.5 cm)

U.S. SUGGESTED RETAIL PRICE: $5,985

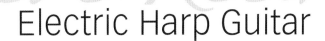

Electric Harp Guitar

S teve Klein's electric guitar designs were even more radical than his acoustic ones. The Klein electric evolved over a 12-year period, with input from Carl Margolis, Ronnie Montrose, and Ned Steinberger. The final designs have headless bodies that place ergonomics over traditional aesthetics (David Lindley dubbed an early prototype "Lumpy"), and they have been championed by such original stylists as Bill Frisell, Henry Kaiser, Lou Reed, Steve Miller, Martin Simpson, Andy Summers, and David Torn. Frisell has said of his Klein Electric, "You can feel the body moving...it's a real instrument and has a real acoustic quality to its tone. I'm really lucky—an all-around guitar that has my sound—I haven't found anything that comes close."

Klein's electric harp guitar, which added a minimalist harp arm with five sub-bass strings to the body of his electric guitar, was made famous by the late Michael Hedges. Hedges was a major force in bringing the harp guitar back to public attention, playing and composing new music for a variety of antique and contemporary acoustic models in addition to his Klein.

317

◀ **Electric Harp Guitar, 1990**
Steve Klein
Vineburg, California
Collection of Jeff Doctorow

Saturn Deluxe Reserve Stock

The Saturn is a double cutaway guitar, built as a showpiece along with the Apollo Artist Reserve Stock (pg. 298) for the 2006 NAMM International Music Products Association show, the oldest and biggest musical instrument and products trade show in the world.

Both the Apollo and Saturn models have set-necks, chambered bodies, bound fingerboards, and Jason Lollar pickups. Briggs's craftsmanship is manifest in the wide variety of neck shapes he offers, which range from traditionally shaped Slim to Colossal and also include three boat-shaped sizes, the soft-vee'd Small Boat, harder-vee'd Full Boat, and the Apollo-only Artist Carve.

♠ Saturn Deluxe Reserve Stock, 2006
Jack Briggs, Briggs Guitars
Raleigh, North Carolina

SPECIFICATIONS

BODY AND SIDE WOODS: 50,000-year-old ancient kauri from New Zealand

TOP WOOD: 45-year-old air-dried flamed redwood

BODY WIDTH, LOWER BOUT: 13⅜ inches (34 cm)

ELECTRONICS: Lollar imperial PAF pickups, 5-way switch, volume and tone controls

NECK WOOD: 30,000-year-old ancient kauri from New Zealand

FRETBOARD MATERIAL: 50-year-old air-dried African blackwood

FRETBOARD INLAY: Paua abalone shell pyramids

HEADSTOCK DECORATION: African blackwood with grain-matched truss rod cover

BRIDGE: Lightweight aluminum wraparound, fully adjustable, from Pigtail Music

NUT AND SADDLE: Delrin slip stone nut

TUNING MACHINES: Grover rotomatic

BINDING: Rippled ivoroid cellulose nitrate on headstock, fingerboard, and body

SCALE LENGTH: 25 inches (63.5 cm)

NECK WIDTH AT NUT: 1¹¹⁄₁₆ inches (4.3 cm)

NUMBER OF FRETS: 22

FINISH: Natural nitrocellulose lacquer

BODY DEPTH: 2 inches (5 cm)

BODY LENGTH: 17¾ inches (45.1 cm)

OVERALL LENGTH: 38¼ inches (97.2 cm)

U.S. SUGGESTED RETAIL PRICE: $7,095

Earlewood

*J*effrey Terwilliger has been repairing and building guitars and basses since 1970, when he was in 7th grade. His Earlewood is the result of years of experimentation, working to create the perfect hybrid electric, a guitar that combines the best guitar designs to optimize playability, appearance, and tone.

As part of his quest, Terwilliger surveyed more than 100 guitarists about their preferences in neck, electronics, top carve, and so on, and then added several innovations of his own to the design.

The top wood is joined to a chambered body with a peaked shape. The 24th fret is a brass plate attached to the end of the fingerboard. "This way you get 24 frets, without knocking the neck pickup out of its sweet spot. Pickups are trimmed with exotic hardwood. The headstock overlay is not merely the same color as the body top wood; we go for broke and cut it from the very same billet. The output jack plate is recessed into an angled bevel and points upward. Knobs are recessed in 'silos.'"

Terwilliger offers 20 different finish colors including Key Lime Green, Caribbean Burst, Reef Teal, Volcano Burst, Hawaiian Fire, Mocha, and Bronze Idol—all of which he coats with clear polyester resin to create a glass-like finish.

SPECIFICATIONS

BODY AND SIDE WOODS: Korina

TOP WOOD: Quilted maple

BODY WIDTH, LOWER BOUT: 13½ inches (34.3 cm)

ELECTRONICS: Per customer order, wide range of choices

NECK WOOD: Three-piece flamed maple

FRETBOARD MATERIAL: Ebony

FRETBOARD INLAY: Mother-of-pearl moon phases

HEADSTOCK DECORATION: Logo and stylized bird at tip

BRIDGE: Tone Pros Tun-o-matic

NUT AND SADDLE: Graph-tech

TUNING MACHINES: Grover top locking 18:1

BINDING: Maple

SCALE LENGTH: 25 inches (63.5 cm)

NECK WIDTH AT NUT: 1¹¹⁄₁₆ inches (4.3 cm)

NUMBER OF FRETS: 24

FINISH: Polyester resin clearcoat

BODY DEPTH: 1¾ inches (4.4 cm)

BODY LENGTH: 18 inches (45.7 cm)

OVERALL LENGTH: 39 inches (99.1 cm)

U.S. SUGGESTED RETAIL PRICE: $5,250

♠ **Earlewood, 2006**
Jeffrey Earle Terwilliger, JET Guitars
Raleigh, North Carolina

Stone Tone Short Scale Baritone Guitar

$\mathcal{T}$his unique blend of wood, stone, and electronics is the product of an unusual collaboration between second-generation Florida stone artisan Robert Di Santo and master luthier John Ingram, who worked with Paul Reed Smith for 25 years.

Di Santo hit on the idea of using a thin slab of stone to top a guitar and brought the concept to Ingram, who was skeptical at first. "My spin was to design a new guitar from the ground up," says Ingram. "The stone has acoustical properties I didn't know existed and to this day, still don't completely understand. There is more midrange than you would expect. The highs really sizzle, and the bass is plentiful, even, and clear. In my view this is a straight-forward, no-nonsense design. Nothing revolutionary, just common sense based on many years' experience."

Ingram says the Stone Tone Short Scale Baritone evolved as it was being designed and built. Most baritone guitars use a scale length between 27 inches (68.6 cm) and 28 inches (71.1 cm), but Eric Johnson, the builder Ingram had been working with, had a jig for slotting a 26.2 inch-scale length, traditionally used for a five-string banjo, sitting around his shop, and they decided to go with that. "It's not that much longer than a normal long scale electric guitar," says Ingram. "The advantage of this scale seems to be that it plays more like a guitar than a 27-inch or 28-inch. And properly strung, it rings similar to a longer scale instrument."

321

SPECIFICATIONS

BODY AND SIDE WOODS: South American mahogany

TOP WOOD: Blue pearl granite

BODY WIDTH, LOWER BOUT: 13 inches (33 cm)

ELECTRONICS: Dual Humbucking/2 vol, 2 tone (push-pull coil split)

NECK WOOD: South American mahogany

FRETBOARD MATERIAL: Brazilian rosewood

FRETBOARD INLAY: Mother-of-pearl dots

HEADSTOCK DECORATION: Vinyl decal

BRIDGE: Leo Quan Badass

NUT AND SADDLE: Bone nut

TUNING MACHINES: Sperzel

SCALE LENGTH: 26.2 inches (66.5 cm)

NECK WIDTH AT NUT: 1¾ inches (4.4 cm)

NUMBER OF FRETS: 22

FINISH: Nitro lacquer

BODY DEPTH: 1⅝ inches (4.1 cm)

BODY LENGTH: 16 inches (40.6 cm)

OVERALL LENGTH: 40 inches (101.6 cm)

U.S. SUGGESTED RETAIL PRICE: $10,000

♠ **Stone Tone Short Scale Baritone Guitar, 2005**
Stone by Robert Di Santo,
built by John R. Ingram, Stone Tone Music
Annapolis, Maryland

Gretsch

G6136 1958 Stephen Stills White Falcon

tephen Stills was one of the first and most prominent guitarists to champion vintage electric and acoustic guitars. His favorite electric guitar was the legendary Gretsch White Falcon, which both he and Neil Young often played on stage with Buffalo Springfield and Crosby, Stills, Nash & Young. This reproduction is a copy of Stills's classic 1958 single-cutaway White Falcon, accurate down to its faded white paint.

Gretsch made some of the biggest and most impressive hollow-bodied electrics of the 1950s, several of which were designed and championed by Chet Atkins. The purposefully over-the-top gold trimmed, 17-inch White Falcon was originally built as a one-off tradeshow showpiece, but it caused so much commotion that it was worked into Gretsch's production line in the mid-1950s. Billed as "the guitar of the future," it was an extravagant instrument back then, listing at the top of Gretsch's line for $600. Original White Falcons command huge prices in the vintage market; a 1958 will set you back around $35,000.

322

● **G6136 1958 Stephen Stills White Falcon, 2000 Gretsch Guitars** Scottsdale, Arizona

SPECIFICATIONS

BODY AND SIDE WOODS: Maple body, oversized f-holes

TOP WOOD: Arched laminated maple

BODY WIDTH, LOWER BOUT: 17 inches (43.2 cm)

ELECTRONICS: FilterTron pickups with Alnico magnets and dual switches, Trademark Falcon volume knobs with red rhinestone markers

NECK WOOD: Three-piece maple neck

FRETBOARD MATERIAL: Ebony, with neoclassical position markers and inlaid Stephen Stills signature between the 18th and 21st fret

FRETBOARD INLAY: Stephen Stills signature between the 18th and 21st fret

HEADSTOCK DECORATION: White falcon, with goldflake Gretsch logo

BRIDGE: Gold-plated, adjustable bridge and Bigsby tailpiece

TUNING MACHINES: Grover Imperial

BINDING: Gold-flecked

Saul Koll

RE 8

aul Koll described this guitar model as an "asymmetrical, ergonomically designed, carved top, headless wonder. As comfortable and great sounding this instrument is," he continues, "it remains somewhat an enigma with only the most daring and brave playing it."

Koll built the original "RE" guitar for Ron Escheté, a master of the seven-string guitar whom *Jazz Times* has called "one of the finest jazz guitarists in L.A." Escheté had played a Klein electric owned by one of his students, and loved the neck angle and how the oddly shaped but ergonomic guitar sat on his leg. He asked Koll to make him something like it, only with seven strings. Because he was playing big traditional archtops at the time, Koll borrowed from that tradition as well as Steve Klein's ideas in coming up with this unique design. The eight-stringed version pictured here was built for Elliott Sharp,

an American multi-instrumentalist, composer, and performer who has been a major player in the avant-garde experimental music scene in New York City for more than 30 years. The RE 8 is primarily built as an electric guitar but also has great acoustics, not unlike a small archtop.

RE 8, 2007 ◖
Saul Koll, Koll Guitar Company
Portland, Oregon
Collection of Elliott Sharp

SPECIFICATIONS

BODY AND SIDE WOODS: Big leaf maple

TOP WOOD: Sitka spruce

BODY WIDTH, LOWER BOUT: 15 inches (38.1 cm)

ELECTRONICS: Lollar custom humbucker

NECK WOOD: Mahogany

FRETBOARD MATERIAL: Ebony

BRIDGE: Floating

NUT AND SADDLE: Lubricated unbleached bone

TUNING MACHINES: Sperzel

BINDING: Celluloid

SCALE LENGTH: Fanned, 25.6 to 26.5 inches (65.1 to 67.3 cm)

NECK WIDTH AT NUT: 2 inches (5 cm)

NUMBER OF FRETS: 22

BRACING: X brace

FINISH: Nitrocellulose lacquer amber shading

BODY DEPTH: 2 inches (5 cm)

BODY LENGTH: 22 inches (55.9 cm)

U.S. SUGGESTED RETAIL PRICE: $5,000

Tornado

*S*aul Koll says that while other kids were out playing sports, he was in the garage taking expensive toys apart and gluing the components into weird new contraptions. He started to play the guitar at 12 and from 1984–1995 played and toured with The Charms, a highly regarded but commercially unsuccessful San Diego-based pop-rock group which recorded several singles and albums before ultimately disbanding.

Koll began built his first guitar while in college and founded the Koll Guitar Company in 1990. Initially, he taught himself, using Irving Sloane's *Classic Guitar Construction* as a guide, and then while working as a repairman under the tutelage of Jon Peterson and Glen Mersat at World of Strings in Long Beach, he began building guitars full time.

This unique instrument was originally built for avant-garde guitarist and composer David Torn, which explains its punning name. Among its many custom features are arm contouring and a tummy cut so that it fits tightly against the player's body.

SPECIFICATIONS

BODY AND SIDE WOODS: Korina

BODY WIDTH, LOWER BOUT: 13 inches (33 cm)

ELECTRONICS: Harmonic Design Z-90, TV Jones Electroflux

NECK WOOD: Korina

FRETBOARD MATERIAL: Brazilian rosewood

BRIDGE: Hipshot Tremolo

NUT AND SADDLE: Lubricated Delrin

TUNING MACHINES: Sperzel

SCALE LENGTH: Fanned, 24.6 inches (62.5 cm)

NECK WIDTH AT NUT: 1 11/16 inches (4.3 cm)

NUMBER OF FRETS: 22

FINISH: Nitrocellulose lacquer

BODY DEPTH: 1 3/4 inches (4.4 cm)

BODY LENGTH: 22 inches (55.9 cm)

U.S. SUGGESTED RETAIL PRICE: $3,000

◆ **Tornado, 2007**
Saul Koll, Koll Guitar Company
Portland, Oregon
Collection of Jeff Doctorow

Delta Wing F01

*G*ary Kramer is best known as a founder of the New Jersey–based Kramer Guitar Company, which produced some of the first and most popular "Super Strats" of the 1980s. Endorsed by Eddie Van Halen, these Kramers introduced the now classic humbucker/single coil/single coil pickup layout in 1984, as well as extra long scale length and a distinctive reverse headstock.

Kramer himself left the company soon after it was founded in 1976 but is now back with a new line of decidedly different-looking instruments. Designed to play easily as well as look cool, the ergonomic Delta Wing features a deeply contoured saddle-like upper-body shape that gives strong support to the picking arm and comes with a detachable leg rest. This custom model Delta Wing is a fretless seven-string.

◄ **Delta Wing F01, 2005**
Gary Kramer and Leo Scala,
Gary Kramer Guitars
El Segundo, California

325

SPECIFICATIONS

BODY AND SIDE WOODS: One-piece Honduran mahogany

BODY WIDTH, LOWER BOUT: 13¾ inches (34.9 cm)

ELECTRONICS: Custom wound Bartolinis, volume, Equalizer, variable coil split

NECK WOOD: One-piece hard rock maple

FRETBOARD MATERIAL: Ebony

FRETBOARD INLAY: Flame maple, purple heart racing stripe

HEADSTOCK DECORATION: Matching color to body (solar yellow)

BRIDGE: Hipshot 7 string

NUT AND SADDLE: Bone

TUNING MACHINES: Lo-pull Sperzels

BINDING: Neck only

SCALE LENGTH: 25.5 inches (64.8 cm)

NECK WIDTH AT NUT: 2 inches (5 cm)

NUMBER OF FRETS: 36 (fretless)

FINISH: Polyurethane

BODY DEPTH: 2 inches (5 cm)

BODY LENGTH: 20 inches (50.8 cm)

OVERALL LENGTH: 40 inches (101.6 cm)

Lapax Cotton Lap Steel

◆ **Lapax Cotton Lap Steel, 2003**
Ville Tyyster, Soitinrakennus Tyyster
Lappeenranta, Finland

SPECIFICATIONS

BODY AND SIDE WOODS: Mahogany

TOP WOOD: Flamed birch

BODY WIDTH, LOWER BOUT: 11¹⁵⁄₁₆ inches (30.3 cm)

ELECTRONICS: Tyyster alnico pickups, undersaddle piezo, stereo output

NECK WOOD: Mahogany

FRETBOARD MATERIAL: Rosewood

FRETBOARD INLAY: Abalone dots

HEADSTOCK DECORATION: Tyyster logo, rosewood and birch binding

BRIDGE: Rosewood, string thru body style

NUT AND SADDLE: Moose shinbone

TUNING MACHINES: Gotoh

BINDING: Rosewood and birch

SCALE LENGTH: 25 inches (63.5 cm)

NECK WIDTH AT NUT: 1⅞ inches (4.8 cm)

NUMBER OF FRETS: 18

FINISH: Polyurethane base, acrylic finish

BODY DEPTH: 1¹³⁄₁₆ inches (4.7 cm)

BODY LENGTH: 19⁵⁄₁₆ inches (49 cm)

OVERALL LENGTH: 36¹³⁄₁₆ inches (93.5 cm)

U.S. SUGGESTED RETAIL PRICE: $4,000

"Hawaiian" lap steels were among the first electric guitars, arising in the midst of America's long obsession with Hawaiian music, which ebbed and flowed from about 1915 into the Eisenhower era of crooner Arthur Godfrey.

Like their acoustic counterparts, electric steel guitars were tuned to open chords and played flat in the player's lap, using a metal bar of some sort to voice chords and slide from note to note. The most commonly used electric steel tuning is C6 (C, E, G, A, c, e), which makes it possible to play a number of chords without moving the bar. Because the bottom three strings are considerably higher than standard tuning, many players use standard A, D, and G strings in those positions.

Electric lap steels became popular in the 1930s, through red hot recordings by Hawaiian virtuosi like Sol Ho'opi'i and "King" Bennie Nawahi, and Western swing masters such as Bob Dunn, Leon McAuliffe, Joaquin Murphey, Noel Boggs, and Jerry Byrd, each of whom created a distinctive personal style of playing.

In addition to several lap steel models, Ville Tyyster also builds acoustic flattops and resonator guitars as well as a variety of solid- and hollow-bodied electrics.

S. B. MacDonald

Resonator Electric

S. B. MacDonald is a refugee from the advertising world who has been building and repairing guitars of every sort since 1990. In addition to being authorized by Gibson, Fender, Martin, Taylor, Ovation, Gretch, and Tacoma for repair and warranty work, he also builds a wide range of his own acoustic and electric instruments.

MacDonald's electric resophonic guitar blends resonator and electric technology to produce a range of sounds he describes as "from deep, full reso-bite to twangle." Each of his resonator electric guitars is made to order, and he gives his clients choices in neck contour, string spacing, nut width, pickups, and colors. He even crafts custom pickguards on request. MacDonald has made resonator electrics for a host of performers, including Lucinda Williams, Robert Hunter (lyricist for the Grateful Dead), John Jackson (guitar player for Kathy Mattea, Bob Dylan, Shelby Lynne), the Last Hombres with Levon Helm, and renowned TV/film composer Mike Post, who is the subject of a Pete Townshend tune on The Who's *Endless Wire* album.

♠ **Resonator Electric, 2004**
S.B. MacDonald, S.B. MacDonald Custom Instruments
Huntington, New York

SPECIFICATIONS

BODY AND SIDE WOODS: Basswood body

BODY WIDTH, LOWER BOUT: 12½ inches (31.8 cm)

ELECTRONICS: Proprietary, active

NECK WOOD: Maple

FRETBOARD MATERIAL: Ebony

FRETBOARD INLAY: Mother-of-pearl

BRIDGE: Biscuit-style resonator bridge

NUT AND SADDLE: Bone nut, ebony saddle

TUNING MACHINES: Grover mini-rotomatics

SCALE LENGTH: 25.5 inches (64.8 cm)

NECK WIDTH AT NUT: 1¾ inches (4.4 cm)

NUMBER OF FRETS: 22

FINISH: Lacquer

BODY DEPTH: 1¾ inches (4.4 cm)

BODY LENGTH: 16½ inches (41.9 cm)

OVERALL LENGTH: 38½ inches (97.8 cm)

U.S. SUGGESTED RETAIL PRICE: $2,000

Transparent Blue Neck, Through the Body Electric

Stephen Marchione embodies the "job description luthier." He makes as wide a variety of guitars and violins as anyone in the trade, including classical guitars, flamenco guitars, archtop guitars, and carved top, neck-through, and tremolo electric guitars. "I adore making violins on the Stradivari and Guarneri patterns," he adds. "I play a jazz, blues, Spanish and Italian classical repertoire, and I'm passionate about flamenco."

Marchione has built more than 300 recording-level custom electric guitars for New York's professional players over the past decade, and his electric guitars have been used in the smash hit *The Lion King* on Broadway and on Bang on a Can's CD *Music for Airports*.

Marchione's neck-through guitar has a fat neck tone and long-ringing sustain. The neck, a three piece rock maple laminate with an African ebony fingerboard, is ultra stable and very fast, thanks to its hand-cut neck contour and smooth fretwork.

SPECIFICATIONS

BODY AND SIDE WOODS: Big leaf maple

TOP WOOD: Big leaf maple

BODY WIDTH, LOWER BOUT: 12½ inches (31.8 cm)

ELECTRONICS: Marchione humbuckers and electronics

NECK WOOD: Sugar maple

FRETBOARD MATERIAL: African ebony

HEADSTOCK DECORATION: Marchione decal

BRIDGE: Marchione steel bridge

NUT AND SADDLE: Micarta

TUNING MACHINES: Sperzel

SCALE LENGTH: 25.5 inches (64.8 cm)

NECK WIDTH AT NUT: 1¹¹⁄₁₆ inches (4.3 cm)

NUMBER OF FRETS: 22

FINISH: Lacquer

BODY DEPTH: 1⅝ inches (4.1 cm)

BODY LENGTH: 17½ inches (44.5 cm)

OVERALL LENGTH: 38½ inches (97.8 cm)

U.S. SUGGESTED RETAIL PRICE: $6,900

329

▲ **Transparent Blue Neck, Through the Body Electric, 2005**
Stephen Marchione, Marchione Guitars
Houston, Texas

Acoustic Electric Hybrid

*T*his at once elegant and provocative new guitar is Michi Matsuda's first acoustic electric. Matsuda's design takes the acoustic/electric concept literally, combining the lower bout of a central sound hole of a flattop guitar with the carved, contoured upper body of a double-cutaway electric.

Matsuda was born in Nagoya, Japan, and raised in Tokyo, and his design sense is strongly influenced by traditional Japanese aesthetics, which emphasize organic form, simplicity, and asymmetry. By grounding his approach in these values, Matsuda has freed himself from many of the conventions of guitar design and consistently produces instruments unlike any one else's. He is also an extraordinary craftsman whose work has been proudly championed by his mentors, Frank Ford, Taku Sakashta, and Ervin Somogyi.

Acoustic Electric Hybrid, 2006 ▶
Michihiro Matsuda
Oakland, California

SPECIFICATIONS

BODY AND SIDE WOODS: Mahogany, koa, redwood

TOP WOOD: Engelmann spruce

BODY WIDTH, LOWER BOUT: 13¾ inches (34.9 cm)

ELECTRONICS: Joe Barden magnetic and Trance Audio acoustic pickup

NECK WOOD: Mahogany

FRETBOARD MATERIAL: Brazilian rosewood

BRIDGE: Brazilian rosewood

NUT AND SADDLE: Bone

TUNING MACHINES: Gotoh 510

BINDING: Rosewood

SCALE LENGTH: 25.25 inches (64.1 cm)

NECK WIDTH AT NUT: 1¾ inches (4.4 cm)

NUMBER OF FRETS: 21

BRACING: Matsuda X bracing

FINISH: Nitrocellulose lacquer

Jolon Model

$\mathcal{A}$ lthough Ric McCurdy specializes in archtops, he also occasionally makes flattop acoustics and electrics. This oddly shaped and headless solid-bodied electric is a one-off he made for himself using a wonderful piece of spalted wood for the body.

Headless guitars are better balanced than their far more common headed relatives, eliminating the weight of the headstock and moving the weight of the tuning machines to the body of the guitar. This is particularly advantageous with bass guitars, which are notoriously top heavy, but can also offer ergonomic benefits for electric and acoustic guitars. Maverick designers Harry Fleishman, Steve Klein, and Ned Steinberger championed headless guitars and basses in the 1980s, and an increasing number of free-thinking luthiers have experimented with headless designs in recent years.

♠ **Jolon Model, 1986**
Ric McCurdy, McCurdy Guitars
New York, New York
Collection of Jeff Doctorow

SPECIFICATIONS

BODY AND SIDE WOODS: Curly maple, all from the same board

TOP WOOD: Curly maple

BODY WIDTH, LOWER BOUT: 13 inches (33 cm)

ELECTRONICS: S. Duncan '59, SS Alnico II and Lil '59 neck

NECK WOOD: Curly maple

FRETBOARD MATERIAL: Gaboon ebony

FRETBOARD INLAY: Asymmetrical pearl blocks

BRIDGE: Custom tuner/vibrato bar

NUT AND SADDLE: Graphite

TUNING MACHINES: Custom 40-1 Tuners

SCALE LENGTH: 25.5 inches (64.8 cm)

NECK WIDTH AT NUT: 1¾ inches (4.4 cm)

NUMBER OF FRETS: 24

FINISH: Gloss Fullerplast

BODY DEPTH: 1⅞ inches (4.8 cm)

BODY LENGTH: 18 inches (45.7 cm)

OVERALL LENGTH: 32 inches (81.3 cm)

U.S. SUGGESTED RETAIL PRICE: $12,000

The Mayan Telecaster
with Larry Robinson Inlay

*L*arry Robinson is one of the great masters of traditional inlay, and this complete transformation of a Telecaster is one of his masterpieces. Robinson also created an equally ornate sister guitar, "Celtic" Tele, which is also owned by the Fender company.

Robinson is completely self-taught as an inlay artist. He began using hand tools in his father's workshop when he was six, and was making furniture with power tools by the time he was 11. He started building guitars in the late 1960s and started doing inlay in 1975 while working with Rick Turner at Alembic. In addition to the custom shops at Fender, Gibson, and Martin, his clients have included Stanley Clarke, Collings Guitars, the Eagles, John Entwistle, David Grisman, Fleetwood Mac, the Grateful Dead, Hot Tuna, Klein Guitars, Led Zeppelin, C.F. Martin & Co., Steve Miller, National Reso-Phonic Guitars, Olson Guitars, Carl Perkins, Ribbecke Guitars, Tony Rice, Santa Cruz Guitar Co., the Tsumura Collection, and U2.

Although many have commented that his work is too precise not to be machine assisted, Robinson works entirely by hand without CAD programs or the CAMs used by so many luthiers and companies today. "Luckily for those of us who only do one-of-a-kind pieces," says Robinson, "it's not cost-effective for computers to do our work."

332

The Mayan Telecaster ♠
with Larry Robinson Inlay, 1994
Fender Custom Shop,
Fender Musical Instruments Corporation
Corona, California
Courtesy of the Collection of Fender Musical Instruments Corporation

SPECIFICATIONS

BODY AND SIDE WOODS: Select ash

TOP WOOD: Select ash

BODY WIDTH, LOWER BOUT: 12¾ inches (32.4 cm)

Expression Baritone

*T*his custom baritone guitar is owned by Mike Mushok of the band Staind. "Mike liked it so much he bought two," says Ralph Novak.

Baritone guitars were first introduced by Danelectro in the late 1950s, but the concept has only recently caught on with many players and luthiers. Baritones are intended to be tuned either a fourth (B, E, A, D, F#, B) or a fifth (A, D, G, C, E, A) lower than a standard six-string guitar. Novak's patented Fanned-Fret design is particularly well-suited to the baritone range, because it allows a longer scale with superior tone, intonation, and feel.

Novak's Expression guitars are designed and built to make maximum use of his patented Fanned-Fret concept, and as he puts it, "they neither nod nor wink at conventional design." Novak explains, "This is a new guitar made for players developing a distinctive style that has no place for compromise." The Expression is balanced in tone, string tension, and weight, and its unique hand-carved body styling is "an ergonomic answer to the player's need for beauty and playability."

Expression Baritone, 2003 ▶
Ralph Novak, Novax Guitars
Eugene, Oregon

SPECIFICATIONS

BODY AND SIDE WOODS: Swamp ash

BODY WIDTH, LOWER BOUT: 12 inches (30.5 cm)

ELECTRONICS: Bartolini pickups, passive, with bass cut switch and 5-way rotary

NECK WOOD: Maple, vertical grain

FRETBOARD MATERIAL: Purple heart

FRETBOARD INLAY: Green abalone, Novax stripe pattern

BRIDGE: Novax proprietary individual bridges with Graphtech saddles

NUT AND SADDLE: Bone

TUNING MACHINES: Gotoh

BINDING: Curly maple

SCALE LENGTH: 30-inch (76.2 cm) bass side, 27.5-inch (69.9 cm) treble, patented fanned-fret system

NECK WIDTH AT NUT: 1¾ inches (4.4 cm)

NUMBER OF FRETS: 22

FINISH: Waterborne

BODY DEPTH: 1¾ inches (4.4 cm)

BODY LENGTH: 18½ inches (47 cm)

OVERALL LENGTH: 39½ inches (100.3 cm)

U.S. SUGGESTED RETAIL PRICE: $2,850

Flat Top Model

*J*im Nunis, company founder, luthier, and designer, tragically succumbed to cancer in 2006, but his four co-workers are continuing his work.

Nunis luthiers begin each of their classic Gibson-influenced guitars by selecting the finest tonewoods available, examining the color, weight, and grain, looking for just the right combination, and typically inspecting 100 or more boards to find two to four usable pieces. After a guitar is built and sanded, Nunis luthiers finish it with 10 to 15 water-thin coats of nitrocellulose lacquer, which Jim Nunis believed was the best guitar finishing material available. "As the finish ages, the tone gets better and better," he wrote. "All the prized vintage Gibsons from the 1950s were done in this same manner."

SPECIFICATIONS

BODY AND SIDE WOODS: Mahogany

TOP WOOD: Eastern flamed maple

BODY WIDTH, LOWER BOUT: 12^{15}/$_{16}$ inches (32.9 cm)

ELECTRONICS: Seymour Duncan distortion trembucker in the bridge position, Fernandez sustainer in the neck, 1k ohm volume pots, 500k ohm tone pots, 3 postion pickup selector switch, mini switches for sustainer on/off and upper harmonic selection

NECK WOOD: 3-piece maple

FRETBOARD MATERIAL: Flamed hard rock maple

FRETBOARD INLAY: Parallelogram black phenolic

HEADSTOCK DECORATION: Eastern flamed maple overlay cut from the same stock as the body top stained black and hand signed

BRIDGE: Gotoh under Floyd Rose patents

NUT AND SADDLE: Gotoh locking nut under Floyd Rose patents

TUNING MACHINES: Chrome Schallers

BINDING: Silver celluloid nitrate

SCALE LENGTH: 24.75 inches (62.9 cm)

NECK WIDTH AT NUT: 1^{11}/$_{16}$ inches (4.3 cm)

NUMBER OF FRETS: 22

FINISH: Nitrocellulose body front, back, sides, and front of headstock; cyanoacrylate blend on the back of the neck and back of the headstock

BODY DEPTH: 1^{13}/$_{16}$ inches (4.6 cm)

BODY LENGTH: 16^{3}/$_{4}$ inches (42.5 cm)

335

♠ **Flat Top Model, 2004**
James Edward Nunis, J. Nunis Custom Guitars
Atlanta, Georgia

Pro Series Electric Guitar

$\mathcal{E}$very part of the hand-carved body of Woody Phifer's Pro Series electric guitar is contoured to fit the player's body. Only the headstock is flat.

Phifer is a meticulous craftsman, and his guitars are full of innovative details and fastidious workmanship. The book-matched headstock and flush-mounted truss-rod cover of this electric are cut from the same wood as the top, and the access panels are carved from the same piece as the back. Both the truss-rod cover and access panel are bound and held in place by one set screw, and a raised Plexiglas pickguard shows off the luster of the wood below. Besides crafing truss-rod covers and access panels, Phifer also makes custom knobs for each instrument. The three hand-turned knobs are made from the same material as the body. With mother-of-pearl inlaid on top and a rubber grip to help tractions (volume swells), the knobs are one of a kind. "Don't worry," Phifer assures, "we make an extra one, just in case." The knobs are also canted to follow the flow of the top.

♠ **Pro Series Electric Guitar, 2003**
Sherwood "Woody" Phifer, Phifer Designs & Concepts
Garnerville, New York
Collection of Jeff Doctorow

SPECIFICATIONS

BODY AND SIDE WOODS: Curly maple

TOP WOOD: Curly redwood

BODY WIDTH, LOWER BOUT: 14¼ inches (36.2 cm)

ELECTRONICS: Gibson 57 Classics

NECK WOOD: Curly maple

FRETBOARD MATERIAL: Ebony

HEADSTOCK DECORATION: Book-matched curly redwood

BRIDGE: Ebony

NUT AND SADDLE: Bone

TUNING MACHINES: Sperzel

BINDING: ABS

SCALE LENGTH: 25.5 inches (64.8 cm)

NECK WIDTH AT NUT: 1¾ inches (4.4 cm)

NUMBER OF FRETS: 22

FINISH: Lacquer

BODY DEPTH: 2½ inches (6.4 cm)

BODY LENGTH: 18⅞ inches (47.9 cm)

OVERALL LENGTH: 38¼ inches (97.2 cm)

U.S. SUGGESTED RETAIL PRICE: $7,200 to $10,000

ELECTRIC

Ken Parker
Original Parker Fly

*K*en Parker's Fly represented a revolution in electric guitar design when it was introduced, the first complete rethinking of the electric solid-body since Leo Fender's Stratocaster 40 years earlier. As Parker says, "the only things on a Fly that will attach to a standard guitar are the strings and the strap button."

To begin with, The Fly weighs a mere 4¾ pounds (2.2 kg), half the weight of previous electrics. Its extraordinarily light weight and unique tonal qualities are made possible by Parker's innovative marriage of unusual woods and space age technology. The guitar's body is poplar, a resonant but lightweight hardwood, while the neck is basswood, a soft wood that would normally be snapped by string pressure. To enable the use of his woods of choice, Parker reinforced the neck with what he describes as an "exoskeleton," a thin but incredibly strong coating of a patented mix of carbon-glass fibers bonded with epoxy. He also crafted the fingerboard from the same composite material and devised a multi-fingered joint to attach the neck to the body.

The guitar's set of magnetic pickups produces a crisp and distinctive electric sound, but Parker had more than that in mind. He enlisted the help of electronics wizard Larry Fishman, who added a bridge-mounted piezo system, which amplifies each string separately to create a realistic amplified acoustic sound. Like the magnetic pickups, the piezos can be used alone or the player can open up a new world of sonic possibilities by combining acoustic and electric tones.

Original Parker Fly, 1994 ▶
Ken Parker, Parker Guitars
Garnerville, New York

338

SPECIFICATIONS

BODY AND SIDE WOODS: Mahogany

TOP WOOD: Mahogany

ELECTRONICS: Mag Pickups, Seymour Duncan Jazz (neck) and JB (bridge)

NECK WOOD: Mahogany

FRETBOARD MATERIAL: Carbon-Glass-Epoxy .020" composite

BRIDGE: Parker custom cast aluminum vibrato bridge, stainless steel saddles

NUT AND SADDLE: GraphTech

NUMBER OF FRETS: 24

FINISH: Polyurethane

Custom 24 Private Stock #184

PRS Private Stock guitars are one-off instruments custom built for individual customers from Paul Reed Smith's own years-in-the-making stash of the finest woods he encountered. The Private Stock guitars were introduced in 1996, and more than 300 have been built to date. The unique waterfall scene on the fingerboard of this guitar was created with mother-of-pearl, paua and paua heart, orange-red spiny oyster shell, and malachite.

The Custom 24 is the same guitar Paul Reed Smith took to his first trade show in 1985, and it remains the core of the PRS line.

Like most PRS electrics, it features a beautifully carved, figured maple top, a concept inspired by Gibson's original Les Paul guitar. One of Smith's many innovations was the development of glasslike, high-gloss finishing techniques that enhance the natural figure of the wood and are offered in an ever-widening array of high-gloss colors, from traditional sunbursts to such PRS specials as Whale Blue, Faded Blue Jean, Abalone, and Cappuccino.

339

SPECIFICATIONS

BODY AND SIDE WOODS: South American mahogany

TOP WOOD: Curly maple

BODY WIDTH, LOWER BOUT: 13 inches (33 cm)

ELECTRONICS: Custom 24 with 5-way rotary

NECK WOOD: South American mahogany

FRETBOARD MATERIAL: Curly rock maple

FRETBOARD INLAY: Depiction of a Norwegian waterfall scene inlaid with mother-of-pearl, paua, paua heart, orange-red spiny, and malachite

HEADSTOCK DECORATION: Private stock eagle inlaid in mother-of-pearl

BRIDGE: Nickel PRS stoptail

NUT AND SADDLE: Rytan nut; adjustable saddle

TUNING MACHINES: Nickel non-locking minis with ebony buttons

BINDING: Natural

SCALE LENGTH: 25 inches (63.5 cm)

NECK WIDTH AT NUT: 1$\frac{11}{16}$ inches (4.3 cm)

NUMBER OF FRETS: 24

FINISH: Slate blue; acrylic urethane

BODY DEPTH: 1$\frac{7}{8}$ inches (4.8 cm)

BODY LENGTH: 17$\frac{1}{4}$ inches (43.8 cm)

OVERALL LENGTH: 38$\frac{1}{2}$ inches (97.8 cm)

U.S. SUGGESTED RETAIL PRICE: $26,000

♠ **Custom 24 Private Stock #184, 2001**
Paul Reed Smith, Paul Reed Smith Guitars
Stevensville, Maryland

Orange Krush Production Model

*T*he genius behind RKS Guitars is Dr. Ravi K. Sawhney, an award-winning product designer who has totally deconstructed and remade objects as diverse as spectrometers, cheese graters, cell phones, and downhill sleds. In each case Sawhney's proprietary, cutting-edge design methodology, Psycho-Aesthetics, has been used to reveal the object's best possible nature and full potential, to enhance the everyday with the extraordinary.

Psycho-Aesthetics fuses art and design, science and experience. "It's a 'sum-of-all-its parts' concept, a spirit of design that when fully and expertly realized, captivates, engages, and delights its audience," Sawhney explains. "Psycho-Aesthetics lives in that rarified space of creating meaningful impressions of a design's intended benefit and the assured delivery of that benefit."

In 2001, Sawhney partnered with Rock-and-Roll Hall of Fame singer/songwriter Dave Mason to launch RKS Guitars, whose unique open-architecture instruments represent one of the most complete re-imaginings of the electric guitar since Leo Fender first gave it life in the 1950s.

♠ **Orange Krush Production Model, 2006**
RKS Guitars
Oxnard, California

SPECIFICATIONS

BODY AND SIDE WOODS: Tenite body, maple and alder core

BODY WIDTH, LOWER BOUT: 13¼ inches (33.7 cm)

ELECTRONICS: Dimarzio pickups, master volume and tone, 5-way pickup selector

NECK WOOD: Northern hard maple, alder

FRETBOARD MATERIAL: Ebony

FRETBOARD INLAY: Custom RKS abalone

HEADSTOCK DECORATION: Chrome plated brass scrolltip

BRIDGE: Hipshot

NUT AND SADDLE: Bone

TUNING MACHINES: Sperzel locking

SCALE LENGTH: 25.5 inches (64.8 cm)

NECK WIDTH AT NUT: 1¹¹⁄₁₆ inches (4.3 cm)

NUMBER OF FRETS: 22

FINISH: UV core polyester, satin urethane

BODY DEPTH: 2¹⁹⁄₃₂ inches (6.6 cm)

BODY LENGTH: 16 inches (40.6 cm)

OVERALL LENGTH: 37 inches (94 cm)

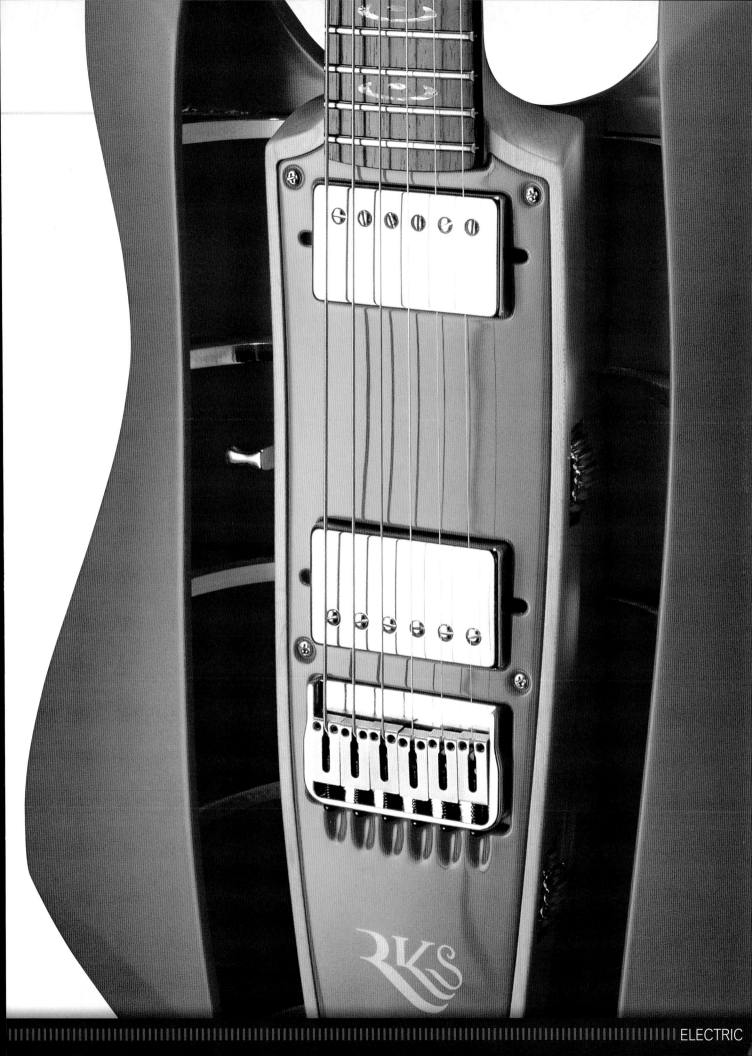

Hollowbody II Doubleneck Guitar, PS #367

Double-necked electric guitars, basically two guitars in one, have been around since the early 1950s, when pioneer electric guitar maker Paul Bigsby custom-built an instrument with six-string guitar and five-string mandolin necks for country singer Grady Martin. Most subsequent electric double-necks have combined six- and 12-string necks, allowing the player to move quickly between the two different types of guitar. This convenience comes at a price however, since the wide body required to carry the two necks makes double-necks heavy instruments, weighing nearly twice a standard solid bodied electric. Gibson introduced the best known electric double-neck, the EDS-1275, in 1958; a solid-bodied SG-style version of that instrument was made famous by Led Zeppelin guitarist Jimmy Page, who used it to play "Stairway to Heaven" onstage in the 1970s.

This one-of-a-kind PRS Private Stock double-neck follows almost all others in putting the 12-string neck on top and the dominant six-string neck on the bottom. Most double-necks are solid bodied; this one's hollow body, with f-holes and a carved top, cuts down on weight. Both fingerboards carry PRS's signature bird inlays, with silhouettes from top to bottom of a flying Peregrine falcon, a marsh hawk, a ruby-throated hummingbird, a common tern, a Cooper's hawk, a kite, a sparrow landing, a storm petrel, and a hawk landing. PRS guitars with 24 frets add a screech owl on a branch on the final fret.

342

SPECIFICATIONS

BODY AND SIDE WOODS: South American mahogany

TOP WOOD: Quilted maple

BODY WIDTH, LOWER BOUT: 16¼ inches (41.3 cm)

ELECTRONICS: Archtop with PRS piezo system

NECK WOOD: South American mahogany

FRETBOARD MATERIAL: Brazilian rosewood

FRETBOARD INLAY: Mother-of-pearl birds with 14-karat gold outlines

HEADSTOCK DECORATION: Mother-of-pearl private stock eagle

BRIDGE: Gold PRS stoptail and gold PRS 12-string bridge

NUT AND SADDLE: Rytan nut; adjustable stoptail

TUNING MACHINES: Gold non-locking minis with ebony buttons

BINDING: Natural

SCALE LENGTH: 25 inches (63.5 cm)

NECK WIDTH AT NUT: 1¹¹⁄₁₆ to 1¾ inches (4.3 to 4.4 cm)

▲ **Hollowbody II Doubleneck Guitar, PS #367, 2004**
Paul Reed Smith, Paul Reed Smith Guitars
Stevensville, Maryland

Dragon 2000

*T*he Dragon 2000 was Paul Reed Smith's fourth Dragon model but the first to move the dragon inlay from the fretboard to the body. Instead of extending the dragon along the length of the neck, the 2000 wraps a big colorful, fire-breathing beast, made of 242 pieces of mastodon ivory, rhodonite, agoya, coral, onyx, sugilite, chrysacola, red, green, and pink abalone, and paua, around the bridge and pickups, covering almost the entire top of the instrument.

Like the previous incarnations of the PRS Dragon, the 2000 was offered in a limited edition of 50 numbered guitars. Yet another PRS Dragon with inlay on the body and extending onto the bottom of the fretboard was introduced in 2002, followed by an over-the-top double-neck six/12 model in 2005, with dragon inlays covering the body and both necks.

◀ **Dragon 2000, 1999**
Paul Reed Smith, Paul
Reed Smith Guitars
Stevensville, Maryland

343

SPECIFICATIONS

BODY AND SIDE WOODS: Mahogany, mastodon ivory, rhodonite, agoya, coral, onyx, sugilite, chrysacola; red, green, and pink abalone; and paua

TOP WOOD: Maple

BODY WIDTH, LOWER BOUT: 12 31/32 inches (32.9 cm)

ELECTRONICS: Dragon 2000 treble and bass

NECK WOOD: Brazilian rosewood

FRETBOARD MATERIAL: Brazilian rosewood

BRIDGE: Stoptail

NUT AND SADDLE: Rytan nut; stoptail saddle

TUNING MACHINES: PRS locking

BINDING: Natural maple

SCALE LENGTH: 25 inches (63.5 cm)

NECK WIDTH AT NUT: 1 11/32 inches (3.4 cm)

NUMBER OF FRETS: 22

FINISH: Black cherry; acrylic urethane

BODY DEPTH: 2 1/16 inches (5.2 cm)

BODY LENGTH: 17 11/16 inches (44.9 cm)

OVERALL LENGTH: 37 1/2 inches (95.3 cm)

U.S. SUGGESTED RETAIL PRICE: $20,000

Centurion Custom

$\mathcal{E}$d Roman has been on what he calls "the bleeding edge" of guitar innovation for more than 30 years and runs the many parts of his "Roman Empire" from "the world's biggest guitar store," Ed Roman Guitars in Las Vegas.

Roman has designed and sold dozens of different guitar models over the years. The Centurion is the top of his current line, with a base price just under $6,000. The guitars are entirely hand built, with direct coupled pickups and a deep-set neck tenon that extends all the way through the body to the bridge to increase sustain and overtone production. Customers can choose from a wide variety of tone woods, fingerboard inlays, and finish colors; this one has a Blue Burst quilted maple body and an intricate vine inlay.

◀ **Centurion Custom, 2006**
Ed Roman, Ed Roman Guitars
Las Vegas, Nevada

344

SPECIFICATIONS

BODY AND SIDE WOODS: Honduran mahogany

TOP WOOD: Honduran mahogany

HEADSTOCK DECORATION: Medallion inlay

BRIDGE: Tone Pros

NUT AND SADDLE: Tusq graphite nut

Paul Reed Smith

Santana II

aul Reed Smith's first marketing attempts came when he twisted the arms of roadies so he could get backstage and show his guitars to headliners like Ted Nugent and Al Di Meola. "One night in ten I'd make a sale," Smith recalls. "I made deals. If someone gave me an order, made a deposit, and then didn't love the finished guitar, I'd give them their deposit back even if I couldn't make my rent the next day. After getting a small following and orders for more than 50 guitars, we built two prototypes. I popped them in the back seat of my truck and cranked it up, calling on guitar dealers up and down the East Coast. After many days and many miles, I came back with enough orders to start a company."

Carlos Santana was among the first musicians who agreed to try one of Paul Smith's hand-built guitars, and he did not ask for his money back. In fact, his first Paul Reed Smith guitar played so well that Santana thought it must have been an "accident of God." After a second guitar proved as good as the first, Santana decided to see what Smith could do with a double-neck guitar. The resulting instrument put any remaining doubts Santana had to rest, and PRS guitars became his signature instruments. Santana's identification with PRS helped bring the company to prominence, and he has remained PRS's most prominent endorsee, with two signature models and even one of the company's standard colors, Santana Yellow, carrying his name.

The Santana II is similar to the first PRS Carlos Santana Model, but adds a three-way toggle switch, volume and tone, artist-grade woods, a Brazilian rosewood fretboard and headstock overlay, and an eagle inlayed on the headstock. The Santana II is made by special order only, using many of the design and construction features Paul Reed Smith employed on the first guitars he hand built for Carlos Santana.

SPECIFICATIONS

BODY AND SIDE WOODS: Mahogany

TOP WOOD: Maple

BODY WIDTH, LOWER BOUT: 13 1/16 inches (33.2 cm)

ELECTRONICS: Santana pickups, volume and tone, 3-way selector

NECK WOOD: Mahogany

FRETBOARD MATERIAL: Brazilian rosewood

FRETBOARD INLAY: Rippled ablaone

HEADSTOCK DECORATION: Eagle, rippled abalone, om on truss rod cover

BRIDGE: Tremelo

NUT AND SADDLE: Rytan nut; adjustable saddle

TUNING MACHINES: Phase II low mass

BINDING: Natural maple

SCALE LENGTH: 24.5 inches (62.2 cm)

NECK WIDTH AT NUT: 1 21/32 inches (4.2 cm)

NUMBER OF FRETS: 24

FINISH: Yellow; acrylic urethane

BODY DEPTH: 2 3/32 inches (5.3 cm)

BODY LENGTH: 16 1/8 inches (41 cm)

OVERALL LENGTH: 37 1/2 inches (95.3 cm)

U.S. SUGGESTED RETAIL PRICE: $8,000

Santana II, 1998 ▶
Paul Reed Smith, Paul Reed Smith Guitars
Stevensville, Maryland

345

ELECTRIC

Ed Roman
Quicksilver

$\mathcal{E}$d Roman bills his Quicksilver Model, which is intended as a direct competitor with Paul Reed Smith's curly maple topped instruments, as "the world's most versatile guitar."

Roman is particularly proud of the many custom options he offers for the guitar, which include bound headstocks, gold or chrome pickup rings, and a vast array of fingerboard inlay materials, colors, and motifs. Quicksilvers can be inlaid in 65 different colors, using abalone, mother-of-pearl, maple, koa, walnut, or just about any other kind of wood. Fingerboard inlay motifs encompass "anything that flies except the trademarked PRS birds"—owls, bats, peacocks, eagles, condors, pterodactyls, ducks, chicken, geese, Pegasus the flying horse, unicorns, flying elephants, flying donkeys, and even flying squirrels—as well as barnyard animals, stars, planets, comets, nebulae, Saturn's rings, moonscapes, seascapes, mountain ranges, prehistoric scenes, the Taj Mahal, pagodas, pyramids, the Sphinx, and more than 10 variations each of lightning bolt and vine inlays.

346

Quicksilver, 2006 ▶
Ed Roman, Abstract Guitars,
a Division of Ed Roman Guitars
Hesperia, California

SPECIFICATIONS

BODY AND SIDE WOODS: Korina and various others

TOP WOOD: Maple and various others

BODY WIDTH, LOWER BOUT: 13 inches (33 cm)

SCALE LENGTH: 25 inches (63.5 cm)

Rockingbat

L as Vegas-based electric guitar designer and entrepreneur par excellence Ed Roman is typically blunt about his Rockingbat. "These guitars are a real pain in the butt to make," he says. "Rest assured we will probably build no more than 25 of these over the next 10 years."

Both the maple top and mahogany back of the solid-bodied guitar are deeply carved to suggest the ribs and skin of a bat wing, while the fingerboard position markers are inlaid bat silhouettes. The headstock resembles a witch's hat, and two small bats distinguish the twelfth fret.

Roman formed Abstract Guitars in the mid-1990s. He acquired a huge supply of body blanks after B.C. Rich went out of business, and then hired a team of talented builders who had worked in the Rich and Jackson factories to build his designs from the blanks. Roman boasts that the Abstract workforce includes "the people who hand carved and built all the USA neck-through guitars for Bernie Rico Jr., and the entire original paint department." Roman says that the company currently builds about 10 highly customized guitars a month, some of them even more outlandish looking than the Rockingbat. Abstract offers customers more than 50 different body designs, a dozen different headstocks, and a wide array of custom inlays and painted finishes.

347

◀ **Rockingbat, 2006**
Ed Roman, Abstract Guitars,
a Division of Ed Roman Guitars
Hesperia, California

James C. Larsen

ShopGirl

James Larsen freely admits that if he was serious about making real money with Girl Brand Guitars he would focus on one or two models and start churning them out in quantity. "I hope to settle down and do that someday," says Larsen, "but for now, I just can't help making each one different from the one before."

And different they are. The pickups are hand built from scratch, the bodies are anodized aluminum over a wooden core, the backs are usually Phenolic or Formica over birch plywood, and the tops are whatever pops into Larsen's head—rusted steel, corroded copper with uncorroded design areas, galvanized steel with the zinc selectively eaten away and left to rust under compost. "I have even, when bored, made some with fancy wood tops, birdseye and burl," Larsen confesses, "but that's the very sort of thing I wanted to get away from."

And each body and neck is festooned with tongue-in-cheek "girl" art by Larsen and/or his partner-in-crime, Janet K. Miller.

Why Girl Brand? "I usually say that it's because guitars, like boats, are always female (for example, B.B. King's "Lucille"), and one can take that pretty far," Larsen explains. "But really I think that 'girl' is just such a terrifically 'loaded' word. A word that's so general and yet so powerfully specific." And so we have HulaGirl, LingerieGirl, ReliquaryGirl ("The Tongue of Robert Johnson, a finger from Maybelle Carter, Charlie Christian, his Femur"), RodeoGirl, SushiGirl (built for Henry Kaiser), and a host of other explorations of vintage "girlness."

ShopGirl is part of Larsen's ongoing "Retro Guy Series," and one of two guitars he has decorated with "Tip2Strip Technology." Like those deliciously risqué nudie pens every guy remembers from the '50s, you just tip the guitar up, and the swimsuit slides off.

SPECIFICATIONS

BODY AND SIDE WOODS: Extruded aluminum sides; linen phenolic back

TOP WOOD: Various materials

BODY WIDTH, LOWER BOUT: 13 inches (33 cm)

ELECTRONICS: 2 pickups/2 transformers, hand wound, hand wired

NECK WOOD: Hard maple

FRETBOARD MATERIAL: Ebony, cocobolo

FRETBOARD INLAY: Mother-of-pearl, abalone

HEADSTOCK DECORATION: Decal

BRIDGE: Standard

NUT AND SADDLE: Bone

TUNING MACHINES: Kluson

SCALE LENGTH: 25.6 inches (65.1 cm)

NECK WIDTH AT NUT: 1⅝ inches (4.1 cm)

NUMBER OF FRETS: 21

BODY DEPTH: 2 inches (5 cm)

BODY LENGTH: 16¼ inches (41.3 cm)

OVERALL LENGTH: 39 inches (99.1 cm)

ShopGirl ▶
James C. Larsen, Girl Brand Guitars
Tucson, Arizona
Courtesy Acme Guitars, St. Louis, Missouri

348

ApocalypseGirl

SPECIFICATIONS

BODY AND SIDE WOODS: Extruded aluminum sides; linen phenolic back

TOP WOOD: Various materials

BODY WIDTH, LOWER BOUT: 13 inches (33 cm)

ELECTRONICS: 2 pickups/2 transformers, hand wound, hand wired

NECK WOOD: Hard maple

FRETBOARD MATERIAL: Ebony, cocobolo

FRETBOARD INLAY: Mother-of-pearl, abalone

HEADSTOCK DECORATION: Decal

BRIDGE: Standard

NUT AND SADDLE: Bone

TUNING MACHINES: Kluson

SCALE LENGTH: 25.6 inches (65.1 cm)

NECK WIDTH AT NUT: 1⅝ inches (4.1 cm)

NUMBER OF FRETS: 21

BODY DEPTH: 2 inches (5 cm)

BODY LENGTH: 16¼ inches (41.3 cm)

OVERALL LENGTH: 39 inches (99.1 cm)

*N*ot all Girl Brand Guitars are lighthearted. Created just after the Iraq War's beginning "shock and awe" bombing, this stark reverse glass painting by Janet K. Miller pairs with Larsen's skeleton fingerboard inlay to create a powerfully disturbing piece of art. Note the toggle switch labeled "wailing/gnashing" and the Arabic script on the treble side horn.

Reverse glass painting is a method of painting backwards on the inside of clear glass. Miller first encountered reverse glass painting in Senegal, where she lived and worked in the early 1980s. It was also practiced in early America, often on clocks. Miller says, "I am often asked if it's tedious or frustrating working inside out and backwards, but I'm left-handed and dyslexic, and for me it feels natural and comfortable. Rather than traditional artist's materials, I use sign painter's enamels. I'm inspired by written and spoken language, African print cloth, my vividly remembered childhood and dreams, Mexican popular culture, and the stark landscapes and extreme weather of the desert where I live. [And], I go to the circus whenever I get the chance."

Larsen's electronics are particularly well thought out. "The idea is to give you Fender and Gibson tone and combinations," he explains. "The current system uses a pair of hand-built transformers which add midrange and low-end beef to the traditionally bright, edgy single-coil tone. The 3-way pickup selector switch plus the three tone taps for each pickup add up to 15 pre-set tones before you ever touch the tone pot. I keep intending to put in an in-phase/out-phase switch which would add, I think, another nine tones, but it seems just one switch too many."

349

♠ **ApocalypseGirl, 2003**
James C. Larsen, Girl Brand Guitars
Reverse glass painting by Janet K. Miller
Tucson, Arizona
Courtesy Acme Guitars, St. Louis, Missouri

Paradis 6s

Rolf Spuler

Paradis 6s, 2006
Rolf Spuler
Gebenstorf, Switzerland

350

Rolf Spuler points out that before Leo Fender created the first widely available solid-bodied electric guitars, what musicians were really looking for was a regular acoustic guitar that could be played really loud. Fender's answer was a mass-produced "industrial" guitar capable of plenty of volume but with an entirely new sound.

"This was the starting point of my vision," Spuler explains. "With the Paradis, I wanted to make available what in 1950 had remained a dream: a stage-friendly guitar, staying true to its natural sound at any volume level, for nylon and steel strings alike."

Spuler's design is as fresh as Fender's was 60 years ago, and, like the Telecaster did, it boldly sets the instrument apart, announcing that it is something new and different. Spuler crafts the bodies from single pieces or book-matched pairs of choice wood, with a tuned cavity that enhances the acoustic properties. The Paradis combines his proprietary piezo pickup system with state-of-the-art electronics and an integrated PolyBass that supplements the guitar's round, acoustic sound with fat sub-octave basses. Additionally, the Paradis has a firewire module, which allows it to be linked directly to a computer and used as a digital guitar.

SPECIFICATIONS

BODY AND SIDE WOODS: Flamed maple, semi-solid

BODY WIDTH, LOWER BOUT: 15 inches (38.1 cm)

ELECTRONICS: Actie, Spuler single string piezo, polybass, firewire connection

NECK WOOD: Solid Indian rosewood

FRETBOARD MATERIAL: Indian rosewood

HEADSTOCK DECORATION: Headstock caps made of flamed maple, removable by magnets

BRIDGE: Indian rosewood, 6 pieces

NUT AND SADDLE: Glass reinforced synthetics

TUNING MACHINES: Modified Gotoh magnum lock

SCALE LENGTH: 25.5 inches (64.8 cm)

NECK WIDTH AT NUT: 1¾ inches (4.4 cm)

NUMBER OF FRETS: 24 + 2 (dropped-D extension)

FINISH: Polyurethane high gloss

BODY DEPTH: 1⅝ inches (4.2 cm)

BODY LENGTH: 18⅓ inches (46.6 cm)

OVERALL LENGTH: 39⅓ inches (99.9 cm)

Gears

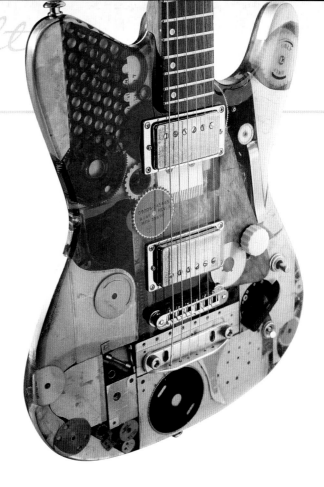

Michael Spalt is a fine artist and guitar maker who covers the tops of his Totem guitars with collages of found objects encased in poured polymer resin. Spalt's collages are influenced by the incomparable German Dada artist Kurt Schwitters, who created masterpieces from scraps of paper and other refuse he found on the streets of his home town.

"In this modern shiny age," says Spalt, "there is a hunger for the authentic and gritty, even to the point where some guitar manufacturers create fake 'authentic relics.' I believe that we need to recycle things and part of my attraction to found objects is the reclamation of their value, beyond their immediate usefulness. I look for the poetry of objects, to weave them into my pieces and let them tell their stories."

Spalt's father is an architect and professor of interior design at the Academy of Applied Art in Vienna, Austria, and he says he grew up surrounded by examples of design of all kinds. He studied art, sculpture, and painting in both the U.S. and Vienna, and has created quite a few Totem bodies which were intended solely as art objects and "will not be turned into guitars."

♠ **Gears, 1998–2006**
Michael Spalt, Spalt Instruments
Los Angeles, California

SPECIFICATIONS

BODY AND SIDE WOODS: Mahogany

TOP WOOD: Resin/assemblage

BODY WIDTH, LOWER BOUT: 12½ inches (31.8 cm)

ELECTRONICS: 2 Lollar Imperial humbuckers (volume/tone/3-way/coil splitter for neck P.V.)

NECK WOOD: Mahogany

FRETBOARD MATERIAL: Brazilian rosewood

FRETBOARD INLAY: Aluminum

HEADSTOCK DECORATION: Pearl logo inlay

BRIDGE: Tone Pros Toneamatic

NUT AND SADDLE: Bone

TUNING MACHINES: Sperzel locking tuners

SCALE LENGTH: 25.5 inches (64.8 cm)

NECK WIDTH AT NUT: 1 11/16 inches (4.3 cm)

NUMBER OF FRETS: 22

FINISH: Lacquer, resin

BODY DEPTH: 2 inches (5 cm)

BODY LENGTH: 16 inches (40.6 cm)

OVERALL LENGTH: 38 inches (96.5 cm)

U.S. SUGGESTED RETAIL PRICE: $3,800

The JD

his unique instrument was commissioned by collector and guitarist Jeff Doctorow, who owns several other Spalt creations. "Jeff basically gave me carte blanche," says Spalt. "He told me 'the wilder the better' and kept encouraging me to push the envelope."

Spalt wanted to make a guitar which would offer some unusual sound-shaping options. To open up tonal possibilities, he glued a wooden "reverse spider," vaguely reminiscent of a resonator guitar's spider, on top, creating a sandwich with the soundboard in the middle.

The saddles are anchored to the spider proper, but they rest on a small plate inserted into a recess at the top of the spider. The strings come straight up from below, through holes in the bridge plate which supports the saddles, and then pass over the saddles to the nut. The spider, like an arched roof structure, distributes the downward pressure towards the rim. The strings pull up vertically on the soundboard, rather than laterally, as in a conventional design.

There are two different anchoring points for the strings and several bridge plates made of various materials which support the saddles. Depending on how the strings are anchored, the strings put pressure on either the soundboard or the back of the guitar. These options also can be mixed—Spalt says he liked to string the three bass strings through the back, and the three high strings through the soundboard using a rosewood bridge plate as saddle support.

The bridge unit is mounted directly into the spider, while the neck unit is supported by a sculpted aluminum piece which floats over the body of the guitar and provides a strap attachment on the upper horn. The other end of the aluminum piece supports the electronics, which float above the guitar body somewhat like a floating archtop pickup/control unit.

352

The JD, 2006 ►
Michael Spalt, Spalt Instruments
Los Angeles, California
Courtesy of the Collection of Jeff Doctorow

SPECIFICATIONS

BODY AND SIDE WOODS: Flame mahogany, Indian rosewood

TOP WOOD: Walnut burl

BODY WIDTH, LOWER BOUT: 14 inches (35.6 cm)

ELECTRONICS: 2 John Birch hyperflux pickups/vol., tone 3 way switch

NECK WOOD: Flame mahogany

FRETBOARD MATERIAL: Ebony

FRETBOARD INLAY: Abalone

BRIDGE: Custom-machined mokume saddles with exchangeable baseplates

NUT AND SADDLE: Bone

TUNING MACHINES: Steinberger banjo style

BINDING: Flame maple (on neck)

SCALE LENGTH: 24 to 26-inch (61 to 66 cm) Novax fanned frets

NECK WIDTH AT NUT: 1¾ inches (4.4 cm)

NUMBER OF FRETS: 24

BRACING: Spruce tone bars

FINISH: Nitrocellulose

BODY DEPTH: 3 inches (7.6 cm)

BODY LENGTH: 22 inches (55.9 cm)

OVERALL LENGTH: 40 inches (101.6 cm)

Junior Brown Guit-Steel

*T*he whole concept was Junior's," says Mike Stevens.

This unique double-necked guitar was a collaboration between guitarist Junior Brown and luthier Michael Stevens. Brown, a virtuoso on both electric guitar and electric steel who draws on such seemingly incompatible influences as Jimmy Bryant, Hoagy Carmichael, Jimi Hendrix, Ernest Tubb, and the Ventures, often shifts between the two instruments several times in the course of a song. He wanted to find a way to combine them so he could navigate between them more easily.

"I was playing both the steel and guitar, switching back and forth a lot while I sang, and it was kind of awkward," says Brown. "But then I had this dream where they just kind of melted together. When I woke up, I thought 'You know, that thing would work!' They made double-neck guitars and double-neck steels, so why not one of each?"

Brown enlisted Stevens's help, and after a few days of experimentation, "Big Yellow," the first Guit-Steel, was born. Stevens says they "rubber-banded" the pieces together to figure out the right balance and distance between the two necks and tried to make the instrument "aesthetically like the old boys at Fender did it." The body was built from four pieces of lightweight ash, which were routed and pinned together. The steel neck is hollow, but the instrument still weighs 12 pounds; for that reason and to get the right angle for his bar technique, Brown had a stand made for it.

Stevens has built two Guit-Steels for Junior Brown and has three more on order from other clients, for which he is scrounging parts.

Junior Brown Guit-Steel, 1985 ♠
Michael Stevens, Stevens Electrical Instruments
Alpine, Texas

SPECIFICATIONS

BODY AND SIDE WOODS: Ash body

ELECTRONICS: Guitar 5-way switch/3-way select guitar or steel/steel stock with blendpot

NECK WOOD: Maple

FRETBOARD MATERIAL: Maple

FRETBOARD INLAY: Plastic dots

BRIDGE: Left-hand strat-style vibrato

NUT AND SADDLE: Bone

TUNING MACHINES: Stock Schallers for guitar; stock Klusons on steel

SCALE LENGTH: Guitar 25.5 inches (64.8 cm); steel short scale 22.5 inches (57.2 cm)

NECK WIDTH AT NUT: 1⅝ inches (4.1 cm)

NUMBER OF FRETS: 22

FINISH: Nitrocellulose lacquer "Blonde"

BODY DEPTH: 1¾ inches (4.4 cm), guitar; 2⅛ inches (5.4 cm), steel

BODY LENGTH: 31¾ inches (80.6 cm)

OVERALL LENGTH: 42 inches (106.7 cm)

U.S. SUGGESTED RETAIL PRICE: $9,500

The Klein Downtown

*T*his collaged electric guitar was the brainchild of Paul Schmidt, who has written books about pioneering California luthier Steve Klein (*Art That Sings: The Life and Times of Luthier Steve Klein*) and archtop masters John D'Angelico and James D'Aquisto (*Acquired of the Angels: The Lives and Works of Master Guitar Makers John D'Angelico and James L. D'Aquisto*). It was Schmidt's idea to have Michael Spalt build a solid-bodied guitar in the shape of one of Klein's distinctive acoustics. Spalt, a longtime admirer of Klein's work, chose a Klein 39.6 as his model for the body form and incorporated a rosewood Klein acoustic neck and bridge that Schmidt had on hand. The top is a collage of objects that Schmidt gathered from Klein's studio; Spalt arranged them and set them in resin.

Schmidt says the guitar plays as well as it looks, delivering a broad array of tones "from sparkly-with-dimension, buttery crooning to full-throttled textured yelling, and everything in between."

354

SPECIFICATIONS

BODY AND SIDE WOODS: Flame maple with cocobolo center strip

TOP WOOD: Resin/assemblage

BODY WIDTH, LOWER BOUT: 16½ inches (41.9 cm)

ELECTRONICS: 2 Fralin jazzbars, volume, 3 way

NECK WOOD: Rosewood/original Klein neck

FRETBOARD MATERIAL: Ebony

FRETBOARD INLAY: Ivory

BRIDGE: Modified Klein acoustic bridge with individual bone saddles

NUT AND SADDLE: Bone

TUNING MACHINES: Rodgers sterling silver

SCALE LENGTH: 25.5 inches (64.8 cm)

NECK WIDTH AT NUT: 1¹¹⁄₁₆ inches (4.3 cm)

FINISH: Oil/resin

BODY DEPTH: 3 inches (7.6 cm)

BODY LENGTH: 19 inches (48.3 cm)

OVERALL LENGTH: 42 inches (106.7 cm)

U.S. SUGGESTED RETAIL PRICE: $15,000

♠ **The Klein Downtown, 2001**
Michael Spalt, Spalt Instruments
Los Angeles, California
Collection of Paul Schmidt

LJ Model

$\mathcal{M}$ichael Stevens was one of the best-known custom-guitar builders of the 1980s, when he created Christopher Cross's Strat-shaped double-neck, Junior Brown's Guit-Steel, the Paul Glasse electric mandolin, and the Roscoe Beck six-string bass. It was during that period that he made this beautiful single cutaway guitar, which is named in honor of his late partner Larry Jameson who died in 1983.

Stevens's career as a luthier began in 1967 when he teamed up with Jameson at the first location of Guitar Resurrection in Oakland, California. In 1974, he decided to leave Guitar Resurrection to pursue a career in his first passion—horses. He trained Arabian show horses for four years before "burning out" and reuniting with Jameson in 1978 at the new Guitar Resurrection in Austin, Texas. He opened his own shop, Stevens Guitars, where he did repair and custom work for guitar greats such as Stevie Ray and Jimmie Vaughan, Albert King, Otis Rush, Hubert Sumlin, Lonnie Mack, Ray Benson, David Grissom, Jerry Jeff Walker, and George Thorogood.

By 1986, his work had attracted the attention of Fender, and when they finally made him an offer that was too good to turn down, he moved to California to become the Founder and Senior Design Engineer of the Fender Custom Shop, working with design engineer John Page. He personally built many of the instruments that Fender's endorsement artists have played including the Eric Clapton, Robert Cray, Yngwie Malmsteen, and Buddy Guy "Strats" and the Danny Gatton and Waylon Jennings "Teles." He moved back to West Texas in 1990, where he continues to ride and rope—and build some of the best electric guitars in the world.

SPECIFICATIONS

BODY AND SIDE WOODS: Honduran mahogany or limba (Korina) body

TOP WOOD: Western maple

BODY WIDTH, LOWER BOUT: 14⅞ inches (37.8 cm)

ELECTRONICS: Passive volume tone, 2 humbucking pickups

NECK WOOD: Match to body wood

FRETBOARD MATERIAL: Rosewood or ebony

FRETBOARD INLAY: Pearl dots, some custom

HEADSTOCK DECORATION: Pearl S logo with decals

BRIDGE: Nashville tunamatic with lightweight bar stop

NUT AND SADDLE: Bone nut

TUNING MACHINES: Schaller or Sperzel

BINDING: Ivoroid

SCALE LENGTH: 24.6 or 25.5 inches (62.5 or 64.8 cm)

NECK WIDTH AT NUT: 1¾ inches (4.4 cm)

NUMBER OF FRETS: 22

FINISH: Nitrocellulose

BODY DEPTH: 2⅜ inches (6 cm)

BODY LENGTH: 18 inches (45.7 cm)

OVERALL LENGTH: 40½ inches (102.9 cm)

U.S. SUGGESTED RETAIL PRICE: $8,500

♠ **LJ Model, 1982**
Michael Stevens, Stevens Electrical Instruments
Alpine, Texas

355

Myka Sungazer

David Myka likes to work very closely with his clients, seeing each guitar he builds as a unique instrument designed to perform a specific set of musical functions. "Each guitar model may serve as a starting point for a new design," says Myka, "or we can start from scratch. Either way the result will be a custom instrument as unique as the vision that guided its construction."

This first Sungazer Goldtop resulted from just such a collaborative effort between Myka and his client Rob Taylor. Taylor came to Myka with a full-scale drawing of his guitar, and envisioned his shape painted to reference the classic Les Paul "Goldtops" of the mid-1950s. Myka added some of his own touches to the tailpiece, f-holes, and overall layout to produce a hollow-bodied Goldtop for the twenty-first century. The instrument proved so sonically and physically appealing that Myka has since produced two more Sungazers for sale and is at work on others.

Myka Sungazer, 2005 ▶
David Myka, Myka Guitars
Orchard Park, New York

SPECIFICATIONS

BODY AND SIDE WOODS: Honduran mahogany

TOP WOOD: Big leaf maple

BODY WIDTH, LOWER BOUT: 13¹¹⁄₁₆ inches (34.8 cm)

ELECTRONICS: Master volume, master tone, LR Baggs control-x piezo preamp

NECK WOOD: Honduran mahogany

FRETBOARD MATERIAL: Figured Indian rosewood

HEADSTOCK DECORATION: Ebony veneer with Gold Pearl logo inlay

BRIDGE: LR Baggs T-Bridge with ebony tailpiece

NUT AND SADDLE: Bone nut, brass piezo saddles

TUNING MACHINES: Sperzel locking tuners

BINDING: Faux maple

SCALE LENGTH: 24.6 inches (62.5 cm)

NECK WIDTH AT NUT: 1¾ inches (4.4 cm)

NUMBER OF FRETS: 22

BRACING: Center block running from neck to underneath the bridge

FINISH: Goldtop with nitrocellulose lacquer

BODY DEPTH: 2¼ inches (5.7 cm)

BODY LENGTH: 18 inches (45.7 cm)

OVERALL LENGTH: 38¼ inches (97.2 cm)

U.S. SUGGESTED RETAIL PRICE: $3,550

Pheo Fracturecaster

𝒫hil Sylvester is a self-taught visual artist whose paintings have been exhibited in the Pacific Northwest and Europe for more than 20 years. He holds a Master of Architecture degree from Princeton, a B.A. in mathematics from Reed College, and a certificate in performance from the Hayes-Marshall School of Theater. He also worked as a professional rock and jazz musician from 1964–1972 and spent two years studying composition and arranging at the Berklee College of Music.

Sylvester says the guitars and amplifiers he makes emerge from questions he has had for years about what makes great guitars sound great, as well as from his need for visual and aural expression. "I work them just as I would my paintings," he explains, "building them, tearing them apart, then rebuilding them, fussing with them until they knock me out. They're not at all about craft, except as it bears upon playability and sound. Like paintings, they are resolved from the front and rough from the back. However these guitars and amps look, I build them to meet or even exceed the performance characteristics of the fine vintage instruments I have had the pleasure to play over the last 35 years."

♠ **Pheo Fracturecaster, 1997**
Philip Sylvester, Art Guitars
Portland, Oregon

SPECIFICATIONS

BODY AND SIDE WOODS: Swamp ash

TOP WOOD: Swamp ash

BODY WIDTH, LOWER BOUT: 14 inches (35.6 cm)

ELECTRONICS: Sylvester custom

NECK WOOD: Rock maple

FRETBOARD MATERIAL: Rock maple

NUT AND SADDLE: Bone nut

TUNING MACHINES: Gotoh

SCALE LENGTH: 25.5 inches (64.8 cm)

NECK WIDTH AT NUT: 1⅝ inches (4.1 cm)

NUMBER OF FRETS: 22

FINISH: Nitrocellulose lacquer

BODY DEPTH: 2 inches (5 cm)

BODY LENGTH: 18 inches (45.7 cm)

OVERALL LENGTH: 40 inches (101.6 cm)

U.S. SUGGESTED RETAIL PRICE: $3,000

Taos Special

*A*ndrea "Manne" (pronounced man-ney) Ballarin has been building high-end electric guitars and basses since 1986. He uses only Italian woods; the spectacularly figured tops of his instruments are made from poplar burl sawn from the bases of centuries-old storm-fallen trees, and the necks are laminated European hornbeam beech framed with rock maple. And, while most builders attach their tops to mahogany, Manne prefers sycamore, which he thinks surpasses mahogany in warmth and sweetness and also has a beautiful texture.

The Taos Special is Manne's top-of-the-line instrument and features his most beautifully colored and figured "Master Grade" tops. Like his other models, the Taos Special features a long upper horn, with the strap pin location on the rear side. "This is a very small particular," says Manne, "but I never saw it on other instruments. Having the pin in this location forces the instrument to angle back towards the player, making it lie against the body and giving a feel of stability and closeness."

358

SPECIFICATIONS

BODY AND SIDE WOODS: Light white korina

TOP WOOD: Italian yew

BODY WIDTH, LOWER BOUT: 12⅜ inches (31.4 cm)

ELECTRONICS: Volume and tone, selector of pickups, push pull for series/parallel operation at bridge and neck pickups

NECK WOOD: Maple with a central beech laminate section

FRETBOARD MATERIAL: Resin

HEADSTOCK DECORATION: Italian yew

BRIDGE: Wilkinson LP

NUT AND SADDLE: Graph tech nut

TUNING MACHINES: Wilkinson EZ lock

SCALE LENGTH: 25.2 inches (64 cm)

NECK WIDTH AT NUT: 1¹¹⁄₁₆ inches (4.3 cm)

NUMBER OF FRETS: 24

FINISH: Durable catalyzed coatings, hand stained

BODY DEPTH: 1¾ inches (4.4 cm)

BODY LENGTH: 19¼ inches (48.9 cm)

OVERALL LENGTH: 37¹³⁄₁₆ inches (96 cm)

U.S. SUGGESTED RETAIL PRICE: $5,100

◆ **Taos Special, 2006**
Andrea Ballarin, Manne Guitars
Schio, Italy

Tesla Seven-String Electric Guitar

Ulrich Teuffel's Tesla is one wild-looking guitar—it even glows in the dark! Even more surprising, it uses seriously radical, state-of-the-art technology to reconnect the guitar with what Teuffel calls "its myth"—the unpredictable noise, distortion, and menace that 1960s guitar gods like Jimi Hendrix, Jeff Beck, and Pete Townshend made part of the electric guitar's sonic vocabulary.

Technical improvements have largely eliminated the annoying humming and squealing feedback produced by early electric guitars, but Teuffel thinks something critical was lost in the bargain. So his instrument, which he named for Nikola Tesla, the legendary inventor and electrical engineer, can produce both modern and primordial guitar sounds.

The Tesla's unusual teardrop shape and construction give it seemingly endless sustain. It is headless, so the strings are clamped behind the nut and tuned with body-mounted tuners, and it also includes a seventh string, a low B which gives the player a wider range of deep bass notes. The Tesla has typical volume and tone control knobs, and the pickup switch lets the player choose either the fat sound of the humbucker or the sweet and

clean neck pickup. But Ulrich's real twist is three push buttons that allow the player to add and control the crazy, archetypal distortions of earlier guitars—the hum of the cord and the output jack, the squealing of pickup feedback, and the breaks in sound caused by loose internal wiring—any time he wants. All this, and then, when you turn out the lights…

359

SPECIFICATIONS

BODY AND SIDE WOODS: Maple and alder

TOP WOOD: Maple and alder

BODY WIDTH, LOWER BOUT: 13⅜ inches (34 cm)

ELECTRONICS: Passiv

NECK WOOD: Birdseye maple

FRETBOARD MATERIAL: Birdseye maple

BRIDGE: Metal Teuffel

NUT AND SADDLE: Metal Teuffel

TUNING MACHINES: Headless Teuffel

BINDING: Natural

SCALE LENGTH: 25.6 inches (65 cm)

NECK WIDTH AT NUT: 1¹¹⁄₁₆ inches (4.3 cm)

NUMBER OF FRETS: 22

BODY DEPTH: 1¹³⁄₁₆ inches (4.6 cm)

BODY LENGTH: 30⁵⁄₁₆ inches (77 cm)

U.S. SUGGESTED RETAIL PRICE: $5,000

♠ **Tesla Seven-String Electric Guitar, 1999**
Ulrich Teuffel
Neu-Ulm, Germany

Taylor

T5 Custom

*T*he T5 is the first electric instrument from a company that has spent 30 years building a reputation for its high-quality acoustic guitars. When asked when Taylor would make an electric, company founder Bob Taylor repeatedly responded, "Somewhere between never and when we can come up with a guitar that's actually unique."

The T5 is a groundbreaking thinline acoustic electric named for its five pickup positions, which allow it to convincingly produce sounds from crunching electric leads to shimmering acoustic strumming. This versatility has led some reviewers to describe it as a Swiss Army Knife for working musicians, five or more guitars in one. Taylor product developer David Hosler says, "This guitar doesn't replace your Les Paul and it doesn't replace your Taylor 810, but there's so much music happening between those two points that this guitar loves to live in."

▲ **T5 Custom, 2006**
Taylor Guitars
El Cajon, California

SPECIFICATIONS

BODY AND SIDE WOODS: Sapele

TOP WOOD: Hawaiian koa

BODY WIDTH, LOWER BOUT: 16 inches (40.6 cm)

ELECTRONICS: Taylor T5

NECK WOOD: Tropical American mahogany

FRETBOARD MATERIAL: Ebony

FRETBOARD INLAY: Taylor T5 "Artist" inlay, mother-of-pearl

HEADSTOCK DECORATION: Ebony overlay, mother-of-pearl Taylor logo

BRIDGE: Ebony

NUT AND SADDLE: Bone

TUNING MACHINES: Taylor gold-plated

BINDING: Multi-layer white with black pinstripes

SCALE LENGTH: 24.9 inches (63.2 cm)

NECK WIDTH AT NUT: 1¹¹⁄₁₆ inches (4.3 cm)

NUMBER OF FRETS: 21

BRACING: T5 custom bracing

FINISH: Gloss

BODY DEPTH: 2³⁄₈ inches (6 cm)

BODY LENGTH: 20 inches (50.8 cm)

OVERALL LENGTH: 40¾ inches (103.5 cm)

U.S. SUGGESTED RETAIL PRICE: $3,798

Birdfish

♠ **Birdfish, 1995**
Ulrich Teuffel
Neu-Ulm, Germany

𝒰lie Teuffel's Birdfish is an experiment in minimalism and variability. Teuffel points out that three fundamental principles—the resonant properties of the body wood, the position of the pickups, and the combination of pickups used—form the character of any electric guitar. If one were to make them variable, he posits, then one could thereby change the character of the instrument.

Making those three fundamental principles variable is the theme of the Birdfish. The body is reduced to two cylindrical resonators, which are available in different materials and are interchangeable by means of a screw-connection. The pickups are arranged on a rail and can be slid to a number of different positions. And five pickup combinations with different characteristics are at one's disposal, offering a wide range of tonal possibilities.

All the components are connected by two aluminum sculptures that Teuffel dubs "bird" and "fish," an apt metaphor for his seemingly incongruous, neither-fish-nor-fowl guitar. "They are bridges of vibration-transfer," he explains, "and establish contact to the body of the player."

SPECIFICATIONS

BODY AND SIDE WOODS: American maple/alder

BODY WIDTH, LOWER BOUT: 12⅝ inches (32 cm)

ELECTRONICS: Passive

NECK WOOD: Birdseye maple

FRETBOARD MATERIAL: Birdseye maple

BRIDGE: Metal Teuffel

NUT AND SADDLE: Metal Schaller

TUNING MACHINES: Headless Teuffel

BINDING: Natural

SCALE LENGTH: 25.6 inches (65 cm)

NECK WIDTH AT NUT: 1¹¹⁄₁₆ inches (4.3 cm)

NUMBER OF FRETS: 22

FINISH: Soft feeling

BODY DEPTH: 2 inches (5 cm)

BODY LENGTH: 31⅛ inches (79 cm)

U.S. SUGGESTED RETAIL PRICE: $7,100

Deluxe Steelcaster

I have always liked the look and feel of old guitars," says James Trussart. "I wanted to somehow emulate the effect of age and history on my own guitars. I wanted to make a guitar that came with a history and a slight element of neglect, of decay, so it had a personality of its own." The varied personalities of his guitars are reflected in the wide range of rock and blues guitarists who have played them, which includes such distinctive stylists and groups as Eric Clapton, Robert Cray, Henry Kaiser, Sonny Landreth, Metallica, Pearl Jam, Joe Perry, Marc Ribot, Keith Richards, Paul Simon, Lucinda Williams, Johnny Winter, and ZZ Top.

Trussart's metal bodied, Telecaster-style Steelcasters are his most popular models. The guitars, available as either a Standard solid body or the Deluxe hollow body seen here, deliver what Trussart calls "a uniquely enunciated sound that, combined with the resonant qualities of the hollow steel body, can range from sweet, crystal clear tones to aggressive full crunch."

The hollow-bodied Deluxe Steelcaster comes in satin, shiny, gold, and copper finishes while the Standard comes in rusty, with surfaces Trussart creates by leaving the bodies outside to corrode and manipulating the surface with his own touches. When he is satisfied with the results, Trussart treats the body to stop the corrosion, sands it to imitate further signs of age and deterioration, and then finishes it with clear satin.

Deluxe Steelcaster, 2006 ▶
James Trussart, James Trussart
Custom Guitars
Los Angeles, California

363

SPECIFICATIONS

BODY AND SIDE WOODS: Hollow steel

BODY WIDTH, LOWER BOUT: 12¾ inches (32.4 cm)

ELECTRONICS: CTS pots/Seymour Duncan Alnico II pro pickups

NECK WOOD: Maple

FRETBOARD MATERIAL: Rosewood

HEADSTOCK DECORATION: Steel recessed headstock

BRIDGE: 6 or 3 compensated saddles/vintage bridge

NUT AND SADDLE: Bone

SCALE LENGTH: 25.5 inches (64.8 cm)

NECK WIDTH AT NUT: 1⅝ inches (4.1 cm)

NUMBER OF FRETS: 21

U.S. SUGGESTED RETAIL PRICE: $4,218

Ron Thorn
Artisan Master #003

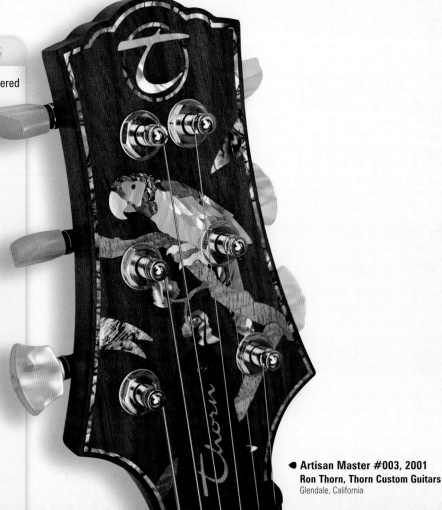

Ron Thorn has a large CNC (Computer Numerical Control) machine that he uses for wood work and two smaller CNCs for his intricate pearl inlay. Even though he is a believer in the use of computer assisted machinery, he is quick to point out that his average total time for a single guitar is five hours and 20 minutes working with a CNC and 69 hours and 30 minutes by hand, not counting the time that might be spent on a custom inlay that he or his father would do by hand with a jeweler's saw and a mini router.

"However small in comparison those five hours and 20 minutes seem," says Thorn, "they are very important to the outcome of the guitar. Accuracy and consistency are unmatched. There are features, such as my double offset purfling, that just can't physically be done by hand. Fret slots are accurate to within 0.0005 of an inch...heck, the wood will expand or contract more than that by the time I turn the lights off in the shop at the end of the day... but it's good to know they are as accurate as can be. Can I build a guitar without a CNC, sure. Would I now if I didn't have one...I doubt it, because I would always feel the guitar isn't as good as it can be with the help of a CNC."

SPECIFICATIONS

BODY AND SIDE WOODS: Honduran mahogany, chambered

TOP WOOD: 1-piece blonde koa

BODY WIDTH, LOWER BOUT: 13 inches (33 cm)

ELECTRONICS: P-90s with matching wood covers

NECK WOOD: Brazilian rosewood

FRETBOARD MATERIAL: Brazilian rosewood

FRETBOARD INLAY: Parrots

HEADSTOCK DECORATION: Parrot

BRIDGE: Thorn 1-piece tremolo

NUT AND SADDLE: Graphtech

TUNING MACHINES: Sperzel

BINDING: Paua offset purfling

SCALE LENGTH: 25 inches (63.5 cm)

NECK WIDTH AT NUT: 1$\frac{11}{16}$ inches (4.3 cm)

NUMBER OF FRETS: 22

FINISH: Natural

BODY DEPTH: 1$\frac{7}{8}$ inches (4.8 cm)

BODY LENGTH: 17 inches (43.2 cm)

OVERALL LENGTH: 38 inches (96.5 cm)

U.S. SUGGESTED RETAIL PRICE: $16,000

◀ **Artisan Master #003, 2001**
Ron Thorn, Thorn Custom Guitars
Glendale, California

Model One

◀ **Model One, 2007**
Rick Turner,
Renaissance Guitars
Santa Cruz, California

ick Turner, who has been building guitars for more than 40 years, is one of the acknowledged masters of electric guitar design. His Model One combines Old World aesthetics with a modern, full-bodied tonal range and is probably his best known design, primarily through its use by Lindsey Buckingham of Fleetwood Mac.

While the Model One looks like an acoustic guitar, it is actually a unique single pickup electric. As a student of guitar history, Turner based the instrument's body shape on a nineteenth-century Viennese acoustic guitar possibly made by Johann Stauffer, C.F. Martin's mentor. The top and back of the guitar are both arched and what appears at first glance to be a sound hole is actually a custom Turner rotating humbucking pickup mounted in a black high-impact Plexiglas plate. The plate can be rotated to change the angle of the pickup and emphasize different tonal characteristics.

With considerable supporting evidence provided by Buckingham's playing, Turner claims that the Model One sounds incredibly acoustic and detailed when it is played clean, "but when the volume kicks up, it screams louder and longer than any guitar you've played…without unwanted feedback or breakup."

SPECIFICATIONS

BODY AND SIDE WOODS: Mahogany

TOP WOOD: Mahogany

BODY WIDTH, LOWER BOUT: 12 inches (30.5 cm)

ELECTRONICS: Sound hole pickup is mounted in rotating black high-impact Plexiglas plate.

NECK WOOD: Eastern rock maple with purple heart and five-layer back of peg head overlay

FRETBOARD MATERIAL: Rosewood fingerboard with full black binding

FRETBOARD INLAY: Paua abalone neck face and side dot market inlays

BINDING: Full edge binding in black vulcanized fiber

SCALE LENGTH: 24.75 inches (62.9 cm)

NUMBER OF FRETS: 24

FINISH: Polyester clear coat over red stain

Twisted Soldato

$\mathcal{M}$ ike Lipe has been building instruments for nearly 30 years although he only began putting his own name on his work a half dozen years ago. Before setting up his own shop, he worked primarily in the custom shops of such major guitar companies as Ibanez and Yamaha, where he built and customized guitars for some of the biggest names in the music business.

Lipe's Twisted Soldato derives part of its name from its angled headstock, which is turned seven degrees from the neck of the guitar. According to Lipe, this eliminates the need for string trees and seats the strings more firmly in the nut, which in turn allows a more even tone across all of the strings. Soldato is the Italian word for soldier, appropriate for a solid-bodied workhorse like this guitar.

Spalted wood is marked by rot caused by various kinds of fungi that live in the forest floor. Under the right combination of warm and wet conditions, fungal rot can create unpredictable but beautiful patterns, typically black, grey, pink, or multicolored streaks that form when competing types of fungus meet each other and try to delineate their own territory. Light colored woods, like the maple this guitar is built from, are the best background for dramatic spalting. Whether it occurs naturally or is induced in an indoor environment, spalting is a dicey business— patterns are completely random, and the rot can weaken the wood beyond use if it is not caught in time.

367

SPECIFICATIONS

BODY AND SIDE WOODS: Alder

TOP WOOD: Spalted maple

ELECTRONICS: RS guitar 280k taper volume with cap.

NECK WOOD: Quartersawn red curly maple

FRETBOARD MATERIAL: Indian rosewood

FRETBOARD INLAY: Pearl dots

HEADSTOCK DECORATION: Burl

BRIDGE: ABM non-trem

NUT AND SADDLE: Vintage bone nut

TUNING MACHINES: Sperzel

BINDING: 3 ply

SCALE LENGTH: 25.5 inches (64.8 cm)

NECK WIDTH AT NUT: 1⅝ inches (4.1 cm)

NUMBER OF FRETS: 22

FINISH: Thin polyester done by Pat Wilkins

BODY DEPTH: 1¾ inches (4.4 cm)

BODY LENGTH: A twisted 15½ inches (39.4 cm)

U.S. SUGGESTED RETAIL PRICE: $3,300

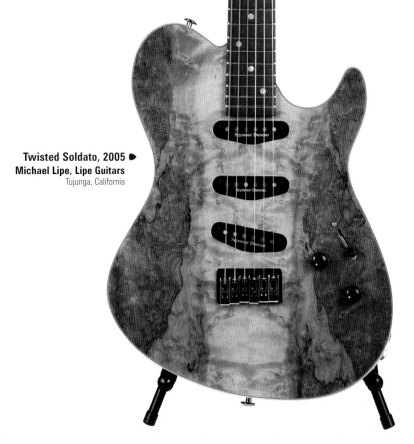

Twisted Soldato, 2005 ▶
Michael Lipe, Lipe Guitars
Tujunga, California

James Tyler
Burning Water

*J*ames Tyler has been building and repairing guitars for more than 40 years, and his list of clients ranges all the way from Michael Bolton to Twisted Sister.

Tyler offers his instruments in a wide variety of finishes, from "classic" colors such as Lake Placid Blue, Candy Apple Red, Shoreline Gold, and Sea Foam Green to his own "wacko colors" and "schmears," which include Fresh Vomit, Psychedelic Vomit, Hazmat Spill Schmear, and Candy Lemon Yellow.

He painted the first Burning Water guitar for Michael Landau, a renowned L.A. session guitarist who has recorded with Miles Davis, Joni Mitchell, James Taylor, and many other top artists. Landau, who had played a Signature guitar that Tyler had built for him for several years, came into Tyler's shop one day and told him he was tired of the paint job. "It was just too happy schmear and festive," Tyler recalls him saying. "He wanted something a little more... a little more... uuuhh... sinister looking. At this time Mike was playing around with his band Burning Water. So I came up with the Burning Water paint job. It was supposed to look like smoke and fire over water, or something. And for those of you who don't think water can burn," Tyler rants, "spare me. Don't call or e-mail. Go read the ninth law of thermodynamics."

◀ **Burning Water, 2000**
James Tyler, James
Tyler Guitars
Van Nuys, California

SPECIFICATIONS

BODY AND SIDE WOODS: Alder; fully painted; mamywo

TOP WOOD: Mamywo

ELECTRONICS: Five-way, volume, mid boost, tone; two virtual vintage single coils at neck and middle, or two JTV single coils, full-size humbucker at bridge; optional Duncan Classic Stacks; mid-boost preamp

NECK WOOD: Quartersawn maple with Indian rosewood fingerboard

FRETBOARD MATERIAL: Rosewood

FRETBOARD INLAY: Pearl

BRIDGE: Wilkinson or Floyd Rose

NUT AND SADDLE: Graph tech

TUNING MACHINES: Sperzel; chrome floating vibrato with locking tuners

SCALE LENGTH: 25.5 inches (64.8 cm)

NECK WIDTH AT NUT: 1⅝ inches (4.1 cm)

NUMBER OF FRETS: 22

MK IV Gryphon High-Tuned 12-String

The Gryphon High-Tuned Unison 12-string is an 18.5-inch scale guitar which is strung with unison pairs of strings and tuned almost a full octave higher (D above standard E) than a standard six-string guitar. The high pitched, doubled strings (custom LaBella GR-12 strings, which are available from any LaBella dealer) provide incredible punch and "cut," with complex, high overtones that bring to mind other midsized fretted instruments with doubled strings, including the Cuban tres, the Puerto Rican cuatro, and the Greek bouzouki. In fact, the Gryphon can provide a reasonable facsimile of the sound of all these instruments, making it what *Guitar Player* magazine described as "an all-purpose 'ethno' axe."

Despite or perhaps because of its diminutive size, the Gryphon is many guitars in one. It is easily played fingerstyle, works equally well as a solo instrument playing single-note leads, and can also take the role of a high-strung Nashville guitar.

◄ MK IV Gryphon High-Tuned 12-String, 2000
Joe Veillette, Veillette Guitars
Woodstock, New York

SPECIFICATIONS

BODY AND SIDE WOODS: Poplar

TOP WOOD: Alaskan spruce

BODY WIDTH, LOWER BOUT: 11 inches (27.9 cm)

ELECTRONICS: Custom under-saddle piezo, D-Tar wavelength preamp

NECK WOOD: Maple

FRETBOARD MATERIAL: Wenge

BRIDGE: Wenge

NUT AND SADDLE: Zero-fret

TUNING MACHINES: Gotoh

BINDING: Black

SCALE LENGTH: 18.5 inches (47 cm)

NECK WIDTH AT NUT: 2 inches (5 cm)

NUMBER OF FRETS: 21

FINISH: Catalyzed lacquer

BODY DEPTH: 2 inches (5 cm)

BODY LENGTH: 13 inches (33 cm)

OVERALL LENGTH: 29¾ inches (75.6 cm)

Tim White
Chrysalis Damsel A-6

orried about what the airline gorillas will do to your guitar when you travel? Then how about an inflatable guitar that folds into a small carrying case and just needs to be assembled and pumped with air?

Tim White, a Yale educated biologist and inventor, has been working on the concept since 1979. His first experiment was replacing the broken top of his 12-string with a graphite grill and putting a weather balloon inside. "The balloon worked OK," White recalls, "but popped too easily. A Mylar K-Mart shopping bag was strong, but did not hold air well. So we put a weather balloon inside a K-Mart shopping bag and stuffed them together under the grill. Inflated tight against the grill, the results were truly amazing—a breathtakingly brilliant sound, significantly louder than an equivalent wooden soundboard 12-string."

The Chrysalis's primarily graphite components snap together with the flip of a lever. The "soundboard" is a latticework "grill" of molded, epoxy-impregnated graphite fibers that resembles the wing of a dragonfly. The graphite has to be lain strand by strand into molds, so each top requires 80 hours of handwork. The Chrysalis can be played "uninflated" as an electric guitar. Inflating the "balloon" creates an acoustic sound chamber akin to the box of a wooden acoustic guitar.

Although White's dream is tomass produce the instrument, fewer than 20 Chrysalis guitars have been built to date, one of which is part of the Boston Museum of Fine Arts' extraordinary collection of musical instruments.

SPECIFICATIONS

BODY AND SIDE WOODS: Inflatable mylar, covered with decorative fabric

TOP WOOD: Lattice-like graphite grillwork

BODY WIDTH, LOWER BOUT: 16½ inches (41.9 cm)

ELECTRONICS: Fishman acoustic matrix natural 1

NECK WOOD: Graphite

FRETBOARD MATERIAL: Wood phenolic laminate

FRETBOARD INLAY: Green abalone

BRIDGE: Graphite

NUT AND SADDLE: Brass

TUNING MACHINES: Schaller M-6 mini

SCALE LENGTH: 25.65 inches (65.2 cm)

NECK WIDTH AT NUT: 1¾ inches (4.4 cm)

NUMBER OF FRETS: 22

BRACING: Lattice-like grillwork

FINISH: 0000 steel wool

BODY DEPTH: 2 inches (5 cm) electric, 6 inches (15.2 cm) inflated acoustic

BODY LENGTH: 18 inches (45.7 cm)

OVERALL LENGTH: 41 inches (104.1 cm)

♠ **Chrysalis Damsel A-6, 2000**
Tim White, Chrysalis Guitars
New Boston, New Hampshire

Black and Blue Electric

*A*lthough Joseph Yanuziello's retro-looking electric guitar appears to be a classic solid body, it actually has an ultra-light hollow body with handmade hardware and custom Lindy Fralin pickups. Yanuziello offers customers a choice of alder, maple, curly maple, South American mahogany, and spruce, as well as several different two-tone color combinations.

Yanuziello also builds similarly styled electric mandolins, mandolas, and mandocellos, and has built an electric with a trapeze tailpiece for jazz notable Bill Frisell. The mandocello is a guitar-sized member of the mandolin family that was popularized by Gibson in the early 1900s as part of its mandolin orchestras. Like the mandolin and its larger cousin the mandola, it has four sets of double strings. It is most often tuned an octave below the mandola (C, G, D, A), although many other tunings are possible.

♠ **Black and Blue Electric, 2000**
Joseph Yanuziello, Yanuziello Stringed Instruments
Toronto, Ontario, Canada

SPECIFICATIONS

BODY AND SIDE WOODS: Alder

TOP WOOD: Maple

BODY WIDTH, LOWER BOUT: 12¾ inches (32.4 cm)

ELECTRONICS: Three Lindy Fralin single coil jazz blues, five-way switch, push pull tone for bridge pickup

NECK WOOD: Maple

FRETBOARD MATERIAL: Rosewood

FRETBOARD INLAY: Corian diamonds and crown

HEADSTOCK DECORATION: Yanuziello decal logo

BRIDGE: Chrome-plated brass with stainless steel saddle inserts

NUT AND SADDLE: Bone nut, stainless steel saddles

TUNING MACHINES: Gotoh, Kluson style

SCALE LENGTH: 25 inches (63.5 cm)

NECK WIDTH AT NUT: 1¹¹⁄₁₆ inches (4.3 cm)

NUMBER OF FRETS: 21

FINISH: Black over metallic blue pre-catalyzed lacquer

BODY DEPTH: 1⅞ inches (4.8 cm)

BODY LENGTH: 15 inches (38.1 cm)

OVERALL LENGTH: 36½ inches (92.7 cm)

ELECTRIC BASS

Leo Fender, who designed the world famous Telecaster and Stratocaster electric guitars, is also the father of the electric bass guitar, which he introduced in 1951. His intention was to create a viable, portable substitute for the cumbersome bass fiddles used in most country and swing bands of the time and, by adding frets, to make an instrument that guitarists could readily learn to play. His four-stringed, solid-bodied Fender Precision Bass was in essence an enlarged version of the Telecaster electric guitar, with a 34-inch (86.4 cm) scale length that put it squarely between the Telecaster's 25½ inches (64.8 cm) and the 40 to 42 inches (101.6 to 106.7 cm) of a typical upright bass.

Although Fender's basses remain the foundation on which all subsequent development rests, bass designers have always felt freer to experiment with form than six-string makers, and the electric bass has taken on extraordinary variety over the years. Most basses still have four strings, like an upright bass, but many builders also offer five- and six-string models, and some build instruments with seven, eight, nine, or even more strings. In addition, contemporary builders also are making unfretted instruments, basses with scrolled headstocks or no head at all, upright electric basses that combine the distinctive sound of an acoustic bass with the portability and playability that Leo Fender pioneered, and more.

Fender

Reissue '51 Precision Bass &
1958 Precision Bass Relic Ltd.

The Fender Precision Bass (P-Bass), the first mass-produced and commercially successful electric bass, was even more revolutionary than its close relative, the Telecaster. Introduced in 1951, the instrument's durability, portability, and booming amplified sound were an immediate hit with bass players who previously had to lug a bulky bass fiddle from gig to gig. It changed the way music was played, and within a few years, it helped change the way music sounded. Combos with electric guitars and basses became the norm in country and rhythm and blues groups across the U.S. during the early 1950s, setting the stage for the explosion of rockabilly and rock and roll that began in the middle of the decade. The P-Bass has been in production since its introduction and remains the most popular bass in the world. Bill Black, who played bass on Elvis Presley's Sun recordings, helped to popularized the P-Bass, and it has also been a favorite of such well-known bassists as Adam Clayton of U2, "Duck" Dunn, John Entwistle, Kim Gordon of Sonic Youth, James Jamerson, George Porter Jr. of The Meters, and Paul Simonon of the Clash.

Fender has reissued the Precision in its original incarnation, and the Fender Custom Shop has recreated the 1958 Precision sunburst, which has long ranked with the original model as a classic. The 1958 Precision, offered in a limited-edition run of 100, has been given Fender's so-called "Relic" treatment, which simulates the natural wear and tear of years of heavy use, with nicks, scratches, worn finish, rusty hardware, and aged plastic parts.

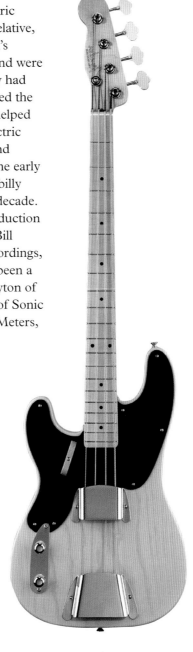

373

● **Reissue '51 Precision Bass, 2005**
Fender Musical Instruments Corporation
Scottsdale, Arizona

● **1958 Precision Bass Relic Ltd., 2005**
Fender Musical Instruments Corporation
Scottsdale, Arizona

SPECIFICATIONS

REISSUE '51 PRECISION BASS

BODY AND SIDE WOODS: Select ash

TOP WOOD: Select ash

BODY WIDTH, LOWER BOUT: 13 inches (33 cm)

1958 PRECISION BASS RELIC LTD.

BODY AND SIDE WOODS: Select alder

TOP WOOD: Select alder

BODY WIDTH, LOWER BOUT: 13 inches (33 cm)

1966 Jazz Bass Closet Classic LTD Builder Select by Mark Kendrick

The Fender Jazz Bass was the second electric bass designed by Leo Fender, joining the Precision in the Fender line in 1960. Originally called the Deluxe Bass, it was renamed the Jazz Bass because Fender thought its narrower neck would appeal to jazz bassists.

Appropriately, the Jazz Bass's best known exponent was the late Jaco Pastorius, whose slippery, virtuosic playing helped define the sound of fusion jazz. Pastorius's favorite instrument was a 1962 Precision he turned into a fretless by removing the frets and patching the fingerboard with wood putty.

This limited edition custom shop edition features Fender's "Closet Classic" treatment—built as if it was bought new in its respective model year, played maybe a few times per year, and then carefully put away. It has a few small dings, a mildly checked finish, lightly oxidized hardware, and aged plastic parts. Mark Kendrick is a Senior Master Builder who has been with Fender since 1990 and has built guitars for the likes of Eric Clapton, Sting, Keith Richards, Marty Stuart, Buck Owens, and Merle Haggard. Instruments he has crafted are in the collections of the Rock and Roll Hall of Fame in Cleveland and the Country Music Hall of Fame in Nashville.

◀ **1966 Jazz Bass Closet Classic LTD Builder Select by Mark Kendrick, 2005**
Master-built in the Fender Custom Shop
Fender Musical Instruments Corporation
Scottsdale, Arizona

SPECIFICATIONS

BODY AND SIDE WOODS: Select alder

TOP WOOD: Select alder

BODY WIDTH, LOWER BOUT: 13½ inches (34.3 cm)

B1 Four-String Fretted Vertical Bass

*L*ee Barker plays bass in two groups, which means at least five hours of playing a week. In the summer of 2002, his wrists began to hurt after only an hour or so of playing his traditional horizontal electric bass. Noting how his wrists were bent as he played, he began to imagine an upright fretted bass that would allow him to use different hand positions. When he discovered that the instrument he envisioned didn't exist, he built one himself.

People noticed the instrument and commented, and, even more important, Barker's wrists were no longer telling him to give up bass playing. He kept tinkering with components, pickup layouts, and different wood and core combinations, always seeking perfection in sound, playability, and feel. "By the time number 30 was built," he says, "I was content with evenness of tone, the low-end growl, and the overall playability of the Barker Bass," and ready to launch his eponymous instrument company.

By adding electric bass guitar electronics to his own chambered body, Barker created an instrument that produces a signature sound unlike either of its parents, combining the ease of playing in the upright position with the speed, precision, and amplifiable signal of an electric bass guitar.

SPECIFICATIONS

BODY AND SIDE WOODS: Alder core and back

TOP WOOD: Cherry

BODY WIDTH, LOWER BOUT: 14 inches (35.6 cm)

ELECTRONICS: Seymour Duncan Basslines, passive, J-bass configuration

NECK WOOD: Maple

FRETBOARD MATERIAL: Rosewood (fretted); ebony (fretless)

HEADSTOCK DECORATION: Laser logo engraving

BRIDGE: Hipshot

NUT AND SADDLE: Graphite from Graphtech

TUNING MACHINES: Gotoh

SCALE LENGTH: 34 inches (86.4 cm)

NECK WIDTH AT NUT: 1½ inches (3.8 cm)

NUMBER OF FRETS: 21

FINISH: Lacquer over toner

BODY DEPTH: 2 inches (5 cm)

BODY LENGTH: 35½ inches (90.2 cm)

OVERALL LENGTH: 64 inches (162.6 cm)

U.S. SUGGESTED RETAIL PRICE: $3,795

🔸 **B1 Four-String Fretted Vertical Bass, 2003–2005**
Lee Barker, Barker Bass
Redmond, Oregon

375

2nd Anniversary Fretless Cortobass

Scott Beckwith, the founder, designer, and self-described "nutty professor" of Birdsong, has been designing and building guitars since 1989. As a professional player, he tried every small bass in existence in the 1980s and 1990s and, finding them all wanting in some way, ultimately decided to build his own. Birdsong, which Beckwith describes as "a team of oddballs making some absolutely kickass little basses," was founded in 2003.

Beckwith's Cortobass is a professional quality short scale bass built for players with small hands (Beckwith himself is a vertically challenged 5 feet, 4 inches) or wanting a smaller, lighter, more compact instrument. While a traditional electric bass has a 34-inch (86.4 cm) scale length, the Cortobass's scale length is only 31 inches (78.7 cm). "These aren't just shrunken copies, a little neck on a big body, or a slapped-together attempt to gain market share," Beckwith says emphatically. "They are a unique marriage of specific design parameters based on over two decades of playing, tweaking, modifying, and repairing electric guitars and basses... and over three decades of being small, with short arms and little hands!"

376

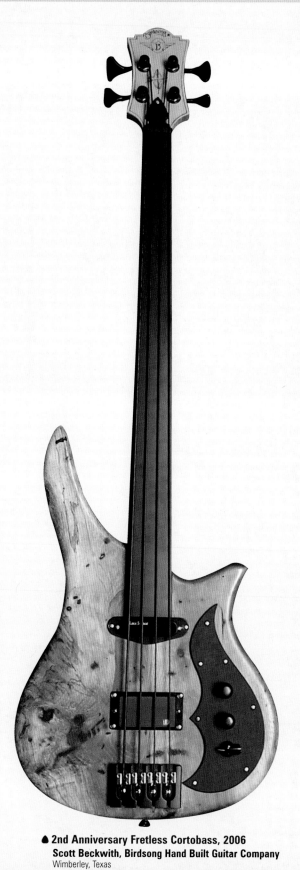

♠ **2nd Anniversary Fretless Cortobass, 2006**
Scott Beckwith, Birdsong Hand Built Guitar Company
Wimberley, Texas

SPECIFICATIONS

BODY AND SIDE WOODS: Spalted Texas pecan

TOP WOOD: Spalted Texas pecan

BODY WIDTH, LOWER BOUT: 12¾ inches (32.4 cm)

ELECTRONICS: Passive lace single and double coil pickups, 2 volumes and a 6 position varitone

NECK WOOD: Maple

FRETBOARD MATERIAL: Ebony

HEADSTOCK DECORATION: Woodburning

BRIDGE: Solid milled brass hipshot style A

NUT AND SADDLE: Hand-carved ebony nut

TUNING MACHINES: Hipshot Ultralites

SCALE LENGTH: 31 inches (78.7 cm)

NECK WIDTH AT NUT: 1½ inches (3.8 cm)

FINISH: Hand-rubbed oil/poly blend

OVERALL LENGTH: 40½ inches (102.9 cm)

Citron AE5 Swallow Signature Bass

$\mathcal{T}$his acoustic electric bass is the result of a true collaboration between luthier Harvey Citron and renowned jazz bassist Steve Swallow, who has been voted the number one electric bassist in the *Down Beat* magazine International Critics Poll since 1983.

According to Jonathan Herrera of *Bass Player* magazine, Swallow's ultimate goal in working with Citron was a bass guitar with genuine acoustic qualities. Starting with the AE5 that Citron first showed Swallow, the two men made change after change. "Since Swallow was happiest with the soloed piezo-pickup sound," says Herrera, "Citron eliminated the AE5's magnetic pickup. Swallow wanted a narrow neck width, but its tendency to shift with the weather found Citron turning to graphite reinforcement. Swallow wanted more warmth and depth, so the body grew deeper, the electronics were placed in the upper bout, and the top was X-braced. The list of revisions goes on."

The AE5 bass is tuned E, A, D, G, C. It is loud enough to be played unplugged, making it an ideal all around instrument, and it is extremely versatile and responsive when amplified.

377

SPECIFICATIONS

BODY AND SIDE WOODS: Honduran mahogany hollowed out

TOP WOOD: Spruce

BODY WIDTH, LOWER BOUT: 13¾ inches (34.9 cm)

ELECTRONICS: 6 piezos, 3 EMG adjustable buffer circuits, EMG BT active EQ master volume

NECK WOOD: One-piece Honduran mahogany

FRETBOARD MATERIAL: East Indian rosewood

HEADSTOCK DECORATION: Sterling silver Citron logo

SOUND HOLE INLAYS: East Indian rosewood

BRIDGE: Rosewood with ebony SOB saddle

NUT AND SADDLE: Bone

TUNING MACHINES: Hipshot Ultralites

SCALE LENGTH: 36 inches (91.4 cm)

NECK WIDTH AT NUT: 1⅞ inches (4.8 cm)

NUMBER OF FRETS: 24

BRACING: X-bracing

FINISH: Catalyzed lacquer

BODY DEPTH: 3 inches (7.6 cm)

BODY LENGTH: 20½ inches (52.1 cm)

OVERALL LENGTH: 45⅞ inches (116.5 cm)

U.S. SUGGESTED RETAIL PRICE: $5,000 without case

⬥ **Citron AE5 Swallow Signature Bass, 2006**
Harvey S. Citron, Harvey Citron Enterprises
Woodstock, New York

Conklin
Vine of Life

▲ **Vine of Life, 2002**
Conklin Guitars and Basses
Springfield, Missouri

SPECIFICATIONS

BODY AND SIDE WOODS: Mahogany back

TOP WOOD: Conklin's exclusive Melted Top completely hand-crafted from birdseye maple, walnut, bubinga, mahogany, and wenge

BODY WIDTH, LOWER BOUT: 13½ inches (34.3 cm)

ELECTRONICS: Lightware systems

NECK WOOD: Laminates of hard maple and bubinga

FRETBOARD MATERIAL: Melted fingerboard

HEADSTOCK DECORATION: Melted headstock cap

BRIDGE: Lightware systems

NUT AND SADDLE: Delrin nut

TUNING MACHINES: Gotoh tuners

SCALE LENGTH: 34 inches (86.4 cm)

NECK WIDTH AT NUT: 2¼ inches (5.7 cm)

NUMBER OF FRETS: Fretless

FINISH: Satin urethane

BODY DEPTH: 1¾ inches (4.4 cm)

BODY LENGTH: 23½ inches (59.7 cm)

OVERALL LENGTH: 46¾ inches (118.7 cm)

U.S. SUGGESTED RETAIL PRICE: $30,000

Conklin specializes in basses with "Melted Tops," created with a unique, secret process that allows Conklin's luthiers to combine several kinds of wood into flowing organic asymmetrical patterns that often run the length of the instrument, from tail to headstock.

Melted Tops represent a radical departure from the standard book-matched, figured maple tops used by most other manufacturers. Conklin's luthiers sort through hundreds of boards from different species of wood—wood that includes buckeye burl; burl and spalted walnut; birdseye, curly, and quilted maple; figured bubinga and cherry; koa; lacewood; purpleheart; zebrawood; and ziecote—and select pieces for their particular grain pattern or color contrast when combined with other woods. Once the boards are chosen and the pattern of intersecting woods is planned, Conklin uses a proprietary process to "melt" each piece into the pattern with airtight joints so precise that it's hard to believe the woods didn't grow that way in nature.

This stunning bass is the most logistically complex Melted Top that Conklin has made. The vine pattern on the top combines five different exotic woods, designed so that the three-octave, fretless fingerboard disappears into the pattern. To keep the hardware as unobtrusive as possible, the guitar also employs a Lightwave optical bridge/pickup system, which eliminates the need for magnetic pickups by using beams of light to detect string motion and convert it into an electrical signal.

378

V2 Cherry Four-String Fretless Vertical Bass

More than a few electric bassists have chosen to play their instruments in a vertical position, both because the top heavy instruments balance better that way and because the position allows them to approach the instrument more like an upright bass than an electric guitar. Ralph Dammann, a bassist who built his first electric bass in 1971, played the second one he built 300 nights a year for seven years.

That instrument was the prototype for his Vertical Bass, which he designed to alleviate the design flaws he found in Fender-style electric basses. "I don't conceive of the electric bass as a four-string guitar tuned down an octave," he explains. "Bass players usually play with their fingers, not picks. So, there is no advantage to having the bass horizontal."

Dammann played classical guitar when he was young and picked up the double bass in his twenties. His experience with these instruments led to his approach to the Vertical Bass—the left hand plays as it does on the double bass, with the thumb behind the neck serving as a pivot, while the right plays somewhat as it does on a classical guitar. Dammann designed the body to provide an armrest so the player doesn't always have to use his thumb as a pivot. The hand is supported over the strings so that the thumb and all the fingers can be used as the player desires. Dammann says he believes that this new design "will, in the hands of a creative musician, lead to that rarest and most prized commodity among musicians—new styles of playing."

**V2 Cherry Four-String ▶
Fretless Vertical Bass, 2004
Ralph Dammann, Dammann Custom Basses**
Charlottesville, Virginia

379

SPECIFICATIONS

BODY AND SIDE WOODS: Cherry

BODY WIDTH, LOWER BOUT: 11⅝ inches (29.5 cm)

ELECTRONICS: Two channel preamplifier by Jacob Joseph with active treble and bass controls and pan pot to control the balance between the Bartollini humbucker and the ABM Piezo bridge

NECK WOOD: Maple

FRETBOARD MATERIAL: Ebony

FRETBOARD INLAY: White mother-of-pearl

HEADSTOCK DECORATION: Dammann Custom Basses trademarked logo in mother-of-pearl

BRIDGE: Piezo active bridge by ABM

NUT AND SADDLE: Ebony

TUNING MACHINES: Gotoh

SCALE LENGTH: 34 inches (86.4 cm)

NECK WIDTH AT NUT: 1⅝ inches (4.1 cm)

NUMBER OF FRETS: 24

FINISH: Nitrocellulose lacquer

BODY DEPTH: 1¼ to 3 inches (3.2 to 7.6 cm)

BODY LENGTH: 15¾ inches (40 cm)

OVERALL LENGTH: 46¼ inches (117.5 cm)

U.S. SUGGESTED RETAIL PRICE: $3,200

C. Brase I – Pink Ivory &
C. Brase I – Fuschias and Hummingbird

Ken Lawrence has been building basses since 1981, when he began working for Moonstone, and founded Lawrence Instruments in 1986. He makes 25 to 30 basses a year and supplements his income as an active live and studio bassist.

Lawrence says he is certain that his extensive gigging has helped enable him to come close in his quest for the perfect bass. "For more than half my life," he explains, "it has been my passion to create the ultimate in bass guitars. I always try to make basses that appeal to me, and I have set very high standards for myself. This has been and continues to be a true labor of love."

Lawrence's Chamberbrase (C. Brase) model is a single cutaway, semi-hollow instrument with a massive, extended upper horn. A number of small narrow sound openings are carved into the horn and left side of the upper bout, forming an elegant decorative pattern that also enhances the instrument's sound.

C. Brase I – Pink Ivory, 2003 ▶
Kenneth Lawrence,
Kenneth Lawrence Instruments
Arcata, California

380

SPECIFICATIONS

C. BRASE I – PINK IVORY, 2003

BODY AND SIDE WOODS: Figured walnut and northern ash

TOP WOOD: Brazilian rosewood

BODY WIDTH, LOWER BOUT: 13⅛ inches (33.3 cm)

ELECTRONICS: Aero single coils in Brazilian rosewood covers, Schertler blue stick under saddle

NECK WOOD: Figured walnut

FRETBOARD MATERIAL: Pink ivory with blue fiber optic mother-of-pearl side position markers

HEADSTOCK DECORATION: Brazilian rosewood

BRIDGE: Pink ivory

NUT AND SADDLE: Pink ivory

TUNING MACHINES: Hipshot Ultralite, black

SCALE LENGTH: 34 inches (86.4 cm)

NECK WIDTH AT NUT: 1¹¹⁄₁₆ inches (4.3 cm)

NUMBER OF FRETS: 26

FINISH: Tung oil and wax

BODY DEPTH: 1⅞ inches (4.8 cm)

BODY LENGTH: 24½ inches (62.2 cm)

OVERALL LENGTH: 47¼ inches (120 cm)

◀ **C. Brase I – Fuschias and Hummingbird, 2003**
Kenneth Lawrence, Kenneth Lawrence Instruments
Arcata, California

SPECIFICATIONS

C. BRASE I – FUSCHIAS AND HUMMINGBIRD, 2003

BODY AND SIDE WOODS: Honduran mahogany

TOP WOOD: Figured Hawaiian koa

BODY WIDTH, LOWER BOUT: 13⅛ inches (33.3 cm)

ELECTRONICS: Custom Seymour Duncan single and dual coil pickups in ebony covers

NECK WOOD: Northeastern ash

FRETBOARD MATERIAL: Indian ebony with blue fiber optic mother-of-pearl side position markers

FRETBOARD INLAY: Fuschias—white, black, and gold mother-of-pearl, sea snail, purpleheart, copper; hummingbird—all black mother-of-pearl

HEADSTOCK DECORATION: Koa headcap

BRIDGE: Ebony with metal saddles

NUT AND SADDLE: Vintage bone nut, metal saddles

TUNING MACHINES: Hipshot Ultralite, black with d-tuner on lowest string

SCALE LENGTH: 34 inches (86.4 cm)

NECK WIDTH AT NUT: 1¹¹⁄₁₆ inches (4.3 cm)

NUMBER OF FRETS: 26

FINISH: Gloss polyester with light amber tint

BODY DEPTH: 1⅞ inches (4.8 cm)

BODY LENGTH: 24½ inches (62.2 cm)

OVERALL LENGTH: 47¼ inches (120 cm)

U.S. SUGGESTED RETAIL PRICE: $12,800

Brase II – Quetzalcoatl

*I*n addition to his skills as a musician and instrument builder, Ken Lawrence is a master of inlay. This five-string bass features an image of Quetzalcoatl, a feathered serpent who was one of the major gods of ancient Mesoamerica. The Olmec, Mixtec, Toltec, Aztec, and Maya worshiped the feathered serpent deity for nearly 2,000 years before the early sixteenth-century Spanish conquest of the region brought an end to Quetzalcoatl's spiritual reign.

Like Larry Robinson, whose work inspired Lawrence tremendously, Ken sometimes adds inlay to the body of an instrument in addition to or instead of its fingerboard and says that inlay on the body is so thin and light that in his experience it never dampens the instrument's sound. He often glues his intricate shell patterns to wax paper with Crazy Glue, then tapes the wax paper to his soundboard material, and uses a scribe and X-Acto knife to cut through the paper and into the board.

♠ **Brase II – Quetzalcoatl, 2002**
Kenneth Lawrence, Kenneth Lawrence Instruments
Arcata, California

SPECIFICATIONS

BODY AND SIDE WOODS: Hawaiian koa and figured northern ash

TOP WOOD: Macassar ebony

BODY WIDTH, LOWER BOUT: 13⅛ inches (33.3 cm)

ELECTRONICS: Aero single coil pickups in ebony covers, custom Seymour Duncan 3-band preamp

NECK WOOD: Birdseye maple

FRETBOARD MATERIAL: Birdseye maple with Indian ebony binding

HEADSTOCK DECORATION: Birdseye maple

BRIDGE: Metal bridge, black finish

NUT AND SADDLE: Vintage bone nut

TUNING MACHINES: Hipshot Ultralite, black finish

SCALE LENGTH: 35 inches (89 cm)

NECK WIDTH AT NUT: 1¹¹⁄₁₆ inches (4.3 cm)

NUMBER OF FRETS: 24

FINISH: Tung oil and wax

BODY DEPTH: 1⁹⁄₁₆ inches (4 cm)

BODY LENGTH: 23¼ inches (59 cm)

OVERALL LENGTH: 46¼ inches (117.5 cm)

U.S. SUGGESTED RETAIL PRICE: $11,500

Dragonetti Five-String Fretless Bass

Les Godfrey has been building electric basses and guitars since 1995. Godfrey has always been fascinated with the double bass, so when he set out to design an electric bass, he made sure his instrument shared motifs and aesthetics with the bass fiddle, while still retaining the functionality of a classic electric bass. Godfrey designed the Dragonetti for great balance and ease of playability. Each instrument is entirely hand carved with an arched-topped, strongly violin-influenced body shape, and elegant violin scrolls on the head and narrow, elongated arms.

The Dragonetti is named for the legendary Italian double bass virtuoso and composer Domenico Carlo Maria Dragonetti (1763–1846). Dragonetti was the first and perhaps the greatest of all bass soloists; his fiery and technically astonishing playing opened the eyes of both Haydn and Beethoven to the possibilities of writing for the instrument, and changed the role of the bass in orchestral music forever.

♠ **Dragonetti Five-String Fretless Bass, 2005**
Les Godfrey, Les Godfrey Custom Instruments
Toronto, Ontario, Canada

SPECIFICATIONS

BODY AND SIDE WOODS: Maple (two-piece body)

BODY WIDTH, LOWER BOUT: 13½ inches (34.3 cm)

ELECTRONICS: Two passive Nordstrand single-coil pickups with two volumes, one tone

NECK WOOD: Maple

FRETBOARD MATERIAL: Rosewood

FRETBOARD INLAY: Aluminum side dots

HEADSTOCK DECORATION: Rosewood veneer with branded "Godfrey" logo

BRIDGE: ⅜-inch (9.5 mm) diameter aluminum rods

NUT AND SADDLE: Corian

TUNING MACHINES: Hipshot Ultralite

SCALE LENGTH: 33 inches (83.8 cm)

NECK WIDTH AT NUT: 1⅞ inches (4.8 cm)

NUMBER OF FRETS: 22

BRACING: Solid body

FINISH: Oil and shellac

BODY DEPTH: 1⅞ inches (4.8 cm)

BODY LENGTH: 22 inches (55.9 cm)

OVERALL LENGTH: 48 inches (121.9 cm)

U.S. SUGGESTED RETAIL PRICE: $3,855

Barcelona VI

*J*erzy Drozd's Barcelona Bass is a semi-acoustic instrument specifically designed for the renowned Spanish jazz/flamenco bass player Carles Benavent, who has been Paco De Lucia's main bass player for more than 25 years and has also played with Miles Davis and Chick Corea. Benavent was a pioneer in finding a role for the bass in flamenco, which is traditionally played only with six-string acoustic guitars.

Drozd says he and Benavent thought a lot about what to name the new instrument. One possibility was "Mars Guitar," the name flamenco audiences gave to the strange instrument with only four thick strings when they first saw Benavent play with Paco de Lucia. But just before they debuted the bass at the Musikmesse 2004 tradeshow in Frankfurt, Benavent said to Drozd, "You know what? Let's call it 'Barcelona'....In the end it is where we both live."

Drozd built his first bass when he was 16. His father thought his interest in playing was a passing phase and refused to buy a bass for him, so he built his own. He followed a how-to book on building a classical guitar and, because he had no access to commercial pickups, he made his own from the little magnets used to hold the doors of kitchen cabinets closed. While he used other designers' pickups for years after he began building professionally, he started building pickups especially suited to the sound and aesthetics of his basses in 2003.

SPECIFICATIONS

BODY AND SIDE WOODS: Spanish cedar

TOP WOOD: Sitka spruce

BODY WIDTH, LOWER BOUT: 15 inches (38.1 cm)

ELECTRONICS: Passive

NECK WOOD: Five-piece maple with wenge runners

FRETBOARD MATERIAL: Ebony

FRETBOARD INLAY: "Ray of Light" made from maple wood

HEADSTOCK DECORATION: Violet rosewood veneer top

BRIDGE: Etimoe wood

NUT AND SADDLE: Ebony

TUNING MACHINES: Hipshot Ultralite chrome plated

SCALE LENGTH: 34 inches (86.4 cm)

NECK WIDTH AT NUT: 1⅝ inches (4.2 cm)

NUMBER OF FRETS: 24

FINISH: Polyurethane satin finish

BODY DEPTH: 1¹¹⁄₁₆ inches (4.3 cm)

BODY LENGTH: 20¼ inches (51.5 cm)

OVERALL LENGTH: 46 inches (116.9 cm)

U.S. SUGGESTED RETAIL PRICE: $3,600

Barcelona VI, 2005 ♠
Jerzy Drozd, Jerzy Drozd Basses
Barcelona, Spain

Novax Mo'B Bass

♦ Novax Mo'B Bass, 2002
Ralph Novak, Novax Guitars
Eugene, Oregon

The tone of an instrument originates with the string," says Ralph Novak, "and the primary factor that controls string tone is scale length." Traditionally, unlike a piano or a harp, all the strings on a guitar have the same scale length, a compromise that can lead to minor but annoying tuning problems. Those problems are compounded on instruments with added strings, such as a five-string bass or seven-string guitar, and they led Ralph Novak to develop his patented NOVAX Fanned-Fret concept.

"Fanning" the frets allows Novak to give each string its optimum scale length; the fanning results from manipulating the scale length of the bass side of the neck relative to the treble side, so that the fret spacing is wider for strings with long scale lengths and closer for those with shorter scales

The Mo'B Bass has five different scale lengths, giving the instrument intonation that Novak claims "You can put up against a grand piano." The added 36-inch (91.4 cm) B-string has a rich voice that would be impossible on a traditional "short scale" 35-inch (88.9 cm) five-string, and the G-string also is sweeter because of its shorter scale.

SPECIFICATIONS

BODY AND SIDE WOODS: Anigre, hand carved

BODY WIDTH, LOWER BOUT: 14 inches (35.6 cm)

ELECTRONICS: Bartolini pickups with Bartolini TBT preamp

NECK WOOD: Paduak, vertical grain

FRETBOARD MATERIAL: Pao ferro

FRETBOARD INLAY: Pearl dot, Novax pattern

BRIDGE: ABM individual bridges

NUT AND SADDLE: Bone

TUNING MACHINES: Gotom, 20:1 ratio

SCALE LENGTH: Patented fanned-fret system, 33.6 to 36 inches (85.4 to 91.4 cm)

NECK WIDTH AT NUT: 1¾ inches (4.4 cm)

NUMBER OF FRETS: 22

FINISH: Waterborne hand-rubbed body, oiled neck

BODY DEPTH: 1¾ inches (4.4 cm)

U.S. SUGGESTED RETAIL PRICE: $3,025

ET Thunderbass

$\mathcal{M}$ ichael Pedulla started out making acoustic and electric guitars in 1975 but soon found that competing with Fender, Gibson, and Martin was a losing battle. Happily, he discovered that bass players were much more open minded about their instruments and a business was born. "Wurlitzer Music in Boston took a couple of basses, and they sold them right away," he recalls, "So I thought, 'Well, it's a matter of logic to make what you can sell.'"

Pedulla's popular Thunderbass was introduced in 1992 and has gone through a number of design changes over the years. Noted for its wide dynamic range and meaty tone, the Thunderbass combines specially devised circuitry with a straightforward control setup of a master volume, active treble and bass boost/cut control knobs, and a pickup-blend knob that governs the two active preamps with three proprietary tone modules specifically designed for Pedulla by electronics wizard Bill Bartolini.

The ET ("Exotic Top") model Thunderbass has laminated wings set to a five-piece neck that includes two thin strips of bubinga. The increased laminating redefines the attack, while the bubinga accentuates the guitar's lower mid-range. The exotic wood top is laminated on a soft maple back, a combination that produces a deep, round tone and a well-defined "sweet" high end. Pedulla says this example's cocobolo top is slightly richer sounding and deeper than other woods he offers. "Tonal differences between top woods are slight," says Pedulla, "but we figure if we appreciate them, chances are you will too."

388

SPECIFICATIONS

BODY AND SIDE WOODS: Maple
TOP WOOD: Cocobolo
BODY WIDTH, LOWER BOUT: 13 inches (33 cm)
ELECTRONICS: Bartolini
NECK WOOD: Maple, bubinga
FRETBOARD MATERIAL: Ebony
FRETBOARD INLAY: Mother-of-pearl
BRIDGE: Machined brass
NUT AND SADDLE: Bone nut
TUNING MACHINES: M.V. Pedulla/Gotoh
SCALE LENGTH: 34 inches (86.4 cm)
NECK WIDTH AT NUT: 1⅞ inches (4.8 cm)
NUMBER OF FRETS: 24
FINISH: Oil, urethane
BODY DEPTH: 1¹¹⁄₁₆ inches (4.3 cm)
BODY LENGTH: 18½ inches (47 cm)
OVERALL LENGTH: 44¼ inches (112.4 cm)
U.S. SUGGESTED RETAIL PRICE: $4,380

ET Thunderbass, 1992 ▶
M.V. Pedulla, M.V.
Pedulla Guitars, Inc.
Rockland, Massachusetts

Pair of Scroll Basses

*H*arry Fleishman, who has been building innovative guitars and basses for more than 40 years, has been called "the Thomas Edison of luthiers." He was a pioneer of headless designs for electric instruments, developed ultra-light (five pound!) electric basses in the 1970s, and first created guitars with multi-scale fingerboards and tops of contrasting woods in the 1980s.

His Scroll Bass, which combines a traditional violin scroll head shape with an elegantly simple, modern-looking body form, is shown here in a matched pair of five-strings, one fretless and the other fretted. The Scroll's volume and tone control knobs are recessed into a slot in the upper edge of the body so they don't break the clean, flowing design, and the bass also features yet another Fleishman invention, a fanned-fret system that he originally developed in the 1970s.

389

♠ **Pair of Scroll Basses, 1975–2005**
Harry Fleishman, Fleishman Instruments
Sebastopol, California

SPECIFICATIONS

BODY AND SIDE WOODS: Curly maple

TOP WOOD: Curly maple

ELECTRONICS: Bartolini with hand-carved pickup covers, ebony

NECK WOOD: Maple

FRETBOARD MATERIAL: Ebony

HEADSTOCK DECORATION: Hand-carved scroll

BRIDGE: Custom Fleishman

NUT AND SADDLE: Brass

TUNING MACHINES: Hipshot

SCALE LENGTH: Multi 34 to 36 inches (86.4 to 91.4 cm)

NECK WIDTH AT NUT: 1¾ inches (4.4 cm)

NUMBER OF FRETS: 24

FINISH: Nitrocellulose lacquer

RKS Guitars

SymBass

$\mathcal{R}$KS Guitars got its start in 2000, when world-renowned industrial designer Ravi Sawhney was taking guitar lessons. He couldn't find a guitar stand that he liked, so he approached one of his designers, Paul Janowski, and said, "Let's design a guitar stand." Janowski half-jokingly replied, "Let's design a guitar!" After mulling the idea over, Sawhney posed the project to his design team and they eagerly went to work. Fifteen pounds of illustrations later, a design emerged based on a human skeletal form.

Rock legend Dave Mason, whom Sawhney met through his brother, became his partner in launching RKS Guitars. Mason, who is best known for his work with Traffic and his song "Feelin' Alright," brought his professional-working-guitar-player's perspective to the project and was key in making the RKS guitar an instrument that the most demanding player could appreciate. After 15,000 hours of design time and obsession, RKS had a guitar that was ready for prime time. (The RKS team did eventually design that guitar stand, too.)

RKS's unique design combines a minimalist neck-through core of headstock, neck, and pickups with a surrounding body shell of either wood or polymer. The body is joined to the "core" with wooden or aluminum ribs that are visible from the front, giving the instruments their distinctive open look. The two halves of the body shell join at the center of the back, which looks far more conventional. The neck-through-body-construction provides clarity and sustain, and then transfers its vibrations to the lively body.

◀ **SymBass, 2006**
RKS Guitars
Oxnard, California

SPECIFICATIONS

BODY AND SIDE WOODS: Swamp ash body

BODY WIDTH, LOWER BOUT: 14 inches (35.6 cm)

ELECTRONICS: Passive, Seymour Duncan basslines

NECK WOOD: Five-piece laminated hard maple

FRETBOARD MATERIAL: Ebony

FRETBOARD INLAY: Abalone dots

HEADSTOCK DECORATION: Chrome-plated brass scrolltip

BRIDGE: Hipshot

NUT AND SADDLE: Bone

TUNING MACHINES: Hipshot Ultralite

SCALE LENGTH: 34 inches (86.4 cm)

NECK WIDTH AT NUT: 1 13/16 inches (4.6 cm)

NUMBER OF FRETS: 24

FINISH: UV cure polyester, satin urethane

BODY DEPTH: 2 19/32 inches (6.6 cm)

BODY LENGTH: 18 inches (45.7 cm)

OVERALL LENGTH: 46 inches (116.8 cm)

U.S. SUGGESTED RETAIL PRICE: $2,999

Vintage Five-String Curl Bass

Johnny Mørch began building electric guitars and basses in 1970, originally teaming with his father Arne in a small production line business. Over the years, Mørch's business evolved in reverse, and he now builds unique instruments completely by hand, working intimately with each client to create guitars and basses that are limited only by "your imagination, technology, and your bank account. In short, whatever shape, color, or sound you want, we'll build it for you!" Instead of specific models, Mørch offers his customers a vast array of choices; as a starting point, his website includes 15 pages of photos of basses he has built over the years, and he maintains an extensive showroom for those who are able to visit him. He has also developed his own pickups, but, as is his wont, offers pickups by other manufacturers should his customers want them instead.

This five-string bass is an example of Mørch's custom work. Like many of his instruments, the non-cutaway bass side of the upper bout ends in a scroll form that Mørch calls the "curl."

393

SPECIFICATIONS

BODY AND SIDE WOODS: Curly mahogany

TOP WOOD: Curly mahogany

BODY WIDTH, LOWER BOUT: 13⅜ inches (34 cm)

ELECTRONICS: Mørch pickups, Mørch active electronics

NECK WOOD: Flamed hard maple, striped with arabutanga mahogany

FRETBOARD MATERIAL: Ebony

HEADSTOCK DECORATION: Mørch logo

BRIDGE: Schaller 5 strings

NUT AND SADDLE: Brass nut

TUNING MACHINES: Gotoh

SCALE LENGTH: 34 inches (86.4 cm)

NECK WIDTH AT NUT: 1¹¹⁄₁₆ inches (43 mm)

NUMBER OF FRETS: 22

FINISH: Nitrocellulose

BODY DEPTH: 2 inches (5 cm)

BODY LENGTH: 18½ inches (47 cm)

OVERALL LENGTH: 45¹¹⁄₁₆ inches (116 cm)

U.S. SUGGESTED RETAIL PRICE: $6,000

Vintage Five-String Curl Bass, 2003 ▶
Johnny Mørch, Mørch Guitars
Ørsted, Denmark

Sugaman Bass DC Model, Five-String

David Minnieweather began building bass guitars for himself when he was in ninth grade. As a professional bassist who has played with such artists as the legendary gospel singer Shirley Caesar, Minnieweather brings a unique perspective to his work as a builder. He says building instruments combines the three things he loves most—woodworking, art, and electronics.

In addition to standard four-string models, Minnieweather often builds basses with five, seven, or nine strings. He likes to work with exotic woods. This example features a mahogany body and redwood burl top. The back is carefully carved to fit the player's body, and the bolt-on neck is made of wenge (pronounced when-gay), an extremely dense lumber with a varied figure of fine, closely spaced dark brown lines.

♠ Sugaman Bass DC Model, Five-String, 2006
David Minnieweather, Minnieweather Custom Bass Guitars
Portland, Oregon

SPECIFICATIONS

BODY AND SIDE WOODS: African mahogany with wenge accent veneer

TOP WOOD: Spalted beech

BODY WIDTH, LOWER BOUT: 14 inches (35.6 cm)

ELECTRONICS: Bartolini custom-radiused pickups, Audere Audio 3ZB Z-Mode onboard preamp

NECK WOOD: Wenge, graphite reinforced

FRETBOARD MATERIAL: Birdseye maple

HEADSTOCK DECORATION: Logo, mother-of-pearl inlay

BRIDGE: Hipshot Style A bass bridge

NUT AND SADDLE: Bone nut

TUNING MACHINES: Gotoh tuners

SCALE LENGTH: 34 inches (86.4 cm)

NECK WIDTH AT NUT: 1⅞ inches (4.8 cm)

NUMBER OF FRETS: 24

FINISH: Catalyzed polyurethane

BODY DEPTH: 1⅝ inches (4.1 cm)

BODY LENGTH: 22 inches (55.9 cm)

OVERALL LENGTH: 44 inches (111.8 cm)

U.S. SUGGESTED RETAIL PRICE: Starting at $3,500

Pagelli

Goldbass

*T*he highly descriptive full name of Claudio Pagelli's Golden Fretless Bass is "Pagelli's Ultra Zero Reduced Three Octave Comfort Balanced Body Fretless Bass (with Hyper Access or U.Z.R.T.O.C.B.B.F.B. (H.A.!)." Its nickname comes from its finish, which is indeed a thin layer of real gold.

Created as a one-off for his own use, the guitar was designed to produce the ultimate fretless sound. The guitar is equipped with a Schertler pickup system, and Pagelli removed everything that could disturb the signal flow. The result, according to the luthier, is a bass with endless sustain and a sound that is "woodier than everything else you ever heard." Pagelli's radical hyper-access cutaway gives the guitar "unbelievable playability till the highest notes," and his own homemade tuners are mounted on the back of the head to keep the design as sleek and unencumbered as possible. By extending the straight lines of the neck to the bottom on the instrument, Pagelli divides the body in half, with unequally sized sides that mirror each other's flowing curves and elongated horn.

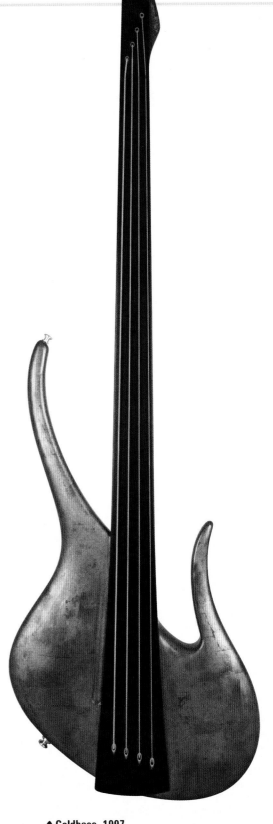

395

SPECIFICATIONS

BODY AND SIDE WOODS: Mahogany

TOP WOOD: Mahogany

BODY WIDTH, LOWER BOUT: 14³⁄₁₆ inches (36 cm)

ELECTRONICS: Schertler custom made

NECK WOOD: Mahogany, neck trough

FRETBOARD MATERIAL: Ebony

HEADSTOCK DECORATION: Ebony

BRIDGE: Ebony

NUT AND SADDLE: Ebony

TUNING MACHINES: Self-made, real mounted

SCALE LENGTH: 33.8 inches (86 cm)

FINISH: Goldplate, then varnish

🔶 **Goldbass, 1997**
Claudio and Claudia Pagelli, Pagelli Guitars
Scharans, Switzerland

Paul Reed Smith

Electric Bass Maple Top, Private Stock #199

Although PRS stopped making basses altogether in 2005, the company created some superb bass guitars over the years. Paul Reed Smith began his career as a bassist, and the first instrument he built was a bass guitar. So it comes as no surprise that his bass designs have been as elegant and unencumbered as the electric guitars on which he built his reputation, with clean, simple lines combined with state-of-the-art electronics.

This unique Private Stock bass employs PRS's second bass design, which was introduced in 2000. The guitar carries a pair of PRS's "high inductance" passive pickups and has a spectacular tiger eye curly maple top on a swamp ash body. The guitar's high-inductance, passive pickups were built specifically for the new bass model and required more than a year of research and development. The whole pickup, which has a built-in thumb rest, is radiussed to follow the arch of the strings, while Smith claims that the solid brass bridge provides enough mass to produce rich harmonics, solid tone, and outstanding sustain.

♠ Electric Bass Maple Top,
Private Stock #199, 2001
Paul Reed Smith, Paul Reed Smith Guitars
Stevensville, Maryland

SPECIFICATIONS

BODY AND SIDE WOODS: Swamp ash

TOP WOOD: Curly maple

BODY WIDTH, LOWER BOUT: 13⅝ inches (34.6 cm)

ELECTRONICS: PRS bass electronics (preamp)

NECK WOOD: Curly rock maple with satin finish

FRETBOARD MATERIAL: Brazilian rosewood

FRETBOARD INLAY: Black onyx bird inlays with 14-karat gold outline

HEADSTOCK DECORATION: Black onyx private stock eagle with 14-karat gold outline

BRIDGE: Gold PRS four-string bass

NUT AND SADDLE: Rytan nut; adjustable saddle

TUNING MACHINES: Gold PRS bass tuners

BINDING: Stained

SCALE LENGTH: 34 inches (86.4 cm)

NECK WIDTH AT NUT: 1⅝ inches (4.1 cm)

NUMBER OF FRETS: 21

FINISH: Tiger eye; acrylic urethane

BODY DEPTH: 1¹¹⁄₁₆ inches (4.3 cm)

BODY LENGTH: 19½ inches (49.5 cm)

OVERALL LENGTH: 43¼ inches (109.9 cm)

U.S. SUGGESTED RETAIL PRICE: $12,000

NS-2J-EX Buckeye Burl Top

S tuart Spector says he started building basses in 1974 simply because he felt he could build something he couldn't afford to purchase. In 1975, Spector met Ned Steinberger, who at the time was designing and building furniture. "Ned moved into our place and became fascinated with the idea that we were nutty enough to make musical instruments," Spector told *Bass Player* magazine. "He said, 'Hey, I think I could design a bass guitar.' I said, 'Great—be my guest.' He came back a week later with the first version of the NS carved-body bass, which we're still making to this day."

This example's mahogany body is topped with distinctively colored and patterned buckeye burl, cut from growths occasionally found on the buckeye, a family of trees that grows throughout North America.

Garry Tallent, who plays bass in Bruce Springsteen's E Street Band, is among the many prominent bassists who play a Spector NS.

397

♠ **NS-2J-EX Buckeye Burl Top, 2005**
Stuart Spector, Spector Basses
Saugerties, New York

SPECIFICATIONS

BODY AND SIDE WOODS: Mahogany

TOP WOOD: Buckeye burl

BODY WIDTH, LOWER BOUT: 12 inches (30.5 cm)

ELECTRONICS: EMG active J pickups, Spector Tone Pump Circuit

NECK WOOD: 3-ply hard maple

FRETBOARD MATERIAL: Pau Ferro

FRETBOARD INLAY: Black mother-of-pearl

HEADSTOCK DECORATION: Abalone inlay

BRIDGE: Hipshot A Style black plated

NUT AND SADDLE: Brass nut

TUNING MACHINES: Black Gotoh

SCALE LENGTH: 34 inches (86.4 cm)

NECK WIDTH AT NUT: 1⅝ inches (4.1 cm)

NUMBER OF FRETS: 24

FINISH: Hand-rubbed oil

BODY DEPTH: 1⅝ inches (4.1 cm)

BODY LENGTH: 19 inches (48.3 cm)

OVERALL LENGTH: 44½ inches (113 cm)

Pagelli
The Splash Bass

$\mathcal{B}$ ass guitar builders have been more inclined to stray from classic design forms than electric guitar builders, probably because their clients are less inclined to be married to traditional designs. Claudio Pagelli describes his Splash Bass as a "four-string fretted orange '60s funkwonder," while *Gitarre & Bass* magazine calls it "an inspiring hint at the possible liberty still to be taken, but yet unexploited" in electric bass design.

The guitar is not only a sinuous and appealing piece of sculpture but also a high-quality instrument built with the Swiss precision Pagelli has become known for since he opened his own shop in 1978. In part because of its extravagant open form, the Splash Bass weighs less than eight pounds (3.6 kg).

◀ **The Splash Bass, 2004**
Claudio and Claudia Pagelli, Pagelli Guitars
Scharans, Switzerland

SPECIFICATIONS

BODY AND SIDE WOODS: Alder

BODY WIDTH, LOWER BOUT: 14³⁄₁₆ inches (36 cm)

ELECTRONICS: Harry Haussel custom made

NECK WOOD: Maple

FRETBOARD MATERIAL: Indian rosewood

BRIDGE: ABM

NUT AND SADDLE: Bone

TUNING MACHINES: Schaller with Pagelli-made knobs

SCALE LENGTH: 33.8 inches (86 cm)

NUMBER OF FRETS: 22

FINISH: 2k

Ultra Vintage J-Bass

*L*ike guitars and basses based on the classic Fender models of the 1950s and early 1960s, Sadowsky's J-Bass draws inspiration from the Fender Jazz bass.

Roger Sadowsky's basses are the result of his many years of experience working with the finest professional guitarists and bassists in New York. He believes that the most important factor affecting the sound of solid-body instruments is the acoustic quality of the wood. "The better a guitar sounds acoustically," says Sadowsky, "the better it always sounds, no matter what pickups, electronics, or amplification are used." He is therefore very particular about his materials, building from woods selected for acoustic resonance, light weight, and beautiful grain. His basses are made from select alder, southern swamp ash, and figured maple tops laminated to swamp ash or alder.

Ultra Vintage J-Bass, 2007 ▶
Roger Sadowsky, Sadowsky Guitars
Brooklyn, New York

399

SPECIFICATIONS

BODY AND SIDE WOODS: Alder

BODY WIDTH, LOWER BOUT: 13½ inches (34.3 cm)

ELECTRONICS: Custom Sadowsky single coil pickups with Sadowsky preamp

NECK WOOD: Maple

FRETBOARD MATERIAL: Brazilian rosewood

FRETBOARD INLAY: Micarta dots

HEADSTOCK DECORATION: Sadowsky logo

BRIDGE: Custom Sadowsky made by Hipshot

NUT AND SADDLE: Ivory

TUNING MACHINES: Sadowsky custom made by Hipshot

SCALE LENGTH: 34 inches (86.4 cm)

NECK WIDTH AT NUT: 1½ inches (3.8 cm)

NUMBER OF FRETS: 20

FINISH: Daphne blue (polyester finish)

U.S. SUGGESTED RETAIL PRICE: $3,675

Welcome & Keefe
Custom Four-String Set Neck

S age Guitars founder and head luthier Ryan Welcome spent years playing and touring as a bassist in the underground Connecticut music scene before deciding to change course and study guitar making under the guidance of master builders William Eaton and John Reuter at the Roberto-Venn School of Luthiery.

Welcome met his partner, Ryan Keefe, while they were both working for Ovation instruments. Welcome says, "It was a big deal allowing someone to become a partner in the business. I've been developing these basses for over eight years and had several other offers before, but Ryan Keefe was the only person that I thought wouldn't drive me crazy."

The two build bolt-ons and set-necks with four to seven strings using a wide variety of woods. This typically well-conceived Sage bass has a sycamore body topped with figured bubinga.

400

♠ **Custom Four-String Set Neck, 2001**
Ryan Welcome and Ryan Keefe, Sage Guitars
Hartford, Connecticut

SPECIFICATIONS

BODY AND SIDE WOODS: Quartersawn sycamore

TOP WOOD: Figured bubinga

ELECTRONICS: Aero humbucking E-series dual coils in custom bubinga covers

NECK WOOD: Flamed maple (3-piece)

FRETBOARD MATERIAL: Cocobolo

HEADSTOCK DECORATION: none

BRIDGE: Hipshot A-style

NUT AND SADDLE: Graphite

TUNING MACHINES: 4 Hipshot D-tuners

SCALE LENGTH: 35 inches (88.9 cm)

NECK WIDTH AT NUT: 1½ inches (3.8 cm)

NUMBER OF FRETS: 26

FINISH: Oil

BODY DEPTH: 1⅝ inches (4.1 cm)

U.S. SUGGESTED RETAIL PRICE: $6,000

EUB (Electric Upright Bass), The Red Rocket

Harry Fleishman

Harry Fleishman has been building EUBs since 1969, constantly experimenting with every aspect of the hybrid instrument. He says that this is one of his favorite designs. "It says everything I wanted it to say, musically and aesthetically," he explains. "However, now that a few years have passed, I'm seeing things I'd change and to that end I am still chasing the elusive EUB. I've chased it since 1969, and I suspect it will be a lifelong pursuit."

This EUB is fairly massive, with the full 42-inch scale of a bass fiddle, so Fleishman wanted to find a way to make it feel lighter and more modern, without losing the touch of traditional aesthetics. The neck is very securely bolted on, but he relieved the joint to make it look more like it is floating. Fleishman also designed an upper bout arm that lets the player feel like they are playing an upright bass. By supporting it on the aluminum bar and letting the ends float, the bass feels solid but looks very light.

Tonally, Fleishman says he was chasing the elusive acoustic bass tone that is so difficult, if not impossible to achieve in an electric upright. Toward that end, he designed a bridge that encompasses piezo elements in a Delrin matrix (Delrin is an acetal resin developed by DuPont), along with six single-coil magnetic pickups in an arched housing, again of Delrin. "Delrin has the interesting property of 'storing' energy very briefly," says Fleishman, "releasing it a bit more slowly than a more rigid material. I find this advantageous for EUBs."

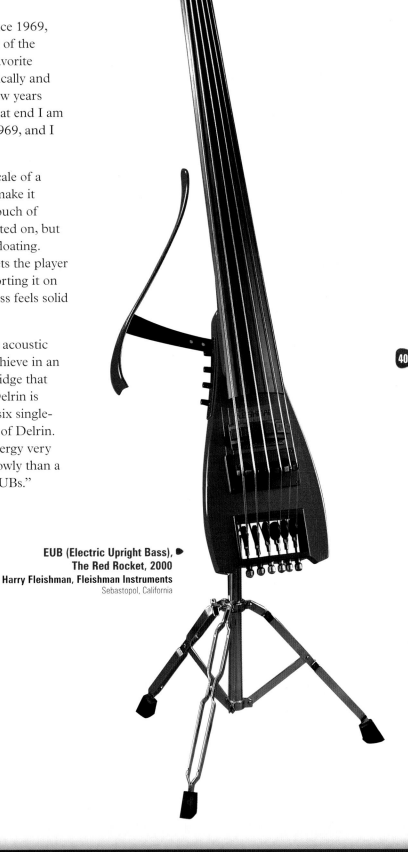

EUB (Electric Upright Bass), The Red Rocket, 2000
Harry Fleishman, Fleishman Instruments
Sebastopol, California

401

SPECIFICATIONS

BODY AND SIDE WOODS: Curly maple

TOP WOOD: Maple veneer

BODY WIDTH, LOWER BOUT: 8 inches (20.3 cm) (approx)

ELECTRONICS: Fleishman pickups and electronics

NECK WOOD: Maple

FRETBOARD MATERIAL: Ebony

BRIDGE: Delrin

NUT AND SADDLE: Ebony

TUNING MACHINES: Fleishman custom

SCALE LENGTH: 42 inches (106.7 cm)

NECK WIDTH AT NUT: 1 15/16 inches (4.9 cm)

FINISH: Nitrocellulose lacquer

ELECTRIC BASS

24-Fret MK IV Four-String Bass

*J*oe Veillette's MK IV acoustic electric bass guitars are intended to bridge the gap between conventional electric basses and classic acoustic uprights. Visually, tonally, and ergonomically, the MK IV combines the best elements of both instruments. The result is an instrument that can fill the roles of both, as well as creating new and unique sounds. *Bass Player* magazine confirmed the success of Veillette's design, calling the MK IV "a beautiful-looking, sounding, and playing instrument," that is "loud and punchy," with "ample bottom-end support" and "a velvety 'mwah'."

Veillette worked as an architectural designer before he got his start in guitar making as an apprentice to Michael Gurian in 1971. He partnered with fellow architecture student and bass designer Harvey Citron in 1975 and worked with Stuart Spector and Michael Tobias in the '90s, after eight years largely focused on his band, the Phantoms, a popular five-piece dance and vocal group that continues to perform both as a full band and an a cappella group. Today, Veillette is assisted by Martin Keith, the son of progressive banjo legend Ben Keith, who does all the electronics, wiring, assembly, and final setup of each instrument. He's also assisted by Ande Chase, a professional bassist, who helps with the building and is "also really good at finding things that have been lost by Joe and Martin."

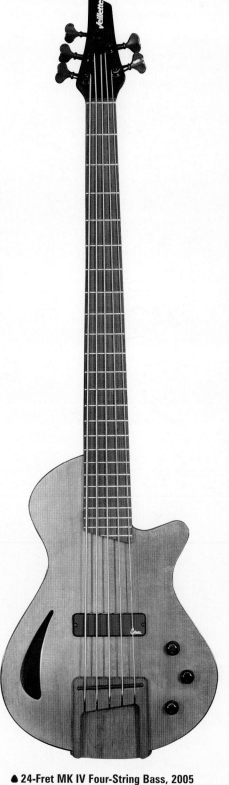

● **24-Fret MK IV Four-String Bass, 2005**
Joe Veillette, Veillette Guitars
Woodstock, New York

402

SPECIFICATIONS

BODY AND SIDE WOODS: Poplar

TOP WOOD: Western red cedar

BODY WIDTH, LOWER BOUT: 12¾ inches (32.4 cm)

ELECTRONICS: Citron pickup, custom under-saddle piezo pickup, D-Tar Eclipse blender preamp

NECK WOOD: Maple

FRETBOARD MATERIAL: Wenge

BRIDGE: Wenge

NUT AND SADDLE: Zero-fret

TUNING MACHINES: Gotoh

BINDING: Black

SCALE LENGTH: 34 inches (86.4 cm)

NECK WIDTH AT NUT: 1¹¹⁄₁₆ inches (4.3 cm)

NUMBER OF FRETS: 24

FINISH: Catalyzed lacquer

BODY DEPTH: 2⅜ inches (6 cm) max.

BODY LENGTH: 17 inches (43.2 cm)

OVERALL LENGTH: 45 inches (114.3 cm)

Spalt Magma 601

ichael Spalt says he started making guitars to get away from writing screenplays, and "at a certain point, I realized I had a lot more fun with guitars. I'm not making these instruments because I want to do something differently from others," Spalt continues.

"The motivation to build them is simply to make something that sounds good, looks cool, and can be played well. I'm just following my own path, doing something that is exciting and interesting to me while I'm making it."

That said, Spalt's Magma bass is different in looks, technology, and sound from anything else being made today. Access to the Magma's electronics, including a battery pack, charging jack with LED monitor, and output jack, is on the backside, and there is a screw on the back of the armrest that allows the player to adjust its angle. Spalt also built LightWave pickup modules, which use a patented infrared light technology to sense string vibration, into the bridge. Unlike conventional pickups that interfere with string vibration, the LightWave Optical Pickup "sees" the vibration of the string without affecting string motion. The system generates virtually no inherent noise, so it produces an almost noise-free, transparent sound at any volume without background hum or buzz, delivering the accurate, full-range sound of each note.

● **Spalt Magma 601, 2004**
Michael Spalt, Spalt Instruments
Los Angeles, California
Collection of Jeff Doctorow

SPECIFICATIONS

BODY AND SIDE WOODS: Sandwich of spalted maple, wenge

TOP WOOD: Bubinga

BODY WIDTH, LOWER BOUT: 16 inches (40.6 cm)

ELECTRONICS: LightWave Optical Pickup system

NECK WOOD: Wenge/maple center stripe

FRETBOARD MATERIAL: Macassar ebony

FRETBOARD INLAY: Pearl

BRIDGE: LightWave monolith type and aluminum base plate

NUT AND SADDLE: Bone nut, LightWave saddle units

TUNING MACHINES: Hipshot ultralite Y

SCALE LENGTH: 34 inches (86.4 cm)

NECK WIDTH AT NUT: 2¼ inches (5.7 cm)

NUMBER OF FRETS: 24

FINISH: Oil/chrome

BODY DEPTH: 3 inches (7.6 cm)

OVERALL LENGTH: 46 inches (116.8 cm)

U.S. SUGGESTED RETAIL PRICE: $5,290

Victor Wooten Yin Yang Monarch

*V*ictor Wooten, who plays bass with the genre bending super group Béla Fleck and the Flecktones, is widely regarded as one of the most innovative bassists at work today. When Wooten asked Fodera to inlay a Monarch bass with a yin-yang symbol, Fodera surprised him by extending the light and dark yin-yang motif to the guitar's entire body and headstock.

The Monarch, introduced in 1983, was Fodera's first bass model and has remained in constant production ever since. Its compact ergonomic form made it an immediate hit with working musicians and it remains a players' favorite. That Wooten and fellow master bassist Marcus Miller have both been playing their Monarchs for more than 20 years is an indication of the design's success.

▲ **Victor Wooten Yin Yang Monarch, 1983**
Vinny Fodera and Joey Lauricella, Fodera Guitars
Brooklyn, New York

SPECIFICATIONS

BODY AND SIDE WOODS: Alder

TOP WOOD: Ebony and holly joined together

BODY WIDTH, LOWER BOUT: 12¹³⁄₁₆ inches (32.5 cm)

ELECTRONICS: Fodera/Pope custom 3 ban equalizer with passive tone with emg p/j pickups

NECK WOOD: Hard maple

FRETBOARD MATERIAL: Maple with ebony inlaid upper register

FRETBOARD INLAY: Ebony dots plus a large mother-of-pearl circle inlay

HEADSTOCK DECORATION: Yin yang style black and white in ebony and holly

BRIDGE: Fodera custom

NUT AND SADDLE: Hand-cut brass

TUNING MACHINES: Fodera

SCALE LENGTH: 34 inches (86.4 cm)

NECK WIDTH AT NUT: 1⁹⁄₁₆ inches (4 cm)

NUMBER OF FRETS: 24

FINISH: Urethane lacquer

U.S. SUGGESTED RETAIL PRICE: $8,619

Quake Fretless Five-String

◆ Quake Fretless Five-String, 2006
Skip Fantry, Knuckle Guitar Works
Seattle, Washington

*K*nuckle's stated intention is to push the limits of traditional instruments "in order to expand their application and usefulness." The company's most radical bass guitar, the aptly named Quake, was designed to explore and facilitate tunings well below contemporary electric basses and to do it with the same tonal expectations traditional registers are held to. To make tunings as low as a full octave below a normal electric bass possible, the Quake has a 39-inch scale length, five inches longer than a standard electric bass and closing in on the 42 inches (106.7 cm) of a bass fiddle. Five strings are standard, and with special strings made specifically for this instrument by LaBella, the normal five-string configuration can be brought down so that the low E is just above 20Hz.

Not surprisingly, the Quake's earthshaking depth and volume can put a real strain on standard bass speakers. Knuckle advises, "The ability to reach E below low E and beyond puts serious demands on most traditional equipment. Care and consideration should be had regarding speakers and your expectations of them." The Quake has a very full and vibrant tone that is heard well on nearly all contemporary gear, but the lowest frequencies are best appreciated with a separate speaker specifically made to handle extremely low frequencies.

405

SPECIFICATIONS

BODY AND SIDE WOODS: Western broad leaf maple

BODY WIDTH, LOWER BOUT: 13 inches (33 cm)

ELECTRONICS: Q tuner magnetic/Graphtech piezo, preamp/magnetic bypass

NECK WOOD: Carbon-reinforced Eastern maple

FRETBOARD MATERIAL: Garolyte

FRETBOARD INLAY: Bone side and top markers

HEADSTOCK DECORATION: Single "K" logo

BRIDGE: ABM single string bridges

NUT AND SADDLE: Garolyte nut

TUNING MACHINES: Hipshot ultralite

SCALE LENGTH: 39.6 inches (100.5 cm)

NECK WIDTH AT NUT: 1¾ inches (4.4 cm)

FINISH: Transparent black burst shellac

BODY DEPTH: 1¾ inches (4.4 cm)

BODY LENGTH: 23 inches (58.4 cm)

OVERALL LENGTH: 48¼ inches (122.6 cm)

Ned Steinberger

Synapse XS-15 FPA Trans Green

*I*ndustrial designer Ned Steinberger stunned the guitar world when he introduced the L-2, his first headless, graphite-reinforced epoxy-bodied bass in 1980. His decidedly non-traditional, reductionist creations, which have been compared to a witch's broom in appearance, remain too radical for many players 25 years later.

Although Les Paul built a headless guitar for himself in the 1940s, the idea was too visually radical to be taken up by many builders before Steinberger. But it makes sense, especially for basses. Traditional bass guitars are not well balanced; the weight of their long necks, oversized wooden headstocks, and large tuning pegs tends to make them droop like unwatered flowers, and they are easily knocked out of tune. By eliminating the head and moving the tuners to the bottom of the instrument, Steinberger balanced his guitar, improved its ability to stay in tune, and also reduced its weight substantially.

The Synapse series is the latest iteration of Steinberger's original concepts, featuring a graphite and three-piece hard maple neck and maple body wings. The fingerboard is phenolic, an extremely stable composite material that is much harder and more rigid than wood, thereby offering a more consistent overall sound quality and completely eliminating the harmonic dead spots that are often a problem with wooden fingerboards.

406

◀ **Synapse XS-15 FPA Trans Green, 2002**
Ned Steinberger, NS Design
Nobleboro, Maine

SPECIFICATIONS

BODY AND SIDE WOODS: Rock maple

TOP WOOD: Flame maple

BODY WIDTH, LOWER BOUT: 9³⁄₁₆ inches (23.3 cm)

ELECTRONICS: EMC Mac. pickups and active equalizer circuit and mixer

NECK WOOD: Rock maple

FRETBOARD MATERIAL: Phenolic

BRIDGE: Piezo pickup

NUT AND SADDLE: Phenolic

TUNING MACHINES: Steinberger in-line

SCALE LENGTH: 34 inches (86.4 cm)

NECK WIDTH AT NUT: 1³⁄₄ inches (4.4 cm)

NUMBER OF FRETS: 24

FINISH: Polymer

BODY DEPTH: 2¹⁄₁₆ inches (5.3 cm)

BODY LENGTH: 15⁹⁄₁₆ inches (39.6 cm)

OVERALL LENGTH: 40⁹⁄₁₆ inches (103 cm)

EU Series Double Bass

*N*ed Steinberger's EU (Electric Upright) Series Double Bass is part of his complete line of electric bowed instruments, which also includes violins, violas, cellos, and bass cellos. The EU Double Bass is molded with concentric laminations of graphite and rock maple that run the entire length of the instrument for maximum sonic integrity, and the back of the neck is curved inward to follow the arch of the graphite fingerboard, resulting in a slim, easy-to-play neck with full access to the upper register.

Steinberger founded NS Design in 1990 with the intent of creating completely new electric bowed instruments. He explains, "Bowed electric instruments have been made since the mid-30s. Unfortunately, most of them are the victims of the misplaced idea that an electric instrument should sound exactly like its acoustic predecessor. I want to take it a step further—to see what these instruments can do when they are set free." NS EU Series Double Basses are currently being "set free" by such well-known bassists as Les Claypool, David Darling, Mark Egan, Colin Greenwood of Radiohead, Tony Levin, Eric Mingus, and Rob Wasserman.

407

SPECIFICATIONS

BODY AND SIDE WOODS: Twenty-seven alternating layers of rock maple and graphite fiber laminated in an epoxy matrix

BODY WIDTH, LOWER BOUT: 6 inches (15.2 cm)

ELECTRONICS: 18-volt active circuit, by Haz Laboratories; mono output

FRETBOARD MATERIAL: Graphite

BRIDGE: Black phenolic

NUT AND SADDLE: Black phenolic nut

TUNING MACHINES: Schaller 20:1 ration, fully encased worm gear tuners, black finish

SCALE LENGTH: 41.7 inches (106 cm)

NECK WIDTH AT NUT: 2 inches (5 cm)

FINISH: Traditional amber stain with clear semi-gloss hand-polished polymer

BODY DEPTH: 4 inches (10.2 cm)

BODY LENGTH: 52 inches (132 cm)

U.S. SUGGESTED RETAIL PRICE: $5,475

◆ **EU Series Double Bass, 2006**
Ned Steinberger, NS Design
Nobleboro, Maine

ACKNOWLEDGMENTS

This book would not have been possible without significant help from all the luthiers who provided images and information about their work (and opinions about each other's). I am indebted to each and every one of them for taking time out from their hectic daily schedules to hunt for photos and answer my many questions.

Special thanks to David Blank, who shared some of his wonderful guitars; Rick Davis, who introduced me to a number of other luthiers and took photos of his shop; Jeff Doctorow, who opened his amazing collection of contemporary guitars to me (and even let me play a few of them); Harry Fleishman, who turned me on to a number of important sources and offered his full support to the project; Ken Parker, who shared the birth of his new archtop with me; Dennis Scannell, who walked me through every step of his complex building process; and Ervin Somogyi, who filled in many blanks in the history of contemporary luthiery.

Thanks to guitar consultants Cliff Cultreri of Destroy All Guitars, Takeshi Hayakawa of Blue-G Guitars, Paul Heumiller of Dream Guitars, Chris Kamen of Classic Guitars International, and Dave Schmidt of Guitar Adoptions for sharing photographs of some of the wonderful guitars they have handled.

Thanks to Steve Riggio at Barnes & Noble, whose idea this all was, and to Carol Taylor at Lark Books, who asked me to tackle the project. At Lark, thanks also to Marthe Le Van, Chris Bryant, Susan Kieffer, Linda Kopp, Jimmy Knight, Mark Bloom, Amanda Carestio, Travis Medford, Julie Hale, Jeff Hamilton, Laura R. Cook, Halley Lawrence, Meghan Wanucha, and everyone else for their support and diligent work on this ambitious and complex project. And special thanks to Paige Gilchrist and Cassie Moore, who made sure it all came together in the end.

Finally thanks to my wife, Nancy, who listened to all the music and shop talk with great patience and unflagging support, and my girls, Emma and Georgia, who had their own ideas about what mattered.

Robert Shaw
Shelburne, Vermont

SELECTED BIBLIOGRAPHY

Achard, Ken. *The History and Development of the American Guitar*. Westport, CT: The Bold Strummer, 1990.

Alexander, Charles and Freeth, Nick. *The Guitar*. Philadelphia: Running Press, 2002.

Bacon, Tony. *Electric Guitars: The Illustrated History*. London: Backbeat Books, 2000.

—(et al). *The Classical Guitar: A Complete History*. London: Balafon Books, 2002.

—*The History of the American Guitar: from 1833 to the Present Day*. New York: Friedman/Fairfax Publishers, 2001.

—*The Ultimate Guitar Book*. New York: Alfred A. Knopf, 1994.

Boak, Dick. *Martin Guitar Masterpieces*. Boston: Bulfinch Press, 2003

Burrows, Terry. *Guitar: A Celebration of the World's Finest Guitars*. London: Carlton Books, 2003.

Carter, Walter. *Gibson Guitars: 100 Years of an American Icon*. Los Angeles: General Publishing Group, 1994

—*The Martin Book*. London: Balafon Books, 1995.

Cumpiano, William R., and Natelson, Jonathan D. *Guitarmaking: Tradition and Technology*. San Francisco: Chronicle Books, 1994.

Evans, Tom and Mary Ann. *Guitars: From the Renaissance to Rock*. London: The Paddington Press, 1977.

Giel, Kate, ed. *Ferrington Guitars*. New York: HarperCollins Publishers and Callaway Editions, 1992.

Gruhn, George and Carter, Walter. *Acoustic Guitars and Other Fretted Instruments: A Pictorial History*. San Francisco: GPI Books, 1993.

— *Electric Guitars and Basses: A Pictorial History*. San Francisco: GPI Books, 1994.

Hartman, Robert Carl. *Guitars and Mandolins in America, Featuring the Larsons' Creations*. Hoffman Estates, IL: Maurer & Co., 1984.

Hiscock, Melvyn. *Make Your Own Electric Guitar*. Hampshire, UK: NBS Publications, 1998.

Kuronen, Darcy. *Dangerous Curves: The Art of the Guitar*. Boston: MFA Publications, Boston Museum of Fine Arts, 2001.

Laskin, William. *A Guitarmaker's Canvas: The Inlay Art of Grit Laskin*. San Francisco: Backbeat Books, 2003.

Longworth, Mike. *Martin Guitars, a History*. Minisink Hills, PA: Four Maples Press, Inc., 1988.

Palmer, Robert. *Rock and Roll: An Unruly History*. New York: Harmony Books, 1995.

Roberts, Jim. *American Basses: An Illustrated History & Player's Guide*. San Francisco: Backbeat Books, 2003.

Schmidt, Paul. *Art That Sings: The Life and Times of Luthier Steve Klein*. Clifton, NJ: Jeff Doctorow/Doctorow Communications, Inc., 2003.

Shaw, Robert. *Great Guitars*. Southport, CT: Hugh Lauter Levin Associates, 1997,

Turnbull, Hugh. *The Guitar, from the Renaissance to the Present Day*. Westport, CT: The Bold Strummer, 1991.

Vose, Ken. *Blue Guitar*. San Francisco: Chronicle Books, 1998.

Washburn, Jim and Johnston, Richard. *Martin Guitars: An Illustrated Celebration of America's Premier Guitarmaker*. Pleasantville, New York: Reader's Digest Books, 2002.

Wheeler, Tom. *American Guitars: An Illustrated History*. New York: Harper Perennial, 1992.

—(et al). *The Electric Guitar: An Illustrated History*. London: Virgin Books, 1993.

GUITAR INFORMATION SITES

Brad's Page of Steel
Everything about steel guitars.
www.well.com/user/wellvis/steel.html

Famous Guitarmaker Internet World Headquarters
www.cybozone.com/fg

Frets.com—A Textbook for Musicians and Luthiers
Frank Ford's massive wonderland of information.
www.frets.com

Gourmet Guitars
Documentary films about the best guitars, makers, and players in the history of luthiery.
www.gourmet-guitars.com

Harp Guitars.net
Gregg Miner's extraordinary pages about harp guitars old and new.
www.harpguitars.net

LUTHERIE LINKS

Charles Fox's Links Page
Incredibly detailed and useful.
www.charlesfoxguitars.com

The Musical Instrument Makers Forum
www.mimf.com

ORGANIZATIONS

American Stringed Instrument Artisans (ASIA)
www.guitarmaker.org

Guild of American Luthiers
www.luth.org

Roberto-Venn School of Luthiery
www.roberto-venn.com

DEALERS AND CONSULTANTS

Blue-G Corporation, Tokyo, Japan
Acoustic guitars.
www.blue-g.com/english.html

Classic Guitars International, Santa Barbara, California
Classical and flamenco guitars.
Chris Kamen
www.classicguitar.com

Rosyne and François Charle, Paris, France
Probably the source for Gypsy jazz guitars, old and new.
www.rfcharle.com

Destroy All Guitars, Raleigh, North Carolina
A collective of outstanding acoustic and electric guitar and amp designers and builders, represented by Cliff Cultreri.
www.destroyallguitars.com

Different City Guitars, Sante Fe, New Mexico
www.differentcity.com

Dream Guitars, Weaverville, North Carolina
Primarily acoustic guitars.
Paul Heumiller
www.dreamguitars.com

Elderly Instruments, Lansing, Michigan
New and old instruments of all kinds, plus recordings, books, and much more.
www.elderly.com

Fine Acoustics, Westminster, Maryland
www.fineacoustics.com

Fine Guitar Consultants, San Diego, California
Boutique guitars of all kinds.
Richard Glick
www.fineguitarconsultants.com

Folkway Music Guelph, Ontario, Canada
www.folkwaymusic.com

G Guitars, New Haven, Connecticut
Electric guitars and basses.
www.gguitars.com

Golden Age Fretted Instruments Westfield, New Jersey
Vintage and new.
John Reynolds
www.goldenageguitars.com

Gruhn Guitars, Nashville, Tennessee
Vintage and new fretted instruments of all kinds from author and expert George Gruhn.
www.gruhn.com

Gryphon Stringed Instruments, Palo Alto, California
Frank Ford
www.gryphonstrings.com

Guitar Adoptions Wonder Lake, Illinois
New and used acoustic and electric guitars.
Dave Schmidt.
www.guitaradoptions.com

The Guitar Gallery, White House, Tennessee
Acoustic guitars.
www.guitargal.com

The Guitar Salon, New York, New York
Classical and flamenco guitars.
Beverly Maher
www.theguitarsalon.com

Henkes & Blazer, Tübingen, Germany
www.antique-acoustics.de

Jacksons Rare Guitars Sydney, Australia
www.jacksonsrareguitars.com

Mandolin Brothers, Staten Island, New York
"The Center of the Acoustic Universe." Fine acoustic and archtop guitars, vintage and new, as well as other fretted instruments.
Stan Jay
www.mandoweb.com

The Music Emporium, Boston, Massachusetts
www.themusicemporium.net

Music Ground Limited Leeds, England
www.musicground.com

Ed Roman Guitars, Las Vegas, Nevada
"The world's largest guitar store."
www.edromanguitars.com

Rudy's Music Shop, New York, New York
Rudy Pensa
www.rudysmusic.com

John G. Stewart Fine Guitars, Seattle, Washington
Archtop and Gypsy jazz guitars.
www.myjazzhome.com

The Twelfth Fret, Toronto, Canada
www.12fret.com

Matt Umanov Guitars, New York, New York
Vintage (and new) guitars since 1965.
www.umanovguitars.com

Vintage and Rare Guitars London, England
www.vintageandrareguitars.com

Zavaleta's la Casas de Guitarars, Tucson, Arizona
Classical and flamenco guitars.
www.zavaletas-guitarras.com

409

PHOTOGRAPHERS INDEX

411

412

413

INDEX & WEB
DIRECTORY

414

415